Spain

WORLD BIBLIOGRAPHICAL SERIES

General Editors:
Robert L. Collison (Editor-in-chief)
Sheila R. Herstein
Louis J. Reith
Hans H. Wellisch

VOLUMES IN THE SERIES

VOLUME 60

Spain

Graham J. Shields
Compiler

CLIO PRESS
OXFORD, ENGLAND · SANTA BARBARA, CALIFORNIA
DENVER, COLORADO

© Copyright 1985 by Clio Press Ltd.

British Library Cataloguing in Publication Data

Shields, Graham J.
Spain: a selected and annotated bibliography. –
(World bibliographical series, v. 60)
1. Spain – Bibliography
I. Title   II. Series
016.946   Z2681

ISBN 1-85109-003-7

Clio Press Ltd.,
55 St. Thomas' Street,
Oxford OX1 1JG, England.

ABC-Clio Information Services,
Riviera Campus, 2040 Alameda Padre Serra,
Santa Barabara, Ca. 93103, USA.

Designed by Bernard Crossland
Typeset by Columns Design and Production Services,
Reading, England
Printed and bound in Great Britain by
Billing and Sons Ltd., Worcester

THE WORLD BIBLIOGRAPHICAL SERIES

This series will eventually cover every country in the world, each in a separate volume comprising annotated entries on works dealing with its history, geography, economy and politics; and with its people, their culture, customs, religion and social organization. Attention will also be paid to current living conditions – housing, education, newspapers clothing, etc. – that are all too often ignored in standard bibliographies; and to those particular aspects relevant to individual countries. Each volume seeks to achieve, by use of careful selectivity and critical assessment of the literature, an expression of the country and an appreciation of its nature and national aspirations to guide the reader towards an understanding of its importance. The keynote of the series is to provide, in a uniform format, an interpretation of each country that will express its culture, its place in the world, and the qualities and background that make it unique.

SERIES EDITORS

Robert L. Collison (Editor-in-chief) is Professor Emeritus, Library and Information Studies, University of California, Los Angeles, and is currently the President of the Society of Indexers. Following the war, he served as Reference Librarian for the City of Westminster and later became Librarian to the BBC. During his fifty years as a professional librarian in England and the USA, he has written more than twenty works on bibliography, librarianship, indexing and related subjects.

Sheila R. Herstein is Reference Library Instruction Coordinator at the City College of the City University of New York. She has extensive bibliographic experience and has described her innovations in the field of bibliographic instruction in 'Team teaching and bibliographic instruction', *The Bookmark*, Autumn 1979. In addition, Doctor Herstein co-authored a basic annotated bibliography in history for Funk & Wagnalls *New encyclopedia*, and for several years reviewed books for *Library Journal*.

Louis J. Reith is librarian with the Franciscan Institute, St. Bonaventure University, New York. He received his PhD from Stanford University, California, and later studied at Eberhard-Karls-Universität, Tübingen. In addition to his activities as a librarian, Dr. Reith is a specialist on 16th century German history and the Reformation and has published many articles and papers in both German and English. He was also editor of the *American Society for Reformation Research Newsletter*.

Hans H. Wellisch is a Professor at the College of Library and Information Services, University of Maryland, and a member of the American Society of Indexers and the International Federation for Documentation. He is the author of numerous articles and several books on indexing and abstracting, and has most recently published *Indexing and abstracting: an international bibliography*. He also contributes frequently to *Journal of the American Society for Information Science, Library Quarterly*, and *The Indexer*.

For Michael and Laura

Contents

Contents

Contents

Introduction

Spain: a brief historical background

The well-known historian Henry Kamen remarked that 'a mixture of legend and reality typifies the blurred view that we still have of Spain's history', and perhaps part of the explanation for this lies in the fact that from earliest times the Iberian Peninsula was a veritable melting-pot of diverse civilizations and cultures. Spain in fact played the unwilling host to numerous invading peoples, including the Phoenicians, Carthaginians, Greeks, Celts, Romans, Visigoths and Moors, all within a relatively short space of time. Many of these races, having arrived and conquered, moved no further into Europe, and thus the mixture of distinct traditions and cultures remained.

The Moors, in particular, were responsible for greatly influencing Spanish civilization. Having invaded from North Africa in 711 AD, they conquered the majority of the Peninsula in just seven years. They actually remained for nearly eight hundred years, and their prolonged stay left Spain culturally very wealthy. It was the slow Christian Reconquest, which proceeded throughout the Middle Ages, which was to act as the impetus that set Spain on the road to future greatness, prosperity and European domination.

The year 1492 (the *annus mirabilis*) marked the beginning of a new era in Spanish history, witnessing not only Columbus' momentous discovery of the New World, but also the final victory over the Moors at Granada, the expulsion of the Jews, and the publication of the first Spanish grammar. Spain was on her way to becoming the greatest imperial power ever, and in the 16th and 17th centuries, under the Habsburgs, the empire continued to expand. Paradoxically, it was as a direct result of their policies that Spain found herself increasingly involved in costly conflicts both at home and abroad, and soon entered a period of economic and political decline from which she never really recovered. Nevertheless, it was during this era that the arts in general, and literature in particular, flourished in what became known as the 'Siglo de Oro' (Golden Age) of Spanish letters.

In 1700 the French Bourbon dynasty acceded to the throne of Spain, and embarked upon the political reform of the country from within. Although a great deal was achieved in this respect, the political decline continued throughout the 18th century, with the failure of the their foreign policy resulting in the loss of most of Spain's European possessions. To make matters worse, the American colonies were now beginning to flex their muscles and establish claims for independence.

The following century was one of major political upheaval and internal strife, culminating in the overthrow of the monarchy in 1868, and its replacement by the short-lived First Republic in 1873. Although the Bourbons were shortly restored, the relative calm of the final quarter of the century was broken by the war of 1898 (the 'year of the disaster') between Spain and the United States, which resulted in the destruction of the Spanish navy and the loss of the last of her American colonies.

The period up to the First World War, in which Spain remained neutral, was characterized by political fluctuations which eventually led to a complete loss of faith in the government, and the establishment of a military dictatorship under General Miguel Primo de Rivera in 1923. Continued civil unrest resulted in the abdication of Alfonso XIII in 1931, the subsequent creation of a Second Republic, and ultimately the outbreak of civil war in 1936. The victory of the nationalists under General Franco was facilitated by support from both Hitler and Mussolini, who used Spain as a testing-ground for troops and weapons later to be employed in the Second World War.

After the ravages of a civil war in which an estimated one million Spaniards lost their lives, Franco was installed as Head of State, and although his authoritarian rule afforded relative peace and stability, individual freedom was severely restricted. For the next decade Spain, already very weak economically, suffered widescale political isolation. However, by the end of the 1940s the Western powers were re-examining their attitude towards the country in the light of what was regarded by many as the far greater threat of communism. In 1953 a defence agreement was signed with the United States, under which Spain would receive economic and military aid in return for allowing the Americans the use of naval and air bases on her territory. Two years later

Introduction

Spain was admitted into the United Nations. The economic growth of the 1960s was paralleled by a growth in the tide of anti-Franco sentiment from a new generation of Spaniards, notably amongst students and the working classes. The internal struggle for power eventually came to a head following the assassination of the Prime Minister, Admiral Luis Carrero Blanco, in 1973, the overthrow of the right-wing régime in Portugal in 1974, and the rapidly failing health of 'el Caudillo'. His death at the end of 1975 secured the restoration of the Bourbon monarchy in the person of Juan Carlos I (Alfonso XIII's grandson), and the renewal of open political debate.

In the last ten years the speed with which the democratization process has advanced, and the success of the government in dismantling the trappings of Francoism, have surprised even those who know Spain well. Naturally, it would be foolish to assume that it has all been plain sailing. Although unsuccessful, the attempted military 'coup' of February 1981 demonstrated just how fragile democracy can be. The king's swift and effective action was the major factor in foiling the threat of another military dictatorship. What remains certain is that, despite the lasting influence of forty years under an authoritarian régime, few people would have predicted that just a decade after Franco's death a freely-elected, socialist government would be poised to take Spain into the European Economic Community (EEC).

Spain today

Modern Spain occupies just over 80 percent of the Iberian Peninsula, and is the second-largest country in Western Europe after France. The total area of all Spanish territory, including the Balearic and Canary Islands, covers 194,897 square miles. A vast tableland (the 'meseta'), which rises to an average of 2,000 feet above sea level, and which is itself traversed by five large mountain ranges, makes Spain the second-highest country in Europe after Switzerland, with Madrid the highest European capital. The north has an Atlantic climate, with cool winters, mild summers and a heavy annual rainfall. The very dry Mediterranean south and east are subject to extremes of temperature in winter and summer, and the climate of central Castile has been aptly described as 'nine months of winter, three months of hell'.

Spain's population of 38 millions, when compared to the size of

Introduction

the country, is very small. In recent years increasing numbers of people have been migrating from the countryside into the towns and cities as a direct result of the decline in agriculture and the lure of better-paid employment in the continually expanding industrial sector. Moreover, many peasants are forced to seek work in other European countries, notably France, and most stay away for three or four years before returning to Spain.

Spanish is now well-established as the fourth major world language after Russian, Chinese and English, and is spoken by over 300 million people. Within Spain the principal language spoken is Castilian. Catalan is widely spoken in the northeast and the Balearic Islands, Basque in the north, and Galician in the northwest. These variations, together with other distinct regional features, make it virtually impossible to define a true national 'Spanish' character. The constitution of 1978 guaranteed the right of Spain's 'nationalities and regions' to autonomy, and much has already been achieved in this direction. Although the Basque Provinces and Catalonia are the traditional 'nationalistic' regions, Galicia and Andalusia also lay claim to historical and cultural independence. The associated terrorist activities of the military wing of ETA (Basque Homeland and Freedom) have now been drastically curtailed due to strong government measures allied to closer links with the French authorities.

The return to democracy has also led to major changes in other areas. Whilst the great majority of Spaniards still belong to the Roman Catholic Church, it is no longer the state religion by law. Indeed, recent reports and articles have shown that fewer people than ever before currently practise the faith. Likewise, a parliamentary monarchy now guarantees freedom to all political parties under the law, and many which were forced to operate clandestinely under the Franco régime have now re-emerged to fight openly in free elections. In a similar way the 1977 Labour Law, amplified by Royal Decree, established the right of workers to form professional associations in order to safeguard their interests.

The industrialization of Spain, largely a post-1950 phenomenon, was initially aided by American investment and military expenditure. The principal industrial areas are centred around the cities of Barcelona and Bilbao, although most important business negotiations are conducted and finalized in Madrid. In recent years tourism has played a major role in the economy, and has become one of Spain's most important industries. The Spanish tourist board's claim that 'Spain is different' enticed more visitors to the country (41.25 millions) in 1983 than the total national population figure. It is therefore hardly surprising that the permanent headquarters of the World Tourism Organization is based in Madrid. Spain's more traditional exports of agricultural produce and raw materials have now been superseded by industrial goods, which account for over 70 percent of the export trade, with half of all exports now going to EEC countries. The return to democracy has also allowed Spain to break down many of the barriers which formerly existed between herself and other nations. In 1977 she joined the Council of Europe, and in 1982 became a member of NATO (although the Prime Minister has promised a referendum on the latter, as many Spaniards are strongly against membership). Ironically, Spain's improved relations with many of her European neighbours have come under some strain recently as the country has moved steadily forward towards full integration into the EEC in 1986. Many current members are deeply concerned at the prospect of Spain's fishing fleet, the biggest in western Europe, being the cause of territorial disputes, and her agricultural sector disrupting the balance of the Common Agricultural Policy (CAP) system. Relations with Britain continue to centre on the age-old problem of Gibraltar which has been under British sovereignty since 1713. Some improvement in the situation took place in February 1985 when Spain lifted restrictions and opened the border fully. In view of the country's increasingly European outlook, the reiterated analogy 'Spain! It hangs like a drying ox hide outside the door of Europe proper' may soon no longer apply.

The bibliography

Spain has always attracted, and will doubtlessly continue to attract, a great deal of interest and study, but despite the large amount of research carried out each year, the only English-language bibliographies available on Spain are those devoted mainly to literature, language and history. Many of these tend to either include Portugal or Latin America, or both. I have therefore attempted to provide what I myself, and I am sure many other Hispanists, have long sought: a large selective and annotated collection covering all subject areas, with the accent on those aspects of Spanish life which, in my view, underline Spain's uniqueness. It contains 982 main items, of which 87 are in Spanish, and 133 subsidiary titles referred to within the annotations.

Introduction

Emphasis has been placed on recently-published literature, but older works of lasting value and importance have also been included. Periodical articles have been incorporated in order to provide a balanced approach where the relevant books stress only one particular aspect of a topic, or where no comparable books on the subject exist. It should be added that articles may sometimes be more readily accessible to the reader, or be preferred for their concise treatment of a specific area. A number of works in Spanish appear in order to avoid bias and provide a balance to the English-language viewpoint.

It goes without saying that selectivity was more difficult for some subjects than for others. The wealth of material available in English on, for example, the Spanish Civil War and Spanish literature had to be carefully sifted in order to maintain a reasonable balance between sections. Works by, and about, specific Spanish writers, artists, composers and film directors have been excluded for the same reason. Major figures are often identified within the annotations of more general works which usually also contain large bibliographies on the more important individuals.

It is hoped that this bibliography will be of use to a wide range of readers. Although it is primarily intended for the informed general reader, it may also serve as a guide for students of Spanish seeking topics for dissertations or other research, by focusing on the quantity, quality and types of literature available in specific fields of interest.

Within the sections items have been listed alphabetically by author, editor or compiler, and in their absence, by title. The only exception to this is the sub-section 'Dictionaries' within the 'Languages and dialects' section, where all appear in title order, as this is how they are most commonly known. The annotations are in the main concise, factual and objective, with critical comment and analysis made where it was felt necessary.

Acknowledgements

Several individuals have facilitated the compilation of this bibliography in the three years it has been in the making. I would particularly like to thank the staff of the Inter-library Loans section of the J. B. Priestley Library at the University of Bradford for their assistance in obtaining much of the included material; John Horton, Deputy Librarian at the University, for his encouragement and advice from the outset; Dr. Rafael Sala,

Introduction

from the School of Studies in Modern Languages, for his help in translating some of the more awkward Spanish titles; my wife Kathryn, who not only typed the manuscript but also provided invaluable assistance, advice and, on many occasions, inspiration; and finally our children, Michael and Laura, both born during the course of its preparation, and without whose help the work would have been completed considerably sooner.

Graham J. Shields
Bradford, West Yorkshire
January, 1985

Chronology

ca.	**15,000-10,000 BC**	Cave paintings at Altamira
ca.	**1,100 BC**	Phoenicians found Cádiz
ca.	**900-650 BC**	Celts migrate to Spain
ca.	**500-400 BC**	Greek colonization and invasion of Carthaginians
ca.	**200 BC-400 AD**	Roman invasion
ca.	**100-300 AD**	Introduction of Christianity
ca.	**400 AD**	Invasion by Vandals and other tribes
ca.	**415 AD**	Invasion by Visigoths
	587 AD	Catholicism becomes official state religion
711-718		Invasion by the Moors
1085		Recapture of Toledo from the Moors marks the turning point in the Reconquest
1094		Valencia recaptured by the Cid
1248		Reconquest of Seville
1348		Black Death
1474		Unification of the Crowns of Castile and Aragón
1478		Establishment of the Inquisition
1492		Recapture of Granada (last stronghold of the Moors) Expulsion of the Jews Discovery of the New World

Chronology

1520-21	Revolt of the Comuneros and Germanía
1545	Discovery of the Potosí mines in Peru
1561	Madrid established as the capital of Spain
1566	Dutch revolt begins
1571	Victory over the Turks at Lepanto
1580	Conquest of Portugal
1588	Defeat of the Armada by the English
1599-1600	Plague
1609-14	Expulsion of the Moriscos
1648	Dutch independence
1668	Portuguese independence
1700-14	War of the Spanish Succession between Britain and Austria
1767	Expulsion of the Jesuits
1805	Defeat by the English at Trafalgar
1808-14	Peninsular War (or Spanish War of Independence) between Spain and the invading French
1812	Cortes of Cádiz proclaims the first liberal constitution
1833-39	First Carlist War
1834	Abolition of the Inquisition
1868	Revolution overthrowing the monarchy
1873-74	First Republic
1898	Spanish-American War (in which Spain loses the last of her American possessions)
1909	Tragic Week
1923-30	Dictatorship of Primo de Rivera
1931-39	Second Republic
1936-39	Civil War

Chronology

1939-75	Franco's dictatorship
1955	Spain joins the United Nations
1975	Restoration of the monarchy
1982	Spain joins NATO
1986	Spain's proposed entry into the European Economic Community

Rulers of Spain

1479-1504	Isabella I of Castile and Ferdinand II of Aragón
1504-06	Philip I and Juana the Mad (daughter of Ferdinand and Isabella)
1506-16	Ferdinand V (II of Aragón)

House of Habsburg

1516-56	Charles I (grandson of Ferdinand and Isabella)
1556-98	Philip II
1598-1621	Philip III
1621-65	Philip IV
1665-1700	Charles II

House of Bourbon

1700-24	Philip V (grandson of Charles II's cousin, Louis XIV of France)
1724	Louis I
1724-46	Philip V
1746-59	Ferdinand VI
1759-88	Charles III
1788-1808	Charles IV (abdicated)
1808	Ferdinand VII
1808-13	Joseph Bonaparte (brother of Napoleon)
1813-33	Ferdinand VII
1833-68	Isabella II (dethroned)
1868-70	Revolution, and coalition of Juan Prim y Prats and Francisco Serrano

House of Savoy

1870-73	Amadeo I (Duke of Aosta, son of the King of Italy) (abdicated)

Rulers of Spain
First Republic
1873-74

House of Bourbon
1874-85   Alfonso XII
1886-1931   Alfonso XIII (abdicated)

Second Republic
1931-39   (1936-39 Civil War)

Head of State
1939-75   General Francisco Franco y Bahamonde

House of Bourbon
1975- .   Juan Carlos I (grandson of Alfonso XIII)

The Country and Its People

1 **The heritage of Spain: an introduction to Spanish civilization.**
Nicholson Barney Adams. New York: Henry Holt, 1959. rev. ed.
380p. maps. bibliog.
A general survey of Spanish history, literature and art, with useful sections on arts
and letters in the 19th and 20th centuries. As many writers do, Adams emphasizes
that the diversity of Spanish culture adds to the richness of its heritage. This is an
excellent introduction to Spain and its artistic achievements over the centuries,
which also contains numerous maps, black-and-white photographs, and an
extensive, partly-annotated bibliography.

2 **The Spanish character: attitudes and mentalities from the sixteenth to
the nineteenth century.**
Bartolomé Bennassar, translated with a preface by Benjamin
Keen. Berkeley, California; Los Angeles: University of California
Press, 1979. 325p. bibliog.
This book represents an excellent attempt to rationalize the very contradictory
nature of the Spanish character. Through chapters on daily life, religion, festivals,
honour, violence and love and dying, Bennassar presents a picture of the
Spaniard as a person who, 'moulded by the peculiar course of Spanish history,
tried to gain power, honour, and riches through brave deeds and an adventurous
spirit rather than by hard work, who would rather fight to conquer existing goods
than work to create new ones, who admired a courageous man more than a
careful one, who chose chance over constancy and favour over merit'. The
Spanish passion for self-analysis and self-criticism is proverbial: their indigenous
pride has gone a long way to enhance the persisting image of 'machismo' amongst
Spanish men. Militarism, the sentiment of honour, and prejudice against labour
were believed to set the Spaniards apart from other peoples. Bennassar studies
these Spanish mental attitudes, and shows them to be the natural result of
historically determined circumstances.

1

The Country and Its People

3 **Spain in the world.**
Saxtone Bradford. Princeton, New Jersey: Van Nostrand, 1962.
121p. 4 maps. bibliog. (Van Nostrand Searchlight Book, no. 3).

The author served as a counsellor at the United States Embassy in Madrid from 1955 until 1957, and this book was 'planned expressly to make Spain more understandable to North Americans'. The work briefly describes the physical features of the country, its history, politics, industry, foreign relations, culture and the character of its people. Although somewhat dated, this remains a useful introductory work for those wishing to understand Spain's importance in the world.

4 **The Spaniard and the seven deadly sins.**
Fernando Díaz-Plaja, translated from the Spanish by John Inderwick Palmer. London: Victor Gollancz, 1968. 223p. bibliog.

The author is a prolific writer on Spanish history and literature, and in this work he takes a witty, unsparing look at his fellow countrymen, their virtues and vices. There are seven chapters, each devoted to a particular sin (pride, avarice, lust, anger, gluttony, envy and sloth), through which an attempt is made to throw light on all aspects of the Spaniard's character and personality. This excellent book includes a bibliography of famous Spanish authors mentioned in the text.

5 **The soul of Spain.**
Havelock Ellis. Westport, Connecticut: Greenwood Press, 1976. 420p.

This well-known work is a reprint of the 1937 edition published by Houghton Mifflin, Boston, Massachussetts. The author first went to Spain in 1891, and died in the same year that the Civil War ended (1939). He writes: 'Spain represents, above all, the supreme manifestation of a certain primitive and eternal attitude of the human spirit, an attitude of heroic energy, of spiritual exaltation, directed not chiefly towards comfort or towards gain, but towards the more fundamental facts of human existence'. Amongst other topics the work includes chapters on the women of Spain, Spanish art and dancing, and the doctor, alchemist and philosopher Ramón Llull (regarded by many as the founder of Spanish mysticism), and it also contains an index.

6 **Spain.**
Robert Goldston. New York: Macmillan; London: Collier-Macmillan, 1967. 138p. map. bibliog. (Nations Today Books).

The author, who lived in the Balearics for ten years, provides general information about Spanish government, geography, history and occupations, and emphasizes the special features of the two Spains: the Spain of heroic legend and the Spain of often grim reality. This is an interesting and very useful book, which introduces the reader to Spain up to Franco's rule. The author also wrote *The Civil War in Spain* (London: Phoenix House, 1967).

7 **Background to Spain.**
   B. J. W. Hill. London: Longmans, 1969. 516p. bibliog.

A general introduction to Spanish history and culture, illustrated with 150 photographs, which traces the connection between the country, its history, its literature and its arts up to the present day. The book is aimed at both students and the non-specialist, encouraging them to seek further information on their own account.

8 **Spain, the land and its people.**
   Carmen Irizarry. London: Macdonald Educational, 1982. rev. ed.
   61p. 2 maps. (Macdonald Countries).

An informative and entertaining introductory study of Spain and her culture, which is excellently illustrated. Topics have been selected which emphasize the history and character of the country, and there is also a short reference section, and a brief gazetteer.

9 **Spain.**
   John Langdon-Davies. London: Batsford; New York: Hastings
   House, 1971. 216p. map.

This work is the opposite, in effect, to a tourist guide, in that it stresses the areas and cultures of regions which are not commonly seen by the majority of tourists. It constitutes a survey of places which give Spain its distinctive character, and of those aspects of life which make it a land of such diversity and fascination. It describes sights, customs, language, dress and scenery, and includes an introductory chapter on Spanish history. Aimed at both the tourist and the 'armchair reader at home', it explodes a lot of the traditional tourist myths about Spain.

10 **Spain and her people.**
   Dorothy Loder. London: Lutterworth Press, 1961. 144p. bibliog.

An easy-to-read introduction to the history and culture of Spain.

11 **Portrait of Spain: British and American accounts of Spain in the
   nineteenth and twentieth centuries.**
   Selected by Thomas F. McGann. New York: Alfred A. Knopf,
   1963. 389p. map. bibliog.

An enthralling collection of twenty-three accounts and descriptions by British and American writers, covering various aspects of Spain and her people over the past 150 years, including pieces by Ernest Hemingway, Robert Graves, George Orwell, Benjamin Disraeli and Somerset Maugham.

12 **Spain and Portugal: Iberian portrait.**
   Donald M. Madden. New York: Thomas Nelson, 1969. 224p.
   map. bibliog.

An excellently-illustrated book for sixth-formers and adults which describes the

The Country and Its People

history, land and peoples of the Peninsula, and contains a brief bibliography, historical highlights and an index.

13 **The presence of Spain.**
James Morris, photographs by Evelyn Hofer. London: Faber & Faber, 1964. 119p. map.

A very evocative work, superbly illustrated with abundant colour and black-and-white photographs, which is described by Gerald Brenan (author of several works on Spain) as 'perhaps the best general book ever written on Spain'. The author and photographer visited every corner of the country, and the style reproduces the atmosphere and fading glory of a land that was once the centre of a huge empire. It provides wide-ranging geographical, historical and cultural perspective to the 'Spanish presence', and includes an index of historical events as well as a general index. This excellent, detailed portrait of Spain loses little by the fact that it is now twenty years old.

14 **The Spaniards: how they live and work.**
Michael Perceval. Newton Abbot, England: David & Charles, 1972. rev. ed. 192p. 2 maps. bibliog. (How They Live and Work).

A good general description of the 'anatomy of Spain', i.e. how the country is run and how the people spend their time at work and play. It discusses contemporary social problems like housing, welfare and education, and includes an appendix entitled 'hints for visitors'. This is an easy-to-read, sometimes whimsical study of Spanish life and customs, and although written during Franco's time, most of it is still relevant to present-day Spain, and is a useful introduction to the basic way of life.

15 **When in Spain.**
Perrott Phillips, illustrated by Alex Brychta. London: Dent, 1974. 72p. 2 maps.

A light-hearted look at the customs, culture and people of Spain, intended primarily as an overview of daily life in Spain for the tourist. Phillips draws on history, customs and folklore to present a fascinating picture, full of interesting facts.

16 **The Spanish temper.**
V. S. Pritchett. London: Hogarth, 1984. 224p. map.

Originally published by Chatto & Windus in 1954, this new edition contains a new introduction by the author. The book describes his personal experiences and observations on Spanish history, life and culture, based on visits made to Spain in 1951 and 1952. Pritchett, a one-time resident of the Peninsula, writes 'of all the foreign countries I have known, Spain is the one that has made the strongest impression on me'.

17 **Living in Spain in the eighties.**
John Reay-Smith. London: Robert Hale, 1983. 207p. 2 maps.
Provides useful information for the growing number of British people who are
considering buying property in, or retiring to, Spain. The volume is well
illustrated, with useful appendixes on the Spanish constitution of 1978; British
government stocks; Spanish inheritance tax; finance; telephones; English schools;
English-language publications; and the British Embassy and consulates. The
author was a practising solicitor in England who decided to go and live in the
south of Spain, and he answers all the probable questions anyone thinking of
going to live in Spain might ask.

18 **Introducing Spain.**
Cedric Salter. London: Methuen, 1967. rev. ed. 239p. map.
This English journalist, who has been a resident in Spain for many years,
describes the country in very general terms. This work is divided into two parts:
one giving general information, and the other describing the country by cities and
regions. The author has also written books on Turkey and Portugal.

19 **Portrait of Spain.**
Tad Szulc. New York: American Heritage Press, 1972. 348p. (A
New York Times Book).
Profusely illustrated, with photographs depicting scenery, architecture, people
and daily life, this is a general survey of the Spaniards, their history, culture and
characteristics by a *New York Times* journalist. Also included is a 'Special
interest guide' to crafts and hobbies, festivals, and fashion and sports, which
provides brief details to the prospective visitor.

20 **The civilization of Spain.**
James Brande Trend. London, New York, Toronto: Oxford
University Press, 1967. 2nd ed. 138p. 4 maps. bibliog. (Oxford
Paperbacks University Series, no. 19).
A concise and valuable study, outlining the history and culture of Spain from the
time of the Phoenicians to the Spanish Civil War. This volume, which contains a
revised bibliography by Henry Kamen, is a standard work for anyone trying to
gain an overall picture of Spanish civilization.

21 **Spain: an introduction to the Spanish nation.**
A. T. Wright. London: University of London Press, 1974. 96p.
A brief survey of Spain, covering daily life, education, institutions, history and
the arts. The book aims to provide a background study of Spain for secondary
school pupils, but it is a useful introduction to all aspects of Spanish life for any
reader.

22 **Spain and her people.**
Jeremiah Zimmerman. London: T. Fisher Unwin, 1906. 350p.
This volume provides impressions of Spain and her people and is illustrated with

5

The Country and Its People

black-and-white photographs. It was written soon after Spain lost her empire in America and her fleet was destroyed. The comments of the author mirror the view of many people at the turn of the century: 'Unfortunately, Spain is not a modern country; her glory is in the past, and she lives and prides herself in her past traditions, as though her glory and her future were not before her. She clings to the past, and rejects the methods that would secure progress and intelligence, and hence it is difficult to forecast the future of Spain. With her seventy per cent. of illiterates, the lack of individual enterprise and patriotism among her people, the need of cohesion among the different provinces, and the constant friction from various quarters; together with the prevailing poverty and a depleted treasury, we confess that the outlook is not promising'. The author's final paragraph predicts the Civil War which followed thirty years after the book was first published.

A hand-book for travellers in Spain and readers at home: describing the country and cities, the natives and their manners; the antiquities, religion, legends, fine arts, literature, sports, and gastronomy: with notices on Spanish history.
See item no. 31.

Iberia: Spanish travels and reflections.
See item no. 39.

Spain, the country, her history and culture.
See item no. 956.

Travellers' Accounts

23 **Spanish quest.**
Ray Alan. London: Collier-Macmillan, 1969. 340p. map. bibliog.
A British journalist, in search of his father (who disappeared when the author was
an infant), journeys around Spain trying to trace records and people who knew
him. The author's comments on the history, land, people and culture of Spain
make this an interesting and very readable work.

24 **Spanish journey or springtime in Spain.**
W. T. Blake. London: Alvin Redman, 1957. 219p.
The author recounts his experiences while travelling in Spain over a period of
thirty-five years. There are thirty-two illustrations, some in colour, and two
appendixes on bullfighting and fishing.

25 **The Bible in Spain.**
George Borrow, with an introduction by Walter F. Starkie. London:
Dent; New York: E. P. Dutton, 1961. 510p. map. bibliog.
(Everyman's Library, no. 151: Travel and Topography).
A classic travel book in which Borrow (1803-81) does not hesitate in stating that
the years he spent in Spain were the happiest days of his life. The work represents
a fascinating record of the author's wanderings through Spain as an agent to the
Bible Society from 1835 to 1839, and stands head and shoulders above all others
as a picture of old Spain. It is not primarily a theological book, but one made up
of memories and colourful anecdotes. At one time Borrow formed close ties with
the gypsies of Badajoz, and he wrote a book on the Spanish gypsies, entitled *The
Zincali* (1841), and also set about translating the Gospel of St. Luke into 'Caló',
their language. He was travelling in Spain at the time of the First Carlist War,
after the death of Ferdinand VII in 1833, and was imprisoned in Madrid in 1838.
Borrow became quite a legend in various parts of Spain, and altogether made four
journeys through the country, the routes of which are shown on the map which is
included in the volume.

Travellers' Accounts

26 The face of Spain
Gerald Brenan. New York: Farrar, Straus & Cudahy, 1951. 310p. map.

The author and his wife returned to Spain in 1949 after an absence of thirteen years, having witnessed, during their last sojourn, the outbreak of the Spanish Civil War. Brenan's mind was full of questions, and he decided to keep a diary in which he recorded everyday experiences and impressions of their travels in central and southern Spain. He states that despite all the events which had occurred during his absence, the character of the people remained remarkably unchanged. His tale of searching for the burial place of the Spanish man of letters, Federico García Lorca (1899-1936), has a classic quality, and the entire book is a joy to read.

27 Journey to the Alcarria.
Camilo José Cela, translated by Frances M. López-Morillas. Madison and Milwaukee, Wisconsin: University of Wisconsin Press, 1964. 139p. map.

This portrayal of provincial Spain, its physical nature and the psychology and values of its people, is an excellent account. The author, a Spanish novelist, describes a walking tour in central Spain, the Alcarria being a territory of New Castile, northeast of Madrid.

28 From Paris to Cadiz.
Alexandre Dumas, translated by Alma Elizabeth Murch. London: Peter Owen, 1958. 216p.

This work was published in the United States under the title *Adventures in Spain* (Philadelphia: Chilton, 1959). This famous French writer (the elder) describes his impressions of Spain whilst visiting the country in order to attend the wedding of the Spanish Infanta. The book is printed as a series of letters, with original illustrations by Gustave Doré. This is a condensed volume of the original four, which retains their essential characteristics, and still manages to convey all the excitement of the Spain of 1846.

29 Spain's magic coast: from the Miño to the Bidassoa; a personal guidebook.
Nina Consuelo Epton. London: Weidenfeld & Nicolson, 1965. 181p.

The authoress, who was born in England, but educated in England, Spain and France, worked for the BBC, and left to take up full-time writing. This book is a personal travelogue of a journey along Spain's northern coast from the River Miño on the Portuguese frontier to the banks of the Bidassoa on the French border. Sadly it contains no map of her journeys, which detracts from the work as a whole, but the volume is illustrated with photographs depicting towns and scenery. Starting in Galicia the work takes the reader across the Asturian, Castilian and Basque coasts and provides useful advice to travellers. Nina Epton also wrote several other travel books, including *Andalusia* (London: Weidenfeld & Nicolson, 1968) which describes her journey through the eight provinces of Spain's southernmost region, and a work entitled *Love and the Spanish* (q.v.).

30 **The Enchanted Mountains: a quest in the Pyrenees.**
Robin Fedden. London: John Murray, 1962. 124p. 2 maps.
bibliog.

This good description of the Spanish Pyrenees, mountain villages and people, is primarily a study of the mountains and mountaineering. It is the story of three journeys made by the author and his wife between 1953 and 1957, and includes several black-and-white photographs of mountain scenery. The exact position of the Enchanted Mountains is indefinite, as the maps do not agree.

31 **A hand-book for travellers in Spain and readers at home: describing the country and cities, the natives and their manners; the antiquities, religion, legends, fine arts, literature, sports, and gastronomy: with notices on Spanish history.**
Richard Ford. London: Centaur Press, 1966. 3 vols. 2 maps.
bibliog. (Centaur Classics).

First published in 1845, this timeless work is a rich mine of information, and has influenced the way English people have seen Spain more than any other book. Although it is over a hundred years old, a great deal of the contents is still valid. Ford was a spirited writer, who in three years travelled over 2,000 miles on horseback around Spain, and spent much of his time recording in sketches, drawings and paintings the scenery through which he passed. Sections within each volume are divided by region, and are a wonderful evocation of the Spain of the 1830s. This edition reproduces the entire text of the original, and is a classic and comprehensive work. Ford also wrote *Gatherings from Spain* (London: Dent, 1970), which is still one of the best one-volume descriptions of old Spain and her people.

32 **A Romantic in Spain.**
Théophile Gautier, translated by Catherine Alison Phillips.
London: Alfred A. Knopf, 1926. 324p.

This French writer (1811-72), poet, critic and journalist visited Spain for five months in 1840, and took the lead in the French appreciation of Goya, whilst the English were lukewarm and preferred the old masters to the modernists. Gautier's book on his travels through Spain has all the colour that characterized his other writings, and was first published in French in 1845.

33 **Familiar Spanish travels.**
William Dean Howells. New York; London: Harper, 1913. 326p.

Confessing that a 'passion for Spanish things' had dominated his boyhood, this American man of letters sets about describing his visit to Spain in 1911, combining the literacy and gusto that marked his long career as author, editor, playwright and poet. Howells taught himself Spanish, and other languages, and wrote many critical articles about several Spanish writers.

Travellers' Accounts

34 As I walked out one midsummer morning.
Laurie Lee. Harmondsworth, England: Penguin Books, 1971. 186p. map.

Much of this excellent autobiographical work describes the author's journey on foot from Vigo to Málaga between July 1935 and July 1936, in which he draws an unforgettable picture of Spain just prior to the Civil War. On first arriving in Spain his knowledge of the country did not extend any further than that 'Seville had a barber, and Barcelona, nuts', and the ability to ask for a glass of water in Spanish. He left only to return via France to join the Republicans during the first winter of the war.

35 A rose for winter: travels in Andalusia.
Laurie Lee. Harmondsworth, England: Penguin Books, 1971. 122p.

A poetic description of a winter spent in Andalusia after an absence of fifteen years. On arrival the author notes that 'it did not take more than five minutes to wipe out fifteen years and to return me whole to this thorn-cruel, threadbare world, sombre with dead and dying Christs, brassy with glittering Virgins'. He notes the changes in a country only too clearly displaying the long-term effects of civil war, and accepts them. This visit does not have as great an impact as the first, described in *As I walked out one midsummer morning* (q.v.).

36 Spain.
John Lomas. London: A. & C. Black, 1925. 2nd ed. 283p. map.

Illustrated with thirty-two colour drawings, this is a description of the author's travels in Spain, leading the reader through all of the country's major cities. It is a highly descriptive work, covering the geography, history, art and architecture of the places visited.

37 Andalucía: a portrait of southern Spain.
Nicholas Luard. London: Century, 1984. 288p.

For eight years Luard and his wife Elisabeth, together with their four children, lived in a remote valley behind the little fishing port of Tarifa. This book is a portrait of the valley, and a vivid personal view of culture and customs. It also represents an excellent traveller's account of southern Spain, a region which García Lorca once described as 'Orient without poison, Occident without action'. Another evocative account of travel in the region is Penelope Chetwode's *Two middle-aged ladies in Andalusia* (London: Century, 1985).

38 Fabled shore: from the Pyrenees to Portugal.
Rose Macaulay. London: Hamish Hamilton, 1973. 200p. map.

An excellent description of a journey made by road along the full length of Spain's eastern and southern coasts, covering the cities, architecture, country and people. It is divided into five sections on: Catalonia; Murcia; Valencia; Andalusia; and the Algarve.

39 **Iberia: Spanish travels and reflections.**
James A. Michener. London: Secker & Warburg, 1968. 818p.
maps. bibliog.

An excellently illustrated, encyclopaedic study of the Peninsula and its people, and the best American interpretation of Spain. The author first visited Spain in 1932, and says that 'During the four decades that I have travelled in Spain I have always wanted to describe the impact this vibrant land has had upon me'. The book contains a wealth of information about Spain from prehistoric times to the 1960s, and is particularly useful for its study of Spanish culture and history. This is one of the most vivid and evocative studies of Spain ever to have been written, and it was reprinted in 1980.

40 **A stranger in Spain.**
H. V. Morton. London: Methuen, 1983. 372p. map. (Methuen Paperback).

This completely original travel book not only recounts the author's journey through Spain in the early 1950s, but also explores Spain's history and culture. The author asserts that 'the stranger who wishes to approach Spain with sympathy and appreciation must do so through its history'.

41 **Images of Spain.**
Mordecai Richler. London: Thames & Hudson, 1978. 191p. map. bibliog.

The author revisited Spain after an absence of twenty-five years, and interviewed several important figures. Eight superb sections define the essence of Spain's history, landscape and culture, and the numerous photographs are enhanced by excerpts from many of the great writers who have been inspired by Spain and her people, including Miguel de Cervantes Saavedra, Lord Byron, Ernest Hemingway, Gerald Brenan and Sachaverell Sitwell.

42 **Railway holiday in Spain.**
D. Trevor Rowe. Newton Abbot, England: David & Charles, 1966. 164p. map. bibliog. (Railway Holiday Series, no. 6).

A first hand survey of the railway system in Spain in the early 1960s, which includes excellent photographs of Spanish locomotives. The author travelled extensively by train, and his descriptions are not limited to historical and technical details about the Spanish railways, but also extend to general comments on the cities he visited and to daily life.

43 **Spain.**
Sachaverell Sitwell. London: Batsford, 1975. 216p. map.

This guidebook is the fruit and accumulation of many journeys made to Spain since 1919. The author emphasizes that, after the Romans, the Spaniards have been the greatest builders, and this graphic work is superbly illustrated with photographic examples.

44 **The road to Santiago: pilgrims of St. James.**
Walter F. Starkie. London: John Murray, 1957. 339p. map. bibliog.

A collection of memoirs of visits to the shrine at Compostela. The journey for Starkie, as for others, holds a peculiar fascination, both for its religious and historical significance, and for its continual reminder 'of the further ghostly journey towards Ultima Thule'. In 813 a tomb was discovered at nearby Padrón, said to be that of the apostle St. James the Great, martyred at Jerusalem in AD 44. According to legend his bones were taken to Spain, where he had formerly evangelized. The discovery of his relics provided a rallying point for Christians in Spain, and Santiago became the most important Christian place of pilgrimage after Jerusalem and Rome during the Middle Ages. 'Sant-Iago' is the Spanish for 'St. James', the city having once been the capital of Galicia. Starkie also wrote *Spanish raggle-taggle: adventures with a fiddle in North Spain* (Harmondsworth, England: Penguin Books, 1961), which describes a summer journey he made alone on foot from San Sebastián to Madrid, earning his living as a wandering minstrel.

45 **Silk hats and no breakfast: notes on a Spanish journey.**
Honor L. W. Tracy. Harmondsworth, England: Penguin, 1962. 189p. map. (Penguin Books, no. 1,822).

Describes a journey in the mid-1950s through the western side of Spain, from Gibraltar to Vigo. The book provides an entertaining account of the travels, the countryside and the people. Tracy also wrote *Winter in Castile* (New York: Random House, 1974), which is an interesting description of travels around the region.

46 **The goodbye land.**
José Yglesias. London: Hutchinson, 1968. 218p.

An evocative picture of Galicia, one of the least known provinces of Spain. This is in part a travelogue and in part a mystery, as the author, (born in Tampa, Florida) travels through the region intent on learning the reasons for his Spanish father's illness and death. He provides a sympathetic and understanding portrait of the land and people. His story was first serialized in the *New Yorker*.

Portrait of Spain: British and American accounts of Spain in the nineteenth and twentieth centuries.
See item no. 11.

The Spanish Pyrenees.
See item no. 61.

South from Granada.
See item no. 457.

Spanish mountain life: the Sierra Nevada.
See item no. 460.

Geography

General

47 **The Spanish plateau: the challenge of a dry land.**
Peter Buckley.   London: Chatto & Windus, 1962. 96p. 5 maps.
(Challenge Books).

A very basic, though useful introduction. Some isolated areas on the Spanish meseta, which covers two thirds of the total area of Spain, have been known to go a whole year without rainfall. The land is very dry, and the climate extreme, but the people survive, and the book tells the story of their long struggle. Although primarily intended as a book for older children, it provides an excellent introduction to the geography of Spain, discussing physical features such as the mountains and rivers, the climate, agriculture, and day-to-day life. The author has travelled extensively in Spain, and there are excellent photographs throughout the book, as well as maps of the Peninsula, the plateau and mountains, rivers, rainfall and demography.

48 **Spain: a geographical background.**
W. B. Fisher, H. Bowen-Jones.   London: Chatto & Windus, 1958.
222p. 18 maps. bibliog.

This is a physical and human geography aimed at sixth-formers and university students. It is divided into three parts, covering the physical basis, human background and regional geography of Spain. This useful general survey is regarded as the first full geographical study in English of Spain, and includes ten black-and-white plates.

49 **The western Mediterranean world: an introduction to its regional landscapes.**
J. M. Houston, with contributions by J. Roglić and J. I. Clarke. London: Longmans, 1964. 800p. 260 maps and diagrams. bibliog. (Geographies for Advanced Study).
Contains a large section (Part 2, p. 164-335) on Spain, which analyzes the structures and landforms, rural landscapes, population and settlement surveying all the regions. The contents include many black-and-white plates, nearly 100 maps and diagrams, a glossary of terms, an extensive selected bibliography and an index. This introductory study describes the Iberian Peninsula as 'a continent in miniature', and contains details on ecology and man's impact upon the land in terms of settlement. The author states that the book may be read at two levels: 'the regional descriptions may be studied first by the sixth form and first year University student, while the advanced student – for whom the book is primarily intended – can study it systematically'.

50 **Some major elements in Spanish placenames.**
B. S. Macaodha. *Geography*, vol. 64, part 1, no. 282 (Jan. 1979), p. 17-20.
Toponomy is important for understanding the link between man and the land, which is particularly strong in Spain, where one community has succeeded another over many hundreds of years. Especially important were the contributions of the Arabs and Romans, whilst elements drawn from older cultures (namely Basque, Celtic, Greek and Phoenician) are also found. The author, Professor of Geography at University College, Galway, Ireland, cites many examples of words and names that cast much light on the land's history and on the cultures of the inhabitants in different epochs. This is a short, introductory article on a fascinating topic, and includes a bibliography.

51 **Western Mediterranean Europe: a historical geography of Italy, Spain and southern France since the Neolithic.**
Catherine Delano Smith. London; New York: Academic Press, 1979. 453p. maps. bibliog.
A study of the geographical past of Mediterranean Europe, mainly concerned with the people, land and land use, and the changing environment. The period studied spans seven thousand years. This is a good general study, which analyzes key aspects of social and economic patterns, and includes numerous maps, plates and figures.

52 **Geografía general de España.** (A general geography of Spain.)
Edited by Manuel Terán Alvarez and Luis Solé Sabaris. Barcelona: Editorial Ariel, 1978. 549p. maps. bibliog.
This excellent and very detailed first volume in a two-volume work, covers the physical geography of Spain (geological characteristics; the meseta; cordilleras; coastline; climate; rivers; lakes; and vegetation) as well as the human geography (rural and urban population; agriculture and livestock; industry; fishing; communications and transport; tourism; and major national socioeconomic

problems). It is well illustrated, and includes a toponomic index and a statistical appendix on the population and economy of Spain, as well as numerous maps.

53 **A geography of Spain and Portugal.**
Ruth Way. London: Methuen, 1962. 362p. maps. bibliog.
A detailed physical and economic geography of the Iberian Peninsula, supplemented with numerous photographs and maps, and including sections on geology, climate, and flora and fauna.

Regional

54 **Galicia.**
Keith Chambers. London: Harrap, 1981. 32p. 3 maps.
(Discovering Spain).
A well-illustrated volume in the series which is aimed at sixth-form students of Spanish, and which covers all aspects of life in Spain. Galicia is one of the poorest parts of the country, where two-thirds of the population still derive their living from the land, and industry is largely confined to food processing. This work studies concisely: the land and the people, including population statistics; the language; the struggle for autonomy; the Galician character; local customs; agriculture; architecture; climate; food and drink; Santiago de Compostela; industry; tourism; and places of interest.

55 **The western Pyrenees: differential evolution of the French and Spanish borderland.**
Daniel Alexander Gómez-Ibáñez. Oxford, England: Clarendon Press, 1975. 162p. map. bibliog. (Oxford Research Studies in Geography).
An analysis of the changes in the geography of the mountains of the western Pyrenees, concentrating on the differences between the French and Spanish parts of the borderland during the last two centuries. This is a useful study, not only for the historical and political geographer, but also for demographers, economic and social historians, and anthropologists. The author spent a year and a half with his family in the Pyrenees gathering material for this wide-ranging work, which covers geography, valley communities, landscape, society, economy and agriculture within their historical settings. Also included are statistics and an extensive bibliography.

56 **Andalusia.**
James Robert Jump. London: Harrap, 1977. 32p. 4 maps.
(Discovering Spain).
A basic, well-illustrated introduction to the region, covering history, geography, population, sport, flamenco, food and drink, agriculture, architecture, and famous Andalusians. As with the other volumes in the series, it is aimed at sixth-form students of Spanish.

15

Geography. Regional

57 The Basque country.
James Robert Jump.   London: Harrap, 1976. 32p. map.
(Discovering Spain).

A general introduction to all aspects of the region, including its people, climate, language, the fight for complete autonomy, Euskadi Ta Askatasuna (ETA), tourism, industry, agriculture, Navarre, food and drink, sports and pastimes (including pelota), music and dancing, regional customs and dress, architecture, and portraits of some famous Basques. The standard of living in the Basque country is twice the Spanish average. The region developed a maritime economy, and since the late 19th century an industrial revolution, based on hydroelectric power, has taken place centred around Bilbao.

58 New Castile.
James Robert Jump.   London: Harrap, 1977. 32p. 4 maps.
(Discovering Spain).

A basic introductory survey of the region and its main characteristics, covering geography, people, industry and handicrafts, agriculture, Madrid, regional customs and places of interest.

59 Old Castile.
James Robert Jump.   London: Harrap, 1977. 32p. 2 maps.
(Discovering Spain).

A companion volume to the book by the same author entitled *New Castile* (q.v.), which briefly looks at: geography; people; food and drink; Segovia; Avila; Burgos; el Cid; Santander; Logroño and the Rioja winefields; the Altamira caves; Valladolid; customs and folklore; and Antonio Machado of Soria.

60 Catalonia.
Heather Elsie Leigh, John R. Leigh.   London: Harrap, 1979. 32p.
5 maps. (Discovering Spain).

Another well-illustrated volume in the series, which discusses the general features of the most industrialized part of Spain, including its: geography; people; history; language; Barcelona; folklore and customs; monasteries (Montserrat); Lérida; Gerona and the Costa Brava; tourism; skiing in the Pyrenees; the Costa Dorada; transport and communications; Tarragona; Antoní Gaudí; and Salvador Dalí.

61 The Spanish Pyrenees.
Henry Myhill.   London: Faber & Faber, 1966. 272p. 8 maps.
bibliog.

An interesting and thorough account of the southern slopes of the range, its peaks and passes, which surveys the Basque, Aragonese and Catalan Pyrenees. The author was a courier with the job of accompanying clients of 'eight of the largest British travel agencies between the Basque coast and the English Channel'. The book records his journeys after he gave up his job to concentrate on travel, and makes many references to fellow travellers who have written about their journeys in this region. There are detailed geographical and historical descriptions, and an appendix giving information on communications, accommodation, maps of the region, and shooting and fishing. Myhill also wrote *The Canary Islands* (London: Faber, 1968), which is a good historical and descriptive guide to the islands.

62 Andalusia.

John Naylon. London: Oxford University Press, 1975. 48p. 7 maps. bibliog. (Problem Regions of Europe).

This series was originally aimed at the sixth-form geography student but, as it developed, it became clear that the works were useful as introductory texts for advanced students of both geography and European studies in general. This volume discusses the development problems of a region which has to contend with the difficulties of Mediterranean drought, wind and flood. The problem is exacerbated by the fact that, although the most populous region in Spain, Andalusia is also one of the poorest. The text includes maps, photographs, and a graph of employment in the area, as well as a useful bibliography which cites works in English and Spanish separately.

63 Geografía regional de España. (The regional geography of Spain.)

Edited by Manuel Terán Alvarez and Luis Solé Sabaris. Barcelona: Ediciones Ariel, 1968. 503p. maps. bibliog.

A book written expressly to deal both with the needs of the university student of Spanish geography and the general reader. The contents cover the geographic regions of Spain as a whole, and each section of this comprehensive study contains its own bibliography. In addition, there is a toponomic index, and a pull-out folder of regional maps.

Physical

64 Soil erosion in Spain.

Hugh Hammond Bennett. *Geographical Review*, vol. 50, no. 1 (Jan. 1960), p. 59-72.

'At the request of the Spanish government, the author spent three months in Spain in 1956 to investigate and report on erosion problems. Field work was confined to the central, southeastern, and southern sections of the country and was carried out with the cooperation of the International Cooperation Administration and the Soil Conservation Service of the Spanish Ministry of Agriculture'. The author was at one time chief of the Soil Conservation Service of the United States Department of Agriculture until his retirement in 1951. The article is divided into sections covering the effects of soil erosion, fragmentation in relation to erosion, and remedial measures involving both consolidation and conservation.

65 **Geomorphology of Europe.**
   Edited by Clifford Embleton. London: Macmillan, 1984. 465p.
   maps. bibliog.

Chapters 11 to 13 (p. 268-340) cover the Iberian Peninsula. This is an excellent and detailed study of the major landforms in Spain, which discusses in particular the geomorphology of the Pyrenees, the Ebro basin, the meseta, the Baetic cordillera and the Guadalquivir basin. All three chapters are written by M. Sala. The book as a whole represents the first comprehensive survey of its kind.

66 **Meseta and campiña landforms in central Spain: a geomorphology of the Alto Henares basin.**
   Bruce G. Gladfelter. Chicago: University of Chicago, Department of Geography, 1971. 204p. maps. bibliog. (University of Chicago, Department of Geography: Research Papers, no. 130).

A scholarly piece of research on the geological formations of the Alto Henares basin, which includes excellent maps, illustrations, tables and a bibliography. This book is based on fieldwork which was conducted from July to December 1967, and will be of great interest to the specialist in the physical geography of Spain.

67 **The rain in Spain.**
   John B. Thornes. *Geographical Magazine*, vol. 46, no. 7 (April 1974), p. 337-43.

Discusses the havoc caused by floods in southeast Spain in 1973, and includes two maps and several colour and black-and-white photographs of the damage caused. Expanding on the events of that year it analyzes what sort of damage flooding causes, and the climatological and geographical problems of the region. It also covers reconstruction and plans for the future which might avert a similar occurrence. However, it should be noted that flooding did take place again in the Alicante-Valencia region in October 1982.

68 **Semi-arid erosional systems: case studies from Spain.**
   John B. Thornes. London: London School of Economics and Political Science, 1976. 79p. maps. bibliog. (London School of Economics Geographical Papers, no. 7).

An introduction to the general nature, principal causes and effects of erosion in semi-arid Spain, explaining how, at the end of the day, the type and extent of action taken against soil erosion should be determined primarily by social and economic criteria. Thornes has also collaborated with A. Gilman on the recently published work in the London Research Series *Land-use and prehistory in southeast Spain* (London: Allen & Unwin, 1984).

69 **Climates of northern and western Europe.**
Edited by C. C. Wallén. Amsterdam; London; New York:
Elsevier, 1970. 253p. maps. bibliog. (World Survey of Climatology,
vol. 5).

Chapter 5 (p. 195-239), by A. Linés Escardó, describes the historical development
of meteorology and its use in understanding the climatic variations of Spain and
Portugal. All aspects of climatology, radiation, insolation, temperature, evapora-
tion, rainfall and winds are covered, and there are numerous maps, figures and
climatic tables to support the text.

70 **Climate and history: studies in past climates and their impact on Man.**
Edited by T. M. L. Wigley, M. J. Ingram and G. Farmer.
Cambridge, England; London; New York: Cambridge University
Press, 1981. 530p. bibliog.

Chapter 15 (p. 356-376) by Angus Mackay is entitled 'Climate and popular unrest
in late medieval Castile', and describes climatic fluctuations in the late mediaeval
kingdom of Castile. It considers aspects of the possible connections between these
fluctuations and mediaeval outbreaks of popular unrest. 'Aspects of weather
factors in the two regions of Old Castile and Murcia are then explained in order
to highlight the differences between the dry-farming lands ("secano") and the
"huertas" of the Levantine coast'. This is a specialized topic, but it gives a useful
insight into the documentation and accounts of the climate in Spain in the 15th
century.

Atlases, maps and gazetteers

71 **Atlas nacional de España.** (Spanish national atlas.)
Madrid: Instituto Geográfico y Catastral, 1965-68. 226p. 100 maps.
Map size: 75×52 cm.

This is the official national atlas of Spain and contains over 100 well-printed
colour map plates covering physical, cultural, economic and political matters. It
also includes a 1:500 physical map, a transparent reference overlay, two bound
booklets describing the geography of Spain, and an index of over 40,000
placenames.

72 **Diccionario geográfico de España.** (A geographic dictionary of
Spain.)
Madrid: Editorial del Movimiento, 1956-61. 17 vols.

A detailed gazetteer of Spanish places, including some long, signed articles with
extensive information on, for example, physical characteristics, climate, vegetation, agriculture, industries, cultural opportunities and history. Questionnaires
were sent out to all the towns and villages of Spain, to be answered by the local

authorities, and the *Times Literary Supplement* of 11 January 1963, described it as providing 'the fullest information about Spain yet collected in a single work'.

73 **Euromap Spain and Portugal.**
Edinburgh: Bartholomew, 1984. Map size: 762×1016 mm. Scale 1:1,250,000 (20 miles to 1 inch).

This is essentially a leisure map, with an inset plan of Madrid and a key in English, French, German and Spanish.

74 **Nuevo atlas de España.** (New atlas of Spain.)
Madrid: Aguilar, 1961. 455p. Map size: 23×52 cm.

A comprehensive atlas of Spain, with maps of the whole country and of the provinces. Also included are special maps on population, agriculture, industry, geology, vegetation and climate, as well as maps of the Spanish colonies and a sixty-page gazetteer with around 30,000 entries.

75 **Spain/Portugal.**
Paris: Michelin. Scale 1:10,000,000.

Carefully-prepared, accurate road maps for all regions.

76 **Spain and Balearic Islands.**
London: Foldex. Scale 1:1,000,000.

A standard road map of Spain and the Balearics.

77 **World travel series map of Spain and Portugal.**
Edinburgh: Bartholomew, 1984. Map size: 762×1016 mm. Scale 1:1,250,000 (20 miles to 1 inch).

An ideal map for the tourist. All classes of roads are shown with road numbering and distances, spot heights in metres, railways, airports, boundaries and hill shading. There is a map of Madrid included as an inset on the scale one mile to one inch.

Tourism and Travel Guides

Tourism

78 **Tourism as an agent of change: a Spanish Basque case.**
Davydd James Greenwood. *Ethnology*, vol. 11, no. 1 (Jan. 1972), p. 80-91.

A useful discussion of how tourism affects the economic development and progress of a region, whilst in the long-term it has an adverse impact on local social and cultural development. The author selects the town of Fuenterrabia in the province of Guipúzcoa for a case study, laying particular emphasis on the effects of tourism on agriculture.

79 **Tourism: Spain's most important industry.**
John Naylon. *Geography*, no. 52 (1967), p. 23-40.

Discusses the growth of Spanish tourism and its significance for the economy. The article also outlines the growth of the industry and the support given to it by the government, and examines future developments and the seasonal problems which accrue in the economy as a result of the tourist trade. The author shows how tourism has expedited the development of good communications links both within the country and between Spain and other nations. Although somewhat dated as regards statistics, the basic premise that the Spanish tourist industry is a major source of revenue for the country remains true.

80 **El milagro turístico.** (The tourist miracle.)
Angel Palomino.   Barcelona: Plaza y Janes, 1972. 293p. 3 maps. (Testigos de España).

A readable and often light-hearted look at the benefits, disadvantages and effects of the annual influx of tourists into Spain. This is a first-hand account based on the author's experiences of living in different tourist regions of Spain since 1955. The topics covered include: the importance of the industry to Spain; transport

21

problems; competition from other European countries, particularly France and Italy; tourism and the State; price control; complaints against hoteliers and tourist operators; financial aid; and opinions on tourism in Spain.

81 **Tourism policy and international tourism in O.E.C.D. member countries.**
Paris: Organisation for Economic Co-operation and Development, 1973- . annual.

This work contains data and comments on: government policy on tourism; tourist flows; the economic importance of tourism; air, rail and road transport; and tourist accommodation. Also included are statistical tables on individual countries. This annual report was first published as *Tourism in Europe* (1960-61), and then as *Tourism in O.E.C.D. Member Countries* (1962-70). In 1971 and 1972 it appeared as *International Tourism and Tourist Policy in O.E.C.D. Member Countries*.

Travel guides

82 **The Basque country.**
Ignacio Aldecoa.   Barcelona: Editorial Noguer, 1963. 61p. map. (Andar y Ver Collection).

One of thirty volumes in a series of profusely-illustrated travel guides to Spain in English, distributed by the International Publications Service of New York, covering in detail the land, the people and their culture. It includes a supplement giving practical information on hotels, museums, libraries, restaurants, routes and places to visit, plus historical notes on the provinces and cities.

83 **Paradores of Spain.**
Sam Ballard, Jane Ballard.   Washington, DC: Ballard's Travel Guides, 1978. 163p. maps.

Beginning in 1928, Spain has gradually established a network of national 'paradores' throughout the country in order to promote her tourist industry. 'Paradores' are government owned and operated inns or hotels, some of which are converted castles, convents or mansions. All 'paradores', 'albergues' and 'hosterías' are listed by region, and details provided on their distinctive qualities and how to reach them. There are numerous maps and photographs, together with brief background details on Spanish history and geography.

84 **The companion guide to Madrid and central Spain.**
Alastair Boyd.   London: Collins, 1974. 477p. 20 maps and plans. bibliog. (The Companion Guides).

The aim of these guides is 'to provide a companion, in the person of the author, who knows intimately the places and people of whom he writes, and is able to communicate this knowledge and affection to his readers'. The author of this volume lived for several years in Spain, and this excellent travel guide, which is easy to ready and well illustrated, covers about a quarter of the total area of the country. He suggests routes which can easily be broken down into sections, encouraging the tourist to use the provincial towns as touring centres. The emphasis is on the culture, history and architecture to be found in the areas of Spain often neglected by tourists in favour of the coast. The author also wrote *The road from Ronda* (London: Collins, 1969), in which he describes his travels with a horse through southern Spain.

85 Spain and Portugal: 1984.
Pat Brooks, Lester Brooks, edited and annotated by Robert C. Fisher. New York: Fisher Travel Guides, 1983. 374p. 13 maps. (Fisher Annotated Travel Guides).

This guide is aimed at the American tourist travelling around Spain and Portugal, and is the first American guidebook to attempt the classification of hotels and points of special interest. Spain covers two thirds of the work, with sections on: planning a holiday; costs; climate; transport (both getting there and whilst in Spain); and formalities and customs. There are also individual chapters on: Madrid; central Spain; Andalusia; Barcelona; the Balearics; and northern Spain. Each chapter covers hotels, restaurants, entertainment, museums and galleries, historic buildings, tours, sports and transportation within each region or city, and there is a special section on Spain today, its culture, food and drink. An interesting note by the editor points out that whereas the majority of Europeans visit Spain purely for its value as an inexpensive place in the sun, North Americans visit mainly for the culture, history and sightseeing. This is a very useful and up-to-date guide, with annotations in the margins.

86 The tastes of travel: northern and central Spain.
Elisabeth de Stroumillo. London: Collins & Harvill Press, 1980. 296p. 4 maps.

This companion to her volume on southern Spain (q.v.) is in five parts, covering: the Basque country and Navarre; Aragón and Catalonia; Old Castile and León; Asturias; and recipes from the regions. There is a map of each region and background historical details are provided.

87 The tastes of travel: southern Spain.
Elisabeth de Stroumillo. London: Collins & Harvill, 1981. 268p. 3 maps. bibliog.

When this book was written, the authoress was a travel correspondent for the *Daily Telegraph*. The four parts cover: the Levant and La Mancha; western Castile and Extremadura; Andalusia; and recipes from around the southern regions. The book provides advice on where to stay, and what particular regional specialities to eat and drink. This is an excellent, though highly personal, work, which notes the history of the places referred to, and also reveals the artistic and architectural treasures to be found in them.

88 **Spain: welcome to Spain.**
  R. A. N. Dixon.   Glasgow: Collins; Chicago: Rand McNally, 1980.
  96p. maps. (Collins Travel Guides/Welcome Guides).

A concise study of Spain for the tourist, divided into two sections. The first contains general information and a gazetteer, and the second has information on the various regions, and regional maps. This extremely useful little book is full of information about all aspects of Spanish customs.

89 **On foot through Europe: a trail guide to Spain and Portugal; also includes Andorra, the Azores, the Canary Islands, Madeira and Mallorca.**
  Craig Evans.   New York: Quill, 1982. 169p. maps.

Packed with information, this 'bible of European hiking opportunities' describes every aspect of hiking, backpacking, ski touring and climbing in Spain and other areas. It is to some extent unfortunate for libraries in that it advises the reader on how to remove separate sections from the book in order to avoid carrying the whole work on expeditions. The chapters cover where and how to go hiking in Spain and Portugal within the different regions, and each section includes brief comments on: flora and fauna; climate; weather; walking information and Spanish walking clubs; maps; guidebooks; camping; mountaineering; skiing; trains and buses; and useful addresses and telephone numbers. All footpaths are graded according to their difficulty. The author is an avid hiker and winter mountaineer, the former editor of *Backpacker* magazine, and an executive director of the American Hiking Society. This very useful guide is unfortunately not indexed.

90 **Mediterranean island hopping: the Spanish islands; a handbook for the independent traveller.**
  Dana Facaros and Michael Pauls.   London: Macdonald, 1981.
  264p. 16 maps. bibliog. (Island Hopping Series).

Covers the three major islands of the Balearics (Majorca, Minorca and Ibiza), and the two largest of the numerous smaller islands (Formentera and Cabrera). Each island is discussed in turn, and information is given on: transport to, and around, them; food, drink and entertainment; sport; and other general and miscellaneous subjects. There is a list of useful words and phrases, as well as a food and drink vocabulary. The word 'Balearic' was the name given by the earliest Greek explorers, and refers to the sling, a weapon which the islanders used with great skill.

91 **Fodor's Spain.**
  London: Hodder & Stoughton. annual. map.

This series was founded by Eugene Fodor in 1936, and is reviewed, revised and updated annually. Background information is provided on history, geography, sport (including bullfighting and pelota) and food and drink, and practical information is supplied on hotels, restaurants, shopping and transport. The work is arranged by region, and includes a map of Spain, with several plans of major cities. This excellent illustrated guide contains an index and an English-Spanish vocabulary.

92 **The companion guide to the south of Spain.**
Alfonso Lowe. London: Collins, 1973. 445p. maps. bibliog. (The
Companion Guides).

Alfonso Lowe is the 'nom de plume' of an English writer who now lives in Spain.
He provides very good descriptions of Spanish architecture, and emphasizes the
importance of the Moorish past. This excellent guidebook, which is compact, easy
to read and well illustrated, includes a useful glossary of terms, and a chronology
of people and events.

93 **Michelin Green Guide: Spain.**
London: Michelin Tyre Co., 1982. 3rd ed. 290p. maps. bibliog.

An indispensable guide for those touring Spain, which, unlike the *Michelin Red
Guide* (q.v.), is not revised annually. It contains all the practical information
which a tourist would require concerning day-to-day life in Spain, routes, maps
and tours, followed by major sections on individual regions, towns and cities.

94 **Free spirits of the Pyrenees: a guide to the Basque country.**
Charles Moore. London: John Gifford, 1971. 106p. map.

A survey of the Basque country, with several colour photographs of views and
buildings, which describes: the geography of the region; the people; folklore and
culture; food and drink; sports; festivals; and tourism. This is a very general, yet
readable book of impressions of a long summer tour made by the author in 1970,
and of two previous visits during the 1960s. Unfortunately, it lacks an index.

95 **Spain: a companion to Spanish travel.**
Edgar Allison Peers. London: George G. Harrap, 1930. 296p.
map. bibliog. (The Kitbag Travel Books).

Divided into four parts covering the different geographical regions of the country,
this book has been written by someone who has spent a good deal of time living
and travelling in Spain, and who makes his love of Spain quite obvious. It is
intended as a 'companion to the tourist in Spain whose aim is to take an
intelligent, though not a specialized, interest in what he sees and hears there, and
who has no previous knowledge of the country beyond a few reminiscences of his
schooldays'. It is hoped to answer most of the questions asked by tourists, and
contains a list of references to some of the 'best books on Spain'. A historical
background is provided, as well as lists of the principal events in Spanish history
since the Moorish invasion, and the sovereigns of Spain up to Alfonso XIII. This
is a clear and readable work, not confused with too much detail, and although
over 50 years old it is still valuable for its portrayal of places of interest which
have changed little in the intervening years.

96 **Spain: the mainland.**
Ian Robertson. London: Benn, 1980. 4th ed. 599p. map. bibliog.
(The Blue Guides).

This guidebook is particularly useful for those planning to tour Spain, and
includes an atlas of the country, a map of the provinces, and town plans of the
major cities. It is a comprehensive guide to the history and the art and

architecture of the country which also includes a useful section covering transport, geography, road maps, customs, currency, hotels and restaurants, and other general information.

97 Spain/Portugal.

Paris: Michelin, Services de Tourisme. annual. (Michelin Red Guides).

Parallel texts are provided in English, French, German, Italian, Spanish and Portuguese. The main section of the guide provides town plans, maps, sights, hotels and restaurants (graded), car agents, and so on. Also included are a map of main roads, distances between major towns, information on food and drink, and a useful dictionary of words most commonly required by tourists.

98 Minorca.

David Wilson Taylor.   Newton Abbot, England: David & Charles, 1975. 206p. 4 maps. bibliog. (The Islands Series).

An easy-to-read, well-organized study of all aspects of the island's history and culture. It is really more than a tourist guide, in that it comprehensively covers such subjects as geology, history (both ancient and modern), and topography. There are also details about the flora and fauna, as well as information on the people, the economy, livelihood, customs and communications, hotels, places to visit and climate. There are three appendixes: information for visitors; a chronology of important events; and a list of the 127 species of birds identified up until 1974. Minorca is the second largest of the Balearic Islands, and the most easterly part of Spain, and was the last place to hold out against Franco.

99 The travellers' guide to the Balearics: Majorca, Minorca, Ibiza and Formentera.

Hazel Thurston.   London: Jonathan Cape, 1979. 366p. 9 maps. bibliog. (Travellers' Guides).

A comprehensive, well-produced and authoritative pocketbook, which provides all the information for an intending traveller to any of the four principal islands. The authoress's comparative treatment emphasizes each island's distinct identity. It is also worth reading *Majorca observed* (London: Cassell, 1965) by Robert Graves, a long-time resident of the largest island, which provides a series of amusing and informative anecdotes.

Spain.
See item no. 9.

Travel in Spain.
See item no. 664.

Paradores of Spain: their history, cooking and wines.
See item no. 874.

Flora and Fauna

100 **The birds of the Balearics.**
David Armitage Bannerman, W. Mary Bannerman.   London:
Croom Helm, 1983. 230p. map. bibliog.
A richly illustrated and excellently written study. Unfortunately Dr. Bannerman, one of the most distinguished ornithologists of the 20th century, died before he had completed this work. However, after 1978 his wife continued writing from her husband's notes and preliminary material. The publishers note therefore that the work could probably have been improved upon by Dr. Bannerman. Nevertheless, it remains an extremely useful book for the many people interested in Balearic birds and seeking a work in the English language. Scottish bird-artist and writer, Donald Watson, painted the twelve colour plates which the book contains. Also included in the volume are: a map of the Balearic Islands; an illustration showing bird topography; an appendix of species requiring confirmation or now extinct; an index of scientific names; and an index of common names.

101 **Bellamy's Europe.**
David Bellamy.   London: British Broadcasting Corporation, 1976.
143p. bibliog.
This book was published to accompany a series of programmes broadcast on British television. Chapter 4 (p. 48-60) is entitled 'Rain in Spain', and the author, in his inimitable style, discusses the climate of Spain and its effect on the flora and fauna. Spain has more than 6,000 species of flowering plants, and also has the greatest diversity of climates of any country in Europe. This is an excellent brief study of natural history in Spain.

Flora and Fauna

102 **Plants of the Balearic Islands.**
Anthony Bonner, translated from the Catalan by Patricia
Mathews. Palma, Majorca: Editorial Moll, 1982. 150p. 6 maps.
bibliog.

This interesting book covers all areas where the flora can be found, and includes
an index of the scientific names of plants, and one of English names. It is intended
for general readers, and obviously the English edition is aimed at the huge
numbers of tourists who visit the Balearics each year. The selection is limited to
the most common, characteristic and interesting plants from among the 1,500 or
so species which are to be found there. There are excellent illustrations by
Hannah Bonner, and some beautiful colour photographs of the flora of the
Islands.

103 **Wild Spain: records of sport with rifle, rod, and gun, natural
history and exploration.**
Abel Chapman, Walter J. Buck. London: Gurney & Jackson,
1893. 472p. map.

A highly readable and thoroughly interesting book. Chapman was part hunter and
part naturalist, and a gifted writer and draughtsman. Having acquired hunting
rights in 'Las Marismas', he was able to become intimately acquainted with the
wildlife of the Coto Doñana region of southwest Spain, and made this area
known to the world through this work. The first part of the book is concerned
with natural history, while the latter half is devoted to sport, and, as far as is
convenient, the chapters follow the change of seasons. There are also: numerous
photographs and illustrations; a glossary of all Spanish words and phrases used in
the text; appendixes on the large game of Spain and Portugal (including deer,
ibex, chamois, bear, wild boar, wolf, fox and lynx); spring migrants to Spain;
supplementary notes on birds; and a very detailed index. Chapman and Buck are
also the authors of *Unexplored Spain* (London: E. Arnold, 1910).

104 **Where to watch birds in Britain and Europe.**
John Gooders, in collaboration with Jeremy Brock. London:
Andre Deutsch, 1970. 299p.

This interesting book is designed to cater for the bird-watcher and traveller in
Europe, and has the basic aim of 'opening the eyes of the would-be traveller to
the possibilities of places he has never heard of, and perhaps persuading him to
go'. The format provides a description of the birds and habitats of each area, a
summary table of birds, and travel directions. The section on Spain (p. 236-253)
covers fifteen different areas, and includes one general map and two regional
maps.

105 **A field guide to the butterflies and burnets of Spain.**
William Bridgeman Lambert Manley, H. G. Allcard. London: E.
W. Classey, 1970. 192p. bibliog.

This detailed guide includes notes on the butterflies and burnets, checklists, an
exhaustive bibliography, a good index, and forty beautiful colour plates. The
authors state that, due to the mountainous nature of much of Spain, collectors

have found it difficult to acquire specimens, but that accessibility is constantly improving.

106 **Portrait of a wilderness: the story of the Coto Doñana expeditions.**
Guy Mountfort. Newton Abbot, England: David & Charles, 1968. 240p. bibliog.

This classic work includes superb photographs (in colour and black-and-white) of the wildlife and vegetation, and primarily the bird-life of the Coto Doñana Nature Reserve in the southwest of Spain. It vividly describes three expeditions (in 1952, 1956 and 1957) to the region, and contains three appendixes on the birds (species and Spanish name) found there, and the animals and reptiles of Andalusia. These expeditions were private ventures by several groups of enthusiasts, under no form of sponsorship, who were brought together through their common interest in ornithology. The area of the Coto Doñana contains half the bird species of Europe, and the principal aim of the trips was to learn the status of the bird populations of the region. Secondly, the plan was to examine their ecological relationship, and to learn about their migratory movements. Time was also given over to the study of the animals, reptiles, insects and flora to be found there. The Coto Doñana had been a hunting reserve of the Dukes of Medina Sidonia for nearly 500 years, and the author (a founder member of the World Wildlife Fund), in an attempt to save the area from development, brought together many conservationists in 1960-61 in order to publicize the objectives of the Fund, using the Coto Doñana as the focal point.

107 **The naturalist in Majorca.**
James Douglas Parrack. Newton Abbot, England: David & Charles, 1973. 224p. map. bibliog. (The Regional Naturalist).

This series is intended to introduce both visitor and resident to the wildlife of an area, and the author visited Majorca over a period of eight years, recording bird migration, and studying the flora and insect life. The contents include: a map of Majorca; a general introduction; geological history; plants; insects; reptiles; mammals; and bird-life. This is a semi-technical work that is nonetheless very readable and interesting, and represents the first account of Majorca's natural history for many years.

108 **Flowers of south-west Europe: a field guide.**
Oleg Polunin, B. E. Smythies. London: Oxford University Press, 1973. 480p. bibliog.

This work is primarily intended for the traveller, as a readily portable guide to the most botanically interesting and most beautiful regions of southwestern Europe. The book includes indexes of popular names, placenames, and plants, and a large bibliography.

109 **Andalusian flowers and countryside.**
Christopher Maitland Stocken. Thurlestone, England: Stocken, 1969. 184p. 17 maps. bibliog.

The author, a Lieutenant Commander in the navy, died in 1966, aged forty-four, and the Danish government provided a memorial to him by naming a mountain

Flora and Fauna

'Stockenbjoerg' in the area of eastern Greenland where he was killed leading a Royal Naval expedition. This is an illustrated work, and includes appendixes on common, wild and naturalized plants, listed by month.

110 Wild flowers of Spain and Portugal.

Albert William Taylor. London: Chatto & Windus, 1972. 103p. map.

'Cut off from the rest of Europe by the Pyrenees and further isolated by range after range of Sierras, the native plants of Spain and Portugal have been to a large extent sheltered from outside influences'. The author hopes that this little book will introduce the interested traveller to examples of the lovely flowers to be found in these two countries. Beautiful colour and black-and-white plates are accompanied by details of where the flowers are found, what they look like, and the time of year they can be seen.

111 Wild Andalusia: Coto Doñana.

Charles A. Vaucher, translated from the French by Douglas J. Gillam. Lausanne, Switzerland: Editions Marguerat, 1967. 209p. map. bibliog.

A description of the natural history of Andalusia, with particular reference to the Coto Doñana National Park and Nature Reserve, which lies around the mouth of the Guadalquivir River. 'Its natural habitat encompasses some 190 square miles of coastal dunes, pine woods, scrubland and the marshland of the Guadalquivir delta. The park is chiefly important as the confluence of bird migration routes between Africa and Europe. Nearly half the bird species (including seasonal visitors) of Europe can be seen there'. The contents comprise fifty-six pages of text, 265 photographs, nine colour plates, and a map of the region. The book describes inhabited Andalusia, wild Andalusia, wildlife habitats, an autumn day, and a winter day. The material for this interesting work was collected during the course of six visits between 1963 and 1966.

112 My life among the wild birds in Spain.

Willoughby Verner. London: John Bale & Danielsson, 1909. 468p.

A detailed study of the birds of Spain, with excellent photographs and sketches to complement the text. Whilst it concentrates on bustards, kites, hawks, eagles and vultures, there are also references to the wildlife and flora of Andalusia in general.

National parks and reserves of western Europe.

See item no. 691.

Archaeology and Prehistory

113   **The Iberians.**
Antonio Arribas Palaus.   London: Thames & Hudson, 1964.
274p. 8 maps. bibliog. (Ancient Peoples and Places, vol. 36).
Studies all aspects of the life and culture of the Iberians. 'Iberians' is a term describing a geographical, and not an ethnic, group, and the author shows how it is impossible to distinguish an Iberian cultural unity. He emphasizes how the classical root of Iberian art, and the uniformity of the alphabet and language, provide the only criteria allowing the use of the collective term 'Iberian peoples'. The work includes ninety photographs, and many line drawings, maps and tables. There is also a chronological table of events covering the period discussed in the book, namely 800-100 BC, i.e. the second period of the Iron Age.

114   **Rock art of the Spanish Levant.**
Antonio Beltrán, translated by Margaret Brown.   Cambridge, England: Cambridge University Press, 1982. 155p. 2 maps. bibliog. (The Imprint of Man).
Originally published in Italian in 1980, this work contains information on the lesser-known rock art of eastern Spain. It covers every aspect from the discovery of rock paintings and the problem of conservation, to the techniques and materials used by primitive man to produce them. The book also includes an excellent study of the paintings themselves. The volume is marvellously illustrated with black-and-white drawings and about one hundred colour photographs of paintings and caves.

115   **Prehistoric man and his art: the caves of Ribadesella.**
Magín Berenguer Alonso, translated from the Spanish by Michael Heron.   London: Souvenir Press; Toronto, Canada: Dent, 1973. 168p. map. bibliog.
The first twelve chapters of this work discuss the general characteristics and art of

prehistoric man, and the final six chapters (which cover half the book) describe prehistoric cavelife and art in Spain. The author concentrates on the more famous caves of Altamira and Ribadesella, and there are numerous sketches, photographs and plans of the individual caves and the paintings therein.

116 **Papers in Iberian archaeology.**
Edited by T. F. C. Blagg, R. F. J. Jones and S. J. Keay. London: BAR, 1984. 2 vols. maps. bibliog. (BAR International Series, no. 193).

This study presents a collection of papers (primarily in English, but with some in Spanish and French) originally given at a conference at the University of Kent at Canterbury in 1981. They intend to reveal something of the particular character of the current archaeological scene in Spain and Portugal, and there has been no attempt to restrict the periods covered, or to find a common theme. The papers cover the period from early prehistory to the mediaeval era, from cave paintings to castles. This is a well-illustrated and scholarly work, which is really only suitable for the specialist.

117 **The Greeks in Spain.**
Rhys Carpenter. London; New York: Longmans, Green and Co., 1925. 180p. bibliog. (Bryn Mawr Notes and Monographs, no. 6). Reprinted New York: AMS Press, 1971.

This short, fascinating study is illustrated with photographs and sketches portraying Greek civilization in the Iberian Peninsula, and includes several appendixes and a chronology of ancient Spain. The author has tried to tailor a piece of documented archaeological investigation so that it can be read by the general reader of ancient history.

118 **The bell beaker cultures of Spain and Portugal.**
Richard J. Harrison. Cambridge, Massachussetts: Peabody Museum of Archaeology and Ethnology, Harvard University, 1977. 257p. maps. bibliog. (American School of Prehistoric Research, Peabody Museum, Harvard University, bulletin no. 35).

A detailed work based on the research of the author in the Iberian Peninsula in 1971, which includes innumerable maps of distribution sites. This work attempts to resolve one of the most perplexing problems in the archaeology of the late Neolithic period in western Europe, namely the formation, distribution and origins of the Beaker folk of Spain and Portugal. Harrison also wrote *The Beaker folk: copper age archaeology in western Europe* (London: Thames & Hudson, 1980). Chapter 6 (p. 126-56) of the latter publication is entitled 'The Iberian Peninsula and North Africa', and puts forward new theories on this enigmatic culture.

119 **The Iberian stones speak: archaeology in Spain and Portugal.**
Paul Lachlan MacKendrick. New York: Funk & Wagnalls, 1969. 238p. 7 maps. bibliog.

An excellent attempt to reconstruct cultural history from archaeological remains. Each chapter considers a particular period, from the cave men (1200 BC) to the

Spanish emperors (AD 138), and the book is abundantly illustrated with maps, plans and sketches, as well as with numerous photographs of archaeological sites and remains. The author emphasizes the persistence of Iberian tradition, and the resistance of the Iberian people under Roman rule.

120 **Full fathom five: wrecks of the Spanish Armada.**
Colin Martin, appendixes by Sidney Wignall. London: Chatto & Windus, 1975. 288p. 15 maps. bibliog.

A discussion in three parts of the excavation of some of the ships which sailed in the Spanish Armada of 1588. This is a good description of the efforts to rescue the remains from the waters around Scotland and Ireland, and conveys the atmosphere of such diving projects well. The work is richly illustrated with photographs of wreck sites, weapons, and other items from these sites. An appendix by Martin provides a full fleet list of the 1588 Armada, showing the order of battle, and briefly describing the subsequent fate of the ships. The book sheds new light on the equipment, weapons and design of the Spanish ships at this time. Both writers are nautical archaeologists whose excavation of Armada wrecks since 1965 has revolutionized our knowledge of the Spanish fleets.

121 **Archaeology under water: an atlas of the world's submerged sites.**
General editor Keith Muckelroy. New York; London: McGraw-Hill, 1980. 192p. maps. bibliog.

A very useful introductory study of certain aspects of underwater archaeology, which includes sections entitled: 'Rome's seaborne trade with Spain' (p. 56-57); 'The Spanish Armada' and 'Two Armada wrecks' (p. 92-95); 'Insights from Aramada pottery' (p. 98-99) and an entire section called 'Shipwrecks in the wake of Columbus' (p. 102-130). These five sections contain many maps, illustrations, diagrams and tables, and provide a wealth of detail that is easy to follow, including case studies of certain wrecks. 'The wrecks of the Spanish Armada provide us with a unique opportunity for studying a wide range of naval, maritime and social affairs in late sixteenth century Europe'.

122 **The ancient Spaniards.**
Gérard Nicolini, translated from the French by Jean Stewart.
Farnborough, England: Saxon House, 1974. 232p. map. bibliog.

This work contains chapters on: Iberian remains in Spain; Iberia in antiquity; Iberian civilization; towns and architecture; sculpture; painted pottery; metalwork; and jewellery. There is a map of the Iberian Peninsula showing the settlements of the early Spaniards, and over 130 illustrations and colour plates. The author attempts to provide examples of the archaeological wealth of ancient Iberia, and although Roman and Greek monuments feature amongst them, he concentrates mainly on the pre-Roman period.

123 **Fossil man in Spain**
Hugo Obermaier. New Haven, Connecticut: Yale University Press for the Hispanic Society of America, 1924; London: Oxford University Press, 1925. 495p. 9 maps. bibliog.

This authoritative work was translated from the original text of *El hombre fósil*

Archaeology and Prehistory

(Madrid, 1916) by Christine D. Matthew. The author has aimed at presenting an overall view of the Old Stone Age period in Spain, through the evidence provided by the geological, palaeontological, archaeological and anthropological sciences. This huge, highly detailed study, abundantly illustrated with photographs, diagrams and maps, covers all aspects relevant to the cultural and bodily development of fossil man in Spain. The appendix extends to ten chapters and represents nearly a hundred pages of notes and bibliography.

124 The world of ancient Spain.
Antonio Pardo, translated by David Macrae.   Geneva,
Switzerland: Minerva, 1976. 140p.

An easy-to-read account of the history and archaeology of ancient Spain, which covers the period from the arrival of the first settlers in the Peninsula to the Roman occupation and the dawn of the Christian era. Good illustrations and colour plates complement the text, exemplifying the artefacts and buildings of the period.

125 The Balearic Islands.
Luis Pericot-García, translated by Margaret Brown.   London:
Thames & Hudson, 1972. 184p. 7 maps. bibliog. (Ancient Peoples and Places, vol. 81).

'The unique legacy of Balearic prehistory to posterity is its megalithic monuments'. The ruins of these stone structures are found in profusion all over the Islands, and this work emphasizes the buildings and architecture at the expense of reconstructing ancient ways of life. The book spans over 4,000 years, from the arrival of the settlers to the Roman conquest, and includes over 100 photographs and line drawings.

126 Spain and Portugal: the prehistory of the Iberian Peninsula.
Hubert N. Savory.   London: Thames & Hudson; New York:
Praeger, 1968. 324p. 23 maps. bibliog. (Ancient Peoples and Places, vol. 61).

The importance of this book is emphasized by the fact that it was one of the first full studies of the subject in Spain. This is attributed to the lack of professional archaeologists fully trained in modern methods of excavation in Spain and Portugal at the time, and the limited facilities for training such people. The situation has now improved, although it is still true that most of the best work done by native archaeologists in Spain has been done in the northern and eastern areas. The author has concentrated on cultural phases which represent the Peninsula's unique contribution to European prehistory, and consequently it is a somewhat selective study.

The Canary Islanders: their prehistory, conquest and survival.
See item no. 160.

Roman Spain: an introduction to the Roman antiquities of Spain and Portugal.
See item no. 167.

History

General

127 **A history of Spain: from the beginnings to the present day.**
Rafael Altamira y Crevea, translated by Muna Lee. Princeton,
New Jersey: Van Nostrand, 1949. 748p. 14 maps. bibliog.

The author is internationally renowned as a historian, educator and jurist, and this book is a good history of Spanish civilization up to the 1930s. A clear and objective approach marks the style of this excellently written and profusely illustrated standard work, which is aimed at university students outside Spain in particular, but also at the non-specialist seeking a basic knowledge of Spanish history. This is a translation of the second Spanish edition, and includes: a large selected bibliography; a list of principal events in Spanish history; a chart of parallel events in the history of Spanish civilization and that of other countries; and nearly 100 illustrations.

128 **A history of Spanish civilization.**
Rafael Altamira y Crevea, translated from the Spanish by
P. Volkov. London: Constable, 1930. 2nd corrected, reprinted
ed.: New York: AMS, 1977. 280p. map. bibliog.

This illustrated work covers the period from the prehistoric era to the outbreak of the First World War, and is written by a most respected and prolific Spanish historian. It is a wide-ranging study of all aspects of Spanish history and culture over the centuries, and emphasizes how the Spaniards were not only pioneers in the discovery and colonization of America, but were also pioneers and explorers in the fields of international law, applied science, navigation and metallurgy. The bibliography provides short notes on the contents of the books listed, and although somewhat dated now, it still represents one of the most important general bibliographies covering all areas of Spanish civilization.

129 **A history of Spain and Portugal.**
William Christopher Atkinson. Harmondsworth, England;
Baltimore, Maryland: Penguin Books, 1960. 382p. map. bibliog.
(The Pelican History of the World).

This volume is of particular interest for its joint treatment of the history of the
two Peninsular countries, and the impact each has had on the other. In attempting
to deal selectively with events in the Peninsula over the past 2,000 years, the
author hoped to present an 'analytical account of the evolution and formation of
the two peoples, to trace the slow and much bedevilled growth of their society'. A
commentary is included on the great Spanish literary and artistic figures over the
years.

130 **The history of Spain.**
Louis Bertrand, Sir Charles Petrie. London: Eyre &
Spottiswoode, 1952. 2nd ed. 432p. 5 maps. bibliog.

An interesting and detailed study, translated from the original French edition.
Part 1, covering the period from the Visigoths to the death of Philip II (1598), is
by Bertrand, and part 2, from the death of Philip II to 1945, is by Petrie. This
second edition includes few changes to part 1, but part two has been updated so
that it covers the events of the Civil War and the history of Spain until the end of
the Second World War. Petrie believes that on many occasions the Anglo-Saxon
presentation of Spanish history has too often been unjust, and the two authors
hope with this book to place events in their correct perspective, and to indicate
the full importance of Spain's civilization and its influence on the modern world.
The work includes: appendixes on the principal events in the history of Spain; a
chronological list of the Spanish sovereigns; tables showing the Spanish succession
in 1700, and the Carlist claim; and a genealogical table of the Christian kings of
Spain.

131 **Diccionario de historia de España.** (A dictionary of Spanish
history.)
Edited by Germán Bleiberg. Madrid: Alianza, 1979. 3 vols.
bibliog. (Alianza Diccionarios).

A reprint of the 1968 edition, published by *Revista de Occidente*, which looks at
Spanish history from its origins up to the Second Republic. This is an excellent
encyclopaedic dictionary, which also includes coverage of Spain's expansion in
Europe and overseas, and external events which influenced Spanish history.
Nearly 6,000 entries appear in the work concerning, for example: prehistory;
kings; statesmen; political leaders; laws; economics; religious movements;
political parties; social movements; wars; battles and peace treaties; religious and
military orders; archaeology; literature; art; linguistics; geography; military
history; and sociology. Volume 3 contains numerous appendixes, including a
chronology and a bibliography extending over twenty pages.

132 **The Spaniards: an introduction to their history.**
Américo Castro, translated by Willard F. King and Selma
Margaretten. Berkeley, California: University of California
Press, 1971. 628p. bibliog.

A scholarly and stimulating introduction to Spanish culture, dealing with the mediaeval background, and assessing the Jewish influence on Spanish history. Although somewhat controversial and heavy-going, the author's interpretation is now established as a classic history of Spain from the earliest times to the end of the Middle Ages. The first English version of this work was entitled *The structure of Spanish history* (Princeton, New Jersey: Princeton University Press, 1954), which was modified and extended in the edition cited here. The author (1885-1972) was also a renowned Spanish philologist and literary critic.

133 **A history of Spain: founded on the 'Historia de España y de la civilización española' of Rafael Altamira.**
Charles Edward Chapman. New York: Free Press; London:
Collier-Macmillan, 1965. 559p. map. bibliog.

This extremely useful work is 'an attempt to give in one volume the main features of Spanish history from the standpoint of America', and was first written in 1918. It studies the growth of Spanish civilization, especially during the period 1479-1808, and is arranged in such a way that the reader can select areas of interest, or periods, in Spanish history and go straight to the relevant chapter(s). It is hoped that, although somewhat dated, the book may serve as a classroom text as well as a useful general introduction to the interested reader. Chapman based this work almost wholly on Altamira's *A history of Spanish civilization* (q.v.), and Altamira himself regards the book as 'a quite faithful portrait of Spain'. The bibliography is extensive.

134 **Spain.**
Stephen Clissold. London: Thames & Hudson, 1969. 211p. 3
maps. bibliog. (New Nations and Peoples Library).

'Each book in the series gives an account of the modern political, social, cultural, and economic conditions of a particular country'. Accordingly, this illustrated summary and analysis of Spanish history emphasizes the thirty years of the Franco régime up to the time of publication. It includes notes on the text, a select bibliography, and a 'Who's who' of people who have been prominent in Spanish affairs, both past and present (i.e. up to 1969). It concludes with an assessment of Spain's place in the world, just six years before Franco's death.

135 **Spain: the root and the flower: a history of the civilization of Spain and of the Spanish people.**
John Armstrong Crow. New York; London: Harper & Row,
1975. 475p. 2 maps. bibliog.

The author first visited Spain in 1928, and has made many subsequent visits. In this history he provides an interpretation of the civilization of Spain from its earliest beginnings. This is a useful and well-written subjective account, which in particular is very critical of the Franco régime up to the early 1960s.

136 **A history of Spain.**
Jean Descola, translated from the French by Elaine P. Halperin.
New York: Alfred A. Knopf, 1963. 483p. map.

This excellent, interpretative account of Spanish history and culture from the earliest times was first published in French in 1959. It contains a chronological summary of events, and genealogical tables of the Spanish monarchy. The author comments 'I do not believe that Spain's destiny throughout the ages evolved in a single direction'. Nor does he believe that 'Spain sprouted like a mushroom on the tip of Europe', for 'no other country has been so wanting in obedience to those rules of continuity that make the writing of history simple for certain nations'.

137 **An historical essay on modern Spain.**
Richard Herr. Berkeley, California: University of California Press, 1974. 308p. 5 maps. bibliog.

Originally published by Prentice-Hall, Englewood Cliffs, New Jersey, in 1971 under the title *Spain*, this is a detailed, scholarly work, which charts Spain's development and transformation from an agrarian, to a predominantly industrial, society. The author seeks to explain the 'country's evolution over the last two centuries', and stresses the changes which have occurred since Franco's death. This very interesting study contains an excellent bibliography.

138 **The Spanish people: their origin, growth and influence.**
Martin Andrew Sharp Hume. London: Heinemann, 1901. 535p. map. bibliog. (The Great Peoples).

An excellent general account of the contribution of Spain to modern civilization up to the end of the 19th century. 'An attempt is made in this book to trace the evolution of a highly composite people from its various racial units, and to seek in the peculiarities of its origin and the circumstances of its development the explanation of its character and institutions, and of the principal vicissitudes that have befallen it as a nation'. This is a classic work by the editor of the *Calendars of Spanish State Papers*.

139 **A concise history of Spain.**
Henry Kamen. London: Thames & Hudson, 1973. 191p. 4 maps. bibliog.

A profusely illustrated, general survey of Spanish history, divided chronologically into sections. The author is a famous historian and has written several works on Spanish history. In this study he emphasizes the importance of the combination of the various distinctive cultures which have influenced the Spanish character.

140 **An explanation of Spain.**
Eléna de la Souchère, translated from the French by Eleanor Ross Levieux. New York: Random House, 1964. 369p. map.

An authoritative account, originally published in French in 1962. The authoress's point of view is liberal and democratic, and thus completely unsympathetic to the Franco régime and to clerical influences. Part 1 describes natural resources, the character of the people, and the social formation of Spain, and goes on to discuss the outstanding features of Spanish history until the end of the 19th century. Part 2 is an account of Spanish history from the beginning of the 20th century to the end of the Civil War, and Part 3 describes the course, objectives and achievements of the Franco régime to 1963.

141 A history of Spain.
Harold Victor Livermore.   London: Allen & Unwin, 1966. 2nd ed. 484p. 8 maps. bibliog.

A good general history of Spain up to the 1950s, which is particularly useful for its concise, accurate summaries of political and institutional matters. Divided into two parts, the first covers the period 'when there was no political unity and "Spain" was no more than a geographical term and an aspiration'. The second deals with Spain since 1474: the modern state. This work is specifically designed for students but will be of interest to any serious reader. Harold Livermore also wrote *The origins of Spain and Portugal* (London: Allen & Unwin, 1971).

142 The Spanish centuries.
Alan Lloyd.   Garden City, New York: Doubleday, 1968. 395p. bibliog. (Mainstream of the Modern World Series).

This accomplished British journalist here presents a work that is both readable and historically accurate, and which concentrates on particular areas of Spanish history. It includes a good bibliography.

143 The culture and history of the Spanish.
Alfonso Lowe.   London: Gordon & Cremonesi, 1977. 225p. map. bibliog.

This well-illustrated and competent work was originally published as *The Spanish: the intrepid nation*. The author, although born in Liverpool, has lived in Catalonia since 1970, and before that practised medicine in Africa until his retirement. His particular technique is the use of short 'thumbnail biographies of historical figures and brief accounts of some surviving monuments'. Lowe also wrote the *Companion guide to southern Spain* (q.v.).

144 A concise history of Spain.
Melveena McKendrick.   London: Cassell, 1972. 224p. map. (Concise Histories).

This book is primarily designed as an introduction to the country, and is useful for the reader with no previous knowledge of Spanish history and culture. It contains many illustrations, some in colour, and a chronology of the most important dates in Spanish history from the earliest times to 1969.

145 The Spaniards in their history.

Ramón Menéndez Pidal, translated, with an introduction, by
Walter F. Starkie. London: Hollis & Carter, 1950. 251p. 3 maps.
bibliog.

This is a fine survey by an eminent Spanish writer, historian and philosopher, who
was born in 1869 and died in 1961. He presents a penetrating examination of the
Spanish character and its relationship to the environment and to history. As in all
his works, he stresses the native roots of Spanish culture, including the Basque,
Gothic and Arabic.

146 A history of Spain and Portugal.

Stanley G. Payne. Madison, Wisconsin: University of Wisconsin
Press, 1973. 2 vols. 12 maps. bibliog.

In this excellent, general account of the Iberian Peninsula the author attempts to
be comprehensive rather than strongly interpretative, emphasizing political
history, with briefer sections on socio-economic and cultural affairs. Volume 1
studies the period from ancient Hispania to 17th-century Spain, and volume 2
covers the period from the 18th century to the Franco era. Each volume is
abundantly illustrated and has its own bibliography. Payne conceived the work for
use as a textbook in courses on Spanish history, but he does not deal in detail with
the rise of the Spanish and Portuguese empires overseas, and places a slightly
greater emphasis on the modern period.

147 A short history of Spain.

Sir Charles Petrie. London: Sidgwick & Jackson, 1975. 128p.
map. bibliog.

A short, but authoritative introduction to the history of Spain, aimed at both the
general reader and the prospective traveller to Spain. The author is a famous
historian.

148 Spain: a companion to Spanish studies.

Edited by P. E. Russell. London: Methuen, 1977. rev. ed. 592p.
2 maps. bibliog.

Contains twelve excellent sections covering all aspects of Spanish language,
history, literature and learning, the visual arts, and music. This is the new version
of a work with the same title which was edited by Professor Edgar Allison Peers,
and which was first published in 1929. Russell states: 'it is hoped that the general
reader, with no particular background or specialization in Hispanic studies, will
also continue to find the book useful for reference; it has been written with his
needs in mind as well as those who wish to start or to extend an existing
knowledge of Spain and its culture'. Each section includes a good bibliography,
designed to encourage further reading. Similar volumes have also been produced
for Germany and France.

149 **Spain: a modern history.**
Rhea Marsh Smith. Ann Arbor, Michigan: University of
Michigan Press, 1965. 508p. 4 maps. bibliog. (The University of
Michigan History of the Modern World).

A concise and interesting account of Spanish history, covering the whole spectrum
from prehistory and including a list of Spanish rulers up to the time of Franco.

150 **Approaches to the history of Spain.**
Jaime Vicens Vives, translated and edited by Joan Connelly
Ullman. Berkeley, California: University of California Press,
1970. 2nd ed. 189p. 4 maps. bibliog.

This book first appeared in Spanish in 1952, and is a brilliant interpretation of all
the major questions of Spanish history, stressing the period before 1500. The
author, a Catalan professor of history who died in 1960, surveys the period
stretching from the first inhabitants to the beginning of the Civil War. The work
includes a section entitled 'Commentary on bibliography' covering nearly thirty
pages, and contains five genealogical tables (Houses of Burgundy, Barcelona,
Trastámara, Austria (Habsburgs), and Bourbon). The author himself attributes
the success of his book to its impartiality and dispassionate analysis of events.

151 **Spain: a brief history.**
Pierre Vilar, translated by Brian Tate. Oxford, England; New
York: Pergamon Press, 1977. 2nd ed. 140p. map. (Pergamon
Oxford Spanish Series).

An excellent introductory work which is both clear and concise, and which studies
the period from 1814 onwards in particular detail. This second edition includes
material added by the author on the Franco régime. The translator's note also
gives a brief resumé of events after Franco's death.

Regional

152 **Catalonia: a profile.**
Víctor Alba. London: C. Hurst, 1975. 258p. 3 maps. bibliog.

The author was born in Barcelona, fought in the Civil War, and spent six years as
a political prisoner. In this work he considers Catalan nationalism from the point
of view of its long and independent history, its language, and its distinct
psychological, cultural and economic characteristics. He traces the history of
Catalonia from its earliest days in the 6th century BC to modern times, and
emphasizes the problems which have arisen as a result of the region's unique
situation within the Spanish State. The author asserts that 'Ever since becoming a
part of Spain, the Catalans have been an oppressed minority'. This is an excellent
exposé of the Civil War and its effect upon the region.

153 **Historia de Galicia.** (A history of Galicia.)
J. C. Bermejo (et al). Madrid: Editorial Alhambra, 1981. 2nd ed.
299p. bibliog.

Very little has been written on Galician history, but this compilation of writings
covers all aspects of Galicia's history including prehistory, the Middle Ages, and
modern-day Galicia. It does not limit itself entirely to history, however, and also
covers social and cultural life. This is a very detailed account, which unfortunately
is not indexed.

154 **A history of Aragon and Catalonia.**
Henry John Chaytor. London: Methuen, 1933. 8 maps. bibliog.

A historical study of these two regions from the time of the Roman occupation to
the 1930s, which concentrates on the mediaeval period. The work represents the
first separate history of Aragón and Catalonia in English. The final chapter covers
literature and learning.

155 **Madrid: the circumstances of its growth.**
P. P. Courtenay. *Geography*, vol. 44 (1959), p. 22-34.

This article discusses the geography and history of the Spanish capital, and
includes sections on: the site of Madrid and its environment; its early
development from prehistoric times; its choice as the capital of Spain in 1561; its
growth up to 1800; and its development in the 19th and 20th centuries. The
author attempts to indicate those factors which have been most significant in
Madrid's rise to supremacy, despite the harsh, poverty-stricken nature of its
environment.

156 **Gibraltar.**
Philip Dennis. Newton Abbot, England: David & Charles, 1977.
152p. map. bibliog. (The Islands Series).

An excellent, easy-to-read introduction to Gibraltar, which is mainly concerned
with its history, and its significance over the years as a disputed piece of territory
between Spain and Britain. It contains a chronology of the history of Gibraltar,
and an appendix dealing with parts of the Treaty of Utrecht (1713) which granted
Gibraltar to the British. Another important study is Howard S. Levie's *The status
of Gibraltar* (Boulder, Colorado: Westview Press, 1983).

157 **Ibiza and Minorca.**
Arthur Foss. London: Faber & Faber, 1975. 209p. 4 maps.
bibliog.

This book completes the author's account of the Balearic Islands which he began
with the work entitled *Majorca* (London: Faber & Faber, 1972). The volume
provides a descriptive history of Ibiza and Minorca, which are amongst the most
popular tourist centres of Spain and the Mediterranean region.

158 **Historia contemporánea del País Vasco: de las Cortes de Cádiz al Estatuto de Guernica.** (A contemporary history of the Basque country: from the Cortes of Cádiz to the Statute of Guernica.) Fernando García de Cortázar, Manuel Montero. San Sebastián, Spain: Editorial Txertoa, 1982. 2nd ed. 224p. 2 maps. bibliog. (Colección Askatasun Haizea, no. 14).

A short, concise study of the political, ideological, social and economic changes which have taken place in the Basque Provinces during the last two centuries. It includes documentary extracts on these subjects, from the Cortes of Cádiz in 1812 (Spain's first constitution) to the Statute of Guernica of 1979. There are also maps, graphs, statistical tables, and an extensive bibliography.

159 **Rock of contention: a history of Gibraltar.**
George Hills. London: Robert Hale, 1974. 510p. 4 maps. bibliog.
Surveys the history of Gibraltar from the earliest times to the beginning of the 1970s. The Rock has been a constant source of conflict between peoples over the centuries, and the author shows how this tiny peninsula is vitally important in relation to the diplomacy between Britain and Spain. To Spain it represented the key to a North African empire, and to 17th-century England the key to both the Mediterranean trade and superiority over France at sea. Hills also wrote *Franco: the man and his nation* (q.v.), and *Spain* (q.v.).

160 **The Canary Islanders: their prehistory, conquest and survival.**
John Mercer. London: Rex Collings, 1980. 285p. 3 maps. bibliog.
An excellent and detailed study of the islands. The author is an archaeologist who has written many works on the Canaries and the Western Sahara (formally Spanish Sahara). Numerous sections cover all aspects of life on the islands, but the emphasis is on their archaeology. The work contains black-and-white photographs and line drawings, and includes appendixes on the autonomy and independence demands of the Canary Islanders, and on radiocarbon datings for the Islands. It is also worth looking at Günther Kunkel's (ed.) *Biogeography and ecology in the Canary Islands* (The Hague: W. Junk, 1976).

161 **Asturias contemporánea 1808-1975: síntesis histórica; textos y documentos.** (Contemporary Asturias 1808-1975: historical synthesis; texts and documents.)
David Ruiz (et al.) Madrid: Siglo Veintiuno de España, 1981. 382p. bibliog. (Historia).
This is a more wide-ranging study than the title suggests. Each author of the individual sections presents a historical summary by way of introduction to each period, followed by selected historical documents and letters. The book is divided into two parts: the first covers important events which occurred in Asturias between 1808 and 1975; and the second concentrates on the economy and social conditions during the same period. Over two hundred documents are included.

Galicia.
See item no. 54.

The western Pyrenees: differential evolution of the French and Spanish borderland.
See item no. 55.

Andalusia.
See item no. 56.

The Basque country.
See item no. 57.

New Castile.
See item no. 58.

Old Castile
See item no. 59.

Catalonia.
See item no. 60.

Minorca.
See item no. 98.

Galicia, nacionalidad histórica: causas de su marginación, su perspectiva.
(Galicia, a historical nation: why it was left behind; its future prospects.)
See item no. 354.

The Basques: the Franco years and beyond.
See item no. 361.

The social structure of Catalonia.
See item no. 362.

Catalonia infelix.
See item no. 368.

The Catalans.
See item no. 370.

Land and society in Golden Age Castile.
See item no. 652.

Early history

162 **Roman mines in Europe.**
Oliver Davies. Oxford, England: Clarendon Press, 1935.
Reprinted, New York: Arno Press, 1979. 291p. 6 maps. bibliog.
(Ancient Economic History).

Chapter 4 (p. 94-139) provides an overall picture of Roman mining, engineering and mineral resources during the Roman occupation of Spain. At one time (between 100 BC and AD 100), Spain was the most important metal-producing country in the world.

163 **V:sigothic Spain: new approaches.**
Edited by Edward James.   Oxford, England: Clarendon Press,
1980. 303p. bibliog.
This book is a collection of papers read at the Visigothic Colloquy, University
College, Dublin, in May, 1975. It is a well-indexed, scholarly study of all aspects
of Visigothic Spain, and comprises articles by scholars from North America,
Spain, France, Germany and the United Kingdom. The work is divided into two
parts: part one studies religion, culture and society; and part two considers
Visigothic Spain in relation to the rest of Europe.

164 **Law and society in the Visigothic kingdom.**
Paul David King.   Cambridge, England: Cambridge University
Press, 1972. 318p. bibliog. (Cambridge Studies in Medieval Life
and Thought, 3rd series, vol. 5).
An investigation into the 'structure and ethos of Visigothic society as it is revealed
in the legal and other sources of the time' which considers the everyday workings
of Visigothic life including: government; defence; early feudalism; crime; the
administration of justice; class ideology; economy; trade; and agriculture. The
author aims to provide an account of this society as the period drew to its close,
and it is interesting to note that it was under Visigothic rule that Catholicism was
made the official religion in 589.

165 **The Romans in Spain 217 B.C.-A.D. 117.**
C. H. V. Sutherland.   London: Methuen, 1939. 264p. 3 maps.
bibliog.
A short, general survey describing the development of Roman Spain. This useful
work is one of the few in English on the Roman period. Roman rule in Spain
lasted until AD 415, when, at the same time as the break-up of the empire, the
Visigoths conquered Spain.

166 **The Goths in Spain.**
Edward Arthur Thompson.   Oxford, England: Clarendon
Press, 1969. 358p. bibliog.
A study of Visigothic rule in Spain throughout the 6th and 7th centuries, in two
parts covering the Arian kingdom and the Catholic. The emphasis is on the
institutions created by the Goths, and their effects on daily life. The author avoids
analyzing the legacy of the Goths, and uses primary sources to back up his
discussion and conclusions.

167 **Roman Spain: an introduction to the Roman antiquities of Spain
and Portugal.**
F. J. Wiseman.   London: G. Bell, 1956. 232p. map.
This interesting study is much more wide-ranging than a straightforward look at
Roman antiquities and architecture, and is primarily aimed at students and
readers of Spanish history rather than of Roman history. It includes many
photographs of Roman remains and buildings in Spain, and an appendix which
lists the Roman emperors relevant to the period of occupation.

The world of ancient Spain.
See item no. 124

Mediaeval

168 **Moors and crusaders in Mediterranean Spain.**
Robert Ignatius Burns.   London: Variorum Reprints, 1978. 318p.
bibliog. (Variorum Reprint: CS73).

A facsimile reprint of sixteen articles which were originally published between 1954 and 1977. The author is a prolific writer on the old kingdom of Valencia and his latest work *Muslims, Christians and Jews in the crusader kingdom of Valencia: societies in symbiosis* (Cambridge, England: Cambridge University Press, 1983) is an excellent study of the settlement of Valencia before and after the Christian reconquest. Both works offer a detailed and scholarly account of many aspects of life in mediaeval Spain.

169 **Muslim Spain: its history and culture.**
Anwar G. Chejne.   Minneapolis, Minnesota: University of
Minnesota Press, 1974. 559p. 3 maps. bibliog.

The Muslims invaded the Iberian Peninsula in 711, the area controlled by them being known as Al-Andalus, and they were not finally driven out until the fall of the city of Granada in 1492. This book is not intended to be a definitive work on the subject of Hispano-Arabic studies, but rather a general study of the history, culture, and intellectual life of Muslim Spain. During the eight centuries of Arab occupation, Spain was by far the most advanced country in Europe, and 'a melting pot of many people: Romans, Visigoths, Berbers, Arabs, Jews and others'. This superb, illustrated work also contains an extensive bibliography. The author also wrote *Islam and the west: Moriscos – cultural and social history* (New York: State University of New York Press, 1982).

170 **In search of the Cid.**
Stephen Clissold.   London: Hodder & Stoughton, 1965. 254p. 2
maps. bibliog.

The Cid's real name was Rodrigo Díaz de Vivar, and the inscription on his tombstone in Burgos gives his dates as 1043-99. He gave his name to the famous *Poema de mío Cid* and Corneille's *Le Cid*, and it is generally believed that this title derived from the Arabic 'Sidi', meaning 'my lord'. He was the legendary hero of Spain in the fight against the Muslims, and Clissold's book represents his search for the true facts behind the legend, poetry and prejudice. Although basically a biography of the Cid's life, this fascinating work provides a greater understanding of events and conflicts between Christians and Muslims in 11th-century Spain.

171 **Early medieval Spain: unity in diversity, 400-1000.**
Roger J. H. Collins.   London: Macmillan, 1983. 317p. 5 maps.
bibliog. (New Studies in Medieval History).

The author emphasizes that, from Roman times to the present, Spanish history has been characterized by a tension between the racial and cultural diversity of its different regions, and the attempts of successive rulers to impose a political and 'national' unity upon it. In this work he offers new interpretations of one of the most crucial phases of the process, between AD 400 and 1000. There is an extensive bibliography included, as well as maps, lists of rulers, and chronological and genealogical tables. This volume forms a companion to Angus Mackay's *Spain in the Middle Ages: from frontier to empire, 1000-1500* (q.v.).

172 **Christian Córdoba: the city and its region in the late Middle Ages.**
John Edwards. Cambridge, England: Cambridge University Press, 1982. 240p. 2 maps. bibliog. (Cambridge Iberian and Latin American Studies).

This book represents a detailed study of Córdoba after its recapture from the Moors in 1236, during the period of Spain's rise to prominence as a European and then a world power. The focal point of this scholarly work is the rivalry between the Crown and the nobility over the control of the affairs of the city and region, and the character of the work is determined by the fact that most of the author's sources are legal or administrative in nature.

173 **Ferdinand and Isabella.**
Felipe Fernández-Armesto. London: Weidenfeld & Nicolson, 1975. 209p. 2 maps. bibliog.

The aim of the book is to portray Ferdinand and Isabella (the Catholic Monarchs) both as rulers and as human beings. The result of their marriage in 1469 is often described as the 'union of two crowns' but in reality the two realms of Aragón and Castile had no common institutions apart from the monarchy, except for the Inquisition which they established in Castile and extended to Aragón. This work studies all aspects of their reigns, intermingling biographical details with historical facts concerning the court, the government, the economy, the conquest of Granada, foreign policy, overseas expansion, and the Church.

174 **Islamic and Christian Spain in the early Middle Ages.**
Thomas F. Glick. Princeton, New Jersey: Princeton University Press, 1979. 376p. map. bibliog.

A full and interesting study of Spain from 900 to 1300, in which the author has adopted a comparative approach. The work is not intended as a general survey of Spain in the Middle Ages, but rather as an analysis of the central issues that contributed to the formation of Islamic and Spanish cultures in the Peninsula.

175 **Spain in the fifteenth century 1369-1516: essays and extracts by historians of Spain.**
Edited by Roger Highfield, translated by Frances M. López-Morillas. London: Macmillan, 1972. 488p. 3 maps. bibliog. (Stratum Series).

This book is made up of fourteen essays on a variety of historical subjects, including the economy of the Catholic Monarchs, law in 15th-century Spain, and the discovery of America. Each essay is written by a Spanish historian, with the exception of one by a Frenchman. It is hoped that these examples will help the reader to understand the history of the Peninsula under the two branches of the Trastámara dynasty from 1369 to the death of Ferdinand in 1516.

176 **The Spanish kingdoms 1250-1516.**
Jocelyn Nigel Hillgarth. Oxford, England: Oxford University Press, 1976-78. 2 vols. 4 maps. bibliog.

A good detailed study of mediaeval Spain, which includes an excellent bibliography. Volume 1 takes the reader up to 1410, while volume 2 spans the period 1410-1516. The author points out that in 1250 Spain did not exist, even as a geographical expression for what we today call Spain, and it can only reservedly be said to have existed in 1516 as a political unity. He also emphasizes the diverse history of the period under scrutiny, and the differences between the various regions.

177 **Muslim Spain: 711-1492 A.D.: a sociological study.**
S. M. Imamuddin. Leiden, Netherlands: E. J. Brill, 1981. 269p. map. bibliog. (Medieval Iberian Peninsula Texts and Studies, vol. 2).

This work is a revised and enlarged edition of *Some aspects of the socioeconomic and cultural history of Muslim Spain 711-1492 A.D.* (Leiden, Netherlands: E. J. Brill, 1965). The aim of this book is to present an outline of the social and cultural activities of Muslim Spain, and is particularly easy to follow, as there are numerous subheadings within each of the major headings or chapters. A good index is also provided. The author also wrote *A political history of Muslim Spain* (Dacca: Najmah, 1961), and is a prolific writer on this period.

178 **The making of medieval Spain.**
Gabriel Jackson. London: Thames & Hudson, 1972. 216p. 6 maps. bibliog. (Library of European Civilization).

A beautifully illustrated survey of the Spanish Middle Ages, up to, and including, the reign of Ferdinand and Isabella. The author emphasizes the achievements and conflicts of the major religious groups, believing that 'by far the most significant aspect of Spanish medieval history was the constant interpenetration of the three distinctive cultures present in the peninsula: the Islamic, the Hebrew and the Christian'. He thus admits to concentrating on cultural and religious questions at the expense of detailed political and diplomatic history. All in all, this is a clear and concise study which reflects the vitality of Spanish history during this period.

179 **The reconquest of Spain.**
Derek William Lomax. London; New York: Longman, 1978. 212p. 6 maps. bibliog.

This history of the struggle of the Christians against the Almoravids, Almohads, Umayyads and Nasrids during the 'Reconquista' (Reconquest) helps us to understand much of what lies behind the 'pride' which became a characteristic of the Spanish. It is interesting to note that the experience of the Christian revolution in the Peninsula gave Spain the expertise, experience and ability to 'Europeanize the populous areas of the New World'. This excellent work sheds much light on the organization and development of society in Spain during an important period in its history. The author also wrote *Another sword for St. James* (Birmingham, England: Birmingham University Press, 1974).

180 A society organized for war: medieval Spain.

Elena Lourie. *Past and Present*, no. 35 (Dec. 1966), p. 54-76.

The Christian reconquest lasted over 700 years, and this article explains how Christian society developed in circumstances which meant that it was conditioned by danger and war. It briefly describes the founding of the Military Orders of Calatrava (1158), Alcántara (1166) and Santiago (1170), and discusses the tactics and equipment that the Christians copied directly from the Muslims. A useful bibliography is also included.

181 Spain in the Middle Ages: from frontier to empire, 1000-1500.

Angus Mackay. London: Macmillan, 1977. 245p. 5 maps. bibliog.
(New Studies in Medieval History).

This work describes the process by which an unstable frontier society developed into a state capable of establishing a vast empire. It studies the emergence of Christian Spain and its civilization, and examines the effects of the Muslim occupation on Spanish society and culture. There is also an excellent bibliography, a glossary, and a list of rulers of the period.

182 The Spain of Ferdinand and Isabella.

Jean Hippolyte Mariéjol, translated and edited by Benjamin Keen. New Brunswick, New Jersey: Rutgers University Press, 1961. 429p. 3 maps. bibliog.

An extremely good study of the period when Spain really began to develop into the greatest power in Europe. It is divided into four main sections covering the reign of Ferdinand and Isabella, institutions, social life and intellectual life. This was a time when industry and trade were encouraged, the arts flourished, America was discovered, and the Caribbean became 'the Spanish lake'. The book was first published in French in 1892, and is recognized by most modern scholars as being the best general study of the political, social, and administrative system under the Catholic Monarchs. The work also contains a useful preface and a bibliographical note by the translator.

183 The castles and the crown: Spain 1451-1555.

Townsend Miller. London: Victor Gollanz, 1963. 379p. map. bibliog.

This book is primarily the story of four people: Isabella I, Ferdinand II, Juana la Loca, and Philip I (the Fair). Its main purpose is to present as clear a picture as possible of their characters, and not a full study of the period.

184 Henry IV of Castile, 1425-1474.

Townsend Miller. Philadelphia; New York: J. B. Lippincott, 1972. 306p. map. bibliog.

This is one of the very few works written on Henry IV, who reigned from 1454 to

1474. It recounts the life and activities of the king chronologically within their historical setting, and describes how his disastrous reign brought economic troubles and violence.

185   A history of medieval Spain.
Joseph F. O'Callaghan.   Ithaca, New York; London: Cornell University Press, 1975. 729p. 8 maps. bibliog.

This massive work provides an excellent narrative history of the Hispanic Middle Ages. It is based on the research and studies of contemporary historians, and extends to the discovery of America in 1492.

186   Isabel of Castile and the making of the Spanish nation 1451-1504.
Ierne Arthur Lifford Plunket.   New York; London: G. P. Putnam's, 1919. 432p. map. bibliog.

Isabella was one of the most remarkable figures in Spanish history, and was responsible for initiating many political, social and religious reforms. She was Queen of Castile from 1474, and of Aragón from 1479, ruling jointly with her husband Ferdinand II of Aragón (Ferdinand V of Castile).

187   History of the reign of Ferdinand and Isabella the Catholic.
William Hickling Prescott, abridged and edited by C. Harvey Gardiner.   London: Allen & Unwin, 1962. 303p. map.

Ferdinand and Isabella's joint reign of Spain, which began in 1479, was one of the most glorious in the annals of Spanish history. The zenith came in 1492, the *annus mirabilis*, when not only did Columbus discover America, but Moorish power was crushed with the fall of Granada, the Jews were expelled from Spain, and Nebrija published his famous grammar. The work covers all areas of Spanish rule, emphasizing the consolidation of the Spanish State and the establishment of Spain's overseas empire. Prescott (1796-1859) gained tremendous recognition with this work, encouraging the pursuit of Hispanic studies amongst other American historians. It has been published more than 150 times in half a dozen languages. This abridged version by Gardiner is based to a large extent on one formulated by Prescott himself, which he executed and then destroyed. Unfortunately, it is not indexed.

188   Curia and Cortes in León and Castile 1072-1295.
Evelyn S. Procter.   Cambridge, England: Cambridge University Press, 1980. 318p. bibliog. (Cambridge Iberian and Latin American Studies).

A scholarly, but by no means definitive, study of specific aspects of government in mediaeval Spain, which includes a glossary and an appendix of legal documents. *Curia regis* was the general name for the assembly which aided the monarch in the work of government during the 11th and 12th centuries. Sadly the authoress died during the final stages of proof correction in March 1980. She also wrote *Alfonso X of Castile: patron of literature and learning* (Oxford, England: Oxford University Press, 1951).

189 **Spain: the rise of the first world power.**
John Fraser Ramsey.   Alabama: University of Alabama, 1973.
341p. 4 maps. bibliog. (Mediterranean Europe Series, no. 1).
The author notes in his introduction that 'of the three great imperial experiments
of western civilization – the Roman, the Spanish, and the British – the Spanish is
the most intriguing and in many ways the most remarkable'. This general survey
of Spanish history up to the early 16th century focuses on the events which shaped
Spain's rise to power.

190 **The Moors in Spain and Portugal.**
Jan Read.   London: Faber & Faber, 1974. 268p. 4 maps. bibliog.
This book is a good general study of the Moorish occupation of, and influence in,
Spain, and is aimed mainly at the general reader. It shows how much the Arabs
contributed to European technology, and describes the indelible stamp left by
them on the culture and national character of Spain and Portugal. It is illustrated,
and contains a comparative chronology of Spain and Christian Europe from 711
to 1614. The author acknowledges the debt he owes to Lévi-Provençal's *Histoire
de l'Espagne musulmane* (Paris: G.-P. Maisonneuve, 1950-53) which is a masterly
work planned as a complete study of Moorish Spain, although at the time of the
author's death only the first three volumes had been completed.

191 **A history of Islamic Spain.**
W. Montgomery Watt, with additional sections on literature by
Pierre Cachia.   Edinburgh: Edinburgh University Press, 1977.
210p. 2 maps. bibliog. (Edinburgh Paperbacks).
A very good and fully illustrated account, providing a brief history of Al-Andalus
during the seven centuries of Arab occupation. It pays particular attention to
social and religious movements, and to intellectual and cultural life. The work is
aimed primarily at the educated reader with little or no previous knowledge of the
subject, and is strongly recommended for university students.

**The troubadour revival: a study of social change and traditionalism in
late medieval Spain.**
See item no. 455.

El ejército de los Reyes Católicos. (The army of the Catholic Monarchs.)
See item no. 570.

Renaissance diplomacy.
See item no. 575.

Habsburgs

192 The emperor Charles V: the growth and destiny of a man and a world-empire.
Karl Brandi, translated from the German by C. V. Wedgwood.
London: Jonathan Cape, 1968. 655p.

This outstanding and minutely detailed work of Charles' reign is primarily concerned with his German problems, and stresses his role as Emperor of the Holy Roman Empire (1519-58) rather than King of Spain (1516-56). The author is considered by many to be the greatest authority on Charles V, having spent a lifetime researching the imperial archives and other major sources.

193 The Mediterranean and the Mediterranean world in the age of Philip II.
Fernand Braudel, translated from the French by Siân Reynolds.
London: Collins, 1972-73. 2 vols. maps. bibliog.

A translation of the French second revised edition of 1966. This colossal masterpiece (over 1,300 pages) spans the reign of Philip II (1556-98), and although it covers the Mediterranean region in general, it is mainly devoted to Spain. Braudel opens up fresh lines of thought and research, and has helped to place the social and economic development of Spain in a far wider, international setting. He says: 'Climate, landscape, diet, rhythms of trade, operations of financiers and the hard life of the peasant and the seamen, all the rich variety and colour of this most magnetic area of human history have their place in a brilliant mosaic'. The work is notable for its huge bibliography and its excellent illustrations alone.

194 Philip of Spain and the Netherlands: an essay on moral judgements in history.
Cecil John Cadoux.   London: Lutterworth Press, 1947. 251p.
bibliog.

A fully documented, scholarly study, which attempts to establish moral judgements regarding the chief protagonists in the revolt of the Netherlands against Spain and Spanish policy-making. It includes a large chronological table and brief descriptions of events in the Netherlands and during the lifetime of Philip II.

195 The secret diplomacy of the Habsburgs, 1598-1625.
Charles Howard Carter.   New York; London: Columbia
University Press, 1964. 321p. 2 maps. bibliog.

Examines the historical background to Spanish foreign policy and to the making of Spanish Habsburg policy. The author discusses intelligence reports and espionage, and emphasizes the importance of the Habsburg intelligence-gathering systems in the formulation of policy decisions. The work opens with the year of the Treaty of Vervins with France (1598) which was also the year of Philip II's death.

196 **The kingdom of Valencia in the seventeenth century.**
James Casey. Cambridge, England: Cambridge University Press,
1979. 271p. map. bibliog. (Cambridge Studies in Early Modern
History).

A scholarly study of the kingdom of Valencia, which analyzes the whole social
and political structure of the province, with a strong emphasis on economic
conditions. In 1238 James the Conqueror (1213-76) seized the city of Valencia
from the Moors, and in 1707 Philip V (1700-46) abolished its autonomy after it
had backed the wrong candidate in a disputed succession to the Spanish throne.
The author attempts to shed some light on the culture and history of the region,
whilst at the same time providing a broad economic, social and political history of
Habsburg Spain. Appendixes include a list of viceroys of the kingdom from 1598-
1700, and several statistical tables and graphs.

197 **The golden century of Spain 1501-1621.**
Reginald Trevor Davies. London: Macmillan; New York: St.
Martin's Press, 1967. 327p. 4 maps. bibliog. (Papermac, no. 49).

A compact history of the century of Spanish ascendancy in Europe, with valuable
analysis of the economic and social aspects. It is useful for both students and the
general reader, and presents an excellent summary of the period.

198 **Spain in decline; 1621-1700.**
Reginald Trevor Davies. London: Macmillan; New York: St.
Martin's Press, 1965. 180p. map. bibliog. (Papermac, no. 139).

The author was a lecturer in Spanish history at the University of Oxford until his
death in 1953. This in-depth study of Philip IV (1621-65) and his son Charles II
(1665-1700) also contains an excellent bibliography and index. His analysis of the
causes – economic, political and military – of the decline of Spain during the
reigns of the last two Habsburg rulers, represents the sequel to *The golden century
of Spain 1501-1621 (q.v.)*.

199 **Daily life in Spain in the Golden Age.**
Marcelin Defourneaux, translated by Newton Branch. London:
George Allen & Unwin, 1970. 256p. bibliog. (Daily Life Series,
no. 13).

This marvellously evocative work was originally published in French, and the
author, through the writings of contemporary travellers in 16th- and 17th-century
Spain, reveals the social life and customs of the country at this time. He
emphasizes a Spanish soul dominated by two sentiments: a profound religious
faith, and a sense of honour. The term 'Golden Age' generally refers to the
Habsburg period when gold and silver from America enabled Spain to launch
greater ventures abroad, and to gain military ascendancy over the whole of
Europe. Notwithstanding this, it also refers to the literary and artistic 'Golden
Century' produced by its flourishing writers and artists, although Spain herself
was in economic decline.

200 **The Golden Age of Spain 1516-1659.**
Antonio Domínguez Ortiz, translated by James Casey. London: Weidenfeld & Nicolson, 1971. 361p. map. bibliog. (The History of Spain).

A structural analysis of society, the economy, the state and cultural institutions, which also discusses the impact on Spain of the colonization and exploitation of America. The whole work leads up to the general period of decline in the middle years of the 17th century.

201 **The decline of Spain.**
John Huxtable Elliott. *Past and Present*, no. 20 (Nov. 1961), p. 52-75.

A superb study of the collapse of the empire, and the end of the 'Golden Age' in Spain during the 17th century. Elliott sees 'the decline in the characters of the rulers, mortmain and vagabondage, contempt for manual labour, monetary chaos and excessive taxation, the power of the Church and the folly of government' as major contributing factors, and notes that most of these ills had been diagnosed in the writings of 17th-century Spaniards themselves. This classic article also discusses such important topics as the demographic history of Castile, which was radically affected by the plague of 1599-60. Also included are useful statistics and a bibliography.

202 **Imperial Spain 1469-1716.**
John Huxtable Elliott. Harmondsworth, England: Penguin Books, 1970. 423p. 6 maps. bibliog.

A balanced, concise study of Spain under the Habsburgs, and of 'the sudden rise of a barren and isolated country to be the greatest power on earth, and of its equally sudden decline'. Together with Lynch's work *Spain under the Habsburgs* (q.v.), this book remains a standard text for any serious study of the period.

203 **The revolt of the Catalans: a study in the decline of Spain (1598-1640).**
John Huxtable Elliott. Cambridge, England: Cambridge University Press, 1963. 623p. 2 maps. bibliog.

This book was originally begun as a study of the political career of Philip IV's favourite and chief minister, Olivares (1587-1645), but at the time a lack of source material forced Elliott to switch emphasis. He explains how the collapse of law and order in Catalonia, and the gradual deterioration of relations between Catalonia and the Madrid government, led to the revolution in 1640. He stresses the importance of the role of Olivares, as many believe that it was his policy (and his established aim) to provoke a revolution in the region. This study also looks closely at the domestic aspects of Spain's decline. Elliott's final sentence notes that 'the revolt of the Catalans at once epitomized and foreshadowed the tragedy of Spain'. The work is almost entirely based on previously unknown documents from Spanish national and local archives.

204 **Richelieu and Olivares.**
John Huxtable Elliott. Cambridge, England: Cambridge
University Press, 1984. 189p. bibliog. (Cambridge Studies in Early
Modern History).

This work is based on the Trevelyan Lectures given at Cambridge University in
1983, and is a comparative study of power and statesmanship in 17th-century
France and Spain. The fortunes of these two great statesmen reflect the outcome
of the great struggle between the two countries. Elliott examines their formative
years, their rise to power, and their political careers, and in particular reveals a
great deal of new material on Olivares. He is presently engaged on a full-scale
political biography of the latter.

205 **Charles V: elected emperor and hereditary ruler.**
Manuel Fernández Alvarez. London: Thames & Hudson, 1975.
220p. 2 maps. bibliog. (Men in Office).

One of Spain's greatest kings, Charles was perhaps the last emperor to attempt to
realize the mediaeval idea of a unified empire embracing the entire Christian
world. This excellent work covers all aspects of his life and reign, both as King of
Spain and Holy Roman Emperor. The book also contains forty illustrations, a
genealogical table, and a select bibliography.

206 **The state, war and peace: Spanish political thought in the
Renaissance, 1516-1559.**
J. A. Fernández-Santamaría. Cambridge, England: Cambridge
University Press, 1977. 316p. bibliog. (Cambridge Studies in Early
Modern History).

This is a useful study of the development and changes in Spanish political thought
in the 16th century. The first part studies mediaeval constitutionalism, Christian
humanism and neoscholasticism (1516-39), and the second covers the decline of
Erasmianism (1539-59). It surveys the contribution of a number of eminent
writers who attempted to apply established ideas to the changing circumstances
brought about by a Habsburg ruler and imperial expansion in the New World.

207 **The Spanish Armadas.**
Winston Graham. London: Fontana, 1976. 256p. map. bibliog.

Most people remember the Armada of 1588, which ended in destruction.
However, far from marking the end of Spanish attempts to conquer and
Catholicize England, it marked a new development, for after that year Spain
launched three further Armadas against England. This is a brilliant account of the
origins and course of the conflict. Winston Graham is also the author of many
famous novels, and his work has been translated into sixteen languages.

208 **Political thought in sixteenth-century Spain: a study of the political
ideas of Vitoria, De Soto, Suárez, and Molina.**
Bernice Hamilton. Oxford, England: Oxford University Press,
1963. 201p. bibliog.

A most valuable study of political theory in Spain, which discusses the opinions of four Jesuit and Dominican philosophers. The work gives biographical details on each of the four theologians, who lectured at universities in Spain and Portugal during the 16th century.

209 Battle of the Spanish Armada.

Roger Hart. London: Wayland; New York: G. P. Putnam's, 1973. 128p. maps. bibliog. (The Documented History Series).

A fascinating, illustrated account which makes use of contemporary documents and illustrations. It describes the defeat of the first Spanish Armada in 1588, and is particularly useful for its vivid illustrations of uniforms, ships, portraits and sketches, as well as its selection of eyewitness accounts.

210 The voyage of the Armada: the Spanish story.

David Howarth. London: Collins, 1981. 256p. map. bibliog.

A brilliant complement to Mattingly's study (q.v.) on the subject, in which the author sets out to establish the truth about events which have been clouded by prejudice. Using original sources he tells the Spanish side of the story, describing the failure of the first Armada (three more were sent before Philip II died) which sailed in 1588. He emphasizes the final stages of the tragedy, when starving men in battered and sinking ships sought refuge in Ireland. The Irish part of the story is covered in *The Armada in Ireland* by Niall Fallon (London: Stanford Maritime, 1978).

211 Spain: its greatness and decay (1479-1788).

Martin Andrew Sharp Hume, revised by Edward Armstrong. Cambridge, England: Cambridge University Press, 1931. 3rd ed. 464p. bibliog. (Cambridge Historical Series).

This work is an overall study of Spanish history from Ferdinand and Isabella to Charles III (1759-88). 'An attempt has been made to present the story with absolute impartiality, and to render it a trustworthy and readable relation of events'. It was first published in 1898, and remains a standard work. The author also wrote *The court of Philip IV* (London: Eveleigh, Nash & Grayson, 1928), and *Philip II of Spain* (Westport, Connecticut: Greenwood Press, 1970, a reprint of the original 1903 edition).

212 Spain 1469-1714: a society of conflict.

Henry Kamen. London; New York: Longman, 1983. 305p. 6 maps. bibliog.

The author stresses the theme of empire, and contends that Spain was economically unfitted for her role as an imperial power, especially in Europe. He also provides a useful and up-to-date account of probably the most interesting period of Spanish history, and notes how Spaniards continued to question and debate: the unification of their country; the conquest of America; the wars in the Netherlands; the role of the Inquisition; and the expulsion of the Moriscos and other aspects of public policy. The work includes two appendixes, one a dynastic table of Spanish rulers 1474-1700, and the other providing economic and demographic statistics.

213 **Spain in the later seventeenth century, 1665-1700.**
Henry Kamen. London; New York: Longman, 1980. 418p. 5
maps. bibliog.

The author comments that most studies on Spain during this period including, for
example, Huguette and Pierre Chaunu's *Séville et l'Atlantique (1504-1650)*, (Paris:
Colin, 1955-60) stop at 1650. This book represents the first total history of Spain
under Charles II. The later 17th century has been considered by many to be the
classic period of the 'decline of Spain', but Kamen presents a different view. He
notes how trade difficulties, inflation and the decline in population and agrarian
production, were problems that began to resolve themselves after mid-century in
a general period of recuperation.

214 **The Spanish Armada.**
Michael Lewis. London: Batsford, 1960. 216p. maps.

This study by an authority and prolific writer on naval history, analyzes the causes
of the defeat of the first Spanish Armada in 1588. It includes an intimate look at
the leaders and the principal characters concerned with diplomatic relations and
military affairs. Illustrated with maps, diagrams and photographs, the volume
discusses all aspects from the human elements to the technical details of guns,
ships and tactics.

215 **Constitutionalism and statecraft during the Golden Age of Spain: a
study of the political philosophy of Juan de Mariana, S. J.**
Guenter Lewy. Geneva, Switzerland: E. Droz, 1960. 199p.
bibliog. (Travaux d'Humanisme et Renaissance, no. 36).

Born in 1535, Mariana was a Spanish Jesuit who taught in Rome and Flanders.
He was the author of *De Rege et Regis Institutione* (1598), a work which linked
him to the school of writers known as the Monarchomachs, and argued that
regicide should be legal. Lewy concentrates on Mariana's thoughts and ideas
rather than on the man, and aims to show the place and significance of his
controversial doctrines in 16th- and early 17th-century Europe.

216 **Spain under the Habsburgs.**
John Lynch. Oxford, England: Basil Blackwell, 1981. 2nd ed. 2
vols. 6 maps. bibliog.

Volume 1 is entitled 'Empire and absolutism, 1516-1598', and volume 2, 'Spain
and America, 1598-1700'. This work provides a fuller treatment of the Habsburg
period than Elliott's (q.v.), especially of the 17th century and the empire. The
author presents a comprehensive and up-to-date survey of the 16th and 17th
centuries, and provides interesting interpretations of the impact of trade with the
empire in America on the economic development of Spain. In this second edition
Lynch has sought to incorporate the results of more recent research, as well as
redrawing maps and providing a new selection of illustrations.

217 **The defeat of the Spanish Armada.**
'Garrett Mattingly. London: Jonathan Cape, 1983. 2nd ed. 384p.
maps. bibliog.

An outstanding work, with the only real flaw being that no precise dates are given
on the planning of the first Armada of 1588. In 1960 Mattingly, an American
scholar, won a Pulitzer special citation for the work. It is written in a most
interesting and readable style, and has been described by the eminent historian A.
L. Rowse as 'a historical masterpiece'; and for the historian J. H. Plumb it was 'a
faultless book, by far the most exciting I have read for many a long time'. There
are excellent illustrations and maps included, as well as general notes on the ships
and their armaments. Mattingly also wrote *The invincible Armada and
Elizabethan England* (Ithaca, New York: Cornell University Press, 1979).

218 **Philip II.**
Geoffrey Parker. London: Hutchinson, 1979. 234p. bibliog. (The
Library of World Biography).

Philip II became King of Spain in 1556, and was known to his age as 'the most
potent monarch of Christendom'. He ruled the greatest empire since the Romans,
and this remarkable portrait of a king who reigned for almost half a century
throws light on the whole history and foreign relations of Spain at the time.
Parker has been fortunate in being able to use information provided by the
monarch's private correspondence ('Altamira Papers'), and he dispels many of
the myths and legends which have surrounded the figure of Philip II for many
years.

219 **Philip II of Spain.**
Sir Charles Petrie. London: Eyre & Spottiswoode, 1963. 318p.
3 maps. bibliog.

From this portrait, Philip II emerges neither as an ogre nor as the champion of
the Counter-Reformation, but as a highly capable and conscientious administrator
with a strong sense of justice, given the standards of his time. It is not solely a
study of the king, but also an evaluation of Spanish history in the second half of
the 16th century.

220 **Philip II of Spain.**
Peter Pierson. London: Thames & Hudson, 1975. 240p. 4 maps.
bibliog. (Men in Office).

A highly interesting and readable account of Philip's life and times which covers:
his education as a prince; his character, family and interests; monarchy and
empire; the court of Madrid and government; and foreign policy. Pierson notes
that 'Philip II thought consciously in terms of dynasty and religion, not of nation-
states'.

221 **History of the reign of Philip II, King of Spain.**
William Hickling Prescott. London: Routledge, 1872. 3 vols. in 2.

This classic work was begun in 1849, but the brilliant Bostonian did not live to
complete his projected four-volume work. However, it ranks alongside his other

classics on the Catholic Monarchs – (*History of the reign of Ferdinand and Isabella* (q.v.) – and the conquests of Mexico and Peru. All were products of the nearly-blind scholar's lifelong devotion to the study of Spanish history. This work, which ends with the construction of the king's 'gloomy pile' of a palace (El Escorial), is written with a distinctive liveliness.

222 **The character of Philip II: the problem of moral judgements in history.**
Edited by John C. Rule and John J. Tepaske. Boston, Massachussetts: D. C. Heath, 1963. 103p. bibliog. (Problems in European Civilization).

Ruling for almost half a century over Spain and her vast empire, Philip II has inspired an immense amount of historical literature. In this book thoughts and opinions on his reign have been put forward by some of the most eminent scholars of Spanish history, including Merriman, Davies, Mattingly and Altamira y Crevea. The volume is divided into sections, presenting: 16th-century views; attacks on his character; reappraisals; modern dissenters; and 20th-century Spanish views. The work also includes short quotations and resumés from the individual authors, which emphasize the conflict of opinion among historians.

223 **Europe and the decline of Spain: a study of the Spanish system 1580-1720.**
R. A. Stradling. London: George Allen & Unwin, 1981. 222p. 5 maps. bibliog. (Early Modern Europe Today).

This work seeks to 'define and illumine some of the major contours of medieval Spain', and also deals with the slow decline of Spanish power. It contains a glossary of Spanish terms, and an excellent bibliographical prologue concerning the problems involved in researching bibliographical data on the subject, and citing all the relevant bibliographical references.

224 **War and government in Habsburg Spain 1560-1620.**
I. A. A. Thompson. London: Athlone Press, 1976. 374p. bibliog.

The greatest military power in 16th-century Christendom was Habsburg Spain, and 'this book is an investigation of government in Spain as an instrument for the organization of war'. The author emphasizes the struggle between the two conflicting systems of administrative control: the first, a system of direct administration by officials and ministers acting for the most part in a public capacity, financed at all levels by the royal treasury; the second, a less cohesive system of indirect administration by non-royal agents. This study of how absolute monarchy in Spain actually worked, looks in particular at the administrative machinery behind Spain's military power during the reigns of Philip II and III.

225 **The great enterprise: the history of the Spanish Armada as revealed in contemporary documents.**
Selected and edited by Stephen Usherwood. London: Bell & Hyman, 1982. 192p.

A useful collection of contemporary documents including letters, dispatches, proclamations and sailing instructions covering the conflict from its beginnings to its aftermath. All the documents are presented in English, and are interspersed with helpful commentaries.

Full fathom five: wrecks of the Spanish Armada.
See item no. 120.

Bourbons

226 **Royal vendetta: the crown of Spain 1829-1965.**
Theo Aronson. London: Oldbourne, 1966. 246p. bibliog.
The central theme of this book is the struggle for the throne of Spain between the Bourbon and Carlist pretenders (supporters of the successors in the male line) which began in 1833. As the author states in his introduction, this is 'a book about people, not politics', though the effects on Spain of the feuds are clearly discussed. There are six chapters covering the principal characters of María Cristina of Naples, Isabella II, Alfonso XII, María Cristina of Austria, and Alfonso XIII, and the throne of Spain (mostly vacant) from 1931 to 1965. Juan Carlos de Borbón y Borbón, groomed by General Franco, is the latest Bourbon to overcome a Carlist pretender to the throne.

227 **A time of triumph and of sorrow: Spanish politics during the reign of Alfonso XII, 1874-1885.**
Earl R. Beck. Carbondale, Illinois: Southern Illinois University Press, 1979. 307p. map. bibliog.
A study of Alfonso's short reign, which gave rise to hopes for a constitutional monarchy in Spain. His two most pressing concerns were ending the civil war begun by the Carlists, and drafting the constitution, and both these problems were settled in 1875-76. The author includes useful material from diplomatic archives, but sometimes exaggerates the political power of the king. The twice Prime Minister, Antonio Cánovas del Castillo, was often the one who determined the pattern of political life during Alfonso's reign. The title reflects the triumph of Alfonso's return to the throne of his ancestors after the First Republic (1873-74), and of Cánovas' political work, and also the sorrow of Alfonso's frustration and untimely demise.

228 **Fascism from above: the dictatorship of Primo de Rivera in Spain 1923-1930.**
Shlomo Ben-Ami. Oxford, England: Oxford University Press, 1983. 454p. bibliog.
Miguel Primo de Rivera's (1870-1930) dictatorship lasted from September 1923 to January 1930. His attempt to unify Spain around the motto 'country, religion, monarchy' was doomed due to his government's failure to create a viable political system. The most popular achievement of his régime was the successful conclusion of the Moroccan War in 1927. He was forced to resign after his chief

source of power, the army, refused to support him. This outstanding book represents the first systematic study of the period, and attempts to re-examine Primo de Rivera's rise to power and the régime itself.

229 The Spanish Bourbons: the history of a tenacious dynasty.

John D. Bergamini. New York: G. P. Putnam's, 1974. 442p. map. bibliog.

This detailed work covers the period from the reign of Philip V, the first Bourbon king of Spain, to Alfonso XIII. The final chapters discuss the abdication of Alfonso, the Franco régime, and prospects for the monarchy in the naming of Juan Carlos as heir apparent. The author notes that Spain has had various Bourbon pretenders to a vacant throne for over forty years – during the Second Republic, the Civil War, and the Franco era. In spite of severe problems (notably the attempted 'coup' of February 1981) Juan Carlos I has shown himself equally tenacious in holding on to, and inspiring support for, the Spanish monarchy.

230 Praetorian politics in liberal Spain.

Carolyn P. Boyd. Chapel Hill, North Carolina: University of North Carolina Press, 1979. 376p. bibliog.

An attempt to explain the relationship between the failure of parliamentary government in Spain and military intervention in political processes, particularly between the years 1917 and 1923. It is an essential work for any serious study of how civil-military relations during a critical period of Spanish history led to a growing reliance upon the military to maintain the political *status quo*, which in turn gave the army stimulus to intervene to protect its corporate interests. It still remains to be seen whether praetorianism can ever be fully eliminated in Spain.

231 Modern Spain 1875-1980.

Raymond Carr. Oxford, England: Oxford University Press, 1980. 201p. map. bibliog.

A concise, yet detailed, study of the political history of Spain during the past one hundred years. An interesting opening paragraph describes how 'the word "liberal", as part of our political vocabulary, comes from Spain' (and was first used to describe a group of radical patriots in Cádiz, refugees from the French invasion of 1808). The book is a re-working of some of the themes written about by Carr over the past twenty years, with a final chapter devoted to Spain's (and western Europe's as a whole) current problems such as inflation, unemployment, terrorism, and the continuing work to maintain a stable democracy. It includes a chronology of the main political events of the period, a glossary of political terms and organizations, and a thorough bibliography.

232 Spain 1808-1975.

Raymond Carr. Oxford, England: Clarendon Press, 1982. 2nd ed. 856p. 5 maps. bibliog. (Oxford History of Modern Europe).

The first edition of this huge standard work was published in 1966, and only went up to 1939. Carr points out the enormous improvements made in Spanish historiography since that time, and this second edition contains five additional essays covering the Franco era, as well as an expanded bibliographical chapter. It is an authoritative account of the political, economic and social conditions in Spain, which attempts to explain the ultimate failure of 19th-century Spanish liberalism.

233 Godoy: master of Spain 1792-1808.

Jacques Chastenet, translated by J. F. Huntington.   London: Batchworth Press, 1953. 249p.

Manuel de Godoy (1767-1851) was a controversial figure, whose policies and character had an important influence on the events leading up to both the Battle of Trafalgar (1805) and the Peninsular War (1808-14). He was a minister to the vacillating Charles IV, a royal favourite, and twice Prime Minister. His disastrous foreign policy contributed to the series of misfortunes and defeats that culminated in the abdication of the king and the occupation of Spain by Napoleon and his armies.

234 The Basque phase of Spain's Civil War, 1833-1835.

John F. Coverdale.   Princeton, New Jersey: Princeton University Press, 1984. 312p. bibliog.

One of the few books in English which deals in detail with the First Carlist War (1833-39), and the only work to properly explain its background and causes. Coverdale explores events leading up to, and the first two years of, the war which was a conflict between conservative northern peasants and the liberal Madrid government. Focusing on these years, when the Basques were the predominant Carlist leaders, the author examines the Carlists' aims, geographic and social bases, and military activities. He concludes that Basque Carlism was the defensive reaction of a still largely intact traditional society against disruptive changes from without and, to some extent, from within.

235 Legacy of glory: the Bonaparte kingdom of Spain 1808-1813.

Michael Glover.   London: Leo Cooper, 1972. 353p. 4 maps. bibliog.

A detailed history of the main events and protagonists of the Spanish War of Independence (1808-14), which tells the story of the French occupation of Spain and the discord between the Emperor Napoleon Bonaparte and his eldest surviving brother Joseph (1768-1844). Joseph was a lawyer, diplomat and soldier, until he was called away from Naples by Napoleon and installed as King of Spain. After being forced to leave Madrid when Spanish insurgents defeated the French at Bailén in 1808, he was later reinstated, and thereafter was kept in a subordinate position that led him on four occasions to offer to abdicate. The book is more a study of the relationship between the two Bonaparte brothers than of the Spanish operations against the French, but is nevertheless useful for providing details on the problems faced by Joseph in his six-year rule of Spain.

236 Eighteenth-century Spain, 1700-1788: a political, diplomatic and institutional history.

W. N. Hargreaves-Mawdsley.   London: Macmillan, 1979. 181p. 4 maps. bibliog.

The work, which constitutes a straight presentation of the facts, opens with an introductory chapter on Spanish governmental institutions during the 18th century, and is followed by three individual sections on the reigns of Philip V (1700-46), Ferdinand VI (1746-59) and Charles III (1759-88). The author has written another work on the same period entitled *Spain under the Bourbons, 1700-1833: a collection of documents* (London: Macmillan, 1973), in which he edits and translates a series of documents dealing with the political, diplomatic, social and cultural aspects.

237 **The Federal Republic in Spain: Pí y Margall and the Federal Republican movement 1868-74.**
Charles Alistair Michael Hennessey.   Oxford, England: Oxford University Press, 1962. 299p. bibliog.

This work was reprinted in 1980 by Greenwood Press. It is a scholarly study of 'intellectualism' in politics and of the federal movement, portraying Pí y Margall as the intellectual and political leader of a difficult period in Spanish politics. The book encompasses the coalition of Juan Prim y Prats and Francisco Serrano (1868-70); the reign of Amadeo I, King of Spain, Duke of Aosta (1870-73); and the First Republic (1873-74), of which Pí y Margall was President. The federal movement is discussed in the context of the spread of Bakuninist ideas, and it is stressed that although the First Republic collapsed within a year, the federal movement continued to exert a growing influence on Spanish anarchism, Catalan regionalism, and on Republican tradition.

238 **The eighteenth-century revolution in Spain.**
Richard Herr.   Princeton, New Jersey: Princeton University Press, 1969. 484p. 5 maps. bibliog. (Princeton Paperbacks).

A good guide to the Spanish Enlightenment, with particular reference to the reign of Charles III (1759-88) and the years of the French Revolution. The volume deals with the apogee of the Enlightenment, the economic advances made under Charles III, and the disruptive effects of the French Revolution on political and religious thinking. This is an authoritative and detailed study of the period when Spain had to come to terms with what was taking place in the rest of Europe, and particularly in France.

239 **The Carlist Wars in Spain.**
Edgar Holt.   London: Putnam, 1967. 303p. map. bibliog.

A concise study of the background to the 19th-century dynastic wars and the present state of Carlism in Spain, which presents a useful account of both the Carlists and the intrigues surrounding Isabella II. The Carlist Wars (1833-39 and 1872-76) 'are the last major European civil wars in which pretenders fought to establish their claim to a throne'. Britain was closely involved in the First Carlist War, sending a mercenary army of 10,000 men in support of the Spanish government and the Queen Regent, María Cristina.

240 **Charles III and the revival of Spain.**
Anthony H. Hull.   Washington DC: University Press of America, 1980. 402p. 4 maps. bibliog.

Charles III, king of Spain from 1759 to 1788, was one of the 'enlightened despots' of the 18th century, who for a short time revitalized Spain. He saw his mission as the reformation of the monarchy and the colonial empire in order to revive Spanish power and influence. The author is a writer of poetry as well as a historian.

241 **Modern Spain 1788-1898.**
Martin Andrew Sharp Hume. London: T. Fisher Unwin, 1899. 574p. map. (The Story of the Nations).

The author has written several standard histories of Spain, and this good general survey charts the story of the nation during 'a century of struggle upward out of the abyss into which despotism and bigotry had sunk it'. It opens with the reign of Charles IV (1788-1808), and concludes aptly with the loss of the colonies in 1898.

242 **The War of Succession in Spain 1700-1715.**
Henry Kamen. Bloomington, Indiana: Indiana University Press, 1969. 436p. bibliog.

A detailed study of the political, social and economic background of the period, which is not a military history as the title might suggest. The childless Charles II (1665-1700) named Philip of Anjou as his heir, but the claim of a Bourbon to the Spanish throne was strongly contested by both Britain and Austria. Austria refused to concede the defeat of its hopes of placing an Austrian candidate on the throne of Spain, and to England a Bourbon king in Spain would disrupt the balance of power in Europe in favour of French hegemony. But by 1714 Philip's control was complete. In the peace settlements Spain lost many of her European possessions (Belgium, Luxembourg, Milan, Sardinia, Naples) including Gibraltar to the British. However, it was during the war that Catalonia was integrated into Spain, thus, paradoxically, creating a unified Spanish State: except for the Basque Provinces and Navarre, the whole of Spain was now under direct royal administration.

243 **Liberals, reformers and caciques in Restoration Spain, 1875-1909.**
Robert W. Kern. Albuquerque, New Mexico: University of New Mexico Press, 1974. 153p. 2 maps. bibliog.

A brilliant study of the domination of liberalism in Spain from 1833 to 1923, with emphasis on the period 1875 to 1909. 'A special class of politicians known as "caciques" practised the boss-type politics of "caciquismo" '. On the other side of the debate stood the reformers, 'convinced either that liberalism had gone astray in Spain, or that democracy, socialism or some new form of technological, positivistic elitism would better serve the Spanish people'. The work centres around Antonio Cánovas del Castillo, who reorganized the liberal parties after the Revolution of 1868.

244 **Napoleon and the birth of modern Spain.**
Gabriel H. Lovett. New York: New York University Press, 1965. 2 vols. map. bibliog.

A detailed, documented history of the Peninsular War/War of Spanish Independence (1808-14), which undermined the Napoleonic system. The invasion of Spain is regarded by many as the greatest error of judgement in Napoleon's career. In volume 1 the author analyzes the revolt of the Spanish people against the French, and the subsequent popular resistance that forced Napoleon to maintain huge forces in the country. Volume 2 describes the struggle against Napoleon, and attempts to show how the war gave birth to a Spain 'perennially burdened with civil strife'. Both volumes contain city plans, campaign maps, and extensive bibliographies.

245 Spain: a modern history.

Salvador de Madariaga.   London: Jonathan Cape, 1961. 736p. map. bibliog.

An objective, general interpretation of Spanish history up to 1944, written with particular emphasis on the reign of Alfonso XIII (1886-1931) and the early days of the Second Republic (1931-39). It provides useful insights into foreign policy, and is especially interesting as the author served as the Second Republic's ambassador to France and to the League of Nations. He later became a professor at Oxford, and was one of Spain's greatest refugee writers. This is a classic study of the end of the constitutional monarchy and the Republic, in which he blames the extremist parties of both sides, and also the king, for Spain's problems. The work includes a large, annotated bibliography.

246 The politics of modern Spain.

Frank E. Manuel.   Westport, Connecticut: Greenwood Press, 1974. 194p. bibliog.

A reprint of the 1938 edition, published in New York by McGraw-Hill in their series 'McGraw-Hill Studies in Political Science'. The author is better known as an intellectual historian of Europe. In this work he covers the period from the 1870s to the Civil War, and although it was written nearly fifty years ago, it still provides a fascinating insight into Spanish politics.

247 The revolutionary Left in Spain, 1914-1923.

Gerald H. Meaker.   Stanford, California: Stanford University Press, 1974. 562p. bibliog.

An important and detailed study of a critical period in Spanish political history, which represents the first comprehensive study of the revolutionary Left in Spain from the beginning of the First World War to Primo de Rivera's military dictatorship. The author notes how in 1914 the Spanish revolutionary Left was uniquely divided between anarchist and socialist tendencies. 'Elsewhere in Europe Bakuninism had been defeated by Marxism . . .' but 'Inspired by Bakuninist principles, a potentially powerful Anarchosyndicalist movement, based mainly in Catalonia, stood on the brink of an era of expansion that would make it a threat to the monarchy and a powerful rival to the smaller, parliamentary Socialist movement . . .'. The author also studies the origins, growth and struggles of the Spanish Communist Party.

248 The Peninsular War.

Roger Parkinson.   London: Hart-Davis MacGibbon, 1973. 208p. 7 maps. bibliog. (The British at War).

Known in Spain as the War of Independence (1808-14), and to the British as the

Peninsular War, Napoleon called the conflict his 'Spanish ulcer'. The author has made use of letters, diaries and eye-witness accounts, to provide a reasonably complete picture of events, and recaptures both the horror and bravery of the fighting during the famous campaign of Sir Arthur Wellesley, Duke of Wellington. This was history's first 'guerrilla' war, when the term (meaning 'little war') was first coined. The book is superbly illustrated, and has an introduction by Ludovic Kennedy, editor of 'The British at War' series.

249 **Fascism: comparison and definition.**
Stanley G. Payne.   Madison, Wisconsin: University of Wisconsin Press, 1980. 234p. bibliog.

This work is a comparative study of fascism, and how the breakdown of the liberal systems in Spain, Portugal and Italy took place at roughly the same time: during the period of the First World War and the years thereafter. It includes a chapter entitled 'Post-fascist survivals: Spain and Portugal', which discusses fascism in Spain from the dictatorship of Primo de Rivera (1923-30) to the Franco régime, and to the official dissolution of the fascist movement by King Juan Carlos in April 1977.

250 **King Alfonso XIII and his age.**
Sir Charles Petrie.   London: Chapman & Hall, 1963. 247p. bibliog.

Alfonso XIII ruled Spain from 1886 (when he was born) to 1931, but until he came of age María Cristina was 'Queen of Spain'. The author was a personal friend of Alfonso, and has endeavoured to convey the king's personal point of view to the reader, underlining how difficult the task of ruling Spain was at the time. The forces which were to lead to the Civil War were already building in Spain, while the constitution (which had been brought before the Cortes in 1876, and which was to remain in force until the 'coup d'état' of General Primo de Rivera in 1923) through which Alfonso was expected to work was quite unsuitable. In the end he left Spain in the hope that by so doing he was preventing a war, but this was merely delayed. He died in Italy in 1941.

251 **King Charles III of Spain: an enlightened despot.**
Sir Charles Petrie.   London: Constable, 1971. 241p. bibliog.

This work is the first book on Charles III (1759-88) in the English language. Charles was the perfect example of the benevolent despot, intensely devoted to the public good. His foreign policy, though securing friendship with France, involved Spain in numerous disasters in America, and his expulsion of the Jesuits from the country and his failure to regain Gibraltar were exploits for which he has been criticized. However, he did transform both the administration and the economic outlook, and had a great deal of success in arresting the decay of Spain before his death in 1788.

252 **The Spanish royal house.**
Sir Charles Petrie.   London: Geoffrey Bles, 1958. 276p. bibliog.

A study of the period from the reign of Philip V (1700-46, founder of the

Bourbon dynasty in Spain) to the 1950s. In this useful history national events provide the background against which the story of the House of Bourbon is set.

253   Alfonso XIII.
Vicente R. Pilapil.   New York: Twayne, 1969. 242p. bibliog.
(Twayne Rulers and Statesmen of the World Series, no. 12).

A history of the life and times of the king who only assumed full authority on his sixteenth birthday in 1902. He sought to enhance the power of the monarchy at the expense of parliament with his constant intervention in politics, and consequently there were numerous plots to assassinate him. In 1923 (a week before a report was to be published on the Spanish defeat at Anual in the Moroccan War in 1921, laying the blame squarely on Alfonso) a 'coup d'état' led by the Captain-General of Barcelona, Miguel Primo de Rivera took place. The coup established a dictatorship in Spain which lasted until 1930. After the elections of 1931 Alfonso was forced to abdicate and leave the country.

254   A queen of Spain: Isabel II.
Peter de Polnay.   London: Hollis & Carter, 1962. 215p. bibliog.

The problems faced by Isabella during her troubled reign can be traced back to her ancestor Philip V, the first Bourbon king of Spain. It was he who brought the Salic Law to Spain from France in 1713. This law specifically forbade female heirs from succeeding to the throne, and was the fundamental cause of the two Carlist Wars. Isabella ascended the throne in 1833, after Ferdinand VII, her father, had issued a pragmatic sanction which revoked the Salic Law and stated that direct succession would be assured even if the newborn were a daughter.

255   Spain's uncertain crown: the story of the Spanish sovereigns 1808-1931.
Robert Sencourt.   London: Ernest Benn, 1932. 399p. bibliog.

The American edition of this work bears the title *The Spanish crown 1808-1931: an intimate chronicle of a hundred years* (New York: Scribner, 1932). It opens with the reign of Ferdinand VII, which was interrupted by Joseph Bonaparte (1808-13), and which ended in 1833 when Ferdinand named his daughter Isabella as heir. Isabella ruled from 1833 to 1868, when she was dethroned. Then followed the two-year coalition of Juan Prim y Prats and Francisco Serrano (1868-70). The short reign of Amadeo I (1870-73) was followed by the First Republic (1873-74), the reign of Alfonso XII (1875-85), and that of Alfonso XIII (1886-1931).

The origins of military power in Spain 1800–54.
See item no. 563.

Hispanismo, 1898-1936: Spanish conservatives and liberals and their relations with Spanish America.
See item no. 577.

Second Republic and Civil War

256 The Spanish Civil War.
Antony Beevor. London: Orbis, 1982. 320p. 10 maps. bibliog.

A highly readable account of the war, which sets out to explain the enmities and
alliances in terms of the three basic forces of conflict: Right against Left, centralist
against regionalist, and authoritarian against libertarian. There is also a
chronology of the war, and a descriptive list of political parties, groupings and
organizations.

257 The origins of the Second Republic in Spain.
Shlomo Ben-Ami. Oxford, England: Oxford University Press,
1978. 356p. bibliog. (Oxford Historical Monographs).

A detailed, scholarly account of the collapse of the monarchy and the coming of
the Second Republic. The author examines the origins and scale of the
Republican movement, which was unleashed by Primo de Rivera's dictatorship
(1923-30), and which culminated in the establishment of the Second Spanish
Republic in April 1931. He presents a picture of the controversial results of the
municipal elections, and also studies the first six months of the Republican
régime.

258 The Spanish revolution: the Left and the struggle for power during the Civil War.
Burnett Bolloten. Chapel Hill, North Carolina: University of
North Carolina Press, 1979. 664p. 5 maps. bibliog.

Earlier editions of this work were entitled *The grand camouflage: the communist
conspiracy in the Spanish Civil War*, and it was first published in 1961. This new
expanded edition incorporates a great deal of new material, presenting a detailed
study of the role of the Communist Party in the anti-Franco forces during the war.
The author explains how the party came to occupy a position of power in May
1937 when the Negrín government succeeded that of Largo Caballero, a socialist
and enemy of the communists. He examines the methods by which the
communists achieved their triumph, and at the same time studies the objectives of
the Soviet Union and the other great powers during the years of war. He also
analyzes the hatred and bitterness which existed between Left and Right before
the Civil War, and the internal strife that ravaged the forces of the Left during the
conflict. Bolloten, who worked as a press correspondent in Spain at the time and
witnessed events at first-hand, makes good use of many primary sources,
including speeches, memoirs, letters and interviews.

259 The Spanish cockpit: an eye-witness account of the political and social conflicts of the Spanish Civil War.
Franz Borkenau. Ann Abor, Michigan: University of Michigan
Press, 1963. 303p. (Ann Arbor Paperbacks, no. AA77).

This book first appeared in 1937, and has since become a classic. It is one of the
first contemporary and mainly first-hand accounts of the early Civil War period,

and the events which led up to it. The Austrian author considered himself a democratic liberal, and having joined the German Communist Party, he obtained a post in the Comintern. Disillusioned both with communism and Marxism due to their 'lack of realism and pedantry,' he then left to become a sociologist, and travelled widely in Republican Spain during the first year of the war. His introductory historical sketch sets the analytical pattern later followed by Gerald Brenan and other writers. The main subject matter is the history of the Spanish Left, its characteristics, achievements and failures. The work also contains a glossary of Spanish parties and terms in use during the period.

260 **The Spanish labyrinth: an account of the social and political background of the Civil War.**
Gerald Brenan. Cambridge, England: Cambridge University Press, 1962. 2nd ed. 384p. 9 maps. bibliog.

The author states that this book was commenced during the conflict 'in order to distract my mind from the horrors and suspense of the Civil War'. Brenan himself sided with the Republicans, and his work represents the best introduction to the Second Republic, and an essential history and interpretation of the social and political structure of 19th- and 20th-century Spain. He writes in such a perceptive manner that later studies have obviously been under his pervasive influence.

261 **The International Brigades: Spain 1936-1939.**
Vincent Brome. London: Heinemann, 1965. 317p. bibliog.

This is the first general account of the Brigades from their beginnings. It is not a comprehensive study, but instead attempts to provide some kind of introductory survey of the composition of these Brigades, and their influence on the fighting.

262 **The revolution and the Civil War in Spain.**
Pierre Broué and Emile Témime, translated by Tony White. London: Faber & Faber, 1972. 590p. 12 maps. bibliog.

This illuminating study was originally published in French, and deals with the international aspects of the war, and the emergence of the nationalist-syndicalist State. The authors frankly admit to siding with the Republican cause (they were ten years old when the Civil War began), although one was 'more in sympathy with the progressive Republicans and the moderate Socialists . . . and the other with the dissident Communists and revolutionary Socialists'. Nevertheless, they have attempted to produce an honest interpretation of the facts, passing a minimum of judgements.

263 **The Comintern and the Spanish Civil War.**
E. H. Carr, edited by Tamara Deutscher. London: Macmillan, 1984. 111p. bibliog.

The author (who died in 1982 at the age of ninety) worked on this book in the last two years of his life, condensing the narrative, whilst maintaining his high standards of research and documentation. He provides a new perspective on relations between Spain and the Soviet Union, and shows how the Communist International (Comintern) was used by Moscow. Whilst Germany and the Soviet

Union were acting, the whole of parliamentary Europe remained impassive as Spain fought what was in fact the first battle of the Second World War.

264　**The Republic and the Civil War in Spain.**
Edited by Raymond Carr.　London: Macmillan, 1971. 275p.
bibliog. (Problems in Focus Series).

Contains many articles by some of the best known historians of the period, and includes chronological tables and a glossary of political terms. The collection stresses political and military history, but also incorporates a very useful section by Hugh Thomas on agrarian collectives during the war. A frequent theme is that the Right and Franco were more firmly established and supported in Spain than Republican sympathizers have noted. The work is particularly useful in providing short summaries on different aspects of Spanish history between 1931 and 1939.

265　**The Spanish tragedy: the Civil War in perspective.**
Raymond Carr.　London: Weidenfeld & Nicolson, 1977. 336p.
7 maps. bibliog.

A very good analytical study which includes a list of governments, a glossary of political terms and a list of main characters, as well as a brief examination of Franco's Spain from 1939 to 1950, and of the economy and political climate between 1951 and 1975.

266　**Communism and the Spanish Civil War.**
David T. Cattell.　Berkeley, California; London: Cambridge University Press, 1955. 290p. bibliog. (University of California Publications in International Relations, vol. 4).

Provides a general account of the Spanish Communist Party's role in the conflict. The major question asked by this book is how valid are the arguments that after the defeat of the Republicans many of them considered the Soviet Union and the Spanish Communist Party the cause of their defeat. There were those, however, who felt that the Republicans only managed to hold out as long as they did due to Russian aid and advice. This work analyzes the internal events in Spain 'and the extent to which Communist policy was motivated by the desire to create a Soviet Republic'. The author also wrote *Soviet diplomacy and the Spanish Civil War* (London: Cambridge University Press, 1957), which discusses how Spain fitted into Russia's foreign policy.

267　**Apprentices of freedom.**
Judith Cook.　London: Quartet Books, 1979. 150p. bibliog.

An easy-to-read and highly interesting study of the working men and women of Britain who joined the International Brigades, less than two hundred of whom are alive today. Unused to travel, and without passports and money, 95 percent of the Britons who fought in Spain during the Civil War came from working-class backgrounds: from the shipyards, the mines and the hunger marches. This book recounts their reasons for going, their experiences in Spain, and the effect it has had on the rest of their lives. It also tells the story of the women, many of them nurses, who pioneered techniques of front-line surgery later to be used in World War II.

268 **The road to Spain: anti-fascists at war 1936-39.**
Edited by David Corkill, Stuart J. Rawnsley.   Dunfermline,
Scotland: Borderline Press, 1981. 164p. bibliog.

An interesting book, which records the motives and experiences of some of the
volunteers for the International Brigades from Britain and Ireland. In a series of
seventeen interviews they speak frankly, vividly and movingly of their lives before
and during their time in Spain. It also contains a chronology of events from 1936
to 1939.

269 **Historical dictionary of the Spanish Civil War, 1936-1939.**
Edited by James W. Cortada.   Westport, Connecticut; London:
Greenwood Press, 1982. 571p. 14 maps. bibliog.

There are about forty contributors to this excellent work, amongst them some of
the most respected of Spanish historians. The need for this type of work is
emphasized by the fact that the war still represents a most popular subject of
study, both because of its importance in Spanish history, and because of its wider
implications with regard to World War II. Research on the subject has increased,
with more archival material becoming available to the historian since Spain's
return to democracy and free elections. Today there are over six books per month
appearing on the subject. This encyclopaedic dictionary contains over 800 entries,
and the principal objective of the volume is to provide quick reference material
on a broad range of subjects. All entries are cross-referenced to suggest other
related topics, and each has its own list of further readings.

270 **The British government and the Spanish Civil War, 1936-1939.**
Jill Edwards, with a foreword by Hugh Thomas.   London:
Macmillan, 1979. 280p. 2 maps. bibliog.

Official British policy was one of non-intervention, as formalized in the agreement
of August 1936. In reality, however, the British government formulated its own
unilateral policy to deal with the immediate problems which the Civil War created
for Anglo-Spanish relations. This study examines the economic, legal and moral
problems, and shows the extent of the British government's commitment to a
nationalist victory in Spain. The work is based on unpublished cabinet, foreign
office, admiralty and private papers, parliamentary debates, the press and
secondary sources. It also includes several documentary appendixes and many
statistical tables. Also worth consulting on the subject of British public opinion of
the war is K. W. Watkins' *Britain divided: the effect of the Spanish Civil War on
British public opinion* (London: Nelson, 1963). For a similar discussion of
Mexico's response to the Spanish Civil War see Thomas G. Powell's *Mexico and
the Spanish Civil War* (Albuquerque, New Mexico: University of New Mexico
Press, 1981).

271 **Miners against fascism: Wales and the Spanish Civil War.**
Hywel Francis.   London: Lawrence & Wishart, 1984. 304p.
3 maps. bibliog.

Welsh miners made up one of the largest contingents within the British Battalion
of the International Brigades. Drawing on numerous interviews with survivors
from the period, as well as more traditional historical sources, the author manages

to paint a vivid picture of the turbulent politics of South Wales in the 1920s and 1930s, the process of volunteering for the Brigades, and the military role played by the Welsh miners. Profusely illustrated, the work also reproduces letters written by volunteers to relatives and friends, which provide an excellent insight into the motives, feelings and politics of the men who went to Spain, thirty-three of whom never returned.

272 **Blood of Spain: the experience of Civil War, 1936-1939.**
Ronald Fraser. London: Allen Lane, 1979. 628p. 7 maps. bibliog.
A fascinating oral history of the war, concentrating on the proletarian parties. The book approaches the subject of the Civil War in a new way, and represents an amalgamation of more than 300 personal accounts. It is fundamentally an attempt to present the subjective experiences of people who participated in the events, and is particularly useful for its comments on the agrarian collectives.

273 **The Spanish Republic and the Civil War 1931-1939.**
Gabriel Jackson. Princeton, New Jersey: Princeton University Press, 1965. 578p. 8 maps. bibliog.
A most useful general history, which is considered by many to take a less biased, more objective view of the conflict than does Hugh Thomas in his work on the Civil War (q.v.). An eminent historian, the author weighs his evidence and judgements carefully, and has produced a well-documented study. The work includes a glossary of organizations and political terms, a detailed chronology of the period, and several appendixes. Gabriel Jackson also wrote *A concise history of the Spanish Civil War* (London: Thames & Hudson, 1980).

274 **Legions of Babel: the International Brigades in the Spanish Civil War.**
Verle B. Johnston. University Park, Pennsylvania: Pennsylvania State University Press, 1967. 228p. 5 maps. bibliog. (Hoover Institution Publications).
A scholarly and well-researched work on the Brigades as a whole, providing a dispassionate history of the volunteer army organized in Paris by the Comintern, and an evaluation of its contribution. According to Johnston, approximately 60 per cent of the members of the Brigades were communists, with the French forming the largest single foreign group (10,000) of a total number of volunteers of between twenty and forty thousand. The Brigades were formally withdrawn from Spain late in 1938 when the Soviet Union's support for the Spanish Republic began to diminish.

275 **They shall not pass: the Spanish people at war 1936-39.**
Richard Kisch. London: Wayland, 1974. 176p. map. bibliog.
The author arrived in Spain in 1936 as a *News Chronicle* reporter. In Barcelona he joined the people's militia, and was involved in the POUM (Workers' Party of Marxist Unification)-anarchist expedition to retake the Balearics, in which he was wounded. Later, as a non-combatant with the International Brigades, he visited factories and rural areas, and spoke to many refugees. When the war finished he edited the Spanish veterans' periodical *Volunteers for Liberty*. Drawing partly on

these experiences he vividly describes particular incidents, and shows how revolutionary changes affected the whole fabric of society, comparing and contrasting the nationalist-held areas with those held by the Republicans. 'No attempt has been made to give a comprehensive detailed account of the military progress of the war in chronological terms. Instead, the outline of military events has been sketched in as the background to the essentially human tragedy of the war'. The title comes from the words of the communist politician Dolores Ibarruri (better known as 'La Pasionaria'): 'No pasarán' – they (the nationalists) shall not pass. A chronology of events during the war is included, as well as lists of the results of the general election of 1936, and the governments between 1936 and 1939.

276 The breakdown of democratic regimes.
Edited by Juan J. Linz, Alfred Stepan. Baltimore, Maryland; London: Johns Hopkins University Press, 1978. 1 vol. bibliog.

Part 2, chapter 5 (p. 142-215) is entitled 'From great hopes to Civil War: the breakdown of democracy in Spain'. Linz attempts to answer the major questions of how and why democratic régimes break down. In Europe the collapse of Spanish democracy was the last in a line of many such collapses elsewhere in the continent. The Republic in Spain (1931-36) was the most short-lived and unstable of the European democracies that failed, and it is the only example in which the final breakdown led to civil war. Linz concludes that the Spanish army was the ultimate cause of the breakdown, although many other factors had already sealed the fate of the democratic régime. This detailed study includes many useful statistics and facts on this period of political instability and insecurity.

277 The Spanish Civil War.
David Mitchell. London: Granada, 1982. 208p. map. bibliog.

This book is based on the BBC television series of the same name, for which the historical consultants were Ronald Fraser and Hugh Thomas. The author is a freelance writer who lived in Spain from 1965 to 1973. His work differs from many other books on the subject in that it does not treat the subject in a strict chronological way; instead he devotes each of the six chapters to a specific aspect of the war. The volume is particularly valuable for the large amount (nearly 100) of eye-witness accounts by mainly Spanish people who lived through the war. It provides an extremely vivid and evocative picture of the conflict.

278 Homage to Catalonia (and looking back on the Spanish War).
George Orwell. Harmondsworth, England: Penguin Books, in association with Martin Secker & Warburg, 1966. 246p.

Orwell vividly documents his experiences as a soldier on the Republican side from 1936 to 1938, and the result is probably the best eye-witness account of the war. He joined the POUM militia (Workers' Party of Marxist Unification) fighting on the Aragón front, and describes the trials and tribulations, discomfort and inefficiency of front-line fighting. This beautifully evocative work combines memoir with analysis, and one of Orwell's most lasting memories is that of the figure of an Italian militiaman representing the spirit of a people struggling against fascism.

279 **Politics and society in twentieth-century Spain.**
Edited by Stanley G. Payne. New York; London: New
Viewpoints, 1976. 244p. bibliog. (Modern Scholarship on
European History).

This useful work comprises eight chapters by leading writers on Spanish history
and politics. The subjects include the Manuel Azaña régime; Popular Front
elections in 1936; Franco's régime; and Spanish political attitudes.

280 **The Spanish revolution.**
Stanley G. Payne. London: Weidenfeld & Nicolson, 1970. 398p.
2 maps. bibliog. (Revolutions in the Modern World).

Payne is the author of several books on Spain. This work represents a powerful
indictment of the Left, with particular emphasis on the 1930s, and is an excellent
historical discussion of distinctly Spanish aspects of the war. The main concern is
with the inner workings of the parties, and the roles of individual leaders. There is
particular criticism of Manuel Azaña (Prime Minister 1931-33, President of the
Second Republic from 1936 to 1939), whom Payne believes appeased the
revolutionary Left. He considers the Right in the Civil War in his books *Falange*
(q.v.) and *Politics and the military in modern Spain* (q.v.), in which he similarly
deals with Rightist extremism.

281 **The coming of the Spanish Civil War: reform reaction and
revolution in the Second Republic.**
Paul Preston. London; New York: Methuen, 1983. 264p. bibliog.
(University Paperbacks, no. 806).

Preston's emphasis is on the roles of CEDA (the Spanish Confederation of
Autonomous Rightist Groups, and the largest political grouping of the legalist
Right) and the PSOE (the Spanish Socialist Workers' Party). He examines the
part played by the Socialist Party, and the resistance it encountered from the landed
and industrial gentry during the Second Republic (1931-36). This important work
attempts to answer the perennial question of who was to blame for the outbreak
of the Civil War.

282 **Revolution and war in Spain, 1931-39.**
Edited by Paul Preston. London; New York: Methuen, 1984.
299p. map. bibliog. (University Paperbacks, no. 834).

A fascinating study which provides a variety of contributions by a number of
experts on the period from Britain, Spain and the United States. Their studies
reflect recent scholarship, and explode the traditional view of the war as a simple
conflict between fascism and communism. In his excellent introductory chapter
Preston notes 'that the reality of Spain in that period is much more complex than
has hitherto been allowed', and the work as a whole shows that the Spanish war
was really many wars. Detailed and vivid accounts are provided not only of the
agrarian problem and political conflicts, but also of the religious, regional and
class confrontations which were taking place in both town and countryside.

283 **Comintern army: the International Brigades and the Spanish Civil War.**
R. Dan Richardson. Lexington, Kentucky: University of Kentucky Press, 1982. 232p. bibliog.

Moving beyond the simplistic view of the Spanish Civil War as a straightforward struggle between 'democracy' and 'fascism', the author focuses on the part played by the International Brigades who fought on the loyalist side. In this work he argues strongly that 'the Brigades were, from beginning to end, an integral part of that interlocking directorate which was the Soviet-Comintern apparatus in Spain, largely sponsored, recruited and controlled by the Communist International for its own purposes'. He also emphasizes that although the Brigades were involved in military exploits which were highly significant and deserving of recognition, they were also an important political, ideological and propaganda instrument for the Soviet Comintern. For the best and most penetrating study of the American battalion, see Cecil Eby's *Between the bullet and the lie: American volunteers in the Spanish Civil War* (New York: Holt, Rinehart, & Winston, 1969).

284 **The origins of Franco's Spain: the Right, the Republic and revolution, 1931-1936.**
Richard Alan Hodgson Robinson. Newton Abbot, England: David & Charles, 1970. 475p. bibliog. (Library of Politics and Society).

The standard general account of the Spanish Right under the Republic, which offers contrasting views to those of Paul Preston (q.v.) on the roles of CEDA and the PSOE. Whilst analyzing the history of the Second Republic and the causes of the Civil War, this work also manages to explain the emergence and development of the various parties, and their relationship with the powerful institutions of the church and the army.

285 **Franco and the Spanish Civil War.**
Laurence E. Snellgrove. London: Longmans, 1965. 135p. maps. bibliog.

An illustrated general account of the rise of Franco and his central role in the war. It includes numerous campaign maps, and a 'who was who' section detailing the principal Republican and nationalist characters of the period.

286 **The Spanish Civil War.**
Hugh Thomas. Harmondsworth, England: Penguin Books, 1977. 3rd ed. 1,115p. 36 maps. bibliog. (Pelican Book).

A mainly military account, this standard text remains the most complete and detailed study of the war. Despite Thomas's claim to objectivity it should be read in conjunction with Gabriel Jackson's *The Spanish Republic and the Civil War 1931-1939* (q.v.), as it shows a distinct Republican bias.

287 **The forgotten men.**
Jesús Torbado, Manuel Leguineche, translated by Nancy
Festinger. New York: Holt, Rinehart & Winston, 1981. 226p.
map.

A translation of the Spanish original best-seller *Los topos* (The moles), which transcribes taped interviews with people who for one reason or another became political refugees during the period of the Spanish Civil War. The personal accounts reproduced here are both detailed and moving, and include memoirs from both nationalists and Republicans, some of whom had been in hiding for over thirty years: their current views and lives are still affected by their past ordeals and hardships. The title refers to the way in which these people were forced to disappear from sight and 'bury themselves in holes', some quite literally.

Carlism and crisis in Spain, 1931-1939.
See item no. 513.

La diplomacia vaticana y la España de Franco (1936-1945). (Vatican
diplomacy and Franco's Spain (1936-1945).)
See item no. 574.

Spain and the great powers 1936-1941.
See item no. 580.

Agrarian reform and the peasant revolution in Spain: origins of the Civil War.
See item no. 649.

Writers in arms: the literary impact of the Spanish Civil War.
See item no. 721.

Bibliography of the Spanish Civil War 1936-1939.
See item no. 963.

Franco

288 **Transition in Spain: from Franco to democracy.**
Víctor Alba, translated by Barbara Lotito. New Brunswick, New
Jersey: Transaction Books, 1978. 333p. bibliog.

A history of modern Spain with the emphasis on the 20th century and Franco's régime. The author points out that since the death of Ferdinand VII, the last absolute monarch of Spain, in 1833, up to the death of Franco in 1975, there had been thirteen changes in political régimes; three dethroned monarchs; two exiled regents; four assassination attempts on the lives of kings; two republics; nine constitutions; five heads of state assassinated; and four civil wars. Within the same period there were 127 governments, 109 in 103 years, and eighteen of them during the thirty-nine-year rule of Franco. In this interesting and informative study, Alba attempts to provide some of the reasons which explain why Spain has had such a distinctive and tumultuous modern history.

289 **Franco and the politics of Spain.**
Edouard de Blaye, translated by Brian Pearce. Harmondsworth, England: Penguin Books, 1976. 576p. bibliog. (Pelican Books).
Originally published in French in 1974, this good general survey of the period provides useful information on the Second Republic and the Franco régime. It includes a large number of appendixes describing the major parties and trade union organizations under the Republic, and a chronology of the period from Franco's birth to his death (1892-1975).

290 **Spain: dictatorship to democracy.**
Raymond Carr, Juan Pablo Fusi Aizpurua. London: George Allen & Unwin, 1981. 2nd ed. 288p. bibliog.
A political, economic and social history of modern Spain, with particular emphasis on political events from 1969 to 1979. Carr and Fusi try to explain the changes that have caused the country's transformation over twenty years from a traditionally agricultural society to a modern industrial democratic state. This is a selective study of the events and institutions of Franco's Spain from 1939 to 1975, which also contains two useful short chapters on Spanish culture 1939-77, and society 1939-77. The final two chapters, revised in the second edition, cover the reign of Juan Carlos I up to 1977.

291 **Franco: a biographical history.**
Brian Crozier. London: Eyre & Spottiswoode, 1967. 589p. 18 maps. bibliog.
A well-written and profusely illustrated eulogistic biography of Franco. Crozier interviewed the Caudillo, and had frequent access to government sources, and this work is an attempt to separate the man from the myth. The author, who was born in Australia, was approaching his eighteenth birthday when the Civil War began. He admits that, on the whole, his conclusions about Franco are favourable, and that as he wrote the book and studied the facts, his feeling for Franco changed 'from antipathy to grudging admiration'. A lot of the book attempts to assess Franco's importance in Spanish and world history. It is a detailed and painstaking study which, although putting forward certain opinions and interpretations of events which to many will appear false or contrived, nevertheless gives an excellent insight into the mind and motivation of one of the world's most written-about characters.

292 **Regimes and oppositions.**
Edited by Robert A. Dahl. New Haven, Connecticut; London: Yale University Press, 1973. 411p. bibliog.
This work includes a chapter by Juan J. Linz entitled 'Opposition in and under an authoritarian regime: the case of Spain' (p.171-259). Linz analyzes the factional opposition to Franco's dictatorship, and shows how the ineffectuality of the official trade unions has been replaced by strong opposition from illegal workers'

councils. The chapter begins with a historical outline of Spain during the 1930s, and moves on to discuss the different forms of opposition to Franco's régime.

293 Spain under Franco: a history.
Max Gallo, translated by Jean Stewart. London: Allen & Unwin, 1973. 390p. bibliog.

A history of the opposition rather than of the régime, which attempts to record in detail the repression that followed under Franco after his victory over the Republicans. Gallo discusses the major factors which have influenced Spain in the recent past, and tries in the course of his book to explain how Franco managed to hold on to the reins of power over such a long period.

294 Franco's prisoner.
Miguel García García. London: Rupert Hart-Davis, 1972. 171p.

The author was born in 1908, and was a lifelong member of the CNT (National Confederation of Workers), the anarcho-syndicalist trade union in Spain. In 1949 he was arrested, tried and sentenced to death, and after thirty-eight days his sentence was commuted to thirty years' imprisonment. Imprisoned for his beliefs in the freedom of open elections, a free press, and a free trade union organization, he always refused to compromise with the prison authorities. He was finally released in 1969, whereupon he left Spain and continued his campaign in Britain on behalf of other Spanish political prisoners. This book describes his experiences under Franco's prison system, and is a savage, yet moving, indictment of the system.

295 Franco: the man and his nation.
George Hills. London: Robert Hale, 1967. 464p. 12 maps. bibliog.

A superb work, which takes no sides and lets the reader decide whether Franco was the evil figure portrayed by his enemies, or the great Christian gentleman painted by his friends. The author had access to family papers, and talked to Franco himself. Over the years he also interviewed relations and associates, as well as enemies and supporters, of Franco. It is therefore a factually reliable biography, and a well-informed critical study of 20th-century Spain.

296 Spain.
George Hills. London: Ernest Benn, 1970. 480p. map. bibliog. (Nations of the Modern World).

A study of the political, economic, social and religious developments which took place in Franco's Spain in the thirty years prior to 1970. The volume also provides background material from previous centuries in order that recent developments can be seen in perspective. The author was formerly a Spanish programme organizer, and correspondent for the BBC.

297 **Spain in transition: Franco's regime.**
Arnold Hottinger. Beverly Hills, California; London: Sage, 1974.
62p. (The Washington Papers, vol. 2, no. 18).

This book was commissioned and written under the auspices of the Center for Strategic and International Studies, and describes the political evolution of the Franco régime from the Civil War to the year before his death. It also discusses Franco's problem of attempting to bring Spain into harmony with the rest of Europe, whilst at the same time not upsetting the balance of power within Spain. The author notes that Franco's greatest success within the political and economic sphere of his thirty-six years in power was his rejuvenation of the Spanish economy through closer links with the economic system of the west.

298 **Authoritarian politics in modern society: the dynamics of established one-party systems.**
Edited by Samuel P. Huntington, Clement H. Moore. New York; London: Basic Books, 1970. 533p. bibliog.

This work includes a chapter by Juan J. Linz entitled 'From Falange to movimiento-organización: the Spanish single party and the Franco regime, 1936-1968' (p. 128-203). Linz portrays Franco's Spain as a weak one-party system which relied on support from the armed forces, the church, the monarchists, the Carlists, the business world, Opus Dei and the Falange. After the Civil War the Falange's influence and role as the régime's political party declined tremendously. Another eminent writer on Spanish affairs, Stanley Payne, wrote that 'Franco conceived of the FET (Falange Española Tradicionalista y de las J.O.N.S.) as the party of the state, but he never thought of his regime as a real party-state'.

299 **Franco.**
Richard Kisch. Hove, England: Wayland, 1977. 96p. map.
bibliog. (Wayland History Makers).

This is a short, up-to-date account of Franco's life and his role as ruler of Spain for nearly forty years. Kisch himself covered the Spanish Civil War as a reporter, and was a member of the International Brigades. His book *They shall not pass* (q.v.) surveys the social background of the Spanish people during the war.

300 **Franco's Spain.**
Stanley G. Payne. London: Routledge & Kegan Paul, 1968.
142p. bibliog.

A concise account, which is generally recognized as one of the most objective general studies of the period. The book is aimed at students of European history, 'serious-minded travelers, and those interested in contemporary affairs'.

301 **Spain in crisis: the evolution and decline of the Franco régime.**
Edited by Paul Preston. Hassocks, England: Harvester Press, 1976. bibliog.

A penetrating analysis of the Franco régime, which first examines the régime forces (the church, the armed forces and the Falange), together with the opposition in the workers' movements. The book subsequently explores the social and economic conditions in which their relations have developed. All the contributors are respected authorities on Spanish history and politics.

302 **Spain in the 1970s: economics, social structure, foreign policy.**
Edited by William T. Salisbury, James D. Theberge. New York: Praeger, 1976. 187p. bibliog. (Institute of International Studies: International Relations Series; no. 5. Special Studies in International Economics and Development).

This volume of essays is the outgrowth of a conference entitled 'Spain in the seventies: problems of change and transition' which was held in June 1973 in Washington DC. The 'purpose of the conference was to examine major aspects of recent political, economic and social changes in Spain'. The preface provides a general summary of the views of the contributors and assesses how far the changes envisaged have been affected by Franco's death in 1975. Part 1 covers the economy of Spain in the 1970s; part 2 looks at Spanish society; and part 3 discusses Spain's relations with Latin America, the United States, and NATO. Although this summary does make predictions, it is firmly based on what has occurred in Spain during the 1960s and early 1970s.

303 **Spain and Franco: the quest for international acceptance 1949-59.**
Edited by J. Lee Shneidman. New York: Facts on File, 1973. 253p. map. (Facts on File).

This study aims to provide a factual account of developments in Spain during the crucial period of 1949-59, when the country emerged from her post-war isolation and made a concerted effort to restore her economy. It opens with a general background to Spain and Spanish foreign policy (1945-48), and moves on to discuss foreign relations, the economy, and trade during the 1950s.

304 **Franco: a biography.**
J. W. D. Trythall. London: Rupert Hart-Davis, 1970. 304p. 5 maps. bibliog.

Like many writers on Franco, the author faces the problem of explaining not so much how Franco attained supreme power in Spain, but how he managed to hold on to it for so long. This volume is much broader than a mere biography, and covers all the major events in Spain from the Civil War up to 1969. The author hopes that by being a non-Spaniard, without strong political convictions, and being born after most of the action the book covers had taken place, he can strip away some of the prejudices and preconceptions which have surrounded Franco and Spain.

305 **Spain: the gentle anarchy.**
Benjamin Welles. New York: Frederick A. Praeger, 1965. 386p. map.

The author, a correspondent for the *New York Times* who worked in Spain in the early 1960s, presents a critical, illustrated account of Franco's Spain. Unfortunately, he devotes a great deal of space to the personalities heading the government and the opposition, and gives little impression of having left Madrid except to interview dignitaries. Nevertheless, it is an understanding, calm evaluation of the people and leaders of Spain in the 1960s, in the light of their historical past, and includes sections on the armed forces, censorship, the Falange, the Catholic Church, and US-Spanish relations.

306 The Franco years.
José Yglesias. Indianapolis, Indiana; New York: Bobbs-Merrill, 1977. 273p. map.

A brilliant work on Spain and the Spanish people since the Civil War, which includes moving interviews with those who lived under Franco's rule, from established political leaders to fugitive terrorists. Whilst providing an excellent social commentary on the times, and a vivid description of how many people merely survived during the 'industrial growth' which occurred under Franco, the author also attempts to separate Franco's life from that of the Spanish people. He argues that much of the economic growth in Spain came not from Franco's economic policies but from American money for the military bases in the country. The whole tone of the work is strongly anti-Franco, and one of the few faults of the book is that all those who are interviewed are plainly anti-Franco as well.

From dictatorship to democracy: Spanish reportage.
See item no. 312.

Falange: a history of Spanish fascism.
See item no. 531.

La diplomacia vaticana y la España de Franco (1936-1945). (Vatican diplomacy and Franco's Spain (1936-1945).)
See item no. 574.

Agony of a neutral: Spanish-German wartime relations and the "Blue Division".
See item no. 579.

Spain and the great powers 1936-1941.
See item no. 580.

Spain and the defense of the west: ally and liability.
See item no. 581.

Post-Franco

307 Spain: conditional democracy.
Edited by Christopher Abel, Nissa Torrents. London: Croom Helm; New York: St. Martin's Press, 1984. 198p. bibliog.

This book is based on a series of public lectures which were held at the University of London. All aspects of the political, social and cultural life of Spain since the death of Franco are examined. In particular, the work covers the role of the armed forces, Spain and NATO, the church, the economy, and the arguments for regional autonomy. There are also important chapters on the cinema and the media after Franco's death, and the Spanish novel from 1972 to 1982.

308 **Spain 1975-1980: the conflicts and achievements of democracy.**
Edited by José L. Cagigao, John Crispin, Enrique Pupo-Walker.
Madrid: José Porrúa Turanzas, 1982. 191p. bibliog. (Ensayos).

A collection of papers delivered at an international symposium, under the same title, held at Vanderbilt University in 1980. The aim of the symposium was to analyze the political, social and cultural evolution of Spain between 1975 and 1980, and this work represents a valuable appraisal of the transitional period. The papers cover all aspects of life since Franco's death: political transition; the Spanish theatre; the Spanish novel; Spanish cinema; the Spanish constitution of 1978; and political parties.

309 **The forces of freedom in Spain, 1974-1979: a personal account.**
Samuel D. Eaton.   Stanford, California: Hoover Institution Press, Stanford University, 1981. 169p. bibliog.

An account of the process of political transition, intermingled with personal anecdotes from the author's experiences as Deputy Chief of Mission of the United States Foreign Service in Spain from 1974 to 1978. Eaton analyzes the functions of the US Foreign Service in Spain, whilst emphasizing how the economic and social progress made in the latter part of Franco's rule aided Spain's democratic transition. He notes that since Juan Carlos became monarch, Spain has established a freely elected bicameral parliament, legalized political parties and trade unions, pardoned political prisoners, held municipal and national elections, and granted some measure of regional autonomy to the Basques and Catalans. Appendixes provide a chronology of the main events 1974-79, a list of principal personalities, and the historical background and characteristics of Spanish constitutions from 1812 to 1978.

310 **The political, economic, and labor climate in Spain.**
Mario Gobbo.   Philadelphia: University of Pennsylvania, Industrial Research Unit, 1981. 134p. map. bibliog. (Multinational Industrial Relations Series; no. 10, European Studies; no. 10- Spain).

The book is divided into three sections, covering politics (history, parties, foreign relations); economics (transport, communications, industries); and labour (labour laws, history, labour organizations). The emphasis is on the post-Franco era, with specific reference to such factors as labour relations, investment and economic developments. There are numerous tables and figures included, to supplement the text.

311 **Spain: change of a nation.**
Robert Graham. London: Michael Joseph, 1984. 326p. map.
bibliog.

A lucid and absorbing analysis of Spain's transitional years, and an extremely good commentary on modern Spanish society. Graham, who was Madrid correspondent for the *Financial Times* from 1977 to 1982, argues that the key to understanding the dramatic switch from Francoism to democracy lies in the social and economic changes that took place from the mid-1950s onwards. He has been able to interview all the leading figures in the nation, and has written a complete survey of the elements that have gone into the making of modern Spain. Another recent study of the transition to democracy is David Gilmour's *The transformation of Spain: from Franco's dictatorship to the constitutional monarchy* (London: Quartet, 1985).

312 **From dictatorship to democracy: Spanish reportage.**
Anatoly Krasikov, translated by N. Shartse. Oxford, England;
New York: Pergamon Press, 1984. 227p.

This book is the result of fifteen years' study of the problems of contemporary Spain, and concentrates on the period of transition. The author is Deputy Director of the TASS news agency, and from 1969 he made regular visits to Spain, and interviewed major participants in political events. It is certainly one of the most readable general studies of Spain's recent history, written from a refreshingly distinct and personal viewpoint. Another recently-published work on the subject is Geoffrey Pridham's (ed.) *The new Mediterranean democracies: regime transition in Greece, Spain and Portugal* (London: Cass, 1984).

313 **Spain and Portugal: democratic beginnings.**
Edited by Grant S. MacClellan. New York: H. W. Wilson, 1978.
228p. bibliog. (The Reference Shelf, vol. 50, no. 5).

A collection of articles and essays on post-Franco Spain and her foreign relations since 1975.

Empire

314 Spain and the loss of America.
Timothy E. Anna. Lincoln, Nebraska; London: University of Nebraska Press, 1983. 343p. bibliog.

A detailed and often controversial explanation of how Spain conserved her overseas empire through specific policies. It is the first comprehensive study of Spain's responses to the American rebellions as a whole, and the author argues that the ultimate explanation of the process of independence must be sought at the highest levels of power in Spain, because it was here that a consensus on political as opposed to military solutions was never reached. It focuses on the policy debates of Ferdinand VII, and the decisions he made with the advice of the high councils and the Cortes between 1808 and 1825.

315 Spain: the 'Spanish problem' and the imperial myth.
Martin Blinkhorn. *Journal of Contemporary History*, vol. 15, no. 1 (Jan. 1980), p. 5-25.

This brilliant article surveys nearly a century of Spanish colonial history, showing to what extent the loss of empire affected the nation. The year 1898, the 'year of the disaster' (i.e. the loss of Cuba), was an important landmark, although Spain lost most of her colonies in the 1820s. Imperial decline led to a great deal of soul-searching and self-examination, in the hope of understanding, if not necessarily solving, what came to be known as 'the Spanish problem'. Blinkhorn notes that 'with hindsight it is not difficult to recognize that the Civil War marked the beginning of the end of Spain's "imperial hangover" '.

316 Mary and misogyny: women in Iberian expansion overseas, 1415-1815: some facts, fancies and personalities.
Charles Ralph Boxer. London: Duckworth, 1975. 142p. bibliog.

A brief account, based on four public lectures, of the place women held in colonial Iberian society. It includes several appendixes of documents and letters of the period, abstracts of these documents in English, and a glossary.

317 **Spain and her Moroccan protectorate 1898-1927.**
James A. Chandler. *Journal of Contemporary History*, vol. 10, no. 2 (Apr. 1975), p. 301-22.

A succinct and interesting account of how Spain, whilst losing the last remaining vestiges of empire in Latin America, set about gaining the territory of Morocco. The conflict lasted nearly thirty years, and caused Spain frequent humiliation. The author examines the motives which led to Spanish interest in Morocco, and their effect on the region. Spain only managed to pacify the Rif rebels through the efforts of Primo de Rivera, in co-operation with the French who feared the spread of unrest to the French protectorate. See also Frances Horace Mellor's work *Morocco awakes* (London: Methuen, 1939), which looks at Spanish-Moroccan relations from earliest times, but with particular emphasis on the period of the Spanish Civil War and the Spanish protectorate in Morocco between 1926 and 1938.

318 **Spain and the empire, 1519-1643.**
Bohdan Chudoba. Chicago: University of Chicago Press, 1952. 299p. 2 maps. bibliog.

A detailed study of the growth and decline of Spanish imperialism on the European mainland in the 16th and 17th centuries. The book begins in 1519, the year when Charles became Holy Roman Emperor, and ends in 1643 with the disastrous defeat of the Spanish army at Rocroi in northeastern France.

319 **Flood tide of empire: Spain and the Pacific northwest, 1543-1819.**
Warren L. Cook. New Haven, Connecticut; London: Yale University Press, 1973. 620p. bibliog. (Yale Western Americana Series, no. 24).

A comprehensive, documented history of Spanish explorations and claims between California and Alaska over a 300 year period. This massive work primarily seeks to portray 'Spanish interaction with the Indians, British, Russians, and Americans . . . competing for hegemony over the same territory'.

320 **The Canary Islands after the conquest: the making of a colonial society in the early sixteenth century.**
Felipe Fernández-Armesto. Oxford, England: Oxford University Press, 1982. 244p. 4 maps. bibliog. (Oxford Historical Monographs).

This is the first attempt to comprehensively portray the life, work and institutions of this early colonial society. The conquest of the Canaries was completed in 1496, and in 1497 the Treaty of Alcáçovas recognized Spanish sovereignty over the Islands. They became an indispensable Spanish base on the sea routes to America, and in 1936 Franco used them as the first base of the nationalist revolution, moving from there to Spanish Morocco.

321 **Viceregal administration in the Spanish-American colonies.**
Lillian Estelle Fisher. Berkeley, California: University of
California Press; London: Cambridge University Press, 1926. 397p.
bibliog. (University of California Publications in History, vol. 15).

A comprehensive analysis of viceregal administration in the Spanish-American
colonies during the whole colonial period. The viceroyalties themselves were
established by the Spanish monarchs after the rule of the 'audiencias' (judicial
tribunals) had proved to be a failure. The viceroy was the highest official in these
colonies, his functions including civil, political and economic administration,
supervision of the royal treasury, the use and conservation of the royal patronage,
and his role as captain-general. The author notes that 'the heritage of Spain in the
New World was the fruit of long lines of able administrators at the head of four
princely kingdoms, through whose official intervention in every detail of life the
transmission of European culture was superintended'. For another view of
Spanish imperial bureaucracy, see 'Authority and flexibility in the Spanish
imperial bureaucracy' by John Leddy Phelan in *Administrative Science Quarterly*,
vol. 5 (June 1960), p. 47-65.

322 **Spain in America.**
Charles Gibson. New York; London: Harper & Row, 1966.
239p. 4 maps. bibliog. (The New American Nation Series).

This book is principally designed for the general reader. It presents a summary of
Spanish America from the time of the earliest explorers to the period of the
conquest, the transition to the colonial era and beyond. The subjects covered
include: the power and influence of the church; the relationship between the
Spanish and the Indians; and social, economic and labour patterns. It also touches
on the fundamental differences between the peoples of North and South America.

323 **The Spanish struggle for justice in the conquest of America.**
Lewis Hanke. Philadelphia: University of Pennsylvania Press;
London: Oxford University Press, 1949. 217p. 2 maps. bibliog.

A fascinating study of Spanish theories of war and colonization, and the efforts to
implement them in the 16th century. This is a basic work on the question of race
relations in the Spanish American empire, which presents an extensive
examination of the proper method of approach to the American Indians. Hanke
emphasizes that no other European people, before or since the conquest of
America, has plunged into such a struggle for justice (as regards the defence of
the rights of the Indians) as the Spaniards. He explains that this unique situation
occurred as a result of the widespread concern felt by soldiers, ecclesiastics and
the crown that all Spain's laws and actions in America should be just, and he
examines how this approach influenced Spanish action there.

324 **The Spanish empire in America.**
Clarence Henry Haring. New York: Oxford University Press,
1947. 388p. map. bibliog.

This is one of the best factual accounts of Spanish-American colonial history,
which is particularly useful for its references to the maritime and financial aspects
of Spanish imperialism. The book has its inception in a series of twelve lectures

delivered in the spring of 1934 at the Instituto Hispano-Cubano of the University of Seville. The Institute's plans to publish the lectures were originally frustrated by the Civil War, but the delay allowed the author to make use of information acquired during the intervening decade. The book also includes an extensive bibliography on all areas of colonial policy.

325 The Dutch Republic and the Hispanic world 1606-1661.
Jonathan Irvine Israel.   Oxford, England: Clarendon Press, 1982. 478p. 4 maps. bibliog.

The works by Israel and Parker (q.v.) represent the standard English texts for any serious study of Spain's conflict with the Netherlands, and the Dutch struggle for independence which lasted from 1556 (when Charles V placed the Netherlands, which was part of the Holy Roman Empire, in the charge of his son Philip II) to 1648 (the Treaty of Münster granting independence). The author attempts to explain why such a prolonged and exhausting struggle took place, despite the fact that there is virtually no doubt that the Spanish crown had by 1606 come to accept the principle of Dutch political and religious independence. For a concise account of the conflict see Israel's article 'A conflict of empires: Spain and the Netherlands 1618-1648' in *Past and Present*, no. 76 (Aug. 1977), p. 34-74.

326 The Spanish conquistadores.
Frederick Alexander Kirkpatrick.   London: Adam & Charles Black, 1963. 366p. 5 maps. (The Pioneer Histories).

First published in 1934, this is a balanced and succinct account of the whole story of the Spanish conquest of the New World, ranging from the discovery of America to the founding of Buenos Aires. The author has also made many contributions to the *Cambridge Modern History*.

327 The government of Sicily under Philip II of Spain: a study in the practice of empire.
Helmut Koenigsberger.   London; New York: Staples Press, 1951. 227p. map. bibliog.

By the middle of the 16th century Spanish power was dominant throughout the Italian peninsula, and Sicily, Sardinia and the kingdom of Naples were all Spanish possessions. This work is a study of the administration of one of these dominions, Sicily, which was originally acquired by the Catalans at the close of the 13th century. During the reign of Philip II (1556-98) the Spaniards and Sicilians balanced the island's role in fulfilling Catholic obligations and imperialist aspirations by preserving many of the facets of its former independence. The author draws primarily on contemporary printed and manuscript sources to provide a detailed picture of the problems of administrating an overseas empire, and perfectly illustrates the workings of Philip II's centralized bureaucratic government.

328 **Columbus: the story of Don Cristóbal Colón, Admiral of the Ocean and his four voyages westward to the Indies according to contemporary sources.**
Retold and illustrated by Björn Landström. London: Allen & Unwin, 1967. 207p. maps. bibliog.

A translation of the Swedish original, which captures the author's contagious enthusiasm. Landström is a painter, lithographer and stage designer, as well as a successful playwright, novelist and critic, and this book is profusely illustrated with colour diagrams, sketches and innumerable maps. The author has used the most important primary source materials available on Columbus (1451-1506) and his voyages to the New World, and has travelled extensively to the actual sites where Columbus and his men first set foot on land. Here he describes Columbus' frantic pursuit of royal patronage, and his search for gold and glory as Admiral of the Ocean and Governor-General of the Indies. The main object of this fascinating work 'has been to give a picture of Columbus' life, his abilities, his thoughts, and his theories, and the deeds which he and his contemporaries performed'. The endpapers give a facsimile of the first printing of Columbus' letter about his discovery, printed in Barcelona in 1493.

329 **Conquest and commerce: Spain and England in the Americas.**
James Lang. New York; London: Academic Press, 1975. 261p. 5 maps. bibliog. (Studies in Social Discontinuity).

A study of the beginnings of the Spanish empire in America, the bureaucratic administration, the royal government, trade, and commercial reform. This is a good general survey of the subject, which is divided into two sections covering Spain in America and England in America.

330 **The fall of the Spanish American empire.**
Salvador de Madariaga. London: Hollis & Carter, 1947. 443p. 2 maps. bibliog.

In this sequel to the following entry, this highly literate and perceptive Spanish historian describes the decline of Spanish power in Spanish America, the inhabitants, and the internal and external origins of the secession from Spain.

331 **The rise of the Spanish American empire.**
Salvador de Madariaga. London: Hollis & Carter, 1947. 408p. 2 maps. bibliog.

This is the first part of a work covering the rise and fall of the Spanish empire in America. The volume provides an 'indispensable background to the life of Simón Bolívar' and to his role in the destruction of Spanish imperialism. The work is divided into four sections objectively studying the background to Spanish imperialism, its evolution in the Habsburg era, its history under the Bourbons, and an estimate of the empire in general.

332 **Spanish Sahara.**
John Mercer. London: George Allen & Unwin, 1976. 264p.
5 maps. bibliog.

A history and description of the region in North Africa which is roughly the same size as Great Britain, and is now known as the Western Sahara. Spain gave up the area in February 1976, after a prolonged dispute which began in 1958. Mercer also wrote 'Confrontation in the Western Sahara' in *The World Today*, vol. 32, no. 6 (June 1976), p. 230-39, which describes the division of the Spanish Sahara between Spain, Morocco and Mauritania in 1975, and mounting opposition to the partition of the disputed territory from the Polisario, supported by Algeria.

333 **The rise of the Spanish empire in the old world and in the new.**
Roger Bigelow Merriman. New York: Cooper Square Publishers, 1962. 4 vols. maps. bibliog.

A large and most useful study of institutional and dynastic history, which contains numerous genealogical tables. This study was first published in 1918, and although now partly outdated by more recent research it remains a fundamental work for any serious study of 16th-century Spain. Merriman systematically examines the domestic history of Spain from the Middle Ages to the end of the 16th century in its setting as the centre of a vast empire in America and central Europe. A newly-published narrative and interpretative history of Spanish and Portuguese exploration and settlement of the New World is Lyle N. McAlister's *Spain and Portugal in the New World: 1492-1700* (Oxford, England: Oxford University Press; Minneapolis, Minnesota: University of Minnesota Press, 1985).

334 **Spain overseas.**
Bernard Moses. New York: Hispanic Society of America, 1929. 114p. (Hispanic Notes and Monographs).

This work was reprinted by Kraus Reprints in 1970, and is a concise survey of the Spanish empire. It offers useful insights into particular areas of Spanish rule in America, including: the bases of Spanish colonial society; Mexico; the Philippine Islands; and Spain's successors in America.

335 **Odious commerce: Britain, Spain and the abolition of the Cuban slave trade.**
David R. Murray. Cambridge, England: Cambridge University Press, 1980. 423p. bibliog. (Cambridge Latin American Studies, no. 37).

Spain's colonial empire witnessed both the beginning and the end of the transatlantic slave trade: the conquest of the Indies led to the beginning of the Atlantic slave trade, and the abolition of the commerce in African slaves preceded the loss of Spain's last American possessions. Throughout the 19th century Cuba was an extremely important market for Spanish exports. The Spaniards believed that the plantation economy of Cuba would be doomed without slave labour, whilst Britain maintained an abolitionist campaign against it. The Cuban slave trade was finally abolished in the 1860s, and the book traces the relations between Britain and Spain at the time.

336 **The army of Flanders and the Spanish road 1567-1659: the logistics of Spanish victory and defeat in the Low Countries' wars.**
Geoffrey Parker.   Cambridge, England: Cambridge University Press, 1975. 2nd ed. 309p. bibliog.

A classic study of Spain's imperial war against the Low Countries, and the mercenary army used unsuccessfully by Philip II to crush the Dutch. 'The book demonstrates how easily a great power can become involved in a ruinous war which it cannot manage to win but cannot bear to abandon'. The book contains sections on the assembly and command of the army, how it behaved in action, and what it was like to be a solider in the 'age of mercenaries'. For a more general account of the conflict, see Parker's *The Dutch revolt* (Harmondsworth, England: Penguin, 1977).

337 **Spain and the Netherlands, 1559-1659; ten studies.**
Geoffrey Parker.   London: Fontana and Collins, 1979. 288p. bibliog.

All the essays in this work have appeared elsewhere. The studies range from general articles on the European and military context, and the consequences of the Dutch revolt, to individual topics. Parker is recognized as the leading authority on Spain and the Netherlands, and is the author of three books on the subject. His main interest is centred around the way in which Spain managed 'to fight such expensive wars, with so many men, so far from her financial and demographic base'.

338 **The Spanish seaborne empire.**
John Horace Parry.   London: Hutchinson, 1966. 416p. 8 maps. bibliog. (History of Human Society).

An excellent account of the growth of Spanish imperialism which is divided into five sections covering the establishment, responsibilities, cost, endurance, disintegration and aftermath of empire. The author attempts to provide a concise account of the relationship between Spain and its American empire from the late 15th to the early 19th century. He tells of Columbus' dreams of fame and fortune in the New World, in the wake of which came the ugly realities of slavery and war. The real strength of the Spanish empire lay in its institutions and its comparatively sophisticated bureaucracy. Parry explains in detail how Spain was able to develop and maintain such a large overseas empire for more than 300 years.

339 **The Spanish theory of empire in the sixteenth century.**
John Horace Parry.   New York: Octagon Books, 1974. 75p. bibliog.

A reprint of the 1940 edition published by Cambridge University Press. The book examines the repercussions of empire, and competently summarizes Spanish imperial doctrine. Parry stresses that 'the Spanish colonial enterprise of the sixteenth century showed all the signs of genuine imperialism – the conviction that the duty of civilised nations is to undertake the political, economic and religious tutelage of more primitive peoples . . .'. However, the author concludes by stating that 'imperialism, more than any other single cause, killed the best political thought of Spain, as it tends eventually to kill all forms of thought'.

340 The Spanish enclaves in Morocco.
Robert Rézette, translated from the French by Mary Ewalt.
Paris: Nouvelles Editions Latines, 1976. 188p. 8 maps. bibliog.

Despite a few typographical errors, this is a useful study of the five Moroccan enclaves under Spanish sovereignty: Ceuta; Peñón de Vélez de la Gomera; Peñón d'Alhucemas; Melilla; and the Chaffarine Islands. The Spanish settlement of all but the Chaffarine Islands (19th century) dates from the 15th and 16th centuries. Like many small 'territories of contention' their importance to the respective parties far outstrips their size. The work is organized in three parts: part one is a history of the 'sovereignty territories'; part two outlines the present-day state of the territories; and part three discusses the Spanish-Moroccan dispute. Spain's possession of these enclaves presents a major hindrance to Morocco's free exercise of sovereignty over her own territories, which she hopes to restore by reuniting them with the sherifian kingdom.

341 The Spanish terror: Spanish imperialism in the sixteenth century.
Maurice Rowdon. London: Constable, 1974. 335p. 7 maps. bibliog.

An illustrated, wide-ranging study of Spanish imperialism and domestic history, which discusses all areas of policy affecting the Spanish American, African and European possessions of Charles V and Philip II. It is a suitable work for the non-specialist as it is easy to read and not too detailed.

342 Imperial Spain: the rise of the empire and the dawn of modern sea-power.
Edward Dwight Salmon. Westport, Connecticut: Greenwood Press, 1971. 154p. bibliog.

Originally published in 1931, this useful work analyzes the foundations of the Spanish empire, its establishment under Charles V, and the faith and sea-power under Philip II. It is primarily aimed at undergraduate students and provides neither a too specialized nor a too elementary account.

343 The early Spanish main.
Carl Ortwin Sauer. Berkeley and Los Angeles, California: University of California Press; London: Cambridge University Press, 1966. 306p. 27 maps. bibliog.

'An introduction to land and life in the first decades of Spanish America'. The whole of the Caribbean area, including the sea, came to be known in English as the Spanish main. The author sets out to study the first Spanish entry into the New World, and detail 'what was seen and thought of the new lands and their inhabitants, how control was taken, and how possession was extended'. This is a detailed and well-documented study, although the literary style is somewhat stilted. For a more popular study, see Peter Wood's *The Spanish main* (q.v.).

Empire

344 **Catalan domination of Athens 1311-1388.**
Kenneth Meyer Setton. London: Variorum, 1975. rev. ed. 325p. bibliog.

First published in 1948, this work is based chiefly on contemporary sources. It discusses the occupation of the city, and the construction of a state by Catalan soldiers of fortune, specifically 'la Companya catalana' (Catalan Grand Company). About 7,000 Catalans, together with their families, occupied the duchy of Athens for three-quarters of a century, until it was captured in 1388 by the Florentines. During the years of occupation, Catalan, together with Latin, was the official language of Athens, but the most important consequence of Catalan rule was the 'inspiration and sense of achievement which this exciting chapter in the history of Catalonia has had on the Catalans', despite the fact that there is nothing of note left behind them in the city today.

345 **The Spanish lake.**
Oskar Hermann Khristian Spate. London: Croom Helm, 1979. 372p. 25 maps. bibliog. (The Pacific since Magellan, vol. 1).

This thorough work does for the Pacific what Braudel has done for the Mediterranean. The starting point is Magellan's (Fernao de Magalhãis) first crossing of the huge expanse of water from east to west in 1520-21, and Spain's subsequent domination of, and imperial designs on, the region. Volume 2 of the series is entitled *Monopolists and freebooters* (London: Croom Helm, 1983), and studies the onslaughts on the Iberian monopoly in the Pacific by the other European powers.

346 **The Spanish main.**
Peter Wood. Chicago: Time-Life Books, 1979. 176p. bibliog. (The Seafarers).

The Spanish Main was the name given in the 16th and 17th centuries to the Spanish possessions along the coast of South America from the Isthmus of Panama to the Orinoco River, but it was applied to the Caribbean area generally. This easy-to-read work is aimed at the general reader, and is beautifully illustrated.

Christopher Columbus and the participation of the Jews in the Spanish and Portuguese discoveries.
See item no. 364.

The church militant and Iberian expansion 1440-1770.
See item no. 422.

The leather jacket soldier: Spanish military equipment and institutions of the late eighteenth century.
See item no. 564.

American treasure and the price revolution in Spain, 1501-1650.
See item no. 591.

Trade and navigation between Spain and the Indies in the time of the Habsburgs.
See item no. 616.

Spanish politics and imperial trade, 1700-1789.
See item no. 622.

Spanish scientists in the New World: the eighteenth-century expeditions.
See item no. 710.

Population

347 Internal migration in Spain.
R. P. Bradshaw. *Iberian Studies*, vol. 1, no. 2 (autumn 1972), p. 68-75.

A discussion of: the history of internal migration in Spain; migration in the 20th century; migration movements 1950-70; the effects of internal migration; and the author's thoughts on the future. Internal migration since the end of the Civil War has led to large-scale rural depopulation, and it is asserted that migration will continue to be an important feature of Spanish life. Also included are three statistical tables on Spanish population, six maps, and a bibliography.

348 Análisis de la población de España. (An analysis of the population of Spain.)
Salustiano del Campo Urbano. Barcelona: Ariel, 1972. 192p. 2 maps. bibliog. (Ariel Quincenal, no. 79).

A short study which summarizes Spanish population trends during this century. It includes a large number of tables and figures, and the various chapters discuss such subjects as the growth and distribution of the population, births and deaths, and emigration.

349 Factors involved in the decline of fertility in Spain 1900-1950.
J. William Leasure. *Population Studies*, vol. 16, no. 3 (March 1963), p. 271-85.

This short article is based on the author's PhD thesis. A statistical analysis is made of the social and economic characteristics associated with the decline of marital fertility in Spain. It is inferred that cultural factors, which may arise from a common historical and linguistic heritage within a region, are apparently closely associated with fertility.

350 **Fertility and nuptiality changes in Spain from the late eighteenth to the early twentieth century. Parts 1 and 2.**
Massimo Livi Bacci. *Population Studies*, vol. 22, nos. 1 and 2 (March/July 1968). Part 1 in no. 1, p. 83-102. Part 2 in no. 2, p. 211-34.

Part 1 opens with a general study of the Spanish population in the 18th century and considers the three censuses which were taken in 1768, 1787 and 1797. The author compares the levels of fertility in the 18th century with those of the 19th and 20th centuries and finds evidence of a substantial drop in marital fertility. Part 2 analyzes the demography of the historical regions: population growth and redistribution; the marriage pattern; and fertility. It also examines population trends in these areas between 1787 and 1910. Statistics show how the proportion of the population remaining unmarried has tended to decrease, mainly because of the decline in numerical importance of the nobility and clergy. In the regions largely affected by migration, the proportion remaining single has remained high or even increased, due to the large numbers of men leaving the regions. The work includes an appendix on birth registration in Spain, statistical tables on population and regional maps.

351 **Rural-urban migration and working-class consciousness: the Spanish case.**
John R. Logan. *Social Forces*, vol. 56, no. 4 (June 1978), p. 1,159-78.

A useful study of the Spanish industrial working class, and how the high concentration of native and migrant workers in new industrial suburbs is one source of class consciousness. The author argues that migrants become increasingly class conscious the longer they remain in the city. The article contains a list of references.

352 **La población española: siglos XVI a XX.** (Spanish population: from the 16th to the 20th century.)
Jordi Nadal Oller. Barcelona: Ariel, 1984. 5th ed. 286p. 25 maps. bibliog. (Ariel Quincenal, no. 56).

This is probably the best general survey of the demographic history of Spain, and it is written by a prolific writer on Spanish sociology, history and economics. He explains, through a synthesized history of Spain, how the 7 million inhabitants of the country at the beginning of the 16th century have now grown to a population of well over 38 million in present-day Spain. Numerous graphs and tables are included.

353 **The changing population structure of Galicia 1900-1970.**
Patrick O'Flanagan. *Iberian Studies*, vol. 5, no. 2 (autumn 1976), p. 61-80.

A detailed study of the structure of Galicia's population, and an analysis of the major factors which affect it. The author stresses the distribution of population in Galicia in the 20th century, but also studies population density, statistics and internal migration. The article includes a bibliography, maps and tables.

Population

La emigración española en la encrucijada: marco general de la emigración de retorno. (Spanish emigration at a crossroads: the general structure of return migration.)
See item no. 377.

The changing faces of rural Spain.
See item no. 453.

Migration, kinship, and community: tradition and transition in a Spanish village.
See item no. 456.

Religion, class, and family in Spain.
See item no. 466.

Comparing nations: the use of quantitative data in cross-national research.
See item no. 475.

Demographic Yearbook.
See item no. 684.

Nationalities and Minorities

354 **Galicia, nacionalidad histórica: causas de su marginación, su perspectiva.** (Galicia, a historical nation: why it was left behind; its future prospects.)
Santiago Alvarez. Madrid: Editorial Ayuso, 1980. 251p. bibliog.
The question of nationalism in Galicia has been largely overlooked by the media and authors in favour of the Basque region and Catalonia. This well-documented work is a political-historical study of Galicia and its struggle for regional autonomy, and includes a chronology of Galician history from the earliest times to 1977.

355 **The Basque country: the national question and the socialist revolution.**
José María Arenillas. Leeds, England: Independent Labour Party National Administrative Council, 1973. 27p. 2 maps. (An Independent Labour Party Square One Pamphlet).
Originally published in the Barcelona journal *La Nueva Era* in April 1937, this English translation contains an introduction by Wilebaldo Solano, editor of the POUM newspaper *La Batalla*. The author was himself a member of the POUM (Workers' Party of Marxist Unification), and was murdered just before the end of the war by Stalinists in Asturias. The essay itself is of great historical interest, being a Marxist analysis of the Basque country and the 1936 revolution, and supplying very valuable background information on the growth of Basque nationalism. It also includes a glossary of acronyms of political parties and movements.

97

356 **Spain, the Jews, and Franco.**
Haim Avni, translated from the Hebrew by Emanuel Shimoni.
Philadelphia: Jewish Publication Society of America, 1982. 268p.
map. bibliog.

A thoroughly researched historical study of the fortunes of Jews in Spain. The emphasis is on attitudes towards the Jews during World War II when 'most other nations in Europe either participated in the onslaught or turned their backs on them'. The author strongly contrasts the events of 1492 (when the Jews were expelled and the Inquisition still persisted) with those of 1939-45, when it is generally agreed that the Franco government saved tens of thousands of Jews. Avni also notes, however, that during this latter period there was still resentment to the setting up of a permanent Jewish community in Spain.

357 **A history of the Jews in Christian Spain.**
Yitzhak Baer. Philadelphia: Jewish Publication Society of America, 1961-66. 2 vols. map. bibliog.

Volume 1 covers the period from the age of the reconquest to the 14th century, whilst volume 2 examines the years from ca. 1300 to the expulsion of the Jews at the end of the 15th century. This work, translated from the original Hebrew, is a highly detailed and thorough study which admirably highlights the real contributions made by the Jews to Spanish economic, social and cultural affairs. Frederic David Mocatta's work *Jews of Spain and Portugal and the Inquisition* (London: Cass, 1981) also describes the problems of the Jews in the Peninsula prior to their expulsion.

358 **The Sephardi heritage: essays on the history and cultural contribution of the Jews of Spain and Portugal.**
Edited by Richard David Barnett. London: Vallentine, Mitchell, 1971- . 2 vols. map. bibliog.

A collection of essays in English, Spanish, French and Hebrew on the Sephardim, who are the Spanish and Portuguese Jews (from the noun 'sepharad', the Hebrew name for Spain). All the essays are written by eminent scholars, and discuss the Jews' distinctive contribution to Spain and Spanish culture. At one time the Jews were a flourishing community in Spain, until their expulsion in 1492.

359 **Ethnicity and nation-building: comparative, international, and historical perspectives.**
Edited by Wendell Bell, Walter E. Freeman. Beverly Hills, California; London: Sage Publications, 1974. 400p. bibliog.

Chapter 24 (p. 341-73) is entitled 'Modern nationalism in old nations as a consequence of earlier state-building: the case of Basque Spain' by Pedro González Blasco. This chapter was originally presented as a paper at the twelfth annual convention of the International Studies Association held in Puerto Rico in 1970, and relates modern Basque nationalism to certain aspects of the earlier state-building period in Spain. It also discusses: the historical context of regionalism; the Basque country in general; the Basque Nationalist Party (Partido

Nacionalista Vasco); and the Basque separatist movement ETA (Euskadi Ta Askatasuna – Basque Homeland and Freedom).

360 **The Basques.**
Henry Camille Blaud. San Francisco: R. & E. Research Associates, 1974. 95p. bibliog.

This is one of a growing number of historical and sociological studies on the Basques and it was originally presented as a thesis in 1957. It concentrates on the origins of the Basques and their complex language (euskara), which is totally unrelated to any other European tongue. The Basques were already established as a distinct people when the Romans completed their conquest of the Peninsula, and in modern times the Statute of Guernica (1979) granted partial autonomy to the Basque Provinces in Spain (Alava, Guipúzcoa, Vizcaya and Navarre).

361 **The Basques: the Franco years and beyond.**
Robert P. Clark. Reno, Nevada: University of Nevada Press, 1979. 434p. 3 maps. bibliog. (The Basque Series).

Within the three sections of this extensive study the author discusses the emergence of Basque nationalism 1876-1936; the Basque Nationalist Party; the Basque language; and ETA. The volume examines the history of the Basques' struggle for linguistic, political and cultural identity, and for regional autonomy: a vitally important subject not just for the region itself but for all of Spain. The author has attempted to deal both sympathetically and analytically with the problem, and this book is essential for any serious study of the topic of Basque nationalism.

362 **The social structure of Catalonia.**
Salvador Giner. Sheffield, England: The Anglo-Catalan Society, 1980. 78p. 2 maps. bibliog. (The Anglo-Catalan Society Occasional Publications, no. 1).

The main aim of this series is to present research and analysis concerning Catalan society, history, language and culture by specialists in these areas, in a form which will be of interest and value to both laymen and scholars. This work includes a map of the Catalan-speaking areas and of the ethno-cultural regions of the Iberian Peninsula. The sense of both Basque and Catalan ethnic identity is based both on distinctive cultural traits and on a consciousness of a common historic, economic and political experience. Catalonia was the first area of Spain to free itself from Muslim domination, and a Catalan state flourished during the 13th and 14th centuries. Present-day Catalans make up Europe's largest and richest minority group.

363 **Rural Catalonia under the Franco regime: the fate of regional culture since the Spanish Civil War.**
Edward C. Hansen. Cambridge, England: Cambridge University Press, 1977. 182p. 3 maps. bibliog.

A study of the effects of Franco's régime on Catalan regional culture, based on the author's observations during his field research there in the 1960s. He argues that Franco's dominance over Catalonia represented a triumph of capitalism over independent national ambitions and claims for regional autonomy.

364 Christopher Columbus and the participation of the Jews in the Spanish and Portuguese discoveries.
M. Kayserling. Folcroft, Pennsylvania: Folcroft Library Editions, 1978. 189p. bibliog.

A reprint of the original edition published in 1894 (New York: Longmans, Green). The author is an eminent 19th-century Jewish historian, and in this book he presents a carefully documented historical study of the role played by Jewish financiers, astronomers, cartographers and seamen in the discovery of the New World.

365 The Basques and Catalans.
Kenneth N. Medhurst. London: Minority Rights Group, 1982. rev. ed. 16p. 2 maps. bibliog. (Minority Rights Group Reports, no. 9).

An attempt to explain briefly the reasons behind Catalan and Basque nationalism. The author also examines the causes and consequences of the repression provoked by nationalist demands. This short study is a very useful introduction to the historical basis for the continuing resistance in these two regions to centralization, and their efforts to achieve full regional autonomy.

366 The Jews in Spain: their social, political and cultural life during the Middle Ages.
Abraham A. Neuman. Philadelphia: Jewish Publication Society of America, 1942. 2 vols. 2 maps. bibliog. (The Morris Loeb Series).

The standard work in English on the Jews in Spain between 1250 and 1450. Volume 1 presents a political-economic study, and volume 2, a socio-cultural one. Whilst describing the social, economic and constitutional aspects of Jewish life in mediaeval Spain, the emphasis is on their institutions, laws and customs. Neuman makes full use of the 'responsa' of the Spanish rabbis (court decisions which various eminent rabbis or heads of academies wrote in reply to written questions addressed to them by their colleagues, rabbinical judges and communal authorities). These 'responsa' shed light on the workings of the governing forces and institutions of the communities, as well as offering tremendous insight into all aspects of Jewish daily life in mediaeval Spain.

367 Basque nationalism.
Stanley G. Payne. Reno, Nevada: University of Nevada Press, 1975. map. bibliog. (The Basque Series).

There is a growing amount of literature on both Basque and Catalan nationalism. This work represents one of the best histories of Basque nationalism, by a respected author of Spanish history and politics. It is an excellent historical account covering the period from the evolution of the Basque principalities to the early 1970s.

368 **Catalonia infelix.**
Edgar Allison Peers. Westport, Connecticut: Greenwood Press, 1970. 326p. map.
This is a facsimile reprint of the original 1938 edition published by Oxford University Press. It is a scholarly history of Catalonia since the Middle Ages, and a work which represents one of the best studies on the Catalan nationalist movement in the late 19th and early 20th centuries. The author outlines the history and achievements of Catalonia within the Spanish state, and clearly regards autonomy for the region as a prerequisite for permanent peace and stability in Spain.

369 **¡Qué gitano!: gypsies of southern Spain.**
Bertha B. Quintana, Lois Gray Floyd, with an introduction by Walter F. Starkie. New York; London: Holt, Rinehart & Winston, 1972. 126p. map. bibliog. (Case Studies in Cultural Anthropology).
This book concerns the gypsies of Andalusia, and in particular of Granada, and analyzes their history, ethos and culture in this region which remains the dominant gypsy 'stronghold' in Spain. The authors deal mainly with the history and traditions of gypsy culture, and with the ways in which it is still changing in response to contemporary pressures. The book is based on fieldwork which was undertaken between 1959 and 1970, and although this is a scholarly work of particular interest to anthropologists, it is still interesting for the general reader.

370 **The Catalans.**
Jan Read. London: Faber & Faber, 1978. 223p. 3 maps. bibliog.
The author has written books on a wide range of topics about Spain. This enthralling work concentrates on the general history of Catalonia from the earliest times to the post-Franco era, but relates it to the Catalan call for regional autonomy. It also looks at the literary and scientific achievements of the region, and the origins of the Catalan language.

371 **The politics of territorial identity: studies in European regionalism.**
Edited by Stein Rokkan, Derek W. Urwin. London; Beverly Hills, California: Sage Publications, 1982. 438p. bibliog.
Chapter 9 (p. 355-87) is entitled 'Urban politics and rural culture: Basque nationalism' and is written by Marianne Heiberg. It presents a good overall picture of the problem, and an analysis of the territorial structure of Spain, in particular the internal divisions within the region. This chapter also gives a short historical background to 'the Spains in their pluralistic unity', whose unifying idea came simply from the period of Christian opposition to the Muslim threat. It goes on to discuss the origins of the Basque 'national' problem, covering the Basque language (euskara), Basque industrialization, the Basque Nationalist Party and ETA. There are tables on the linguistic situation of the Spanish Basque country in 1975, parliamentary elections in the Basque Provinces during the Second Republic, and elections in the region in the post-Franco period. Chapter 10 (p. 389-424) is entitled 'The politicization of Galician cleavages' and is the work of César E. Díaz López. The author provides an analysis of post-Franco Galicia

which demonstrates how Galicia, whilst retaining its own cultural identity, must still rely heavily on central government, which up to now has ignored the fundamental economic problems of the region. The Galicians have their own language (gallego), from which modern Portuguese originated, and which was once the foremost literary language of the Iberian Peninsula.

372   **A history of the Marranos.**
Cecil Roth, with an introduction by Herman P. Salemon.   New York: Schocken Books, 1975. 4th ed. 424p. bibliog. (Schocken Paperbacks on Judaica).

This book was originally published in 1932. 'Marranos' was the term used to designate Jews who converted to the Christian faith to escape persecution, but who continued to practice Judaism secretly. The term also applies to their descendants. They were often called the 'secret Jews of the Peninsula', and this is a very full and detailed look at their history in Spain, from the beginnings of Marranism to the decline of the Inquisition. The epilogue goes on to describe the Marranos in the first quarter of the 20th century.

373   **Linguistic minorities in western Europe.**
Meic Stephens.   Llandysul, Wales: Gomer Press, 1976. 796p. 15 maps. bibliog.

Chapter 14 (p. 603-74) covers Spain, and describes the cultural and political situations of the Galicians, the Basques and the Catalans. These three plus Andalusia make up the four autonomous regions of Spain. The author provides a good survey of each region, with broad sketches of the major problems facing them and the central government.

Catalonia: a profile.
See item no. 152.

Historia contemporánea del País Vasco: de las Cortes de Cádiz al Estatuto de Guernica. (A contemporary history of the Basque country: from the Cortes of Cádiz to the Statute of Guernica.)
See item no. 158.

The ghosts of 1492: Jewish aspects of the struggle for religious freedom in Spain 1848-1976.
See item no. 420.

Emigration

374 Amerikanuak: Basques in the New World.
William Anthony Douglass, Jon Bilbao. Reno, Nevada:
University of Nevada Press, 1975. 519p. 2 maps. bibliog. (The
Basque Series).

The term 'Amerikanuak' refers to 'the Americans', i.e. those Basques who have
settled in the United States and Latin America. Many Basques still contend that
their ancestors discovered the New World before Columbus. In addition,
Columbus' first expedition was dependent upon Basque ships and sailors, and
from 1492 onwards the Basque presence permeated the conquest and colonization
of Latin America and the American west. They are also credited by some with the
founding of Montevideo and Buenos Aires. One of the earliest works on the
subject is 'L'émigration Basque' by Pierre Lhande (Paris: Nouvelle Librairie
Nationale, 1910), in which Lhande states that in order to be an authentic Basque
there are three requirements: 'to have a sonorous name which states its origin,
speak the language of the sons of Aitor, and . . . have an uncle in America'.
Douglass and Bilbao trace the emigration history of the Basques, and study their
influence in the countries of Latin America and the western region of the United
States.

375 Exiles and citizens: Spanish Republicans in Mexico.
Patricia Weiss Fagen. Austin, Texas; London: University of
Texas Press for the Institute of Latin American Studies, 1973.
250p. bibliog. (Latin American Monographs, no. 29).

A well-documented study of Spanish emigrés to Mexico from 1939 to 1968. The
author notes how a significant portion of the intellectuals and professionals of
Spanish society escaped into exile with the outbreak of the Civil War in 1936 and
the defeat of the Republicans in 1939, and shows how they profoundly affected
academic and cultural life in Mexico.

Emigration

376   **La emigración española a Bélgica en los últimos años.** (Spanish
emigration to Belgium in recent years.)
E. García Manrique.   Zaragoza, Spain: Departamento de
Geografía Aplicada del Instituto Elcano, 1964. 192p. 5 maps.
In 1964 the number of Spanish emigrés in Belgium was approximately 20,000.
This detailed analysis looks at the emigration process, the work situation, and the
groupings of Spaniards in different regions of Belgium.

377   **La emigración española en la encrucijada: marco general de la
emigración de retorno.** (Spanish emigration at a crossroads: the
general structure of return migration.)
Compiled by José A. Garmendia.   Madrid: Centro de
Investigaciones Sociológicas, 1981. 459p. bibliog. (Colección
'Monografías': no. 38).
A general survey of the Spanish population, and an analysis of the reasons for
emigration to such countries as West Germany, France and Switzerland during
the 1960s and 1970s. The major part of the book is devoted to the study of the
return of emigrants.

378   **Spanish immigration to the United States.**
R. A. Gómez.   *Americas*, vol. 19 (July 1962), p. 59-78.
A short, yet detailed, investigation of Spanish emigration to the United States,
and an examination of the pattern of Spanish settlement there. The movement of
large numbers of Spaniards to the USA was particularly strong during the last
decades of the 19th century and the first decades of the 20th century. The article
also discusses the settlement of Spaniards in Latin America, the reasons for
emigration, and emigration procedures. Bibliographical references are included.

379   **The Spanish in Australia.**
Albert Jaime Grassby.   Melbourne, Australia: A. E. Press, 1983.
102p. map. bibliog. (Australian Ethnic Heritage Series).
An entertaining and highly interesting description of the Spanish contribution to
the discovery and settlement of Australia. The early Spanish seafarers of the 16th
and 17th centuries, and the flow of Spanish-speaking settlers since, have had a
considerable influence on Australia. There are now over 150,000 people of
Spanish-speaking origin in the continent, and they have included famous farmers
and aviators, the first Labour Prime Minister, and even the co-inventor of the
Australian meat pie!

380   **Los españoles en Francia: inmigracion cultura.** (Spaniards in
France: immigration and culture.)
Guy Hermet.   Madrid: Guadiana de Publicaciones, 1969. 294p.
bibliog. (Colección Ayer, Hoy y Mañana de España, no. 6).
Originally published in French as *Les espagnols en France* (Paris: Editions
Ouvrières, 1967), it is the first book to be written on this subject, and provides a
general description of the geographical distribution of Spaniards, and their

104

problems of integrating into French society. The author analyzes their values, needs and ambitions, and includes three case studies detailing personal experiences. The work includes over twenty pages of statistical data. Another useful study is *La emigración española a Francia* (Spanish emigration to France) by Javier Rubio (Barcelona: Ariel, 1974), with the emphasis on emigration for economic reasons.

381 **The invisible immigrants: a statistical survey of immigration into the United Kingdom of workers and dependants from Italy, Portugal and Spain.**
John Stuart Macdonald, Leatrice D. Macdonald. London: Runnymede Industrial Unit, 1972. 62p. (Runnymede Industrial Unit Special Publication).

This short study makes excellent use of the statistics provided by censuses and official immigration data, spanning the 1960s and early 1970s. It discusses: the historical background; the geographic distribution of Spanish immigrants; settlement and return migration; and employment patterns. An appendix notes how in 1971, with strong pressure on the government due to the rising number of unemployed, the issue of work-permits in industry for unskilled and semi-skilled workers from all countries other than the EEC, Norway and Denmark was prohibited. Since this time the regulations have been tightened further still.

382 **Emigración española en Europa.** (Spanish emigration in Europe.)
Andrés Sorel. Bilbao, Spain: Zero, 1974. 214p. bibliog. (Biblioteca Promoción del Pueblo; Serie P; no. 69).

A useful, general analysis of the principal reasons for, and characteristics of, Spanish emigration to other countries in Europe, followed by individual chapters on Spaniards in West Germany, Switzerland, France and Holland. It is also worth consulting *Emigración española a Europa* (Spanish emigration to Europe) by Francisco Sánchez López (Madrid: Confederación Española de Cajas de Ahorros, 1969), which is a large and detailed study with a preponderance of statistical tables on Spanish emigration.

383 **Beyond death and exile: the Spanish Republicans in France, 1939-1955.**
Louis Stein. Cambridge, Massachussetts; London: Harvard University Press, 1979. 306p. bibliog.

It is generally believed that around 500,000 Spanish Republicans sought refuge in France after Franco's victory in the Civil War, preferring exile to imprisonment or death. Although often herded into makeshift concentration camps, many were sent to work at defence factories and farms with the outbreak of World War II, whilst others joined the Foreign Legion or the regular French army. After the German occupation of France, about 13,000 Spaniards (described by Hitler as presumptive enemies) were captured and sent to the Mathausen concentration camp. Their main hope of return to Spain was that when the Nazis were defeated the Allies would then turn to removing Franco from power. However, during the Cold War Franco was regarded as essential to western security, and the Spanish Republicans, left out in the cold, turned to guerrilla warfare within Spain. The

Emigration

author has interviewed many refugees and researched French, Spanish and Catalan sources making this a fascinating work.

Mediterranean family structures.
See item no. 478

Languages and Dialects

General

384 **The Spanish language: together with Portuguese, Catalan and Basque.**
William J. Entwistle. London: Faber & Faber, 1962. 2nd ed.
367p. 8 maps. bibliog. (The Great Languages).
This is the standard history of the development of the Spanish (Castilian) language. Sections cover Iberian dialects and languages from the earliest times to their extension overseas, in line with the Spanish and Portuguese conquests.

385 **Spanish personal names: principles governing their formation and use which may be presented as a help for cataloguers and bibliographers.**
Charles F. Gosnell. New York: H. W. Wilson, 1938.
Republished Detroit, Michigan: Blaine Ethridge, 1971. 112p.
bibliog.
Although primarily intended for librarians, certain sections of this book (particularly chapter 4) are useful for anyone interested in the historical background to the origin and evolution of Spanish names. At the same time a certain amount of Spain's national civilization is reflected in the growth and formation of names.

386 **Historia de la lengua española.** (A history of the Spanish language).
Rafael Lapesa. Madrid: Editorial Gredos, 1981. 9th ed. 690p.
(Biblioteca Románica Hispánica, III: Manuales, no. 45).
This book is the most useful full-scale historical account of the development of Spanish and is a standard work on the language from pre-Roman times to the present.

387 **Spanish: phonology: descriptive and historical.**
I. R. MacPherson. Manchester, England: Manchester University
Press; New York: Barnes & Noble Books, 1975. 181p. bibliog.

Aimed principally at university students of Spanish, this is an up-to-date
introductory course on phonetics and phonology. It is presented in a graded
format, with each chapter followed by a set of exercises. Line drawings, sound-
charts and word and sound indexes complement the clear, well-organized text.

388 **Around the world in Spanish.**
Ralph Penny, Dorothy Severin. *Geographical Magazine*, vol. 50,
no. 5 (1978), p. 322-28.

Spanish is the fourth major language grouping in the world after English, Russian
and Chinese, with around 300 million people having it as their mother tongue.
The authors survey its spread from Europe to the Americas, and from the
Philippines to the northwest of Africa. They chart its rise in status from being one
of a number of rural dialects to the language of culture and administration
throughout the country, and the speech of the educated classes everywhere. The
birth-rate is high in the Spanish-speaking countries of America, so the number of
Spanish speakers can only increase, and it is therefore safe to forecast that
Spanish as a world language will continue to grow in importance.

389 **How Spanish grew.**
Robert K. Spaulding. Berkeley, California; Los Angeles:
University of California Press, 1965. 259p. map. bibliog.

A useful survey of the evolution and structure of the Spanish language. Spaulding
traces its origins from pre-Roman times to the period of modern Spanish,
stressing the influence of social and political events on the language's
development. The final chapter deals with slang, popular Spanish and various
Spanish dialects (including Leonese, Aragonese and Andalusian). This book is
intended for anyone interested in the history and development of language, and is
an absorbing and clearly presented work.

390 **The Spanish language today.**
C. H. Stevenson. London: Hutchinson University Library, 1970.
146p. bibliog. (Modern Languages).

The author seeks to explain some of the greater complexities of Spanish, a verb-
centred language of free word order. Spanish is the most faithful descendant of
classical Latin, and this is a succinct, but detailed, survey of the language rather
than a grammar.

391 **The Basque language.**
Antonio Tovar, translated by Herbert Pierrepont Houghton.
Philadelphia: University of Pennsylvania Press, 1957. 112p.
bibliog.

Describes and illustrates all aspects of the history of the language and its
structure. Written in particular for students of Basque, it is one of the few works
in English discussing the major features of the Basque language. Tovar is also the

author of *The ancient languages of Spain and Portugal* (New York: S. F. Vanni, 1961), which offers a scholarly history of the older languages and dialects of the Peninsula.

392 **The language and history of Spain.**
James Brande Trend.   London: Hutchinson House, 1953. 189p. bibliog.

A thoroughly documented historical survey of the rise, changes and spread of Spanish languages from their Latin foundations to present-day Spanish in Spain and Latin America. Trend does not indulge in technicalities, and the work is therefore suitable for the general reader.

Linguistic minorities in western Europe.
See item no. 373.

Romance linguistics and the Romance languages: a bibliography of bibliographies.
See item no. 958.

A sourcebook for Hispanic literature and language: a selected, annotated guide to Spanish, Spanish-American, and Chicano bibliography, literature, linguistics, journals, and other source materials.
See item no. 959.

Modern Iberian language and literature: a bibliography of homage studies.
See item no. 964.

M.L.A. International Bibliography of Books and Articles on the Modern Languages and Literatures.
See item no. 969.

Bibliografía de la lingüística española. (A bibliography of Spanish linguistics.)
See item no. 974.

The Year's Work in Modern Language Studies.
See item no. 977.

Grammars

393 **Spanish step-by-step.**
Charles Berlitz.   New York: Everest House, 1979. 336p.

A reasonably presented self-instruction textbook, which will provide the beginner with quite an extensive vocabulary. It aims to guide the reader in speaking correct colloquial Spanish through the presentation of short, easy-to-follow conversational patterns. There are twenty-five lessons in all, and an English-Spanish dictionary section is included.

394 **Master Spanish.**
R. Clarke. London: Macmillan, 1982. 322p. bibliog. (Master Series).

Designed primarily for adult beginners working without a teacher, this work contains an introductory chapter on the alphabet and pronunciation designed to be used in conjunction with the accompanying cassette. This is followed by twenty teaching units, each concerned with a particular subject or aspect of life, with emphasis on the acquisition of the spoken language.

395 **The basis and essentials of Spanish.**
Charles Duff. London: Nelson, 1969. 4th ed. 180p. (Basis and Essentials Series).

The author wrote several foreign-language handbooks, which are particularly useful for students and travellers. He died in 1966, having completely revised and rewritten this work which was first published in 1933. The main object of this compact and practical book is to provide those interested in the language with a basic grammar and vocabulary for most everyday situations.

396 **Beyond the dictionary in Spanish: handbook of colloquial usage.**
Arthur Bryson Gerrard. London: Cassell, 1967. 4th ed. 160p.

The author attempts to bridge 'the gap between the written word as acquired from grammar books and the living speech as spoken by a native'. The Spanish-English dictionary section includes valuable commentary on word usage (e.g. olé), special vocabularies, and an English-Spanish cross-reference index.

397 **Introductory Catalan grammar: with a brief outline of the language and literature, a selection from Catalan writers, and a Catalan-English and English-Catalan vocabulary.**
Joan Gili. Oxford, England: Dolphin, 1974. 4th ed. 251p. map.

A classic work, revised in this fourth edition, which includes a new chapter on pronunciation and spelling by Max Wheeler. It thoroughly illustrates and explains the Catalan language with examples from the early chroniclers to 20th-century writers.

398 **Spanish grammar.**
Eric Viele Greenfield. New York: Barnes & Noble, 1972. 4th ed. 236p. (College Outline Series, no. 42).

A succinct grammar which contains only the prime essentials. Its 'one and only purpose is to serve as a textbook for those beginning the study of Spanish'. All the basic principles of Spanish grammar are presented in a clear and simplified form.

399 **A manual of modern Spanish.**
L. C. Harmer, F. J. Norton.   London: University Tutorial Press,
1957. 2nd ed. 623p.

Originally conceived as a course covering the fundamentals of all aspects of
grammar, the book was expanded to include the intricacies of Spanish syntax. The
work also contains excellent sections on the conjugation of verbs and Spanish-
English/English-Spanish vocabularies.

400 **Spain after Franco: language in context.**
Juan Kattán-Ibarra, Tim Connell.   Cheltenham, England: Stanley
Thornes, 1984. 2nd ed. 179p. map. bibliog.

This work was written for students of Spanish 'opting to study the background to
Spanish society rather than literature, and who have an interest in current affairs'.
The presentation remains unaltered from the first edition (1980) and the four
main sections (transition towards democracy; changes in society; Spain and the
modern world; economic difficulties) are introduced in English, and then followed
by reading and comprehension exercises. There is also a 'Who's who' and a
'What's what' section, and a chronology up to 1983. Unfortunately there are no
audio-visual aids to accompany the text, which draws on material from the
Spanish press. However, the work has been popular enough to go into a second
edition, and is useful for private study, adult education, sixth-formers, and the
initial stage of undergraduate study.

401 **Invitación: Spanish for communication and cultural awareness.**
Angela Labarca, with the collaboration of Elmer A. Rodríguez.
New York: Holt, Rinehart & Winston, 1983. 431p.

A basic textbook for higher level students of Spanish at college or university.
Although leaning towards the American college system as well as towards Latin
American Spanish, it is nevertheless up-to-date and useful for all aspects of
contemporary Spanish language.

402 **The evolution of Spanish: an introductory historical grammar.**
Thomas A. Lathrop.   Newark, Delaware: Juan de la Cuesta,
1980. 172p. bibliog. (Juan de la Cuesta Hispanic Monographs,
no. 1).

A comprehensive study of the evolution of the Spanish language, aimed at the
novice. 'Since the University student who becomes interested in the Spanish
language frequently does not come equipped with a knowledge of classical Latin,
the first chapter deals with the major features of this language, especially with
those which are important to the development of Spanish'. The remainder of the
book deals with distinctive features in the development of modern Spanish.

403 **A concise Spanish grammar.**
R. N. de M. Leathes.   London: John Murray, 1984. 166p.

A clearly set out and easy-reference grammar, which is particularly helpful for the
beginner or tourist, whilst at the same time providing more specific information

for advanced students. It also contains some notes on Latin American variants and on colloquial Spanish.

404 Living Spanish.
R. P. Littlewood. London: Hodder & Stoughton, 1979. 2nd ed. 358p.

This book is intended for all students of the Spanish language, and is based largely on material that has been used in evening classes over a number of years. Every attempt has been made to provide the reader with a fairly broad background to the language. The major part of the work is made up of stories in Spanish, and the author's aim is to cover the more elementary points.

405 Guide to Spanish idioms: a practical guide to 2500 Spanish idioms.
Raymond H. Pierson. Cheltenham, England: Stanley Thornes, 1981. rev. ed. 174p. bibliog.

Primarily intended to supplement texts, grammars and dictionaries, this guide was prepared in response to a general demand for lists which collect into convenient form several categories of information. It is a well-organized analysis, aimed mainly at English-speaking students beginning Spanish, but is also of use to teachers, libraries and tourists.

406 An essential course in modern Spanish.
H. Ramsden. London: Harrap, 1959. 416p.

A useful standard work for university students, 'essential' in vocabulary, idioms and grammar. The course is divided into twenty-five lessons and eight review and development sections, each with its grammar, vocabulary and exercises.

407 A textbook of modern Spanish: as now written and spoken in Castile and the Spanish American republics.
Marathon Montrose Ramsey, revised by Robert K. Spaulding. New York: Holt, Rinehart & Winston, 1956. rev. ed. 692p. bibliog.

A standard work, first published in 1894, which comprehensively covers all aspects of Spanish grammar. This edition has a completely new section on phonology, a revised section on morphology, and an updated section on syntax. Strictly speaking there is no 'Spanish' language, and diversities of dialect are so great that Catalan, Andalusian and Galician are mutually unintelligible. The central position of Castile, and the political ascendancy it had acquired by the 11th century, have caused the Castilian dialect to be acknowledged as the typical language of Spain.

408 Essential Spanish grammar.
Seymour Resnick. London: Teach Yourself Books, Hodder & Stoughton, 1975. 127p. (Teach Yourself Books).

This useful textbook is aimed specifically at those people wishing to speak and understand simple, everyday Spanish, and who only have limited time. It provides grammatical rules and structures which are amply illustrated with phrases and sentences. The work as a whole lists over 2,500 words which are identified as nearly identical in Spanish and English.

409 Catalan.
Alan Yates. London: Hodder & Stoughton, 1975. 381p. bibliog. (Teach Yourself Books).

Catalan is the mother tongue of nearly 7 million people, with more people speaking Catalan than Danish, Norwegian or Irish. The book is aimed principally at the interested traveller who wishes to learn the first language of the Catalan regions, and the student of romance languages in general and Catalan specifically. It contains a large Catalan-English and English-Catalan vocabulary after the thirty lessons and exercises, and is certainly the best work on this subject available at present.

Dictionaries

410 Appleton's new Cuyás English-Spanish and Spanish-English dictionary.
Arturo Cuyás, revised and enlarged by Lewis E. Brett, Helen S. Eaton. New York: Appleton-Century-Crofts, 1972. 5th rev. ed. 1,277p.

A good standard dictionary for the serious student, which contains more than 130,000 entries. In this latest revision the compilers have: added new words from all fields of interest; dropped those words that are no longer in current use; and have modified those that have acquired new meanings or more precise equivalents in Spanish or in English.

411 Cassell's Spanish-English, English-Spanish dictionary.
Revised by Anthony Gooch, Angel García de Paredes. London: Cassell; New York: Macmillan, 1978. 7th ed. 1,109p.

A standard dictionary which incorporates many Latin American terms and idioms, with appendixes on English and Spanish verbs. It was originally edited by Edgar Allison Peers, and although thoroughly revised is less practical than the Collins dictionary (q.v.).

412 Collins Spanish-English, English-Spanish dictionary.
Colin Smith, in collaboration with Manuel Bermejo Marcos and Eugenio Chang-Rodríguez. London: Collins, 1971. 1,242p.

A well-organized, up-to-date dictionary which embraces British and American English, and Peninsular and South American Spanish. According to many lexicographers this is the best desk-format dictionary in the field, particularly as it aims to be 'a dictionary of modern current English and Spanish'. It contains about 50,000 entries, including proper names, and is very reasonably priced.

413 **Diccionari català-anglès, anglès-català.** (Catalan-English, English-Catalan dictionary.)
Jordi Colomer del Castillo. Barcelona: Editorial Pòrtic, 1981. 768p. (Col·lecció Diccionaris).

An enlarged edition of the original first published in 1973, which includes sections on verbs and abbreviations. The third edition of the compact version was published by French & European Publications, New York, 1981.

414 **Diccionario de le lengua española.** (A dictionary of the Spanish language.)
Madrid: Real Academia Española, Espasa-Calpe, 1984. 20th ed. 2 vols.

This is the standard authority on current usage published by the Spanish Royal Academy which has also published the *Diccionario histórico de la lengua española* (A historical dictionary of the Spanish language) (Madrid: Real Academia Española, 1972- .), a compilation of the different usages of each word through the centuries. The Academy's first dictionary was the *Diccionario de la lengua castellana* (A dictionary of Castilian Spanish) (Madrid: Gredos, 1979. 3 vols. facsimile ed. (1726-39)), which is commonly regarded as a masterpiece, and is still an important source for contemporary researchers.

415 **Harrap's concise Spanish and English dictionary.**
Clare Mulderrig. London: Harrap, 1985.

A new dictionary which has not yet been published but which should be available in the autumn of 1985.

416 **Nuevo diccionario ilustrado de la lengua española.** (A new illustrated dictionary of the Spanish language.)
Barcelona: Editorial Ramón Sopena, 1982. 1,232p.

An encyclopaedic dictionary with 250,000 entries, 5,000 illustrations and thirty-two colour plates, which also contains a section on synonyms and antonyms. All entries have been vetted by the Spanish Royal Academy for language.

417 **Simon and Schuster's international dictionary: English-Spanish, Spanish-English.**
Edited by Tana De Gámez. New York: Simon & Schuster, 1973. 1,605p.

Although somewhat weak on Spanish regional vocabulary, this dictionary is nevertheless highly recommended for the more than 200,000 entries it does contain. The pronunciation of English entry words is indicated according to the International Phonetic Alphabet, and distinction has been made between American and British pronunciation and usage. The publishers also produced a concise international dictionary in 1975, which represents an abridgement of the above work, with the addition of some new material.

418 **The Williams Spanish and English dictionary.**
Edwin Bucher Williams.   London: Nelson, 1974. expanded ed.
1,244p.

First published in 1963, with the American edition published in New York by
Holt, Rinehart & Winston, this work contains 125,000 main entries, and is up-to-
date and easy to use. It is also a well-organized reference work which is fuller in
points of grammar than some other dictionaries.

**A bibliography of Hispanic dictionaries: Catalan, Galician, Spanish,
Spanish in Latin America and the Philippines.**
See item no. 961.

Religion

419 Religion in the Republic of Spain.
C. Araujo García, Kenneth G. Grubb. London; New York;
Toronto: World Dominion Press, 1933. 109p. 3 maps.

An analysis of the growth of the Reformed and Evangelical churches of Spain
during the years of the Second Republic.

420 The ghosts of 1492: Jewish aspects of the struggle for religious freedom in Spain 1848-1976.
Caesar C. Aronsfeld. New York: Columbia University Press,
1979. 86p. bibliog. (Jewish Social Studies Monograph Series,
no. 1).

A work mainly concerned with the little-known aspects of the Jewish struggle for
civil liberties and religious freedom during the last century and a half. Religious,
racial and even anti-aristocratic class prejudices combined to create an obsession
with 'purity of blood' ('limpieza de sangre') which became manifest in the 16th
and 17th centuries. In 1492 about 170,000 Jews were expelled from Spain but
those who remained became 'conversos' (i.e. practising Catholics), and played a
prominent part in every aspect of Spanish religious and intellectual life. The work
also covers Spanish-Israeli relations, and notes the memorable event in 1968 when
the first officially sanctioned synagogue was opened in Spain since 1350.

421 Spanish and Portuguese monastic history 600-1300.
Charles Julian Bishko. London: Variorum Reprints, 1984. 336p.
bibliog. (Collected Studies Series, no. CS188).

'The history of the rise, survival, diffusion and operation of ideas, institutions,
spirituality and culture'. These thirteen detailed and scholarly studies, the
majority referring to Spain, are essentially reprints of articles by the author
written between 1941 and 1983. They provide a wealth of information on the

116

history, institutions and factors of growth in Spanish secular and religious life. Bishko has also written *Studies in medieval Spanish frontier history* (London: Variorum, 1980) in the same series.

422 The church militant and Iberian expansion 1440-1770.

Charles Ralph Boxer. Baltimore, Maryland; London: Johns Hopkins University Press, 1978. 148p. bibliog. (The Johns Hopkins Symposia in Comparative History, no. 10).

Based on four lectures given in 1976, this work focuses on the aims and attitudes of the Spanish branch of the Roman Catholic Church towards the empire, and the problems posed by the education and formation of an indigenous clergy among peoples of different ethnic origins and cultural backgrounds. Spanish missionaries were well aware that they were the vanguard of the church militant, as well as loyal subjects of the Spanish crown, and they played a vital role in the overseas expansion of Europe.

423 Church, politics and society in Spain, 1750-1874.

William James Callahan. Cambridge, Massachussetts; London: Harvard University Press, 1984. 325p. 2 maps. bibliog. (Harvard Historical Monographs, vol. 73).

The author states that 'few institutions have played so central a role in the history of a people as has the Spanish Church', and goes on to examine why the subject of the church has aroused such controversy over the years, and how its involvement in political and social conflicts has made it a focus of much attention and research. The book begins in 1750, when the process of political, economic and social reform was reaching its height, and concludes in 1874 with the collapse of the First Republic and the restoration of the Bourbon monarchy.

424 Apparitions in late medieval and Renaissance Spain.

William A. Christian. Princeton, New Jersey: Princeton University Press, 1981. 349p. 3 maps. bibliog.

The author has studied about one hundred cases of Spanish divine visions from 1399 to the present, and has visited most of the villages discussed in this work, and been present at a number of contemporary visions. The main bulk of the text comprises a series of verbatim reports of celestial visions by, for example, working people, children, farmers, shepherds' wives and servants during the 15th century.

425 Local religion in sixteenth-century Spain.

William A. Christian. Princeton, New Jersey: Princeton University Press, 1981. 283p. map. bibliog.

This study of religious belief and practice is based on responses to a questionnaire sent out by Philip II's chroniclers to the towns and villages of New Castile in the years 1575 to 1580. It discusses the two levels of Catholicism existing at the time: the Church Universal based on the sacraments, liturgy and the Roman calendar; and a local one based on particular sacred places, ceremonies, images, relics and locally chosen patron saints. The latter is the main subject of this excellently-documented work.

426 Person and God in a Spanish valley.
William A. Christian. New York; London: Seminar Press, 1972. 215p. maps. bibliog. (Studies in Social Discontinuity).

A study of the religious life of the people of the Nansa valley of northern Spain in the province of Santander (the site of apparitions of the Virgin and St. Michael in the early 1960s), which is based on a year spent living within that community. The opening section describes the people, their society and their culture in this agricultural base in the Cantabrian mountains, and the remainder of the work is given over to describing the forms of religion they practise.

427 Catholicism and the Franco régime.
Norman B. Cooper. Beverly Hills, California; London: Sage Publications, 1975. 48p. bibliog. (Sage Research Papers in the Social Sciences; Contemporary European Studies Series, no. 90-019).

A concise study of the role of Catholicism in Franco's Spain, which also discusses the 1953 concordat, Opus Dei (founded in 1928 under the dictatorship of Primo de Rivera), and the relationship between Spain and the Vatican.

428 The oppression of Protestants in Spain.
Jacques Delpech. London: Lutterworth Press, 1956. 114p.

A useful introduction to the problems of Spanish Protestants, and a thorough documentary account of Protestant-government relations in Spain during Franco's rule, especially since the decree of 1948 which demonstrated the stiffening of official policy towards them. The author is a French Huguenot minister who spent thirty years visiting and talking to the scattered Protestant communities throughout Spain, and he concludes that Spanish Protestants under Franco did not enjoy the toleration that the régime originally promised them in 1945 in Article 6 of the 'Fuero de los Españoles'.

429 Spanish anticlericalism: a study in modern alienation.
John Joseph Devlin. New York: Las Americas Publishing Company, 1966. 271p. bibliog.

An account by an American Catholic and Professor of Spanish Literature of the reactions of liberal Spanish authors to the 'confessional state' in Spain. He explains the differences between anticlericalism and anti-religious attacks in the church, and provides a general summary of the criticisms made of the Spanish church over the centuries. He also discusses in detail the anti-clerical movement from the middle of the 19th century to the present.

430 **Iglesia, dictadura y democracia: catolicismo y sociedad en España (1953-1979).** (Church, dictatorship and democracy: Catholicism and society in Spain, 1953-79.)
Rafael Díaz-Salazar.   Madrid: Ediciones Hoac, 1981. 526p.
3 maps. bibliog. (Ediciones Hoac, no. 45).

This large volume studies the relationship between Catholicism and Spanish society during a period which included both Franco's rule and the transition to democracy, and a new constitution. It is one of the best Spanish interpretations of the Catholic Church's role in modern Spanish society. A large bibliography covers the socio-historical analysis of Catholicism in Spain, and the sociological and theological study of religion and Catholicism in particular.

431 **Church and State in Franco Spain.**
William G. Ebenstein.   Princeton, New Jersey: Center of International Studies, Woodrow Wilson School of Public and International Affairs, Princeton University, 1960. 53p. bibliog. (Princeton University: Center of International Studies; Research Monographs, no. 8).

The topics covered include: the Spanish Catholic Church; its position in world Catholicism; the clergy and religious orders; and Opus Dei and the concordat of 1953. Concentrating on the church's ties with the Franco régime, the author emphasizes that the church was the single most important source of stability and respectability during the Franco period.

432 **Religious freedom in Spain: its ebb and flow.**
John David Hughey.   London: Carey Kingsgate Press, 1955. 211p. bibliog.

A general survey of Protestantism and Catholicism in Spain since the 15th century, written by a Baptist scholar who lived there for four years. He attempts to describe and analyze the official Spanish attitudes and policies towards Protestantism over the years, and stresses how members of minority religions in Spain have always experienced persecution, toleration and freedom at different times. Unfortunately the work is very poorly indexed.

433 **The thirty thousand: modern Spain and Protestantism.**
Carmen Irizarry.   New York: Harcourt, Brace & World, 1966. 399p. bibliog.

The work opens with a brief historical outline of Erasmism and Lutheranism, and moves on to the 1930s to discuss attempts to break the centuries-old power of the Catholic Church. The title refers to the number of Protestants believed to be practising their religion in Spain at the time this book was written, and demonstrates how they have been persecuted over the years. The authoress argued strongly for religious liberty at a time when the links between Franco's state and the Catholic Church were very strong.

Religion

434   **The Spanish Inquisition.**
Henry Kamen.   London: Weidenfeld & Nicolson, 1965. 339p.
map. bibliog.

An excellent study representing the synthesis of previous research on the subject.
Kamen discusses the question of how much the Inquisiton contributed to the
decline of Spain, and proposes the controversial point that it served to bolster the
power of the landed gentry and aristocracy. He quotes extensively from records of
the time made by the Inquisition, in which every word and gesture was written
down by a secretary present at a torture. The Inquisition was created in 1478, and
was only abolished by Royal Decree in 1834.

435   **A history of the Inquisition of Spain.**
Henry Charles Lea.   New York; London: Macmillan, 1922.
4 vols. bibliog.

Despite its age and bias, this work remains a classic of both research and
interpretation, and is written by a prolific author on religion in the Europe of the
Middle Ages. This massive study looks at all aspects of the Inquisition from its
inception in the 15th century as an ecclesiastical tribunal. Lea also wrote *The
Moriscos of Spain: their conversion and expulsion* (Westport, Connecticut:
Greenwood Press, 1968).

436   **Spanish church and society, 1150-1300.**
Peter Linehan.   London: Variorum Reprints, 1983. 336p. bibliog.
(Collected Studies Series; CS184).

A collection of nine essays, some in English and some in Spanish, which were first
published between 1969 and 1982. They investigate the related themes with which
the author was concerned in his earlier work *The Spanish church and the Papacy
in the thirteenth century* (London: Cambridge University Press, 1971). The work
describes the internal condition of the church in Spain, and its relations and
conflicts with the State.

437   **The clerical confrontation with the Enlightenment in Spain.**
C. C. Noel.   *European Studies Review*, vol. 5, no. 2 (Apr. 1975),
p. 103-122.

A discussion of the dilemma faced by Spanish clerics to enlightened thought
before 1789, and their reactions to what basically signified the end of the true
Catholic tradition of unity and authority. 'Well disposed and intelligent Catholics,
both laymen and clerics, were caught in this dilemma: could they accept the
desirable practices of improvement without risking the destruction of their faith
by intellectual freedom'. The author emphasizes that this article is only an
introduction to an area which requires further study.

438   **Spanish Catholicism: an historical overview.**
Stanley G. Payne.   Madison, Wisconsin; London: University of
Wisconsin Press, 1984. 263p. bibliog.

This respected scholar emphasizes the importance of religion in Spanish history
through a comprehensive study of Catholicism in Spain from mediaeval times to

the present, with particular reference to the political and socioeconomic issues involved. Through a well-ordered, chronological approach Payne dissects its institutions and relations with the state. The work contains an excellent bibliography.

439 Spain, the church and the orders.
Edgar Allison Peers. London: Eyre & Spottiswoode, 1939. 218p. bibliog.

A general study of the church in Spain, and of the religious orders (Augustinian, Dominican, Franciscan and Jesuit) from 1700 onwards. Although detailed, it is suitable for any reader interested in this subject.

440 The Spanish Inquisition.
Jean Plaidy. London: Book Club Associates, 1978. 544p. bibliog.

A somewhat superficial study by the famous historical novelist, which will be of particular use to the general reader rather than the specialist historian. It primarily analyzes the personalities involved in the Inquisition from the instigators to the victims, and also describes how attempts were made to establish the Inquisition in the Spanish colonies.

441 The Spanish Inquisition.
Cecil Roth. New York: W. W. Norton, 1964. 316p. bibliog.

A historical and religious study of the Inquisition, which looks at the causes which led to its formation, and the religious background of 14th-century Spain. As in Kamen's work (q.v.) the author emphasizes the fact that the methods of torture employed by the Inquisition were on the whole 'conservative and unoriginal', although there were examples of extremely brutal methods being employed to obtain a confession of heresy. Several appendixes provide transcripts of trials.

442 Anticlericalism: conflict between church and State in France, Italy, and Spain.
Jacob Salwyn Schapiro. Princeton, New Jersey: Van Nostrand, 1967. 207p. bibliog. (Anvil Books: Ideas, Ideals, Ideologies, no. 91).

A concise study of the Catholic Church as a social and political institution. The major aim of the book is to describe and explain the conflict between clericalism and anticlericalism in Catholic France, Italy and Spain that arose at the close of the 18th century and continued into the 20th century, and which revolved around the power and privileges that the Catholic Church enjoyed.

443 The tragic week: a study of anticlericalism in Spain, 1875-1912.
Joan Connelly Ullman. Cambridge, Massachussetts: Harvard University Press, 1968. 448p. bibliog.

'La semana trágica' (the tragic week) started as a general strike in protest against conscription for an unpopular war in Morocco, and became a rebellion in which workers burned and looted convents, churches, church schools and other religious éstablishments in Barcelona and its suburbs. This study tries to explain the reasons behind the distrust and dislike of the clergy by both workers and much of the middle class. The authoress makes a strong case for 1909 (the year of 'the tragic week') being the critical turning point toward the failure of the constitutional monarchy.

The road to Santiago: pilgrims of St. James.
See item no. 44.

Religion, class, and family in Spain.
See item no. 466.

Religious conflict and consensus in Spain: a tale of two constitutions.
See item no. 539.

La diplomacia vaticana y la España de Franco (1936-1945). (Vatican diplomacy and Franco's Spain (1936-1945).)
See item no. 574.

Philosophy

444 Historia crítica del pensamiento español. (A critical history of
Spanish philosophy.)
José Luis Abellán.   Madrid: Espasa-Calpe, 1979-. 4 vols. map.
bibliog.
The author has written many books on Spanish culture and thinking. In this work
volume 1 discusses methodology, and provides a historical introduction; volume 2
covers the Golden Age; and volume 3 examines the Baroque period. At the time
of writing volume 4 (covering 19th and 20th-century Spanish philosophy) had still
not been published. Each volume contains indexes and appendixes on the writings
of individual philosophers.

445 Contemporary Spanish philosophy: an anthology.
Translated, and with an introduction by, A. Robert Caponigri.
Notre Dame, Indiana; London: University of Notre Dame Press,
1967. 383p. bibliog.
An anthology of works by eleven contemporary Spanish philosophers, who have
attempted to reintegrate Spanish and European culture in their writings. The
selection represents Spanish philosophy in the past, as well as current themes and
problems in Spanish thinking.

446 Is there a Spanish philosophy?
José Ferrater Mora.   *Hispanic Review*, vol. 19, no. 1 (Jan. 1951),
p. 1-10.
A brief, scholarly article which sets out to explain why there is a definable Spanish
philosophy. True to the traditions of philosophy, the author asks almost as many
questions as he answers.

Philosophy

447 **The Krausist movement and ideological change in Spain, 1854-1874.**
Juan López-Morillas, translated by Frances M. López-Morillas.
Cambridge, England: Cambridge University Press, 1981. 2nd ed.
180p. bibliog. (Cambridge Iberian and Latin American Studies).
A translation of the author's book which first appeared in 1956 in Spanish. The
work studies the relatively obscure intellectual movement which was current in
Spain between 1850 and 1880, and evolved from the work of the little-known
German philosopher Karl Christian Friedrich Krause (1781-1830). Krausism did
in fact deeply affect the religious, political and philosophical thoughts of a
generation of Spanish liberals, including the 19th-century novelist Benito Pérez
Galdós. It represented a lifestyle exemplified by sober dress and the cultivation of
taciturnity. The work of Krause (who believed himself to be the only true
interpreter of Kant) was brought into Spain by Professor Julián Sanz del Río. The
more committed members of the movement wanted a republic 'that is at once
reformist and conservative'. Their wish came true in 1931, but was short-lived,
with authoritarian Catholicism crushing what not only Krausists saw as a
movement towards a more open and humane society.

448 **Presence and absence of existentialism in Spain.**
Julián Marías Aguilera. *Philosophy and Phenomenalogical
Research*, vol. 15 (1954), p. 180-91.
Although thirty years' old, this article remains useful for the information it
provides on 20th-century Spanish philosophy, with particular emphasis on the two
major tendencies of philosophy in the 1950s: neoscholasticism and existentialism.
References are included.

449 **The rhetoric of humanism: Spanish culture after Ortega y Gasset.**
Thomas Mermall. New York: Bilingual Press, 1976. 135p.
bibliog. (Studies in the Literary Analysis of Hispanic Texts).
This book is a study of the dominant ideas and philosophies in Spanish culture
since the Civil War, and represents both an enquiry into the different types of
humanism in Spain, and a study of the 'rhetoric' of humanism. Part 1 covers
conservative humanism and the work of Pedro Laín Entralgo and Juan Rof
Carballo. Part 2 studies socialist humanism and the work of Enrique Tierno
Galván and José Luis Aranguren. Aimed at graduate students and teachers of
Spanish literature, culture, history and philosophy, this is the first serious attempt
in English to assess the importance of the Spanish essay after José Ortega y
Gasset.

450 **Studies in Spanish Renaissance thought.**
Carlos G. Noreña. The Hague: Martinus Nijhoff, 1975. 277p.
bibliog. (International Archives of the History of Ideas, vol. 82).
A collection of essays on Spanish philosophers from the end of the 15th century to
the first decades of the 17th, aiming to draw attention to the many different
aspects of Spanish intellectual life at that time. This volume concentrates in
particular on the works of: Francisco de Vitoria (1492?-1546), one of the greatest
of Spanish theologians, and adviser to the Emperor Charles V; Fray Luis de León
(1527-91), the greatest Spanish prose writer of the 16th century, and one of

Spain's greatest poets; and Juan Huarte de San Juan (1529-88), a moralist, and one of the boldest writers on the naturalistic philosophy of man.

451 **On the various kinds of distinctions.**
Francisco Suárez, translated by Cyril Vollert. Milwaukee, Wisconsin: Marquette University Press, 1947. 67p. bibliog. (Medieval Philosophical Texts in Translation, no. 4).

Suárez (1548-1617), a Spanish theologian and philosopher, was the most important figure of the second flowering of scholasticism. His principal work, *Diputationes metaphysicae*, was used for over a century as the textbook of philosophy in most European universities, Protestant and Catholic alike, and is presented here translated from the Latin.

452 **Vives' 'Introduction to wisdom': a Renaissance textbook.**
Edited by Marian Leona Tobriner. New York: Teachers College Press, Columbia University, 1968. 159p. (Classics in Education, no. 35).

Juan Luis Vives (1492-1540) was a Spanish humanist and student of Erasmus, who travelled to England in 1523 to lecture on philosophy at Oxford. He advocated the use of the vernacular in schools, argued for the building of academies, supported the education of women, and recommended a reorganization in teaching methods. Tobriner gives a detailed study of Vives' life and works, and this is followed by the preface to Richard Morison's first English translation of Vives' book in 1540, and the text of *Introductio ad sapientiam* itself.

Constitutionalism and statecraft during the Golden Age of Spain: a study of the political philosophy of Juan de Mariana, S. J.
See item no. 215.

Society

General, and social structure

453   The changing faces of rural Spain.
Edited by Joseph B. Aceves, William Anthony Douglass.
Cambridge, Massachussetts: Schenkman; New York, London:
John Wiley, 1976. 205p. bibliog.

A selection of essays centred around the major topic of the mass exodus of the peasantry to Spanish cities and foreign countries. There is also discussion of other subjects such as the impact of emigration, modern expatriation, and rural development and planning on different regions of modern Spain. All the contributors are well-known writers in the fields of Spanish anthropology, ethnology and rural sociology.

454   Social change in a Spanish village.
Joseph B. Aceves.   Cambridge, Massachussetts; London:
Schenkman, 1971. 145p. 3 maps. bibliog. (The Schenkman Series
on Socio-economic Change).

A detailed study of the village of El Pinar, between Segovia and Valladolid, in which the author aims to 'introduce the general reader to the problems of rural Spain'. El Pinar was one of the first villages in Spain to benefit from land reform and rural development programmes. 'This book begins with a description of the village area, the social life and values of the people, and goes on to discuss change programmes and their effects on El Pinar and its area'. The author is himself the son of an ex-inhabitant of the village who emigrated to the United States.

455 **The troubadour revival: a study of social change and traditionalism in late medieval Spain.**
Roger Boase. London: Routledge & Kegan Paul, 1978. 219p. bibliog.

The original troubadours first appeared in Provence and northern Spain, and were lyric poets of chivalric love who flourished from the 11th to the 13th century. The author notes, however, that courtly love was much more than a poetic convention: 'it was a literary and sentimental ideology'. He believes that the large amount of amatory verse composed in Spain in the 15th century, and its uniform and deliberately archaic character, support his argument that a 'troubadour revival' occurred during that time.

456 **Migration, kinship, and community: tradition and transition in a Spanish village.**
Stanley H. Brandes. New York; London: Academic Press, 1975. 220p. 3 maps. bibliog. (Studies in Social Discontinuity).

A useful work which aims to assess the nature and impact of depopulation on Becedas, a small peasant village in southwestern Castile. In particular the author stresses how emigration from the community has radically altered land tenure arrangements, standards of living, marriage patterns and so on, and Becedas, like many other villages, has had to adapt. The author spent almost eighteen months in the village researching his subject.

457 **South from Granada.**
Gerald Brenan. London: Hamish Hamilton, 1974. 282p. map.

An absorbing account of life in the village of Yegen, in the Alpujarra, between 1920 and 1935, describing customs and folklore in vivid detail. Together with J. Pitt-Rivers' *People of the Sierra* (q.v.), it represents one of the few books which have been written in English on Andalusian mountain life. The book contains not only the author's reflections on Spanish society, but marvellous accounts of visits to his mountain home by his friends Lytton Strachey, Virginia Woolf, David Garnett and Roger Fry. It was originally published in 1957, and has since been published by Penguin Books (1963) and by Cambridge University Press (1980).

458 **The city and the grassroots: a cross-cultural theory of urban social movements.**
Manuel Castells. London: Edward Arnold, 1983. 450p. bibliog.

Part 5 of this book (p. 213-88) is entitled 'The making of an urban social movement: the citizen movement in Madrid towards the end of the Franquist era'. The social mobilization around urban issues that occurred in the neighbourhoods of most Spanish cities in the 1970s was regarded by most experts as the largest and most significant urban movement in Europe since 1945. A thorough analysis is made of planning policies, building programmes, and the mobilization of citizens demanding more say in these policies and programmes in order to alleviate the urban crisis. The section also includes tables and maps.

459 **Compromising relations: kith, kin and class in Andalusia.**
John R. Corbin, Marie P. Corbin. Aldershot, England: Gower, 1984. 153p. 3 maps. bibliog. (Studies in Spanish Anthropology, no. 1).

A detailed analysis of Ronda society, which begins with a general description of the city, its social structure and the social inequality and conflict observed. The authors then present their study of personal relations, their compromising effect on the impersonal system of state and market economy, and their link with social class. Comparing their own findings with those of other studies of Andalusia, they conclude by commenting on the effects of different perspectives on interpretations of social class in southern Spain. This study of Andalusian anthropology is continued in volumes 2 and 3 of the series: *Urbane thought; culture and class in an Andalusian city* (Aldershot, England: Gower, 1985), and *The anarchist passion: class conflict in southern Spain, 1810-1965* (Aldershot, England: Gower, to be published in 1986).

460 **Spanish mountain life: the Sierra Nevada.**
Juliette de Baïracli-Levy. London: Faber & Faber, 1955. 131p.

An evocative personal travel account of life in this area of southern Spain over a period of eight months, which looks at the customs and social structure of the region.

461 **Daughters of the Reconquest: women in Castilian town society, 1100-1300.**
Heath Dillard. Cambridge, England: Cambridge University Press, 1984. 272p. bibliog. (Cambridge Iberian and Latin American Studies).

A scholarly study of the vital participation of women in the shaping of Hispanic society during the Reconquest and the mediaeval expansion of Christian 'Spain'. It looks at all aspects of life and customs, and provides a fascinating insight into social history during a crucial period of growth and development.

462 **Echalar and Murélaga: opportunity and rural exodus in two Spanish Basque villages.**
William Anthony Douglass. London: C. Hurst, 1975. 222p. map. bibliog.

A study of two small agrarian communities in the Basque Provinces, which analyzes the relationships between these communities and the interplay between traditional peasant societies and industrialization. The main problem discussed is one that arises particularly in Mediterranean agriculture-based societies (Greece, Spain, Portugal, Italy) where there is a challenge to the village inhabitants, especially the young, between choosing the agrarian tradition into which they were born or the new urban-industrial lifestyle. This book attempts to combine the results of an anthropological field study with archival research of social, economic and demographic changes in Echalar and Murélaga during the 20th century. Douglass is also the author of *Death in Murélaga: funerary ritual in a Spanish Basque village* (Seattle, Washington; London: University of Washington

Press, 1969), a detailed study of the social structure of the rural community and the elaborate ceremony surrounding death.

463 Love and the Spanish.

Nina Consuelo Epton. London: Cassell, 1961. 216p.

A highly readable historical analysis of the private and public morality of the Spanish people throughout the country. Epton also wrote *Madrid* (London: Cassell, 1964), a description and study of the social life and customs in Spain's capital.

464 The pueblo: a mountain village on the Costa del Sol.

Ronald Fraser. London: Allen Lane, 1973. 285p. bibliog.

An illuminating study of some of the more important aspects of modernization in the region of the village of Tajos in the province of Málaga, describing the changes in society during Franco's rule. The book is based on visits made to the village in 1957 and 1971, and basically consists of interviews with villagers on specific subjects of interest.

465 The pasiegos; Spaniards in no man's land.

Susan Tax Freeman. Chicago, London: University of Chicago Press, 1979. 291p. 6 maps. bibliog.

The inhabitants of the village of Vega de Pas in the Province of Santander ('pasiegos') are mainly a cattle-herding community. They have been classified amongst the 'despised peoples' of northern Spain, and this genealogical and historical analysis of them is combined with field study research. Freeman also wrote *Neighbors: the social contract in a Castilian hamlet* (Chicago, London: University of Chicago Press, 1970), a study of the village of Valdemora, and a sensitive examination of the nature of the contracts which bind the villagers to one another. Again, it is a combination of field study and documentary research.

466 Religion, class, and family in Spain.

Charles F. Gallagher. Hanover, New Hampshire: American Universities Field Staff, 1973-74. 4 vols. maps. bibliog. (West Europe Series).

This easy-to-read work comprises four small pamphlets, each covering a different aspect of Spanish life: Spanish Catholicism; factors affecting fertility; regional considerations; and the roads to democracy. The emphasis is on religion and population trends. Valuable statistics are included.

467 The people of the plain: class and community in lower Andalusia.

David D. Gilmore. New York; Guildford, England: Columbia University Press, 1980. 247p. map. bibliog.

The author focuses on class relations and traditional culture in Fuenmayor, a farming town between Seville and Córdoba. The whole study is based on fieldwork, and supported by statistical data, and many aspects of Andalusian rural life are portrayed during the final years of Franco's régime.

129

468* **Continuity and change: the social stratification of Spain.**
Salvador Giner. Reading, England: University of Reading, 1973.
2nd ed. 39p. 2 maps. bibliog. (University of Reading Graduate
School of Contemporary European Studies; Occasional
Publication, no. 1).

A short but useful piece of work which provides a very broad outline of modern
Spanish class structures, and attempts to describe some of the principal
characteristics and trends in the stratification of Spanish society beween 1808 and
1973. The author concludes that modernization has been slower in the Iberian
Peninsula than in any other western European country, due in many respects to
social stratification.

469 **El femenismo en España, hoy.** (Feminism in Spain today.)
Anabel González. Bilbao, Spain: Zero; Madrid: ZYX, 1979.
312p. bibliog. (Biblioteca 'Promoción del Pueblo', no. 37).

This book offers a clear view of the current state of the feminist movement in
Spain, and includes discussion and interviews with Spanish feminists. It brings out
into the open their major concern with all aspects of life, whether political, social,
organizational or cultural. The feminist movement has only really taken off in
Spain in recent years, having lain dormant because of repression under Franco
(when large meetings of any kind were forbidden) and the very conservative and
traditional nature of Spanish society. The work includes statistical appendixes on
women in Spain, broken down into five sections: population; women and family;
women and education; women and work; and sexuality. It also contains a forty-
page comprehensive bibliography, and lists feminist organizations in Spain by
town or city.

470 **Remaking Ibieca: rural life in Aragon under Franco.**
Susan Friend Harding. Chapel Hill, North Carolina; London:
University of North Carolina Press, 1984. 221p. 3 maps. bibliog.

A study of social change in the village of Ibieca in northeastern Spain between
1950 and 1975, which was largely the result of the expansion of capitalist
agriculture brought about by agrarian reform measures enacted under the Franco
régime. The emphasis is on the agricultural development of the village, and the
consequent social ramifications.

471 **Captive cities: studies in the political economy of cities and regions.**
Edited by Michael Harloe. London; New York: John Wiley,
1977. 218p. bibliog.

Chapter 10 (p. 187-211) is entitled 'Urban movements in Spain' by Jordi Borja, in
which he studies six different types of urban movement and their aims and
achievements. The author presents a perceptive analysis of urban social
movements which have arisen over the last twenty-five years, despite the
authoritarian régime which existed for most of that time. He assesses the urban
consequences (the concentration of population, and the creation of the
underemployed urban labour force) of Spain's economic transformation which,
the author believes, have led to tight planning control and property speculation.

As a result city centres have become deserted, and the suburb or 'barrio' has appeared as the unit of social cohesion and force.

472 **Culture and society in contemporary Europe: a casebook.**
Edited by Stanley Hoffman, Paschalis Kitromilides. London: George Allen & Unwin, 1981. 237p. bibliog. (Casebook Series on European Politics and Society, no. 2).

The section covering Spain (p. 152-67) is entitled 'Spain: a culture in transition' by Antonio Bar. It primarily assesses the development of cultural affairs from 1939 to the present day, and demonstrates how Spanish culture is well on the way to recovery after the critical years of Franco's censorship. The author shows how culture is linked to society as a whole as well as to events within the economic and political spheres.

473 **A Spanish tapestry: town and country in Castile.**
Michael Kenny. London: Cohen & West, 1961. 243p. 2 maps. bibliog.

A vivid and detailed study which contrasts life in the village of Ramosierra in the province of Soria with that in the urban parish of San Martín in Madrid. It complements the research undertaken by Julian Pitt-Rivers in *The people of the Sierra* (q.v.), which studies an Andalusian community through a similar approach.

474 **Belmonte de los Caballeros: a sociological study of a Spanish town.**
Carmelo Lisón-Tolosana. Oxford, England: Clarendon Press, 1966. 369p. 2 maps. bibliog.

A sociological interpretation of life and traditions in a particular town, based upon fieldwork carried out between 1958 and 1960. The author tries to interpret the background, as well as the present and future of a small Aragonese community, and also examines its structure and organization. This presentation is more wide-ranging than that of Freeman, Kenny or Pitt-Rivers, in that the author discusses both the history of the town and the social changes occurring at the time of writing.

475 **Comparing nations: the use of quantitative data in cross-national research.**
Edited by Richard L. Merritt, Stein Rokkan. New Haven, Connecticut; London: Yale University Press, 1966. 584p. bibliog.

Includes a chapter entitled 'Within-nation differences and comparisons: the eight Spains' (p. 267-319) by Juan J. Linz, which analyzes the social structure and mobility of the population under Franco, and stresses regional differences. Numerous maps and tables are included in this study.

Society. General, and social structure

476 **Sociology in Spain.**
Jesús M. de Miguel, Melissa G. Moyer. *Current Sociology*, vol.
27, no. 1 (spring 1979), p. 1-299.
A special 'Trend Report' issue, with separate sections covering different aspects
of sociology in Spain. The most important aspect of the work is its massive
bibliography (1,380 items) of sociology in Spain up to 1979. The work is divided
into subsections covering: the sociology of sociology; sociological theory and
knowledge; social change; social stratification, class, and mobility; demography
and population; urban and regional studies; rural sociology; sociology of work,
bureaucracy, and organization; political sociology; sociology of the family,
women, youth and sex roles; sociology of education and science; sociology of
religion; sociology of law; sociology of medicine, and social psychiatry; mass
communications, sociology of literature, and sociolinguistics; sociology of art,
sport, and leisure; minorities, deviance, and social control; social psychology;
methodology, research techniques, and statistics.

477 **Honour and shame: the values of Mediterranean society.**
Edited by J. G. Peristiany. London: Weidenfeld & Nicolson,
1965. 265p. bibliog. (The Nature of Human Society).
Includes a chapter entitled 'Honour and shame: a historical account of several
conflicts' (p. 79-137) by Julio Caro Baroja, translated from the Spanish by R.
Johnson. The author examines the evolution of the concept of honour in Spanish
society since the Middle Ages and the chapter is based both on fieldwork and
literary texts. He also examines the political, economic and religious reasons for
changes in the conception of honour, which to the present day exerts a
considerable influence on Spanish society.

478 **Mediterranean family structures.**
Edited by J. G. Peristiany. Cambridge, England: Cambridge
University Press in association with the Social Research Centre,
Cyprus, 1976. 414p. bibliog. (Cambridge Studies in Social
Anthropology, no. 13).
Contains a section comprising three articles on Spain (p. 305-46): 'The ethics of
inheritance' by Carmelo Lisón-Tolosana examines the relation between family
types, morality and inheritance in Galicia; 'Ritual kinship in the Mediterranean:
Spain and the Balkans' by Julian Pitt-Rivers compares the nature and function of
ritual kinship in Spain, Greece, Cyprus and Serbia; and 'Observations on
contemporary Spanish families in Mexico: immigrants and refugees' by Michael
Kenny studies the Spanish family in Mexico, and how Spanish emigrants adapt to
their new environment and different roles in society.

479 **Power and pawn: the female in Iberian families, societies, and
cultures.**
Ann M. Pescatello. Westport, Connecticut: Greenwood Press,
1976. 281p. bibliog. (Contributions in Intercultural and
Comparative Studies, no. 1).
A scholarly study which attempts to summarize and interpret the female's

historical experience in Spain and Portugal and their colonies. The title itself refers to the dual interpretation of woman's place in history: one theory views woman as the wellspring of power and wielder of influence in all areas of activity in society; the other suggests that the female has always been a pawn in a world dominated by males.

480 **Aristocrats and traders: Sevillian society in the sixteenth century.**
Ruth Pike. Ithaca, New York; London: Cornell University Press, 1972. 243p. bibliog.

This is the first study in English of Seville's colourful social history, and attempts to show how the social classes were affected by the new ideas and values arriving from the New World. The authoress strongly emphasizes the importance of trade to the city during this period, and makes full use of both archival and manuscript, as well as literary, sources of the time.

481 **The people of the Sierra.**
Julian A. Pitt-Rivers. Chicago, London: University of Chicago Press, 1971. 2nd ed. 232p. bibliog. (Phoenix Books, no. P55).

Originally presented as a doctoral thesis in 1954, this is a valuable sociological study of the village of Grazalema in the mountains of the province of Cádiz (the first edition used the pseudonym of Alcalá de la Sierra). The author spent a large amount of time living in the village during the early 1950s, and his principal conclusion drawn from the study of patterns of life there was that the society was basically egalitarian. The book also aims to throw light on the culture and traditions of Andalusia generally.

482 **The city as context: urbanism and behavioral constraints in Seville.**
Irwin Press. Urbana, Illinois: University of Illinois Press, 1979. 303p. map. bibliog.

After living in Seville for fifteen months, the author here provides a study of the urban phenomenon, using Seville as his example. The book presents a minutely detailed study of social conditions and daily life in the city, dealing specifically with: neighbourhoods; families and kinship; sex roles; class and social differentiation; religion; housing; financial matters; and health.

483 **The peasants of the Montes: the roots of rural rebellion in Spain.**
Michael R. Weisser. Chicago, London: University of Chicago Press, 1976. map. bibliog.

This detailed study of the rural economy and society encompasses the structure of peasant communities, their morality and their religion during the 16th and 17th centuries. Amongst other topics Weisser discusses the criminal activity recorded in the rural region of the Montes de Toledo. There is also a helpful appendix on the use of local archives in Spain.

Person and God in a Spanish valley.
See item no. 426.

Social problems

484 Treatment of young delinquents in Spain and the Basque country from 1936 to 1978.

Antonio Beristain. *International Journal of the Sociology of Law*, vol. 8, no. 3 (Aug. 1980), p. 277-96.

This article discusses the development of penal legislation and practices in Spain since the outbreak of the Civil War under three principal headings: characteristics of the treatment of juvenile delinquents in Spain from 1936 to the death of Franco in November 1975; new treatment of young people from 1975 to 1978; and the outlook for the future. It also contains several statistical tables and a bibliography.

485 El sistema penitenciario español. (The prison system in Spain.)

Francisco Bueno Arus. Madrid: Publicaciones Españoles, 1971. 37p. bibliog. (Temas Españoles, no. 513).

This short work studies: the basic philosophy behind depriving people of their liberty; the classification of prisoners; prisoner discipline and treatment; the legal status of inmates; and how prisoners are regarded once set free. It was written at the time when Franco was still Head of State, and despite the fact that many of the figures and statistics used in the book are completely out of date, this book is still useful for the basic facts it imparts on the reasoning behind the prison system under Franco and its administration.

486 Alcohol problems and alcohol control in Europe.

Phil Davies, Dermot Walsh. Beckenham, England: Croom Helm; New York: Gardner Press, 1983. 320p. bibliog.

Chapter 17 (p. 186-93) discusses alcohol-related problems in Spain and policies for their control, and also provides figures and data on alcohol consumption. An attempt has been made to develop, examine and assess a public health perspective on these alcohol problems.

487 Crime and the law: the social history of crime in western Europe since 1500.

Edited by V. A. C. Gatrell, Bruce Lenman, Geoffrey Parker. London: Europa, 1980. 381p. bibliog. (Europa Social History of Human Experience).

Chapter 3 (p. 76-96) is entitled 'Crime and punishment in early modern Spain' by Michael Weisser. It is a useful outline of the problem of crime in Spain during the 16th century, and provides a general discussion on how criminal justice operated through the institutions and office of the 'corregidor', a royal officer who after 1480 represented the crown in all administrative and political affairs. Royal criminal statutes were contained within the law codes *Novísima recopilación de las leyes de España*, which have been reprinted (1976) from the original 1805 Madrid publication. The article also covers the activities of the quasi-military brotherhood

'Santa Hermandad', organized by Ferdinand and Isabella, and looks at the types of crimes committed in towns, cities and rural areas.

488 Crime and society in early modern Seville.
Mary Elizabeth Perry. Hanover, New Hampshire: University Press of New England, 1980. 298p. 2 maps. bibliog.

The authoress thoroughly explores the relationship between criminal subcultures and the 'respectable' society of Seville in the 16th and 17th centuries. She argues that crime must be studied as an integral part of society rather than as an isolated aberration, and shows that crime encompassed everyday activities performed by ordinary people in marginal areas where crime and respectability often meet: commerce; charity; military service; prisons; public entertainment; and the church.

489 Penal servitude in early modern Spain.
Ruth Pike. Madison, Wisconsin: University of Wisconsin Press, 1983. 204p. 3 maps. bibliog.

Throughout the 16th and 17th centuries convicted criminals were sentenced to terms of hard labour on the galleys, in the mercury mines of Almadén, and the military 'presidios' (garrisons or forts) in North Africa. After the abolition of the galleys in 1748, penal labour in the form of the 'presidio' sentences became the most common form of punishment. This book is an excellent account of the history of penal servitude in early modern Spain, with emphasis on the changing purposes for which penal labour was intended to serve. Part 1 covers the 16th and 17th centuries, and part 2, the 18th century.

490 Report of an Amnesty International mission to Spain 3-28 October 1979.
London: Amnesty International, 1980. 64p.

This report considers the treatment of people detained in Spanish police stations. Important changes have taken place since Franco's death in the areas of constitutional and criminal law, notably the introduction of a new constitution in 1978. However, Amnesty International has established that torture and maltreatment are still occuring, particularly in Barcelona and the Basque country. In their view this deterioration in the treatment of prisoners has been facilitated by these new laws and internal procedures. This detailed study raises numerous questions regarding police procedures and the state of prisons in Spain.

491 Child labour in Spain: a general review.
Susan Searight. London: Anti-slavery Society, 1980. 54p. bibliog. (Child Labour Series, report no. 3).

This report is based on a four-week visit to Spain in June 1979, followed by two further visits in the same year. Surprisingly, post-Franco Spain is still the home of one of the largest populations of working children in Europe, with the extent of the problem varying from region to region. Many sources, including individuals and organizations within Spain, were interviewed by Searight, and she provides a useful yet disturbing background study to the problem, and offers some recommendations for improvement in the situation without social upheaval.

There are few books on the subject of children and their welfare in Spain. Juan Luis Morales' work *El niño en la cultura española: ante la medicina y otras ciencias; la historia, las letras, las artes y las costumbres* (Madrid: Talleres Penitenciarios, 1960) (Children in Spanish society: as regards medicine and other sciences; history, learning, the arts and customs) represents the best introduction to the history of children in Spain, and includes a detailed bibliography of paediatrics.

492 Juvenile delinquency trends in Spain.

A. Serrano Gómez. *International Criminal Police Review*, vol. 35, no. 334 (Jan. 1980), p. 16-27.

This study is the first part of a paper submitted at the eighth International Criminology Congress which met in Lisbon in September 1978. The aim of the article is to provide a general view of the main aspects of juvenile delinquency in Spain. There is a strong emphasis on statistics to illustrate the major trends, which, in common with most west European countries, the author sees as providing conclusive proof of ever increasing juvenile crime in Spain.

493 A map of crime in sixteenth-century Spain.

I. A. A. Thompson. *Economic History Review*, vol. 21 (1968), p. 244-67.

The article points out how 'an analysis of the incidence and distribution of crime has obvious and important implications for the more general social and economic picture'. It includes two maps and statistical tables on the distribution of crime and criminals in Spain at the time, together with a bibliography.

Social welfare

494 The problem of confinement: an aspect of poor-relief in eighteenth-century Spain.

William James Callahan. *Hispanic American Historical Review*, vol. 51 (1971), p. 1-24.

'In eighteenth-century Spain few problems disturbed government authorities and educated opinion more than the presence of mendicants, vagabonds and the idle poor in virtually every city and town of the realm'. After 1750 the Spanish crown attempted to develop a system of poor-relief designed to limit the distribution of alms to the deserving poor and to impose severe restrictions upon the beggars, with the establishment at the same time of institutions of confinement. This article details the problems and policies which were involved.

495 **Psychiatry in Spain: past and present.**
John Chatel, Barbara Joe. *American Journal of Psychiatry*,
vol. 132, no. 11 (Nov. 1975), p. 1,182-86.
A short article which surveys the history of psychiatry in Spain, and discloses pioneering efforts in the establishment of mental institutions. Nevertheless, the authors note how Spanish psychiatrists today are less innovative than their counterparts in other countries. The importance of the church, attitudes towards the family, and other sociocultural factors are emphasized.

496 **La antropología médica en España.** (Medical anthropology in
Spain.)
Edited by Michael Kenny, Jesús M. de Miguel. Barcelona, Spain:
Editorial Anagrama, 1980. 353p. bibliog. (Bibliotecas Anagrama
de Antropología, no. 15).
Both authors are prolific writers in the field of sociology and anthropology. This perceptive study represents the first attempt to analyze the social anthropology of Spain from the point of view of health and sickness. The work comprises fifteen important studies by specialists in the field, half the papers having been written by non-Spaniards.

497 **Poverty and welfare in Habsburg Spain: the example of Toledo.**
Linda Martz. Cambridge, England: Cambridge University Press,
1983. 266p. bibliog. (Cambridge Latin American Studies).
This is the first book in English to focus on poor-relief in 16th and 17th-century Spain. The first part of this detailed and scholarly work discusses national issues and attitudes and the second part is devoted to Toledo, one of the most densely populated and important regions of Castile. Basing her account on primary sources, the authoress describes the services offered to the poor and the types of people who used them.

498 **Health in the Mediterranean region: a comparative analysis of the
health systems of Portugal, Spain, Italy, and Yugoslavia.**
Jesús M. de Miguel. Ann Arbor, Michigan: University
Microfilms, 1976. 2 vols.
A comparative analysis of three main variables: social class, rural-urban strata, and regional differences. This work was presented as the author's doctoral thesis at Yale University in 1976. For a more specific account see his 'Health in the Mediterranean region: the case of Spain' in *Revista Internacional de Sociología*, no. 5-6 (1973), p. 83-137.

499 **The Spanish health planning experience 1964-1975.**
Jesús M. de Miguel. *Social Science and Medicine*, vol. 9 (1975),
p. 451-59.
A critical analysis of health reform processes during these years of economic development. See also the author's 'The role of the medical profession in a non-

democratic country: the case of Spain' in *Health and the division of labour* edited by Margaret Stacey *et al.* (London: Croom Helm, 1977, p. 41-59).

Monopolistic structures and industrial analysis in Spain: the case of the pharmaceutical industry.
See item no. 635.

World Health Statistics Annual.
See item no. 689.

Politics

General (post-Franco)

500 **Franco's political legacy: from dictatorship to façade democracy.**
José Amodia. London: Allen Lane, 1977. 348p. map. bibliog.
This work, whilst attempting to dissect the institutions of Francoism, also provides an overall view of the Spanish political system 'at a key point in its history, when Franco's life is nearing its end and the structures of government he has created will have to stand by themselves'. It is useful for the information it imparts on many areas of political life under Franco.

501 **The Spanish political system: Franco's legacy.**
Ergasto Ramón Arango. Boulder, Colorado: Westview Press, 1978. 293p. bibliog. (Westview Special Studies in West European Politics and Society).
This work is divided into four parts covering the pre-Franco era, the Civil War, the Franco régime, and the post-Franco period. However, the bulk of the book is concerned with Spain under Franco, and provides a comprehensive analysis of the political system created by him.

502 **Democratic politics in Spain: Spanish politics after Franco.**
Edited by David S. Bell. London: Pinter, 1983. 203p. bibliog.
This work contains nine commissioned essays, whose linking theme 'is not so much the peculiarity of Spain as the comparability with parallel trends and factors in other parts of western Europe'. It is not only valuable for those interested in Spanish politics and political parties, but for anyone wishing to gain a greater understanding of the effects of transitional politics on many facets and institutions of Spanish life. The author also wrote *Eurocommunism and the Spanish Communist Party* (q.v.).

139

Politics. General (post-Franco)

503 **The political transformation of Spain after Franco.**
John F. Coverdale. New York; London: Praeger, 1979. 150p.
3 maps. (Praeger Special Studies).

The emphasis of this study is on the speed with which Spain has changed in the years since Franco's death in 1975. It discusses how the changes to democracy were made, with information gleaned from the press and conversations with Spaniards 'ranging from Prince Juan Carlos to taxi drivers'. In his conclusion the author assesses the problems which faced (and at the time of writing still face) the government of the day, with particular regard to economic problems, regionalism and unemployment. The author also wrote *Italian intervention in the Spanish Civil War* (Princeton, New Jersey: Princeton University Press, 1975).

504 **El proceso electoral.** (The electoral process.)
Jorge de Esteban. Barcelona, Spain: Editorial Labor, 1977. 384p.
bibliog. (Politeia).

This study was written at a time when Spain was holding its first free elections for forty years. As the author comments, to participate in the elections one needs to be informed politically, and this work sets out to provide information on the electoral process to a Spanish public which had grown ignorant of what elections really meant.

505 **The other western Europe: a political analysis of the smaller democracies.**
Earl H. Fry, Gregory A. Raymond, in collaboration with David E. Bohn, James L. Waite. Santa Barbara, California; Oxford, England: ABC-Clio Information Services, 1983. 2nd ed. 288p. bibliog. (Studies in International and Comparative Politics, no. 14).

The book as a whole aims to introduce students to the political systems of western European countries normally neglected in most texts on European politics. The second edition is revised and expanded from the first, which was published in 1980. The work includes a chapter entitled 'Iberian politics: beyond corporatism?' (p. 11-51), which looks at the two authoritarian régimes which had endured for decades in the Iberian Peninsula. Both came to an end in the mid-1970s. The chapter sets contemporary Spanish political behaviour in its historical, geographical and cultural contexts, and emphasizes the ethnic, linguistic and religious diversities which have played an important role in the Spanish party system.

506 **The Spanish public in political transition.**
Peter McDonough, Antonio López Pina, Samuel H. Barnes.
British Journal of Political Science, vol. 11, part 1 (Jan. 1981), p. 49-79.

A useful article which emphasizes the importance of the king in the political transition. The factors behind the relative smoothness of the transition are studied, with the analysis being based on national surveys conducted in 1978 and 1980.

507 **Political cleavages in Spain and the 1979 general election.**
José M. Maravall. *Government and Opposition*, vol. 14, no. 3
(summer 1979), p. 299-317.
With reference to the general election of March 1979 (the first constitutional
general election since the death of Franco in 1975), the author illustrates how the
transition from dictatorship to democracy in Spain highlights 'the ideological
moderation of the electorate . . . the continuities with past political cleavages
between Left and Right' and 'the threat to the new democracy coming from the
political violence of Basque separatists and from the activities of Francoist
groups'.

508 **The transition to democracy in Spain.**
José M. Maravall. London: Croom Helm; New York: St.
Martin's Press, 1982. 213p. bibliog.
A detailed analysis of the political development of Spain during a crucial period,
by the Professor of Political Sociology at the University of Madrid. It is divided
into three major sections, with a fourth smaller section as a conclusion. The first
covers political alignments and elections in Spain during the transition to
democracy; the second, ideological and material foundations of democracy; and
the third discusses the socialist alternative in Spain: socialism, communism and
the trade union movement.

509 **Spain: the struggle of democracy today.**
Constantine Christopher Menges. Beverly Hills, California;
London: Sage Publications, 1978. 80p. bibliog. (The Washington
Papers, vol. 6, no. 58).
A concise study which assesses the changes for the survival of democracy in Spain
after the 1977 elections, and also examines the political parties and system in
detail. It provides a useful insight into the struggle for real democracy in Spain
and summarizes the political progress made since Franco's death.

Politics and society in twentieth-century Spain.
See item no. 279.

Los militares en la transición política. (The armed forces during the
political transition.)
See item no. 565.

The press and the rebirth of Iberian democracy.
See item no. 905.

Political parties, groups and movements

510 Operation Ogro: the execution of Admiral Luis Carrero Blanco.

Julen Agirre. New York: Quadrangle and New York Times Book Co., 1975. 196p.

An excellent and full account of ETA (Basque Homeland and Freedom) from the inside, based on the transcripts of taped interviews with four young Basques who came to Madrid, lived in the city for a year, and on 20 December 1973 assassinated Carrero Blanco (the Prime Minister, and a close friend of General Franco) by dynamiting his car. The word 'Ogro' (meaning 'ogre') was the nickname given to Carrero Blanco because of his bushy eyebrows.

511 The Communist Party in Spain.

Víctor Alba, translated by Vincent G. Smith. New Brunswick, New Jersey; London: Transaction Books, 1983. 475p. bibliog.

A translation of the author's prize-winning work which was first published in Spanish in 1979. It is the first comprehensive English-language analysis of the social history of the Communist Party in Spain from its founding in 1920 to the resignation of its secretary-general, Santiago Carrillo, in 1982.

512 Mediterranean challenge 2: Eurocommunism and the Spanish Communist Party.

David S. Bell. Brighton, England: Sussex European Research Centre, 1979. 76p. bibliog. (Sussex European Papers, no. 4).

The author researched this subject in Spain from 1976 to 1979 and he emphasizes the distinctive characteristics of the Spanish Communist Party in contrast with those of other west European communist parties. The first part of the study deals with the history and development of the PCE (Partido Comunista Español) up to and including the 1979 elections. The second and third parts look at the theory and practice of communist doctrine and party organization, which the Spanish communists have altered, and their views on European integration and defence.

513 Carlism and crisis in Spain, 1931-1939.

Martin Blinkhorn. Cambridge, England: Cambridge University Press, 1975. 394p. map. bibliog.

'Carlism represents the outstanding example of a popular movement of the ultra-conservative, as distinct from the fascist right'. This is the first study in English of that movement, which originally sought to restore a religiously inspired corporative monarch focused on Don Carlos, heir presumptive to the Spanish throne in 1833. The Carlists' activities during the 1930s began with their plotting against the Second Republic, and participation in the rising of 1936. The author studies Carlism's internal politics and ideology, and its relations with other elements in the Spanish Right.

514   **The Spanish anarchists: the heroic years 1868-1936.**
Murray Bookchin.   New York: Free Life Editions, 1977. 344p.
map. bibliog.

The first comprehensive account in English of the largest anarchist movement in the world, which began with the Italian anarchist Giuseppi Fanelli's visit to Spain in 1868, a time of great political unrest. Small groups of working-class intellectuals in Barcelona and Madrid, originally followers of Pí y Margall's federalist movement, were converted to revolutionary socialism. The important anarchist union, the CNT (National Confederation of Workers), was founded in 1910, and by 1936 had a membership of around one million. Bookchin's work analyzes thoroughly the theories, heroes, conflicts, repression and evolution of the movement. Another interesting work on the anarchists is *A new world in our hearts* edited by Albert Meltzer (Sanday, Orkney: Cienfuegos Press, 1978), which, in the course of seven articles, offers a brief history of Spanish anarchism, and examines its aims and achievements.

515   **Dialogue on Spain.**
Santiago Carrillo.   London: Lawrence & Wishart, 1976. 222p.

A transcript of a conversation between Carrillo and Régis Debray and Max Gallo, just prior to Franco's death in 1975. Carrillo was secretary-general of the Spanish Communist Party from 1960 to 1982, when he resigned after his party's poor showing in the 1982 elections. He was a staunch supporter of Eurocommunism, a fact which often led him into conflict with other members of the party. In this book he responds to questions put to him covering his life, political thoughts, recollections of the Civil War, and his party's domestic and foreign policies.

516   **The Basque insurgents: E.T.A. 1952-1980.**
Robert P. Clark.   Madison, Wisconsin; London: University of
Wisconsin Press, 1984. 328p. 6 maps. bibliog.

A perceptive and fascinating work (and the first in English), which describes, analyzes and interprets one of Europe's leading insurgent movements, which has been fighting for more than twenty years for the independence of the Basque provinces of Spain and France. This volume is intended as a sequel to the author's earlier work *The Basques: the Franco years and beyond* (q.v.). It is divided into two main sections, the first covering the origins and ideology of ETA, and the second providing detailed information on the patterns of ETA violence, and the organization's relationship with the Basque people and the Spanish State.

517   **Political parties of the world.**
Compiled and edited by Alan J. Day, Henry W. Degenhardt.
Harlow, England: Longman, 1980. 432p.

The section on Spain (p. 301-06) lists all the major Spanish political parties with the dates they were established, their history, membership, orientation, structure, publications and international affiliates.

Politics. Political parties, groups and movements

518 **Historia de E.T.A.** (The history of ETA.)
José Mari Garmendia. San Sebastián, Spain: Haranburu, 1979-
80. 2 vols.

A comprehensive two-volume study of the Basque terrorist-freedom organization.
Volume 1 covers the period from 1958 to 1967, and analyzes its political
evolution; volume 2 covers from 1968 to the present, and the ultimate split into
two factions. Proclamations and letters issued by ETA itself are also included.

519 **The European Left: Italy, France, and Spain.**
Edited by William E. Griffith. Lexington, Massachussetts: D. C.
Heath, 1979. 260p. bibliog.

This useful survey developed as a result of a conference of the Left in Latin
Europe, which was held at the Bologna Center of the School for Advanced
International Studies at the Johns Hopkins University in September 1978. The
Left in Spain virtually appeared from hibernation after the long reign of General
Franco, with Spanish socialism and communism being forged in the underground
and exile struggle against him. The editor comments that it would be highly
unlikely for the PSOE (Spanish Socialist Workers' Party) to form a government in
the near future in Spain: three years later it did so.

520 **The Communists in Spain: study of an underground political
movement.**
Guy Hermet, translated from the French by S. Seago,
H. Fox. Farnborough, England: Saxon House; Lexington,
Massachussetts: Lexington Books, 1974. 238p. bibliog. (Saxon
House Studies).

A full and objective study of the Spanish Communist Party under Franco's
régime, tracing the origins of the party in the 1920s to its workings up to 1971.
Whilst studying the party as an underground clandestine organization in the days
of Franco, it also provides an extremely useful and detailed analysis of the politics
of the period generally.

521 **Spanish separatism: E.T.A.'s threat to Basque democracy.**
Peter Janke. London: The Institute for the Study of Conflict,
1980. 19p. map. bibliog. (Conflict Studies, no. 123).

This short study explains how, despite Juan Carlos's and the government's efforts
in transforming Spain into a constitutional monarchy with democratic institutions,
the problems posed by ETA have remained. It charts the course of the violence
from its beginnings to its often dramatic heights, examines ETA's aims and
support, assesses the threat it poses to the nation and how the State has
responded.

522 **Anarchists of Andalusia 1868-1903.**
Temma Kaplan. Princeton, New Jersey: Princeton University
Press, 1977. 266p. bibliog.

The only sustained mass movement based on anarchism which has occurred anywhere flourished in Andalusia, particularly in the province of Cádiz, from about 1868 to 1903. This detailed study focuses on the social and economic context of the movement, and the authoress has used police reports in local archives to reconstruct the lives of over 300 rank-and-file anarchists. The Andalusian movement is shown as one which was highly organized and dedicated to defending workers' rights through a wide range of organizations, including trade unions, workers' circles and women's societies, all of which favoured general strikes rather than terrorism. Kaplan also wrote the chapter entitled 'Women and Spanish anarchism' in *Becoming visible: women in European history* edited by Claudia Koonz and Renate Bridenthal (Boston, Massachussetts: Houghton Mifflin, 1977), and 'Spanish anarchism and women's liberation' in the *Journal of Contemporary History*, vol. 6, no. 2 (1971), p. 101-10.

523 **Red years/black years: a political history of Spanish anarchism, 1911-1937.**
Robert W. Kern. Philadelphia: Institute for the Study of Human
Issues, 1978. 335p. 6 maps. bibliog.

The book opens in 1911 with the emergence of the CNT (National Confederation of Workers), and the foundation of the FAI (Iberian Anarchist Federation) in 1927. It proceeds to look at the early attempts to organize the working classes, the exile of the anarchists (declared illegal during the dictatorship of Miguel Primo de Rivera), and the collapse of the movement in 1937. The emphasis is on anarchist politics, although the author comments that to some extent 'the book is a group biography of the major Spanish anarchists, for I felt that this biographical technique might capture nuances of the movement that might otherwise be lost'.

524 **Political forces in Spain, Greece and Portugal.**
Beate Kohler, translated by Frank Carter, Ginnie Hole. London:
Butterworth Scientific, 1982. 281p. bibliog. (Butterworths
European Studies).

This book is an analysis of the political parties of the three countries which applied for membership of the European Economic Community after emerging from dictatorial political régimes. Part 1 is devoted to Spain, and in particular the transition to democracy, together with the alignment of political forces and the political development in the country in the perspective of EEC membership. It describes the various parties, assesses their historical development, current policies and future prospects.

525 **The communist parties of Italy, France and Spain: postwar change and continuity: a casebook.**
Edited by Peter Lange, Maurizio Vannicelli. London: Allen & Unwin, 1981. 385p. bibliog. (Casebook Series on European Politics and Society, no. 1).

A basic study of Eurocommunism, with a wide-ranging presentation of the major documents of the communist parties of these three countries. Fundamentally, the volume provides a comparative study of the development of the parties since the Second World War. The documents are arranged into five sections covering general strategy, alliances, party organization, international policy and policy towards the communist movement. The work is aimed at teachers, students and researchers of comparative European politics.

526 **Conservative politics in western Europe.**
Edited by Zig Layton-Henry. London: Macmillan, 1982. 352p. bibliog.

Chapter 12 (p. 292-317) is entitled 'Spanish conservative politics' by Kenneth Medhurst, in which the author seeks to examine Spanish conservative politics in the light of the idea that 'in this century forces of moderate conservatism have appeared readily to yield to more intransigent modes of right-wing activity'. It also discusses the reasons for the re-emergence, since Franco's death, of a more distinctly conservative style of politics. The various sections cover: the 19th- and early 20th-century background; the crisis of the 1930s; Franco's régime; political change in the Franco era; the post-Franco era; and the conservative parties in contemporary Spain.

527 **Les partis politiques en Espagne.** (Spanish political parties.)
Pierre Letamendia. Paris: Presses Universitaires de France, 1983. 127p. bibliog. (Que Sais-je?, no. 2051).

A detailed and well-organized history of political parties in Spain, which looks at the history of the Spanish party system from 1812 to 1975, and the restructuring of the system between 1975 and 1977. Each of the major parties of present-day Spain is looked at individually: the UCD (Union of the Democratic Centre); the PSOE (Spanish Socialist Workers' Party); the PCE (Spanish Communist Party); the AP (Popular Alliance); and the nationalist and regional parties of Catalonia and the Basque Provinces. In conclusion the author offers his views on the relative strengths and weaknesses of the parties after the 1982 elections.

528 **Party systems and voter alignments: cross-national perspectives.**
Edited by Seymour Martin Lipset, Stein Rokkan. New York: The Free Press; London: Collier-Macmillan, 1967. 554p. bibliog. (International Yearbook of Political Behavior Research, vol. 7).

Chapter 5 (p. 197-282) is entitled 'The party system of Spain: past and future' by Juan J. Linz which studies the reasons for the weakness of the traditional Spanish parties before 1936, comparing the situation in Spain with that existing in Italy in the early 1920s. Linz believes that by closely analyzing the elections between 1910 and 1936 it is possible to gain a key understanding of the complex politics of the period.

529 **Moderates and conservatives in western Europe: political parties, the European Community and the Atlantic alliance.**
Edited by Roger Morgan, Stefano Silvestri. London: Heinemann Educational Books, 1982. 280p.

'The Spanish centre parties' (p. 135-61) by Antonio Marquina Barrio studies the two principal parties of the centre-Right in Spain, Alianza Popular (Popular Alliance) and Unión del Centro Democrático (Union of the Democratic Centre), examining their policies and attitudes towards the development of the European Economic Community and the Atlantic alliance. The author is Professor of Political Science at the Complutense University of Madrid.

530 **Communism and political change in Spain.**
Eusebio Mujal-León. Bloomington, Indiana: Indiana University Press, 1983. 274p. bibliog.

The Communist Party in Spain was a clandestine organization for four decades prior to Franco's death in 1975, until it was officially legalized in April 1977. This detailed work covers the past twenty-five years of its history, and analyzes its failure to provide the most effective opposition force in the country after Franco. In the 1982 elections the communists received only 3.8 per cent of the popular vote, compared with the socialists' 46 per cent. The author concludes by speculating on the prospects for communism in Spain.

531 **Falange: a history of Spanish fascism.**
Stanley G. Payne. Stanford, California: Stanford University Press; London: Oxford University Press, 1962. 316p. bibliog.

This is the standard work in English offering a thorough analysis of the effects of fascism on Spain. The Falange was the creation of José Antonio Primo de Rivera (son of the dictator Miguel) in the early 1930s. The author attempts to provide a balanced and objective account, describing the background of the movement, the life of Primo de Rivera, and the influence of the Falange on politics in Spain between 1936 and 1960. This book provides the other side to the picture which is lacking in Gabriel Jackson's *The Spanish Republic and the Civil War 1931-1939* (q.v.).

532 **Electoral participation: a comparative analysis.**
Edited by Richard Rose. London; Beverly Hills, California: Sage, 1980. 354p. bibliog. (Sage Studies in Contemporary Political Sociology).

'The new Spanish party system' (p. 101-89) by Juan J. Linz presents a detailed study of the party system in Spain under the new democracy, using public opinion and electoral data to characterize the different parties and their social bases. Events in Spain are also related to developments in other Mediterranean countries. Numerous tables are included, presenting detailed information and statistics on electoral behaviour and the political parties themselves.

Politics. Political parties, groups and movements

533 **Spanish political parties: before and after the election.**
Jonathan Story. *Government and Opposition*, vol. 12, no. 4
(autumn 1977), p. 474-95.

This general survey considers the political parties before and after the 1977
elections, in which 156 were registered, presenting a total of some 6,000
candidates for 557 seats in the Cortes (the Spanish parliament).

534 **Reappraisals of fascism.**
Edited by Henry A. Turner. New York: New Viewpoints, 1975.
238p. bibliog. (Modern Scholarship on European History).

This work contains a chapter by Stanley G. Payne entitled 'Spanish fascism in
comparative perspective' (p. 142-69). In it he considers the question of which
individuals and groups in Spain could properly be regarded as fascist throughout
the course of the 20th century. Another historical study of fascism in Spain has
been made by Paul Preston in *Fascism in Europe*, edited by S. J. Woolf (London;
New York: Methuen, 1981). Preston's analysis (p. 329-51) covers many aspects of
the Spanish Right in the 1930s, and particularly the strongly debated role of the
authoritarian Catholic CEDA (Spanish Confederation of Autonomous Right).

535 **Anarchism: a history of libertarian ideas and movements.**
G. Woodcock. Harmondsworth, England: Penguin Books, 1963.
492p. bibliog.

Reprinted in 1983, this work contains a chapter entitled 'Anarchism in Spain' (p.
335-75) which traces the history and development of Spanish anarchism to the
strength it had achieved by the time of the Civil War. It was quickly destroyed,
however, when in March 1939 nationalist troops marched into Barcelona (the
focal point of Spanish anarchism) without a single worker going on strike or a
single shot being fired. In 1976 the CNT (National Confederation of Workers),
the anarcho-syndicalist trade union, re-emerged, and in May 1977 was officially
given legal status. The CNT is now seen by many as the largest radical
organization in Spain, rather than the smallest of the major union centres.

The Spanish revolution.
See item no. 280.

**The coming of the Spanish Civil War: reform reaction and revolution in
the Second Republic.**
See item no. 281.

**The origins of Franco's Spain: the Right, the Republic and revolution,
1931-1936.**
See item no. 284.

**Authoritarian politics in modern society: the dynamics of established one-
party systems.**
See item no. 298.

148

Constitution and Legal System

Constitution

536 **Constitución española: edición comentada.** (The Spanish
constitution: a critical edition.)
Madrid: Centro de Estudios Constitucionales, 1979. 413p.

A collaborative work by many specialists involved in studying in detail the
significance of the recent (1978) changes to the Spanish constitution. This
'commentary' tries to explain what the constitution actually means and how it
operates. It comments individually on all 169 articles, and includes a
comprehensive index relating all aspects to the relevant article in the text of the
constitution.

537 **Las constituciones de España.** (The constitutions of Spain.)
Jorge de Esteban.   Madrid: Taurus, 1982. 343p. bibliog. (Textos
Auxiliares, no. 1).

The author has written many works on Spanish constitutional history. This
particular book, which is a preliminary study, is aimed at two groups of readers:
the first being students of law, and students of Spanish history and politics; the
second, the general reader, in order to provide an overall picture of constitutional
history. The work analyzes the evolution and significance of the Spanish
constitutional process from its beginnings to the present day, and includes the
texts of all Spanish constitutions.

538 **The Spanish constitution.**
H. R. G. Greaves.   London: Hogarth Press, 1933. 47p. bibliog.
(Day To Day Pamphlets, no. 15).

The volume was published by Leonard and Virginia Woolf through the Hogarth
Press and the author was a lecturer at the London School of Economics and

Political Science. This is a short but clear description of the origins and significance of Spanish constitutions, and in particular the constitution of 1931.

539 **Religious conflict and consensus in Spain: a tale of two constitutions.**
Richard Gunther, Roger A. Blough. *World Affairs: a Quarterly Review of International Problems*, vol. 143, no. 4 (spring 1981), p. 366-412.

This article compares the manner in which important church-State relations were treated by the framers of Spain's two most recent democratic constitutions of 1931 and 1978. It also attempts to explain why these two constitutions are so dramatically different in their treatment of religious issues. The authors conclude that "unlike their predecessors in 1931, the contemporary Spanish elites have produced 'a Constitution born out of the cooperation of all political forces' ".

540 **The Cortes and the king: constitutional monarchy in the Iberian world.**
Francis J. D. Lambert. Glasgow: University of Glasgow Institute of Latin American Studies, 1981. 25p. bibliog. (Occasional Papers, no. 32).

Iberian constitutional monarchies have been neglected by researchers until recently, and this concise work is a comparative study of constitutional monarchy in Spain, Portugal and Brazil. The author discusses the differences and shared features of the three, and sees the restoration of the monarchy in Spain as providing new order and freedom (which in 1981 had still to prove itself).

541 **Aproximación al derecho constitucional español: la constitución de 1978.** (An approach to Spanish constitutional law: the constitution of 1978.)
Manuel Martínez Sospedra. Valencia, Spain: Fernando Torres, 1980. 314p. bibliog. (Colección Ciencias Sociales, no. 5).

This detailed work is aimed at the general reader and university student alike, in that, through its clear and easy-to-understand style, it presents an objective analysis of the constitution of 1978, and avoids the over-use of legal terminology. It is divided into four parts covering: the fundamental laws of the constitution; the territorial structure of the State (statutes related to the autonomous regions); bases of power (the monarchy, parliament, the government and judicial power); and constitutional guarantees. It includes three appendixes covering referenda, electoral legislation and the general elections of 1977 and 1979.

542 **Constituciones y períodos constituyentes en España (1808-1936).**
(Constitutions and constituent periods in Spain, 1808-1936.)
Jordi Solé Tura, Eliseo Aja. Madrid: Siglo Veintiuno Editores, 1979. 5th ed. 175p. bibliog. (Estudios de Historia Contemporánea, Siglo XXI).

Solé Tura was a member of the committee charged with drawing up the constitution of 1978. This book represents a thorough constitutional history of

Spain, and includes a section which provides documents relating to the 1845, 1869, 1876 and 1931 constitutions.

543 **The Spanish constitution of 1978.**
Madrid: Servicio Central de Publicaciones/Presidencia del Gobierno, 1978. 45p. (Documentación Administrativa, no. 180).
The complete constitution in English, published by the government, and available from the Spanish Embassy in London. Unfortunately it contains many typographical errors, and does not include an index. The new constitution established a parliamentary monarchy, with legislative power vested in the Cortes, a bicameral parliament composed of the Congreso de Diputados (Congress of Deputies-lower house) and the Senado (Senate-upper house). The Congress has not less than 300 and no more than 400 members, who are all elected in a proportional system in relation to the population of each province. The members of the Senate are elected in a majority system and executive power is vested in the president (i.e. the Prime Minister).

544 **Manual of Spanish constitutions 1808-1931: translation and introduction.**
Arnold R. Verduin. Ypsolanti, Michigan: University Lithoprinters, 1941. 99p. bibliog.
An excellent work for following the political evolution and constitutional developments in Spain over nearly a century and a half. The author provides an introduction to each constitution, placing it in context, and giving the full text in English. The work contains: the constitution of 1808; 1812 (Cortes of Cádiz); the Royal Charter of 1834; the constitution of 1837; the constitution of 1845; the constitutional project of 1856; the constitution of 1869; the republican project of 1873; the constitution of 1876; and the constitution of 1931. It was published in a small edition and may be hard to come by.

The influence of international labour conventions on labour law and social change in Spain.
See item no. 668.

Legal system

545 **Fresh winds on rotted sails: Spanish legal reforms, American parallels, and the Cuban socialist alternative – a reply to Antonio Beristain.**
James P. Brady. *International Journal of the Sociology of Law*, vol. 9, no. 2 (1981), p. 177-200.
This scholarly article 'critically evaluates contemporary Spanish legal reforms in the light of Spanish history and political economy and in comparison with similar

reforms undertaken at the turn of the century in the U.S.A.'. It is basically a reply to Beristain's article concerning the treatment of delinquents (q.v.). Brady argues that 'liberals like Beristain' praise the legal reforms which occured after Franco's death oblivious to the fact that these reforms 'are easily recognized as the same tattered "solutions" enacted long ago in more developed western nations where they have failed to provide either fairness or security'.

546 **Lawsuits and litigants in Castile, 1500-1700.**
Richard L. Kagan.   Chapel Hill, North Carolina: University of North Carolina Press, 1981. 274p. map. bibliog.

The author explores the dramatic rise in litigation procedures in the course of the 16th century, and the importance of lawsuits in Castile during the 16th and 17th centuries. Part 1 is principally concerned with the economic, social, legal and political changes in Castile which precipitated an increase in the volume of civil litigation. Part 2 tries to establish why Castile's 'legal revolution' ran out of steam, leading to a decline in litigation and the stagnation of the courts and tribunals.

547 **Hispanic law: until the end of the Middle Ages.**
Eelco Nicolas Van Kleffens.   Edinburgh: Edinburgh University Press, 1968. 382p. bibliog.

A Dutch lawyer traces the origins and development of Hispanic law, emphasizing the ethnic, linguistic and historic characteristics of Hispanic jurisprudence and its influence after the 16th century in Spain, the Americas, Asia and Africa. The study provides a thorough analysis of the development of Spanish law under Alfonso X ('el Sabio' – the Wise), and in particular 'Las Siete Partidas' (a seven-part code of the varied laws of the time, which were basically of Gothic origin) and their later influence. They defined the roles of religion and the church, emperors, kings and noblemen, justice, marriage and blood relations, contractual obligations, last wills and estates, and penal law. Appendixes list the contents of the 'Fuero Juzgo', 'Fuero Real de Castilla', and 'Las Siete Partidas'.

548 **Spain and the rule of law.**
Geneva, Switzerland: International Commission of Jurists, 1962. 153p.

A report which is concerned with the extent of the observation of the rule of law in Spain between 1936 and 1962. Despite its age, the report remains useful for its factual and documentary material on the legal system under Franco.

549 **The Spanish judiciary: a sociological study. Justice in a civil law country undergoing social change under an authoritarian regime.**
José-Juan Toharia.   Ann Arbor, Michigan: University Microfilms, 1975. 692p. map. bibliog.

Originally presented as the author's doctoral thesis at Yale University in 1974, this is a sociological analysis of judges and the legal system under Franco. It was later published in a revised form in Spanish as *El juez español* (The Spanish judge) (Madrid: Tecnos, 1975).

Law and society in the Visigothic kingdom.
See item no. 164.

International Labour Review.
See item no. 675.

Protective legislation and equal opportunity and treatment for women in Spain.
See item no. 676.

Guide to the law and legal literature of Spain.
See item no. 971.

Government and Administration

550 **Las fuerzas del orden público.** (The forces of public order.)
M. Ballbé, M. Giró. Barcelona, Spain: Dopesa, 1978. 79p.
(Colección 'Los Marginados').

A short study of all aspects of the Spanish police force, in which the authors argue strongly for a democratization of the forces of public order in line with the political system in Spain since Franco's death, and a movement away from the virtual integration of the police into the armed forces. Another work, *La policía y sus sindicatos en España* (The police force and its trade unions in Spain) by Mauricio Moya Lucendo (Madrid: Editorial Fundamentos, 1982), looks in particular at the USP (Union of Police Forces' Trade Unions), of which the author was a founder member.

551 **La administración española: estudios de ciencia administrativa.**
(Spanish administration: studies in administrative science.)
Eduardo García de Enterría. Madrid: Alianza Editorial, 1972.
165p. bibliog. (El Libro de Bolsillo; Sección: Humanidades,
vol. 389).

The author is the driving force behind the continuing study and reappraisal of administrative science in Spain since the 1920s. The above work presents a basic history of administration in Spain, discussing its history, structure and problems, both regional and national.

552 **The Spanish public service.**
Alberto Gutiérrez Reñón. *International Review of Administrative Sciences*, vol. 35, nos. 2-3 (1969), p. 133-40.

Although this article is now quite old, it still remains useful for its background information on the organization of public administration in Spain during Franco's rule. The author provides a brief general survey, and discusses the number and classes of public employees, the framework of laws and regulations, recruitment and aspects of the career of the public servant. The author also contributed to the book *Estudios sobre la burocracia española* (Studies on Spanish bureaucracy) (Madrid: Instituto de Estudios Políticos, 1974).

553 International Review of Administrative Sciences, vol. 46, no. 1 (1980).

This journal is published by the International Institute of Administrative Sciences in three editions (English, French, Spanish). This particular issue (134p.) is wholly devoted to public administration and administrative laws in Spain. All the articles are in Spanish with summaries in English, and cover all aspects of the subject in the post-Franco era.

554 How Spain is run.

James Robert Jump. London: Harrap, 1981. 32p. map. (Discovering Spain).

A short general study of government and administration in Spain. The transition to democracy is observed through sections on the monarchy, parliament, the welfare state, law and order, the armed forces, foreign relations, taxation, consumer protection and industry.

555 The Spanish ministerial elite, 1938-1969.

Paul H. Lewis. *Comparative Politics*, vol. 5, no. 1 (Oct. 1972), p. 83-106.

An attempt to analyze the ministerial administration of the Council of Ministers under Franco over three decades. It charts: the trends in recruitment to the council; staff turnover; the average age of ministers between 1938 and 1968; length of tenure in office; the average age of promotions; occupational background of ministers; and regional representation on the council. The author concludes that the Franco régime displayed more adaptability to change than that of other dictatorships in its bureaucratic workings.

556 Government in Spain: the executive at work.

Kenneth N. Medhurst. Oxford, England; New York: Pergamon Press, 1973. 256p. bibliog. (The Commonwealth and International Library. Governments of Western Europe).

A thorough dissection of the institutions of Francoism, with sections on the political system; the workings of the government; the civil service; ministerial departments; national and local administration; and the legal system.

557 The government and administration of metropolitan areas in western democracies: a survey of approaches to the administrative problems of major conurbations in Europe and Canada.

Alan Norton. Birmingham, England: University of Birmingham, Institute of Local Government Studies, 1983. 60p.

This book contains a short chapter entitled 'Spain: the metropolitan administration of Greater Barcelona and Madrid' (p. 33-42) which analyzes the two largest metropolitan areas of Spain, and looks at their finances, services and problems.

558 **Sociología de la administración pública española.** (The sociology of Spanish public administration.)
Madrid: Centro de Estudios Sociales de la Santa Cruz del Valle de los Caídos, 1968. 392p. (Anales de Moral Social y Económica, vol. 17).

There are over a dozen contributors to this work, which represents one of the best sources of information on public administration in Spain. All aspects are covered, including: historical structure; ideology; social stratification; age of public servants; salaries; administrative reform; public and private bureaucracies; and a comparison of public administration in Spain with that of other European countries.

Curia and Cortes in León and Castile 1072-1295.
See item no. 188.

War and government in Habsburg Spain 1560-1620.
See item no. 224.

The government of Sicily under Philip II of Spain: a study in the practice of empire.
See item no. 327.

Armed Forces

559 **Buques de guerra españoles 1885-1971.** (Spanish warships 1885-
1971.)
Alfredo Aguilera. Madrid: Editorial San Martín, 1972. 2nd ed.
147p. bibliog.

Spain is a country with a great naval history, and this richly illustrated book
covers all types of ships and submarines of the said period (which begins with the
year in which steam ships really took over from sailing vessels). Along with
general comments, there are also technical details on displacement and size,
speed, propulsion, armaments, protection and crew numbers.

560 **Historia política del ejército español.** (A political history of the
Spanish army.)
José Ramón Alonso. Madrid: Editora Nacional, 1974. 567p.
bibliog.

The author was at one time director of Radio Nacional de España (Spanish
National Radio). This study describes how the army has played, and continues to
play, a vital role in Spain's political history, and spans the years 1700 to 1931. It
emphasizes just how much influence the army in general, and individual officers,
have exerted on all areas of Spanish life. Alonso traces its development,
organization, successes and failures, and provides a bibliography of nearly forty
pages, containing one thousand references. It should also be noted that the first
volume of a nine-volume work on the military history of Spain has just been
published and the whole work will provide the most comprehensive study of the
subject in Spanish: Ricardo de Cierva y de Hoces' *Historia militar de España* (A
military history of Spain) (Barcelona: Planeta, 1984- .).

Armed Forces

561 Spanish and Portuguese military aviation.
John M. Andrade. Leicester, England: Midland Counties
Publications, 1977. 120p. map.

This book is primarily intended for the aviation historian, but it is also of interest
to those who wish to know more about the historical background and current
state of Spanish military aviation. It includes over thirty pages of photographs
showing aircraft of the Spanish Air Force and the Spanish Naval Air Service,
together with a map of Spanish and Portuguese military airfields, and a glossary of
military terms. In his introduction the author refers readers to the Spanish
aviation monthly *Flaps*, which is available from specialist aviation bookshops in
this country.

562 El militar de carrera en España: estudio de sociología militar.
(The professional soldier in Spain: a study of military sociology.)
Julio Busquets Bragulat. Barcelona, Spain: Ediciones Ariel,
1971. 2nd ed. 298p. 6 maps. bibliog. (Demos: Biblioteca de
Sociología). (Publicaciones del Departamento de Sociología de la
Universidad de Madrid: Estudios y Monografías).

An extremely important study of military sociology by a former army major,
whose actions and writings in defence of democracy caused him to be arrested six
times. After retiring from the army, he ran as a candidate in the 1977 elections,
and was elected as a deputy for the Socialist Party of Catalonia. This work, which
was originally banned by Franco, offers a thorough analysis of the emergence and
transformation of the military profession in Spain. It is divided into two parts: the
first discusses the Spanish armed forces from 1808 to 1936; the second covers the
period under Franco from 1939 to 1969.

563 The origins of military power in Spain 1800-1854.
Eric Christiansen. London: Oxford University Press, 1967. 193p.
map. bibliog. (Oxford Historical Monographs).

An excellent study of the political influence of the army up to the First Carlist
War (1833) and during the decade before the 1854 revolt. It does not attempt to
provide a definitive military history of Spain, nor a social history of the Spanish
army. Rather, it analyzes the political activities of the army, which are considered
chronologically from the emergence of a political army between 1800 and 1832, to
the military opposition 1848-54, and the role of the generals in the Cortes. For an
easy-to-read general study of the Spanish army during the War of Independence
(1808-14) see Otto von Pivka's *Spanish armies of the Napoleonic wars* (London:
Osprey, 1975), which discusses all aspects of the army, including uniforms, the
number of soldiers and fighting capabilities.

564 The leather jacket soldier: Spanish military equipment and institutions of the late eighteenth century.
Odie B. Faulk. Pasadena, California: Socio-Technical
Publications, 1971. 80p. bibliog.

A general consideration of the role and equipment of the Spanish soldier in the

Spanish borderlands of western America. Although the Spaniards never conquered the Indians, they succeeded in holding them at bay so that the Spanish frontier did not recede. The author also discusses the social conditions under which the 'soldados de cuero' existed. For a more detailed and scholarly study of the history of a particular regiment operating in the borderlands, see Janet R. Fireman's *The Spanish Royal Corps of Engineers in the western borderlands: instrument of Bourbon reform 1764 to 1815* (Glendale, California: Arthur H. Clark, 1977).

565 **Los militares en la transición política.** (The armed forces during the political transition.)

Carlos Fernández Santander. Barcelona, Spain: Argos Vergara, 1982. 348p. bibliog. (Primera Plana, no. 12).

The author is the son of a notable military man, and has written several articles on military affairs in Spain. This book represents an objective study and analysis of the role of the army in the recent political transition, from the death of Franco in November 1975 to the end of 1978 and the new constitution. It highlights in particular the numerous military moves, statements and policies which influenced, and were influenced by, events which occurred at this time of radical political change.

566 **The Mediterranean naval situation 1908-1914.**

Edited by Paul G. Halpern. Cambridge, Massachussetts: Harvard University Press, 1971. 415p. bibliog. (Harvard Historical Studies, vol. 86).

Chapter 10 (p. 280-313) is entitled 'Spain and Russia: ambitious naval powers', and discusses how Spain set about renewing her fleet during the crucial period leading up to the outbreak of the First World War. The bulk of the Spanish navy had been destroyed in 1898 by the Americans at the time of the loss of Cuba. In 1908 a naval law provided for the construction of a number of ships which were to form the nucleus of a new Spanish fleet. Although a minor naval power, Spain represented a potentially important factor in the Mediterranean in the years before 1914.

567 **The geo-strategic importance of the Iberian Peninsula.**

Stewart Menaul. *Conflict Studies*, no. 133 (1981).

This study comprises the whole issue (25p.) and is a concise study of Spain's armed forces and their role in the European sphere. Although written before Spain actually became a member of NATO, the information it imparts on Spain's military and geo-political importance remains useful. The author argues that Spain's armed forces will make a significant contribution to the defence of the west – her air defence system being especially important. There is also an appendix providing statistics on the armed forces of Spain and Portugal.

568 **Politics and the military in modern Spain.**
Stanley G. Payne. Stanford, California: Stanford University
Press; London: Oxford University Press, 1967. 574p. 6 maps.
bibliog.

This book remains the standard work on the influence of the army on the
government of Spain during the last 150 years (centring on the period 1898 to
1939). Payne's conclusion is as relevant today as it was when it was first written:
'in the second half of the twentieth century, as during the preceeding one hundred
and fifty years, the role of the Spanish military remains dependent not upon the
ambition of generals but upon the stability of government institutions and the civil
maturity of Spanish society as a whole'.

569 **Los ejércitos españoles: las fuerzas armadas en la defensa nacional.**
(The Spanish armed services: the armed forces and national
defence.)
César Ruiz-Ocaña Remiro. Madrid: Editorial San Martín, 1980.
447p. 7 maps. bibliog.

A very useful study, and one of the few which encompasses all branches of the
armed forces in Spain: the air force, the army and the navy, as well as the state
security forces such as the Civil Guard and the national police. The author
considers the costs of defence as a proportion of GNP; NATO and the EEC
alliances; and relations between the armed forces and the State during the past
century.

570 **El ejército de los Reyes Católicos.** (The army of the Catholic
Monarchs.)
Jorge Vigón. Madrid: Editora Nacional, 1968. 274p. bibliog.
(Mundo Científico: Serie Castrense).

An informative and illustrated work, covering all aspects of the army of
Ferdinand and Isabella including recruitment, organization, training, discipline,
weapons and their fabrication. In particular the author emphasizes how important
the army was in the context of providing solutions to the many political problems
of their reign. An interesting table on soldiers' pay from 1407 to 1517 is included.

A society organized for war: medieval Spain.
See item no. 180.

Praetorian politics in liberal Spain.
See item no. 230.

**The army of Flanders and the Spanish road 1567-1659: the logistics of
Spanish victory and defeat in the Low Countries' wars.**
See item no. 336.

Foreign Relations

571 **Spain in the twentieth-century world: essays on Spanish diplomacy, 1898-1978.**
Edited by James W. Cortada. Westport, Connecticut: Greenwood Press; London: Aldwych Press, 1980. 294p. bibliog. (Contributions in Political Science, no. 30).

'The purpose of this book is to provide a perspective on Spain's position in world affairs today', with individual chapters being written by eminent specialists on contemporary Spanish affairs. 'Each essay, while based on historical perspective, provides a definition of the issues that have defined and will probably continue to define, political, economic, and cultural ties between Spain and the rest of the world'. This excellent study, edited by the foremost authority on Spain's foreign relations, complements his bibliography on the subject (q.v.). Part 1 considers the historical perspectives, and comprises two essays on Spanish foreign policy 1898-1936, and 1936-1978. Part 2 looks at Spain in the world, with essays on her relations with western Europe, North Africa, the Middle East, eastern Europe, the Soviet Union, Latin America, the Far East and the United States.

572 **Two nations over time: Spain and the United States 1776-1977.**
James W. Cortada. Westport, Connecticut; London: Greenwood Press, 1978. 305p. bibliog. (Contributions in American History, no. 74).

The definitive work on Spain-United States relations over the past two centuries. Whilst Cortada studies the general themes prevailing in these relations, the basic purpose of his book is to help clarify the issues and basic tenets involved. He also covers the cultural and economic relations, emphasizing how after the war between them in 1898 Spain became more and more orientated towards Europe. Another excellent study of Spain-United States relations, this time over the past forty years, is Richard R. Rubottom's and J. Carter Murphy's *Spain and the United States since World War Two* (New York: Praeger, 1984).

573 **Spain: N.A.T.O. or neutrality?**
H. P. Klepak. Kingston, Ontario: Centre for International
Relations, Queen's University, 1980. 224p. bibliog. (National
Security Series, no. 1/80).

Although written before Spain joined NATO in 1982, this report remains useful
for its examination of the implications of Spain's entry from both the perspective
of the Alliance and that of Spain. In the NATO context the author sets out the
political and military advantages and disadvantages for the Alliance. From the
Spanish viewpoint, the author emphasizes the difference of opinion on the NATO
decision between the domestic political factions. Indeed, the controversy in
present-day Spain is whether or not she should remain in NATO.

574 **La diplomacia vaticana y la España de Franco (1936-1945).**
(Vatican diplomacy and Franco's Spain, 1936-45.)
Antonio Marquina Barrio. Madrid: Consejo Superior de
Investigaciones Científicas, 1983. 710p. bibliog. (Instituto Enrique
Flórez: Monografías de Historia Eclesiástica, vol. 12).

This huge work analyzes in great detail the diplomatic relations between the
Vatican and Spain during the Civil War and the Second World War. The author
stresses the importance of the Vatican's official recognition of the Franco régime
to the Caudillo and the régime itself. The author studies the negotiations beween
the Vatican and the Franco government, and provides an extremely useful
documentary appendix of 150 items, covering nearly 400 pages.

575 **Renaissance diplomacy.**
Garrett Mattingly. Harmondsworth, England: Penguin
University Books, 1973. 313p. bibliog.

Although Spain is referred to throughout the book, chapters 14 and 15 (p. 131-45)
specifically examine Ferdinand's foreign policy and methods of diplomacy.
Ferdinand was the first Spanish monarch to experiment with resident ambassadors
and a real diplomatic code of conduct. 'As he watched his foreign service at work,
and as one European crisis after another increased his reliance on it, he remedied
its weaknesses'. During his reign (1474-1516) the most impressive diplomatic
service in Europe was built up, and remained dominant for well over a century.

576 **The Mediterranean challenge, 6: Spain, Greece and community
politics.**
G. Minet, J. Siotis, P. Tsakaloyannis. Falmer, England: Sussex
European Research Centre, University of Sussex, 1981. 161p.
bibliog. (Sussex European Papers, no. 11).

The first essay in this book (p. 1-83) is entitled 'Spanish and European diplomacy
at a crossroads' and is the work of G. Minet. It deals with the foreign polcy
implications of Spain's entry into the EEC by 1 January 1986. The author
discusses broadening the Community's diplomatic horizons to the Spanish-
speaking world at a time when Spain is also trying to balance her foreign policy
through increased contact with Latin America. The major question asked by

Minet is whether 'the Spanish posture is compatible or not with the European interest'. The chapter includes a list of references and an appendix on 'Spain's foreign trade' with the world as it was in 1980.

577 **Hispanismo, 1898-1936: Spanish conservatives and liberals and their relations with Spanish America.**
Frederick Braun Pike.   Notre Dame, Indiana; London: University of Notre Dame Press, 1971. 486p. 2 maps. bibliog. (University of Notre Dame International Studies of the Committee on International Relations).

A useful study of the cultural rivalry after the Spanish American War of 1898, centred on the concept of 'hispanismo': 'the conviction that through the course of history Spaniards have developed a lifestyle and culture, a set of characteristics, of traditions, and value judgements that render them distinct from all other peoples'. The work looks in detail at the ideology of 'hispanismo' with specific reference to Spain's relations with Spanish America up to the Spanish Civil War. There is also a chapter on Spanish emigration to South America between 1900 and 1930.

578 **Spain, the E.E.C. and N.A.T.O.**
Paul Preston, Denis Smyth.   London: Routledge & Kegan Paul, 1984. 96p. (Chatham House Papers, no. 22).

This work analyzes the paradoxical situation whereby NATO member states were happy to receive Spain into the Alliance in 1982, whilst many Spaniards had become firm opponents of participation in NATO defences. In contrast, widespread public support exists in Spain for integration into the European Community, at the same time as serious resistance (principally from France) remains within the EEC itself. The authors consider possible solutions to these problems currently affecting Spain's relations with two major strategic and economic blocs. Denis Smyth is also author of the forthcoming book *Diplomacy and strategy of survival: British policy and Franco's Spain, 1939-45* to be published by Cambridge University Press.

579 **Agony of a neutral: Spanish-German wartime relations and the 'Blue Division'.**
Raymond L. Proctor.   Moscow, Idaho: Idaho Research Foundation, 1974. 359p. 7 maps. bibliog.

This book represents an excellent and detailed analysis of Spanish-German relations, and Franco's success in avoiding German (and Allied) violation of Spanish territory. The author served in the United States army and air force throughout the Second World War, and prior to his retirement from military service was Director of Intelligence for the United States Defense Forces in Spain, Morocco and the western Mediterranean. Techically, the Spaniards fighting in German uniforms during the Second World War were members of the 250th Spanish Volunteer Infantry Division. However, from its inception to this day they have been known as the 'Blue Division', stemming from the blue shirts they wore as they made their way from Spain to Germany in order to fight on the northern sector of the Russian front from October 1941 to October 1943. The use of the 'Blue Division' is of central importance, as it symbolizes an aspect of the strained, almost tortured, series of events that constituted the wartime relations between Spain and Germany. These relations, which derived from the policies of the two countries during the Spanish Civil War, frequently raised questions about Spain's neutrality. The existence of the division was called into question during the United Nations' inquiry of 1946 into the so-called 'Spanish Question', and contributed to Spain's condemnation and temporary diplomatic isolation.

580 **Spain and the great powers 1936-1941.**
Dante Anthony Puzzo. New York; London: Columbia University Press, 1962. 296p. bibliog.

Puzzo sets Spain's relations with the great powers around the framework and events of the Spanish Civil War. He explains how Spain became the centre of world interest at that time, and how other countries were sucked into the conflict with Spain eventually becoming an 'axis satellite'. This discussion of Spain's domestic and international trials and tribulations involves an examination of the roles played by the six major powers: Great Britain; France; the United States; Germany; Italy; and the Soviet Union. Herbert Feis's book *The Spanish story: Franco and the nations at war* (New York: W. W. Norton, 1966) covers the same ground, but extends to 1944, and concentrates in detail on Spanish-United States relations during this period.

581 **Spain and the defense of the west: ally and liability.**
Arthur Preston Whitaker. New York: Harper, 1961. 408p. 2 maps. bibliog.

Published for the Council on Foreign Relations, the central theme of the study is the relationship, from 1945 onwards, between the United States and Spain under the agreements made in 1953 for the establishment of several joint air and naval bases in Spain. Whitaker also provides a perceptive look at the domestic evolution of Spain during the first two decades of Franco's rule.

Gibraltar.
See item no. 156.

Rock of contention: a history of Gibraltar.
See item no. 159.

The secret diplomacy of the Habsburgs, 1598-1625.
See item no. 195.

The Comintern and the Spanish Civil War.
See item no. 263.

Spain and Franco: the quest for international acceptance 1949-59.
See item no. 303.

Spain and Portugal: democratic beginnings.
See item no. 313.

The geo-strategic importance of the Iberian Peninsula.
See item no. 567.

Spain, Portugal and the European Community.
See item no. 618.

The enlargement of the European Community: case-studies of Greece, Portugal and Spain.
See item no. 619.

A bibliographic guide to Spanish diplomatic history, 1460-1977.
See item no. 960.

Economy

582 The political economy of modern Spain: policy-making in an authoritarian system.
Charles William Anderson.   Madison and Milwaukee, Wisconsin; London: University of Wisconsin Press, 1970. 282p. bibliog.

An informed discussion of the changes in Spain's economic policy in the 1950s and 1960s, which finds the patterns of development more like those of western democracies than one might expect. The study focuses on the years 1957 to 1967, a decade of major economic growth in Spain under Franco.

583 The economic transformation of Spain and Portugal.
Eric Nicolas Baklanoff.   New York; London: Praeger, 1978. 211p. bibliog. (Praeger Special Studies).

This book emphasizes the close inter-dependence of politics and economics. Spain's economic and political evolution from the end of the Civil War (1939) until 1975 was dominated by Franco. Under him 'Spain was transformed from an autarkic corporate state into an outward-looking, modified capitalist market economy'. The major theme of this book is the interplay of economic systems and economic growth. Part 1 considers the economic evolution of Spain, with emphasis on the period since the Civil War; part 2 studies Portugal; and part 3 compares the two.

584 Spain to 1990.
Brinsley Best.   London: Euromoney, 1984. 242p. (Euromoney Special Study).

This specially commissioned study is a comprehensive analysis of the risks and prospects of Spain's economic performance for the rest of this decade. It argues that the country will achieve one of the highest economic growth rates in Europe by 1990, with, or without, entry into the EEC. The study also takes a detailed look at banking and finance structures and the industrial sector.

585 **The Fontana economic history of Europe: contemporary economies, part 2.**
Edited by Carlo M. Cipolla. London: Fontana, 1976. 402p. bibliog. (The Fontana Economic History of Europe, vol. 6, part 2).

This standard work on European economic history contains a chapter entitled 'Spain 1914-1970' (p. 460-529) by Josep Fontana and Jordi Nadal Oller, translated by C. E. de Salis. It presents a succinct account of 20th-century Spanish economic and social history, with special reference to the long periods of economic stagnation, and the years of gradual stabilization and growth revolving around the development of Spanish industry. The volume contains an excellent statistical appendix.

586 **The Fontana economic history of Europe: the emergence of industrial societies, part 2.**
Edited by Carlo M. Cipolla. London: Fontana, 1973. 845p. bibliog. (Fontana Economic History of Europe, vol. 4, part 2).

This Fontana volume contains a chapter entitled 'The failure of the industrial revolution in Spain 1830-1914' (p. 532-626) by Jordi Nadal Oller, translated by John Street. The book deals with the impact of the industrial revolution on individual countries, and this chapter shows how economic growth in Spain between 1830 and 1914 was very unbalanced, and how efforts to rapidly industrialize the country were largely unsuccessful. Nadal argues that this 'failure' arose from a lack of native capital to invest in productive enterprises, due largely to the effect of mistaken government policies.

587 **Economic Report.**
Bilbao, Spain: Banco de Bilbao Research Department, 1970- . annual.

An abridged (usually around one hundred pages) English version of the original Spanish report, the *Informe económico*. The Banco de Bilbao was established in 1857, and this report looks at all areas of the Spanish economy, and contains numerous statistical tables.

588 **Economic Surveys: Spain.**
Paris: Organisation for Economic Co-operation and Development, 1961- . annual.

Compiled by committees of the OECD for each of its member countries, these detailed surveys present an analysis of the economic policies and main economic trends of the year, and the prospects and potential policies for the coming year. Appendixes include a wide range of comparative and annual statistics. The report on Spain for 1984 contains sixty-nine pages.

Economy

589 **Early economic thought in Spain 1177-1740.**
Marjorie Grice-Hutchinson. London: Allen & Unwin, 1978.
189p. bibliog.

An exploration of the subject of economic thought and monetary history in Spain in the presence of Christian, Islamic and Jewish communities. The authoress provides a good economic history of the period, and extols the value of the work of the old Spanish economists – the shrewd observers who felt the effects of inflation at first hand.

590 **Public policy in a no-party state: Spanish planning and budgeting in the twilight of the Franquist era.**
Richard Gunther. Berkeley, California: University of California Press, 1980. 361p. 2 maps. bibliog.

This work is based on a series of ninety-seven interviews with Spanish government officials, and analyzes public expenditure at a time when Spain had the smallest public sector in Europe, and the government spent amazingly little on defence and education. The explanation for this lay in the composition of the governing élite, and in the political processes by which economic decisions were made (i.e. in a political vacuum).

591 **American treasure and the price revolution in Spain, 1501-1650.**
Earl J. Hamilton. New York: Octagon Books, 1970. 428p. map. bibliog. (Harvard Economic Studies, vol. 43).

A classic study of the rise and fall in Spain's economic fortunes in the 16th and 17th centuries, which describes and assesses the impact of American silver on the Spanish economy. The work has been the subject of considerable criticism for some of its interpretations. Nevertheless, it remains a fundamental study for its information and statistics on prices and wages, and on the silver shipped to Spain. Hamilton's article 'The decline of Spain' (*Economic History Review*, vol. 8 (1937-38), p. 168-79), although nearly fifty years old, remains a classic account of the economic decline of Spain in the 17th century. For a more detailed study of this subject see the massive work by Ramón Carande *Carlos V y sus banqueros* (Charles V and his bankers) (Madrid: Sociedad de Estudios y Publicaciones, 1967. 3 vols.), which analyzes the Spanish empire from the viewpoint of the cost of its maintenance, and concludes that the price of the empire led eventually to the ultimate economic decline of Castile.

592 **The Spanish economy in the twentieth century.**
Joseph Harrison. London: Croom Helm, 1984. 207p. map. bibliog. (Contemporary Economic History of Europe).

For most of the 20th century the Spanish economy has remained isolated and backward, but it is becoming increasingly important with her impending membership of the EEC. A growing number of multinational companies are finding Spain an attractive country in which to invest, due to the relatively cheap labour and weak trade unions. This superb study provides a good account of Spain's economic growth and problems, and links them to relevant political events. Harrison has also written *An economic history of modern Spain* (Manchester, England: Manchester University Press, 1978), which examines and

168

interprets the factors influencing the economic and social development of Spain since the beginning of the 18th century.

593   **The economic history of Spain: (under the Umayyads 711-1031).**
S. M. Imamuddin.   Dacca, Bangladesh: Asiatic Society of
Pakistan, 1963. 537p. 2 maps. bibliog. (Asiatic Society of Pakistan
Publication, no. 11).

A revised English version of the author's PhD thesis, originally written in Spanish and submitted to the University of Madrid. It is a very useful and original work, and the most comprehensive study in English of Spain's economy under the Muslims.

594   **The contemporary Spanish economy: a historical perspective.**
Sima Lieberman.   London: Allen & Unwin, 1982. 378p. bibliog.

A study of economic conditions, and political and historical events since 1939 (although contemporary Spanish agriculture is placed in its historical perspective before that date). The author also discusses Spain's 'industrial revolution', the restoration of free trade unions, and the problems of inflation and unemployment. It is argued that traditional institutions, political, economic and social, all have a major role to play in future Spanish economic development, and there is a look ahead to the implications of Spain joining the EEC.

595   **Money, prices and politics in fifteenth-century Castile.**
Angus Mackay.   London: Royal Historical Society, 1981. 184p.
3 maps. bibliog. (Royal Historical Society, Studies in History
Series, no. 28).

An economic and monetary history of mediaeval Spain, which complements the studies made by Hamilton (q.v.) on similar topics regarding early modern Spain. It contains two major chapters on the supply of precious metals to the kingdom, and the prices and wages structure. The author also provides three appendixes showing copies of original economic documents of the period.

596   **Ciudad Real, 1500-1750: growth, crisis and readjustment in the**
Spanish economy.
Carla Rahn Phillips.   Cambridge, Massachussetts; London:
Harvard University Press, 1979. 190p. 6 maps. bibliog.

A work which charts the years of Spanish economic and military dominance to the years of economic and colonial decline, focusing on the effects of the downfall of Spanish power on one Castilian city. It first considers the general history of the city and region, and then moves on to examine the population, agriculture, industry, taxation and patterns of investment. The authoress demonstrates how Ciudad Real's economy grew from around 1500 to 1580 and then endured stagnation through the major part of the 17th century, only re-establishing a viable economy in about 1750.

Economy

597   **Quarterly Economic Review of Spain.**
London: Economist Intelligence Unit, 1952- . quarterly.

Compiled by an independent research and advisory organization, these quarterly
reviews aim to interpret, as well as report on, current trends in the economies of
the world. Spain is covered in one of a series of over eighty such reviews. There
are useful summaries on current events in the Spanish political arena, along with
facts, interpretations and statistics on the Spanish economy. An annual
supplement provides a summary of general information on Spain's economy.

598   **Regional development policy and planning in Spain.**
Harry Ward Richardson.   Farnborough, England: Saxon House;
Lexington, Massachussetts: Lexington Books, 1975. 250p. map.
bibliog. (Saxon House Studies).

The author has written several articles on regional planning in Spain, and this
work presents a critical assessment of Spanish regional economic policies. He
notes that regional development problems are perennial, but is nevertheless
critical of the policies adopted in the mid-1970s and concludes that 'despite the
inexorable march of events, it is most unlikely that the analysis in this book will
become quickly outdated'.

599   **Madrid and the Spanish economy, 1560-1850.**
David R. Ringrose.   Berkeley, California: University of
California Press, 1983. 405p. 18 maps. bibliog.

A highly detailed and scholarly work, which offers a new perspective on the
economic history, decline and stagnation of early modern Spain. Castile was
expanding in the 16th century, and in 1561 Madrid became the capital of Spain
and the Habsburg empire, and was a large metropolis by 1630. By the middle of
the 17th century the city dominated the interior, and other urban centres had
declined in importance. 'The uneven distribution of urban income directed
demand toward agricultural staples from the interior and quality merchandise
from the ports, discouraging diversification in the regional economy'. The
author's study helps to explain Spain's slow industrialization, and how Madrid
helped to create an inflexible economy and a political class that tried to insulate
the economy from modernization.

600   **The limits of economic growth in Spain.**
Manuel Roman.   New York; Washington; London: Praeger,
1971. 186p. bibliog. (Praeger Special Studies in International
Economies and Development).

This work aims to identify the 'main structural obstacles to the process of
industrial growth (economic) initiated in Spain after the Spanish economy opened
itself to the international market forces stemming from the E.E.C.'. It looks at
the economic history of Spain since 1939 and pays particular attention to
agriculture, tourism, emigration and the limits of expansion under Franco.

601 **Spain: Economic Report.**
London: Lloyds Bank, 1980- . annual.
A rich source for an annual summary of economic developments in Spain, and the most detailed produced by any British bank. Each report gives background information on Spain, with more detailed sections on: the economy; production industry (agriculture, manufacturing, mining, transport, housing, tourism, banking and finance); and foreign trade. The 1984 edition contains 27 pages, and includes a map and appendixes on the Balearic Islands, Canary Islands, and the Spanish enclaves in North Africa (Ceuta, Melilla, and the Chaffarine Islands).

602 **Banking, railroads, and industry in Spain 1829-1874.**
Gabriel Tortella-Casares. New York: Arno Press, 1977. 707p.
bibliog. (Dissertations in European Economic History).
A reprint of the author's doctoral thesis submitted to the University of Wisconsin in 1972, which deals in minute detail with the banking system, the industrial sector, the railway network, and their mutual interplay during the central decades of the 19th century. The emphasis is on the banking structure and the economic history of Spain during this period. Statistics are included in numerous appendixes.

603 **An economic history of Spain.**
Jaime Vicens Vives, with the collaboration of Jorge Nadal Oller, translated by Frances M. López-Morillas. Princeton, New Jersey: Princeton University Press, 1969. 825p. maps. bibliog.
Translated from the original Spanish edition of 1955, this is the most reliable general study of Spanish economic history. Vicens Vives' pioneeering and monumental work surveys and analyzes the economic and social development of Spain since the earliest times. The book grew out of the author's course on the economic history of Spain at the University of Barcelona. It is divided into six main parts, which study the: primitive and colonial economy; feudal and seigniorial economy (the economy of al-Andalus from the 8th to 12th centuries); urban economy; mercantilist economy from the discovery of America to the economic transformation in the 18th century; and the impact of the industrial revolution. The bibliography runs to over fifty pages.

604 **The economic development of Spain.**
World Bank. Baltimore, Maryland: Johns Hopkins Press, 1963.
416p. 19 maps.
The report of a mission organized by the World Bank at the request of Spain in the early 1960s. Although over twenty years old, it remains useful for its study of how public policy and planning under Franco operated, and how the World Bank's recommendations and advice attempted to assist the Spanish administration in the preparation of a long-term development programme designed to expand and modernize the Spanish economy (something Franco was always keen to achieve). It includes a useful thirty-nine page summary covering all sections.

Economy

605 **The Spanish economy: 1959-1976.**
Alison Wright. London: Macmillan, 1977. 195p. map. bibliog.
The authoress lived in Spain between 1970 and 1972, and has written quarterly economic reviews on the Spanish economy for the Economist Intelligence Unit (q.v.). In this important study she discusses the rapid growth of the Spanish economy under Franco, but does not assess the political development which accompanied it.

Spain, Portugal and the European Community.
See item no. 618.

The enlargement of the European Community: case-studies of Greece, Portugal and Spain.
See item no. 619.

Spanish mercantilism: Gerónimo de Uztáriz – economist.
See item no. 621.

The Mesta: a study in Spanish economic history 1273-1836.
See item no. 648.

Land and society in Golden Age Castile.
See item no. 652.

Transportation and economic stagnation in Spain, 1750-1850.
See item no. 665.

Finance and Banking

606 **Banking structures and sources of finance in Spain and Portugal.**
The Banker Research Unit.   London: Financial Times Business
Publishing, 1980. 94p.

'In recent years the Spanish financial system has been subject to a transformation
process, which is having the effect of changing its traditional features'. This
transformation has been inspired by a general wish to see a more flexible system
offering competition between the different institutions which make it up. This
study outlines these changes and how they have affected the financial system as a
whole. Although it is not over-technical, an awareness of banking language is a
distinct advantage. The section on Spain covers roughly half the book, and
includes a list of banks operating in Spain, with their addresses and telex
numbers.

607 **Banking and economic development: some lessons of history.**
Edited by Rondon Cameron.   New York; London: Oxford
University Press, 1972. 267p. bibliog.

Chapter 4 (p. 91-121) by Gabriel Tortella-Casares, is entitled 'Spain 1829-1874'
and is an invaluable study of 19th-century Spanish banking. Tortella himself
helped to found, and at one time headed, the Economic History Group in the
Bank of Spain Research Department. He notes how 'Spain in the 1850s
undertook an intensive programme of railway construction and financial
promotion. The result was disastrous and set back industrialization and economic
development for years'.

608 **The dawn of modern banking.**
Center for Medieval and Renaissance Studies/University of
California, Los Angeles. New Haven, Connecticut; London:
Yale University Press, 1979. 321p. bibliog.

All the essays in this book were prepared for a conference held at the UCLA in
September 1977, under the sponsorship of its Center for Medieval and
Renaissance Studies. The work includes a chapter on 'Banking and society in late
medieval and early modern Aragon' (p. 131-67) by Manuel Riu Riu, which
studies the early banking systems and organization in the region.

609 **European financial reporting: 5, Spain.**
P. J. Donaghy, J. Laidler. London: Institute of Chartered
Accountants, 1982. 181p.

This study is designed to enable the reader with a British accounting background
to understand and interpret Spanish company accounts. It also gives detailed
information on business organizations and taxation, and contains a glossary of
English-Spanish and Spanish-English accounting terms. The text is complemented
by numerous charts, tables and extracts from the accounts of Spanish companies.

610 **Historia de la moneda española.** (A history of Spanish currency.)
Octavio Gil Farrés. Madrid: [s.n.], 1959. 415p. bibliog.

An excellent monetary history of Spain, and a study of numismatics from the
earliest times to 1937. A very useful and minutely detailed study which includes
numerous plates illustrating the coins used in Spain over the centuries.

611 **La banca y el Estado en la España contemporánea (1939-1979).**
(Banking and the State in contemporary Spain, 1939-79.)
Antonio González Temprano, Domingo Sánchez Robayna,
Eugenio Torres Villanueva. Madrid: El Espejo, 1981. 260p.
bibliog. (Colección EE, no. 27).

A detailed analysis which sets out to demonstrate the internal relations of private
Spanish banking, its predominant role in the Spanish economy, and its links with
the State. It contains numerous figures, charts and graphs plus a large number of
appendixes supplying a wealth of statistical information on public and private
banking.

612 **Spanish banking schemes before 1700.**
Earl J. Hamilton. *Journal of Political Economy*, vol. 57 (1949),
p. 134-56.

Hamilton is an expert on Spain's financial and economic history, and this is a
useful short article studying the finance policy and banking schemes under the
Spanish monarchs up to 1700. He also wrote 'The foundation of the Bank of
Spain' (*Journal of Political Economy*, vol. 53 (1945), p. 97-113).

613   **Foreign finance in continental Europe and the United States, 1815-1870: quantities, origins, functions and distribution.**
D. C. M. Platt.   London: George Allen & Unwin, 1984. 216p. bibliog.

The chapter on Spain (p. 106-39) studies British, Dutch and French investment in Spain, and Spanish domestic finance and public credit. It presents a concise examination of the history of foreign finance in the country during a crucial period, and the author notes how most of Spain's 'limited resources of disposable capital were chanelled primarily into the state and Spanish railways when, under happier circumstances, they might have taken a larger part in the growth of the national economy'.

614   **The early history of deposit banking in Mediterranean Europe.**
Abbott Payson Usher.   Cambridge, Massachussetts: Harvard University Press, 1943. 649p. bibliog. (Harvard Economic Studies, vol. 75).

This huge work provides a general analysis of banking and credit systems in the western Mediterranean. Part 1 studies the structure and functions of the early credit system, and part 2 looks at banking in Catalonia between 1240 and 1723.

Spain to 1990.
See item no. 584.

Money, prices and politics in fifteenth-century Castile.
See item no. 595.

Banking, railroads, and industry in Spain 1829-1874.
See item no. 602.

Trade

615 Doing business in Spain.
Ian S. Blackshaw. London: Oyez, 1980. 198p.

Spain is becoming increasingly important as a major west European country for overseas business and investment, and this work is aimed at providing an English-language text which will give company executives, businessmen and entrepreneurs a clear and concise introduction to the legal, fiscal and exchange control aspects of conducting business in Spain.

616 Trade and navigation between Spain and the Indies in the time of the Habsburgs.
Clarence Henry Haring. Gloucester, Massachussetts: Peter Smith, 1964. 371p. map. bibliog.

This classic book, which was first published in 1918, carefully describes the details and difficulties of trade and navigation between Spain and the New World in the 16th and 17th centuries. Haring notes how in spite of the volume of gold and silver produced in the mines in America, 'the Habsburgs could not have played the political rôle to which they aspired in the sixteenth and seventeenth centuries without the assistance of foreign capitalists and bankers'. The volume also contains an excellent section on the 'Casa de Contratación' (House of Trade) which was set up in Seville in 1503 as an agency which administered economic relations between Spain and the Indies.

617 Spain: business opportunities in the 1980s.
Metra Consulting and International Joint Ventures. London: Metra Consulting Group, 1980. 292p. 3 maps.

A detailed report which was actually written by Ben Box and Michael Wooller, with the view that Spain would have joined the EEC by the mid-1980s (1 January 1986, is now the projected date). The study aims to provide relevant information on what Spain requires, and how the country's economic system is organized, for those preparing to trade with Spain. It also looks in detail at recent Spanish economic history.

618 **Spain, Portugal and the European Community.**
Edited by Joyce Rushworth. London: University Association for Contemporary European Studies, 1979. 75p. map.
This publication contains the papers presented at the UACES conference organized in conjunction with the Iberian Centre, St. Anthony's College, Oxford, in 1978. It discusses the national and regional problems faced by Spain and the EEC in relation to trade, as a consequence of Spain's proposed entry into the Community in 1986, and looks at the position of the Spanish economy, industry and agriculture within an enlarged market. Much of Spain and Portugal's industry lags far behind that of their proposed European partners, and consequently competition may prove difficult.

619 **The enlargement of the European Community: case-studies of Greece, Portugal and Spain.**
Edited by José Luis Sampedro, Juan Antonio Payno. London: Macmillan, 1983. 263p. bibliog. (Studies in the Integration of Western Europe).
The section on Spain (p. 187-241) comprises three chapters which look at the characteristics of the Spanish economy, and Spain's motives in seeking entry into the EEC. These chapters explain why Spain is committed to membership, the probable effects of full membership on Spanish agriculture, and the implications for Spanish industry.

620 **The rise of the Spanish trade in the Middle Ages.**
Charles Verlinden. *Economic History Review*, vol. 50 (1939-40), p. 44-59. (Studies in Sources and Bibliography, no. 7).
This article represents a short study of the history of mediaeval Spanish trade, and is a 'resumé of a series of lectures delivered at the Institut des Hautes Études de Belgique at Brussels in 1937 and of a communication presented to the International Congress of Historical Sciences at Zurich in 1938'.

621 **Spanish mercantilism: Gerónimo de Uztáriz – economist.**
Andrés Villegas Castillo. Philadelphia: Porcupine Press, 1980. 193p. bibliog.
Originally published in 1930, this study aims to draw attention to the existence of Spanish economic writers who both expanded and applied the doctrines of the mercantile system. It discusses the historical aspects of Spanish internal and external trade, and demonstrates just how important foreign trade was to Spain during the 15th and 16th centuries. Uztáriz (1670-1732) was the first Spaniard to write a real economic treatise, in which he basically held that national wealth would be attained and preserved by bringing about a state of affairs in which the country exported more than it imported.

Trade

622 **Spanish politics and imperial trade, 1700-1789.**
Geoffrey J. Walker. London: Macmillan, 1979. 297p. 2 maps.
bibliog.

A thorough analysis of Spain's trading relationship with her American empire,
and the policies which affected it during the 18th century. The author charts
Spain's ultimately unsuccessful struggle to retain commercial control of her
colonies against growing economic and diplomatic pressures from France and
Great Britain, and describes in detail the voyages of Spain's transatlantic trade
fleets.

Conquest and commerce: Spain and England in the Americas.
See item no. 329.

Aristocrats and traders: Sevillian society in the sixteenth century.
See item no. 480.

Spain: Economic Report.
See item no. 601.

**Foreign finance in continental Europe and the United States, 1815-
1870: quantities, origins, functions and distribution.**
See item no. 613.

**The Spanish industry in (the) face of its integration into the European
Community.**
See item no. 629.

Foreign technology and industrialization: the case of Spain.
See item no. 636.

La agricultura española y el comercio exterior. (Spanish agriculture and
foreign trade.)
See item no. 645.

Directory of the Spanish industry, export and import.
See item no. 943.

Industry

623 **The Spanish oil industry.**
Mario Alvarez-Garcillán. *Petroleum Review*, vol. 25, no. 294
(June 1971), p. 209-15.
A short study which outlines the history of the Spanish petroleum industry, and
makes the point that Spain was the first of the so-called western countries to be
involved with petroleum – it was the Arabs who developed ways of distillation
which they introduced into western Europe through Spain.

624 **Spanish oil: a study of Spain's new oil frontier.**
H. S. Bluston. Bedford, England: Energy Consultancy, 1978.
59p. bibliog.
Spain started to produce oil from her Mediterranean fields in 1973, over two years
before the first British oil came on stream. The author attempts to present a
unified account of the subject, tracing the discoveries of oil up to the production
stage, and describing the production regions in the Gulf of Valencia individually.
Some problems such as deepwater production, and the effects of pollution and
tourism, are also discussed. Bluston concludes with an overall assessment of
Spanish offshore oil production, and its prospects for the future. Amongst other
works on the subject, he has also written *Spain's offshore oil technology: Spain's
advances in offshore technology* (Bedford, England: Energy Consultancy, 1979).

625 **Cooperation at work: the Mondragon experience.**
Keith Bradley, Alan Gelb. London: Heinemann Educational,
1983. 102p. bibliog.
An interesting and detailed study of the growth and achievements of the
Mondragón group of industrial cooperatives in the Basque Provinces, which
emphasizes how the worker cooperatives have increased workplace consensus.
Mondragón is exemplified as the largest, most complete, and perhaps most

179

successful, cooperative in a capitalist economy, and the authors argue that its experience contributes much to the debate on the directions which industrial relations in Europe should follow.

626 **Honor, commerce and industry in eighteenth-century Spain.**
William James Callahan. Boston, Massachussetts: Harvard Graduate School of Business Administration, 1972. 79p. bibliog. (Kress Library of Business and Economics, no. 22).

A scholarly study of the attempt to raise the social esteem of commerce and the manufacturing industry in 18th-century Spain. The work describes the efforts which were made by the State, and much of educated opinion, to eradicate the aversion of Spaniards of all social classes towards work in commercial, manufacturing and artisan occupations.

627 **Mondragón 1980.**
Alastair Campbell. London: Industrial Common Ownership Movement, 1980. 23p. (Industrial Common Ownership Movement, pamphlet no. 9).

A succinct account of how industrial democracy has succeeded at the now famous town of Mondragón in the Basque Provinces, in which the author also provides a concise history of the aims and operations of the worker-owned enterprises. Father Arizmendi-Arrieta, the acknowledged leader and inspirer of the movement (who died in 1977), stated that his aim was 'to provide a means by which people could create work for themselves and work in harmony with one another'. Campbell also wrote *Worker-owners, the Mondragón achievement: the Caja Laboral Popular and the Mondragón co-operatives in the Basque provinces of Spain: a report* (London: Anglo German Foundation for the Study of Industrial Society, 1977).

628 **Spain's iron and steel industry.**
Ronald H. Chilcote. Austin, Texas: Bureau of Business Research, University of Texas at Austin, 1968. 174p. 7 maps. bibliog. (Bureau of Business Research: Research Monograph, no. 32).

An excellent, comprehensive survey and analysis of a vital industry in Spain's economy, which includes appendixes, tables, numerous maps and charts, and an extensive bibliography. Spain has been a centre for the production of iron and steel for centuries, and this study relates the industry to Spain's economic and political history as a whole. It studies: raw materials; power; water and transportation; labour; trade; the largest companies; and the role of heavy industry in Spain. Although central government policy has changed since this work was written, it is still very useful for the detailed picture it provides.

629 **The Spanish industry in (the) face of its integration into the European Community.**
Juergen B. Donges. *Economia Internazionale*, vol. 33 (Nov. 1980), p. 399-415.

This volume of the journal reprints the seminar presentations on 'The problems of the international trade and investment in the 80s' held at the Ministry of Commerce and Tourism in Madrid in April 1980. The paper on Spain discusses the possible effects of entry into the EEC on Spanish manufacturing industry as regards world trade. Donges basically proposes a gradual industrial reform policy for Spain, with the belief that 'the expectations of the [Spanish] manufacturing sector in the context of an enlarged Common Market may be influenced positively'.

630 **The origins of modern industrialism in the Basque country.**
Richard J. Harrison. Sheffield, England: University of Sheffield Department of Economic and Social History, 1977. 18p. bibliog. (Studies in Economic and Social History, no. 2).

This short study covers the years from the late 19th to the early 20th century, when the real growth of Basque regional industry began, marking a clear turning point in the region's economic development. Present-day industries in the region include nuclear power plants, and industrialists in this field, as in others, face the constant threat of possible abduction by members of ETA.

631 **The Rio Tinto Company: an economic history of a leading international mining concern 1873-1954.**
Charles E. Harvey. Penzance, England: Alison Hodge, 1981. 390p. map. bibliog.

The Rio Tinto Company was formed in 1873 to work the ancient mines in southern Spain in the province of Huelva, and rapidly became the world's leading supplier of sulphur and copper. Harvey describes the growth of the company, up until the mines were finally sold to local interests in 1954, and relates it to the course of events in Spain. Since 1954 the company has become a fully-fledged multinational industry. This excellent study complements David Avery's *Not on Queen Victoria's birthday: the story of the Rio Tinto mines* (London: Collins, 1974), which is more a socio-political history.

632 **The rise of Spain's automobile industry.**
Richard I. Hawkesworth. *National Westminster Bank Quarterly Review*, (Feb. 1981), p. 37-48.

A short history of the growth in car production in Spain, from the establishment of Fiat's first factory in Barcelona between 1950 and 1953, to 1980 when it ranked fifth of the west European car producers. Another article on Spain's car industry is 'Ford fiesta Spain: a case study of international investment and trade' by François Vellas (*Journal of World Trade Law*, vol. 13, no. 6 (Nov.-Dec. 1979), p. 481-94), which discusses the American Ford Motor Corporation's role in increasing the size and variety of the Spanish automobile industry.

633 **The development of the Spanish textile industry, 1750-1800.**
James Clayburn La Force. Berkeley and Los Angeles, California:
University of California Press, 1965. 210p. map. bibliog.
(University of California, Los Angeles: Publications of the Bureau
of Business and Economic Research).

This work offers a detailed analysis of the textile industry, and, in the wider
context, of Spain's early attempts at economic development and progress. It is a
fully documented and comprehensive study of attempts by the Spanish crown to
restore Spain's vitality in textile manufacturing – all four Bourbons of the 18th
century constructed, owned, and operated textile factories. However, except for
its remarkable development in Catalonia and Valencia, the industry responded
disappointingly, even though it received preferential treatment over any other
sector of the economy during this period.

634 **A history of Spanish firearms.**
James Duncan Lavin. London: Jenkins; New York: Arco, 1965.
304p. bibliog.

A superbly illustrated history of the firearms industry from the introduction of
gunpowder into Spain in the 14th century, to the death of the last great Spanish
royal gunsmith, Isidro Soler, in 1825. This is the first comprehensive study of the
subject in English, and includes a glossary of Spanish firearms' terms and a list of
Spanish gunmakers. Another useful general survey is William Keith Neal's
Spanish guns and pistols (London: G. Bell, 1955).

635 **Monopolistic structures and industrial analysis in Spain: the case of
the pharmaceutical industry.**
Félix Lobo. *International Journal of Health Services*, vol. 9, no. 4
(1979), p. 663-82.

This article is a summary of various aspects of the author's doctoral thesis
prepared in 1977, and provides a useful examination of the structure of the
Spanish pharmaceutical industry. Technology, the effects of advertising, and
financial and economic considerations are all taken into account. The relationship
between the industry, public and private health care, and the quality of health
services generally in Spain are also discussed.

636 **Foreign technology and industrialization: the case of Spain.**
Peter O'Brien. *Journal of World Trade Law*, vol. 9, no. 5 (Sept.-
Oct. 1975), p. 525-52.

In this article the author has drawn upon material in the UNCTAD (United
Nations Conference on Trade and Development) report entitled *Major issues
arising from the transfer of technology: a case study of Spain*. Noting the rapid rise
in industrial output in Spain since the 1960s, he examines the background to, and
growth of, Spanish industry since the Civil War. Special emphasis is placed on the
role of foreign investment, and the conditions under which foreign technology has
been transferred and utilized in the industrial sector.

637 **The cork oak forests and the evolution of the cork industry in southern Spain and Portugal.**
James J. Parsons. *Economic Geography*, vol. 38, no. 3 (July 1962), p. 195-214.

Whilst Portugal represents the leading producer and exporter of cork bark, Spain has over fifteen per cent of the world's cork forests, principally in Andalusia and Extremadura. The author (who spent 1959-60 travelling around Spain and Portugal surveying the forests) looks at: corkwood production and forest management; the origins of 'cork' manufacturing and the export trade; the cork stopper industry in Spain; the use of cork for insulation; and the decline of the industry in recent years.

638 **A look at Spain.**
John Pullin. *Engineer*, vol. 248 (May 1979), p. 30-55.

A very competent and concise survey of industrial development and individual industries in post-Franco Spain. The author visited several industries and institutions, and charts Spain's rise as an industrial power. He examines the: car industry; chemical industry; steel industry; energy industry (including new nuclear power stations); and shipbuilding.

639 **La industria española en los años ochenta.** (Spanish industry in the eighties.)
Antonio Robert. Madrid: Moneda y Crédito, 1980. 151p.
(Monografías de Moneda y Crédito, no. 3).

An overall analysis of Spanish industry in relation to the growth and general situation of world industry. The author tries to project how Spanish industry will develop in the next ten years, by looking principally at the oil, chemical, steel, car, and electronics industries, as well as the railways, dockyards and other smaller industries. The book contains numerous statistical tables.

640 **Spain.**
World Fishing, vol. 24, no. 9 (1976), p. 19-43.

An illustrated article on the Spanish fishing industry, which analyzes its difficult situation at the time of writing, and its future plans. The changes in fishing limits on Spain's traditional fishing grounds, deficiencies of the fishing fleet, and an inadequate system for the commercialization of the catches, all pose problems for the government in its attempt to revitalize the industry. More recently (together with the wine-producing industry) it has given rise to problems in the negotiations for Spain's accession to the EEC, with other member states feeling threatened by the prospect of large Spanish fleets gaining access to their national fishing grounds. For detailed annual statistics on Spain's fishing industry, see the *F.A.O. Yearbook of Fishery Statistics* (Rome: Food and Agriculture Organisation, 1947- . annual.), and the *Review of Fisheries in O.E.C.D. Member Countries* (Paris: Organisation for Economic Co-operation and Development, 1967- . annual.). The latter, as well as providing detailed statistics, provides a brief summary of the current problems faced by the industry, the structure of the fishing fleet, and government policy towards the industry as a whole.

Industry

641 **Mondragon: an economic analysis.**
Henk Thomas, Chris Logan. London: George Allen & Unwin, 1982. 218p. bibliog.

This study was published in co-operation with the Institute of Social Studies at The Hague. The Mondragón group of co-operatives, which was started in 1943, has achieved much success and world-wide interest. The authors have based their analysis on extensive research and several months of fieldwork in Mondragón itself. The emphasis is on the operation of the industrial self-management system, and Mondragón's potential for growth in the industrial sector. It examines industrial relations, and implies that new roles now exist for trade unions in worker education and the sharing of new responsibilities.

642 **The industrialization of the continental powers 1780-1914.**
Clive Trebilcock. London; New York: Longman, 1981. 495p.
7 maps. bibliog.

Chapter 5 (p. 292-384) is entitled 'The powers of deprivation: Italy, Austria-Hungary, Spain'. It surveys the industrialization of Spain from the late 18th century to the outbreak of the First World War, and represents a comparative study of the country's under-developed industrial economy.

643 **Historia de la empresa española: la evolución empresarial dentro de la economía española.** (A history of Spanish industry: commercial development within the Spanish economy.)
Pedro Voltes Bou. Barcelona: Editorial Hispano Europea, 1979. 510p. bibliog. (Biblioteca de Dirección, Organización y Administración de Empresas).

An excellent overall study of Spanish industry from the earliest times, aimed primarily at university students, and specialists in any of the industries discussed. This large work is divided into small manageable sections, each with its own bibliography, and discusses: agriculture; mining; fishing; handicrafts; finance; textiles; metals; railways; insurance; chemicals; electricity and gas; construction; shipbuilding; cars; newspapers; advertising; air transport; tourism; cinema; and industry in general, both during and after the Civil War. The author also wrote *Historia de la economía española en los siglos XIX y XX* (A history of the Spanish economy in the 19th and 20th centuries) (Madrid: Editora Nacional, 1972-74. 3 vols.).

Spain to 1990.
See item no. 584.

Transporte marítimo y construcción naval en España.
(Maritime transport and shipbuilding in Spain.)
See item no. 661.

Planning for national technology policy.
See item no. 713.

Silk textiles of Spain: eighth to fifteenth century.
See item no. 832.

Edición y comercio del libro español, 1900-1972. (The Spanish publishing and book trade, 1900-72.)
See item no. 896.

Publishing in Spain.
See item no. 898.

Kompass (Spain): register of Spanish industry and commerce.
See item no. 946.

Agriculture

644 **Agricultural policy in Spain.**
Paris: Organisation for Economic Co-operation and Development, 1974. 49p. (Agricultural Policy Reports).
Spain has a rich and varied agriculture, and this publication presents a concise study of Spanish agricultural policy under Franco in the 1960s and 1970s, considering all the major aspects of production, labour, trade and finance. A new study of the changes that have taken place in the ten years since Franco's death would now be most useful.

645 **La agricultura española y el comercio exterior.**
(Spanish agriculture and foreign trade.)
Fritz Baade. Madrid: Instituto de Desarrollo Económico, 1967. 308p. bibliog. (Estudios de Economía, no. 1).
A highly detailed analysis of over twenty Spanish agricultural products in respect of their possible export value, and a survey of economic development plans and regional agriculture. The work includes a 100 page appendix, which provides detailed statistics on the varieties of Spanish agricultural produce.

646 **Unrewarding wealth: the commercialization and collapse of agriculture in a Spanish Basque town.**
Davydd James Greenwood. Cambridge, England: Cambridge University Press, 1976. 223p. 2 maps. bibliog.
An agricultural history of Fuenterrabia between the years 1920 and 1969. Greenwood describes how the farmers changed subsistence farms into commercial enterprises in response to the demand created by tourism and industrialization. He returned to the town in 1973 to find that the collapse of agriculture was virtually complete, with many of the young Basques leaving the farms for factory work in the larger towns and cities.

647 **Reforestation in Spain.**
Henry A. Kernan.   Syracuse, New York: State University College
of Forestry at Syracuse University, 1966. 52p. maps. (World
Forestry Publication, no. 3).

A study by an American expert of the twenty-five year old reforestation
programme in Spain under Franco. The author makes the important point that
over half of Iberia is unsuitable for sustained agriculture, which is notable for
Spain's economy in the past has always been agriculture-based.

648 **The Mesta: a study in Spanish economic history 1273-1836.**
Julius Klein.   Port Washington, New York: Kennikat Press, 1964.
444p. map. bibliog.

This is a reprint of the scholarly 1920 study of the Castilian sheep-raising guild
(formerly recognized in 1273) whose economic power and influence, particularly
in the 16th century, stretched as far as the Spanish-American colonies. The full
name of the guild was the 'Honrado Concejo de la Mesta' (Honourable Council
of the Mesta), and it was fundamentally a society composed of all the sheep
rearers in Castile. The origin of the word comes from either the Spanish 'mezcla'
(mixture), a reference to the mixture of sheep, or from the Arabic 'mechta',
meaning winter pastures for sheep. Some historians blame the Mesta for Spain's
underdevelopment compared to that of the rest of Europe, with many of Spain's
other industries being neglected in favour of agriculture and stock breeding. It is
also significant that Spain continued to export raw materials and import
manufactured goods well into the 19th century – the Mesta was only dissolved in
1836.

649 **Agrarian reform and the peasant revolution in Spain: origins of the
Civil War.**
Edward E. Malefakis.   New Haven, Connecticut; London: Yale
University Press, 1970. 469p. 11 maps. bibliog.

This book represents a definitive history of the all-important agrarian issue during
the Second Republic, and its primary purpose is to explore the reasons why the
Republic's agrarian reform programme failed so badly. The author analyzes the
historic roots of the agrarian problem, and shows it to be one of the fundamental
causes of the Civil War.

650 **Labourers and landowners in southern Spain.**
Juan Martínez-Alier.   London: Allen & Unwin, 1971. 352p.
4 maps. bibliog. (St. Antony's College, Oxford, Publications,
no. 4).

A sociological and economic analysis of the Spanish experience of latifundia (vast
estates dating from the Reconquest, which largely supplanted small farms) and
land reform as seen in the agricultural areas of Andalusia. It describes the conflict
between labourers and landowners, noting how the labourers, although
subscribing to the tenet 'we who work' must always clash with landowning classes,
also realize that 'we the poor *must* work'.

187

Agriculture

651 **Agrarian structures in north western Iberia: responses and their implications for development.**
T. P. O'Flanagan. *Geoforum*, vol. 11, no. 2 (1980), p. 157-69.
A scholarly study of the mixture of different agrarian structures in Galicia, which the author believes is one of the principal reasons why the full potential of a physically fertile region has not been achieved. At the same time he shows how government rural policies are gaining little for the area, and concludes that prospects are bleak for Galicia without the implementation of integrated, rural, structural reform.

652 **Land and society in Golden Age Castile.**
David E. Vassberg. Cambridge, England: Cambridge University Press, 1984. 263p. 4 maps. bibliog. (Cambridge Iberian and Latin American Studies).
An analysis of the economic decline of Spain from an agricultural perspective. The main source of economic wealth for the Habsburg Empire in the 16th century was the revenue created by agriculture in Castile, when eighty per cent of the Castilian population lived in villages or small towns. The author has researched into Spanish legal and administrative documents to discover more about the rural customs and institutions of the region during the Golden Age. He studies the various forms of land ownership in rural areas (public, ecclesiastical, noble, urban middle-class and peasant), and the changes that took place in ownership and agriculture generally.

653 **El problema de la tierra en la España de los siglos XVI-XVII.**
(The land problem in Spain during the 16th and 17th centuries.)
Carmelo Viñas y Mey. Madrid: Consejo Superior de Investigaciones Científicas, 1941. 242p. bibliog.
During this period the physical development of the Iberian Peninsula underwent great changes, and new institutions grew up which left a permanent imprint on the country, leading to many of the peculiarities and complexities of the land problem in Spain. One of the author's primary aims is to produce a work, not solely concerned with economic and agrarian history, but one which interweaves all the relevant social, political and economic material to provide a complete history of the period. The study is based principally on contemporary accounts by writers and economists. Viñas y Mey also wrote *La reforma agraria en España en el siglo XIX* (Agrarian reform in Spain in the 19th century) (Santiago, Chile: El Eco Franciscano, 1933), which considers the subject of Spanish land tenure.

Remaking Ibieca: rural life in Aragon under Franco.
See item no. 470.

The cork oak forests and the evolution of the cork industry in southern Spain and Portugal.
See item no. 637.

Transport and Communications

654 **Steam on the Sierra: the narrow gauge in Spain and Portugal.**
Peter Allen, Robert Wheeler. London: Cleaver-Hume Press,
1960. 203p. 6 maps.
A well-illustrated work which describes narrow gauge railways throughout Spain,
and provides full details of the lists of rolling stock and locomotives of the public
narrow-gauge lines. Most of the book is concerned with Spain (180p.). The
enthusiasm of the authors for their subject is more than apparent.

655 **The railways of Spain.**
George L. Boag. London: Railway Gazette, 1923. 129p. bibliog.
This book is based on knowledge gained by the author during several years of
practical experience in the management of a railway in Spain. Although over sixty
years old, the work is still useful for the detailed information it gives on the
Spanish railway system in the 1920s.

656 **Inland waterways of Europe.**
Roger Calvert. Hassocks, England: Flare Books, 1975. 2nd ed.
259p. 6 maps. bibliog.
Very little information exists in English on this type of transport system in Spain.
The section on Iberia (p. 188-97) provides useful details on both the navigable
rivers and canals.

657 **El transporte aéreo en España.** (Air transport in Spain.)
Gabriel Cano García. Barcelona: Editorial Ariel, 1980. 240p.
bibliog. (Colección Elcano; la Geografía y sus Problemas: Serie de
Monografías, no. 2).
A good general account which underlines how air transport in Spain is closely

189

Transport and Communications

linked with the tourist trade. The topics covered include: the history of air travel in Spain; the national airline (Iberia); tourism and international traffic; and freight transport by air. Unfortunately it is not indexed, although the contents page lists sub-headings within each chapter.

658 **El 'affaire' de las autopistas.** (The motorway 'affair').
Bernardo Díaz Nosty. Bilbao, Spain: Zero, 1975. 192p. bibliog.
(Biblioteca 'Promoción del Pueblo': Serie P., no. 76).

A discussion of the problems and intrigues surrounding the design and construction of motorways and toll roads in Spain in the early 1970s, with particular attention to the roles of the government and multinational business concerns. It provides detailed facts about road tolls, construction costs and traffic predictions. The author also poses the question why, at a time when the energy crisis had taken its own toll on the world economy in general, and on the Spanish economy in particular, did Spain embark on a programme of road construction costing more than one billion pesetas.

659 **Last steam locomotives of Spain and Portugal.**
M. J. Fox. London: Ian Allan, 1978. 138p. map. bibliog.

'A pictorial souvenir of the last years of steam locomotives operation in Spain and Portugal', and a fascinating study for the true steam enthusiast. Black-and-white photographs (covering 130p.) of Spanish and Portuguese locomotives span approximately the last fifteen years of steam on the RENFE (Red Nacional de los Ferrocarriles Españoles, i.e. Spanish National Railways Network).

660 **El transporte colectivo urbano en España.** (Collective urban transport in Spain.)
Edited by José Jané Solá. Barcelona: Ariel, 1972. 342p.
(Colección Demos: Biblioteca de Ciencia Económica).

This book presents the views of a number of experts on the most important aspects of urban transport in Spain. The rapid growth of the large towns and cities in Spain, due in part to the continually escalating numbers of people moving from the countryside into industrial areas, has produced very serious problems as regards 'collective' transport, i.e. all public and private modes of travel.

661 **Transporte marítimo y construcción naval en España.**
(Maritime transport and shipbuilding in Spain.)
Pedro Sancho Llerandi. Madrid: Ediciones de la Torre, 1979.
188p. bibliog. (Nuestro Mundo, no. 3: Serie Economía).

A study of the shipbuilding industry, the ports, and the problems of maritime transport, which has been written for both the specialist in Spanish naval transport, and the general reader.

662 **Steam on the R.E.N.F.E.: the steam locomotive stock of the Spanish national railways.**
Lawrence Geoffrey Marshall. London: Macmillan, 1965. 195p. map.

The companion volume to *Steam on the Sierra* (q.v.). The author discusses the history of the national railway network, which in its modern state came into being in 1943. He gives details of the locomotives themselves, and their manufacturers who represent builders all over Europe and the USA. The book is aimed at railway enthusiasts, and includes full technical details and conversion tables, and over 150 photographs of the locomotives.

663 **Las telecomunicaciones en España.** (Telecommunications in Spain.)
Francisco Molina Negro. Madrid: Publicaciones Españoles, 1970. 43p. 3 maps. bibliog. (Temas Españoles, no. 509).

This short, illustrated study looks at the growth and development of telegraph and telephone systems in the country over the past one hundred years.

664 **Travel in Spain.**
Michael Thomas Newton. London: Harrap, 1976. 32p. 2 maps. (Discovering Spain).

A basic survey of transport systems in Spain, described through the eyes of two people who travelled to Spain from England, and then journeyed across Spain, and back to England. The volume looks at ferry crossings, train journeys, buses, cars and aeroplanes. This short and very general work is aimed at students of Spanish, but is marred by several printing errors.

665 **Transportation and economic stagnation in Spain, 1750-1850.**
David R. Ringrose. Durham, North Carolina: Duke University Press, 1970. 171p. 14 maps. bibliog.

The basic premise for this work is that the lack of an adequate transportation system was a primary cause of the political and economic stagnation of the country in the 19th century. The author describes the inadequacies of the roads in Spain before the railway age, and emphasizes how all areas of transport are linked to the implicit belief that economic growth and development are impossible without a ready supply of specialized transport. This stimulating study provides a new understanding of the prerequisites in transport technology for an industrial revolution.

666 **Stanley Gibbons stamp catalogue: part 9, Portugal and Spain.**
London: Stanley Gibbons, 1980. 313p.

This famous catalogue has been in continuous publication since 1865, and is commonly regarded as the philatelists' 'bible'. In this volume the section on Spain (p. 154-228) is followed with further information on issues from her former colonies (p. 229-311). There are detailed descriptions, illustrations (approximately 600), and prices of Spanish stamps issued between 1850 and 1979.

667 **Historia de los ferrocarriles españoles.** (A history of Spanish railways.)
Francisco Wais y San Martín.   Madrid: Editora Nacional, 1974. 2nd ed. 728p. (España en Tiempos).

A superb history of all aspects of the Spanish rail network, by an engineer who dedicated his life to the technical and historical study of the railways. He looks at the origins of the system in Spain in 1848, and studies its growth and development prior to 1970.

Railway holiday in Spain.
See item no. 42.

Banking, railroads, and industry in Spain 1829-1874.
See item no. 602.

Labour and Trade Unions

668   **The influence of international labour conventions on labour law and social change in Spain.**
Joaquín Albalate Lafita.   *International Labour Review*, vol. 118, no. 4 (July-Aug. 1979), p. 443-57.
This short article discusses how the influence of international labour standards can be clearly seen in the 1978 Spanish constitution and the reform of labour law which is now taking place. The author makes the distinction between indirect influence exerted through public opinion and trade union action, and the direct influence of obligations contained in ratified conventions. He cites a number of examples where legislation was adjusted in order to facilitate the implementation of laws concerning administration and labour relations, employment policy, working conditions, social security and the protection of certain categories of workers.

669   **Collective bargaining and class conflict in Spain.**
John Amsden.   London: Weidenfeld & Nicolson and the London School of Economics and Political Science, 1972. 204p. bibliog.
A scholarly study of the working of the official trade unions under Franco in the period 1961 to 1968, which begins with a brief history of the labour movement in Spain, and moves on to examine collective bargaining and industrial relations in general. The work also analyzes the operation of the 'jurados de empresa' (the factory committees which were introduced by law in 1953), and includes a case study made by the author whilst working in a Spanish factory.

670 **The anarchist collectives: workers' self-management in the Spanish revolution 1936-1939.**
Edited by Sam Dolgoff, with an introductory essay by Murray Bookchin. New York: Free Life Editions, 1974. 192p. map. bibliog.

Although there is a huge amount of literature on the Spanish Civil War, there are relatively few books devoted to the subject of workers' self-management, 'which constituted one of the most remarkable social revolutions in modern history'. The first section provides background information on the nature of the Spanish revolution; the collectivist tradition; the development of the libertarian labour movement in Spain; and the historical events leading up to and culminating in the destruction of the collectives. The major second section deals with the social revolution itself, describing life in the collectives, how the new institutions were established, and how they functioned. The concluding evaluation cannot help but be biased, as Dolgoff describes himself as an active 'anarcho-pluralist' deeply involved in the radical labour movement. Another work on the topic is Gaston Leval's *Collectives in the Spanish revolution* (London: Freedom Press, 1975), a richly detailed study of the workers' collectives during the Civil War, which at times struggles to be impartial. It has been translated from the French by Vernon Richards.

671 **The labor movement in Spain: from authoritarianism to democracy.**
Robert M. Fishman. *Comparative Politics*, vol. 14 (Apr. 1982), p. 281-305.

This paper deals with the development of the labour movement after Franco's demise, concentrating on an analysis of the 1978 trade union elections, the first to be held under the new régime.

672 **Spain: the workers' commissions: basic documents 1966-71.**
Edited by David Fulton, translated by Vicente Romano (et al.). Toronto, Canada: Canadian Committee for a Democratic Spain, 1973. 95p.

The first permanent workers' commissions were established at the beginning of 1961. The documents contained in this work provide an important introduction to the background of the commissions, and the emergence of this significant workers' movement in Spain. The introduction traces the growth of labour struggles from the end of the Civil War up to the 1970s.

673 **The current evolution of trade unionism in Spain.**
Juan N. García-Nieto París. *Labour and Society*, vol. 4, no. 1 (Jan. 1979), p. 26-48.

The laws prohibiting any kind of free association in trade unions which were in force under Franco were repealed in April 1977. Before this time only a single, official, government-controlled trade union organization existed, membership of which was compulsory. This work presents a good general survey of the trade union situation in Spain before and after Franco, and includes details of the new legal provisions made in 1977. The latter covered, for example, laws concerning the right to strike, collective bargaining, trade union elections, and the formation of major trade unions. Trade unionism is still developing in Spain, and has recovered far more rapidly after Franco's suppression than was expected.

674   **Manpower and education in Franco Spain.**
Morris A. Horowitz.   Hamden, Connecticut: Archon Books, 1974. 164p.

An original look at manpower policy and education in Spain, which analyzes the size and composition of the labour force and educational development, and their effects on the economic growth of the country. It includes a huge collection of statistical tables on both areas.

675   **International Labour Review, vol. 105, no. 3 (Mar. 1972).**

The entire issue of this journal is devoted to Spain, and contains a collection of articles which examine, from different viewpoints, the effects of the Trade Union Act passed in 1971, and the extent to which the trade union rights of Spanish workers were affected.

676   **Protective legislation and equal opportunity and treatment for women in Spain.**
María de los Angeles Jiménez Butragueño.   *International Labour Review*, vol. 121, no. 2 (Mar.-Apr. 1982), p. 185-98.

A historical review of developments in legislation designed to achieve the equality of rights between the sexes at work, the culmination of which was the Workers' Statute of 1980. The authoress examines the position and problems of women workers in several fields (maternity protection, employment opportunities, equal pay, family responsibilities), and concludes that labour legislation, and particularly social security legislation, still contains discriminatory provisions, some of which are favourable and some unfavourable to women. For a more detailed account see the recently published study by María Pilar Alcobendas Tirado entitled *The employment of women in Spain* (Luxembourg: Commission of the European Communities, 1984).

677   **Affluence, class structure, and working-class consciousness in modern Spain.**
John R. Logan.   *American Journal of Sociology*, vol. 83, no. 2 (Sep. 1977), p. 386-402.

A concise assessment of the political effects of improvements in the standard of living of the working class. The author surveyed a group of textile workers in Barcelona, and concluded that, as living standards rise, a growing proportion of the more affluent workers become more class conscious, in the sense that they become more class militant and politically aware.

678 Dictatorship and political dissent: workers and students in Franco's Spain.

José M. Maravall. London: Tavistock, 1978. 199p. bibliog.
(Tavistock Studies in Sociology).

An extremely valuable analysis of the re-emergence of the working-class movement under Franco. It studies the resistance mounted by working-class organizatons and students from three angles: the social and political tensions between Franco's régime and a process of rapid capitalist development; the persistence of traditions of political militancy in certain parts of society; and the survival and reappearance of underground political organizations, mainly socialist and communist.

679 Report of the study group to examine the labour and trade union situation in Spain.

Geneva, Switzerland: International Labour Organisation, 1969. 253p.

A detailed and officious study which is useful for gaining an understanding of the labour situation in Spain under Franco. The work is divided into six parts comprising: a general introduction and terms of reference of the study group; an outline economic history of Spain up to 1939, 1939-59, and 1959-69; the labour situation; and trade unions prior to, and since, 1936. The group visited Spain at the suggestion of the Spanish government, and was critical of the progress made towards the full representation of trade unions. Although they put forward some ideas for improving the situation, the study group tends to withdraw from stating the obvious fact that Franco did not want to consider granting any kind of real freedom to the workers.

680 El movimiento obrero en la historia de España. (The labour movement in Spanish history.)

Manuel Tuñón de Lara. Madrid: Taurus; Barcelona: Laia, 1977. 3 vols. maps. bibliog.

This massive and comprehensive work has become a standard source for historical data on the workers' movement in Spain. The author is a prolific writer on Spanish economic and social history, and this particular study was first published in Madrid by Taurus in 1972. Volume 1 covers the period 1832-99; volume 2, 1900-23; and volume 3, 1924-36. Each section is preceded by a brief chronological history of the period, and historical data.

681 Workers and the Right in Spain, 1900-1936.

Colin M. Winston. Princeton, New Jersey: Princeton University Press, 1985. 361p. 2 maps. bibliog.

An excellent contribution to this field, with the history of the 'Sindicatos Libres' (Free Trade Unions) forming the bulk of the work. For seven years they were the second-largest group of unions in Spain, playing a decisive role in the development of the Spanish labour system from 1919 to 1931. The author traces their emergence following the collapse of Catholic syndicalism in Catalonia (Spain's most industrialized region), and shows how, in the period up to the Civil

War, they moved from radical Carlism to a form of proletarian fascism. He attributes their success, in contrast to the failure of the syndicalism supported by the Catholic Church, to their willingness to engage in nonreligious, straightforward unionism, and to their strongly adversarial relationship with the employers.

682 **Labor policy and practices in Spain: a study of employer-employee relations under the Franco régime.**
Fred Witney.   New York; London: Praeger, 1965. 103p. bibliog.
(Praeger Special Studies in International Economics and Development).

This short work describes the problems which arise when a government, particularly a dictatorship, has absolute power over labour affairs. It is a good survey of another aspect of Franco's complete control over internal affairs, and analyzes the government's total domination of employer-employee relations. The right to collective bargaining was only recognized in 1958, and not until 1962 were workers granted the right to express lawfully a collective complaint to their employers.

The revolutionary Left in Spain, 1914-1923.
See item no. 247.

Child labour in Spain: a general review.
See item no. 491.

The Spanish anarchists: the heroic years 1868-1936.
See item no. 514.

Anarchists of Andalusia 1868-1903.
See item no. 522.

Red years/black years: a political history of Spanish anarchism, 1911-1937.
See item no. 523.

Anarchism: a history of libertarian ideas and movements.
See item no. 535.

Cooperation at work: the Mondragon experience.
See item no. 625.

Honor, commerce and industry in eighteenth-century Spain.
See item no. 626.

Mondragón 1980.
See item no. 627.

Mondragon: an economic analysis.
See item no. 641.

Labourers and landowners in southern Spain.
See item no. 650.

Statistics

683 **Anuario Estadístico de España.** (Statistical Yearbook of Spain.)
Madrid: Instituto Nacional de Estadística, 1912- . annual.

This publication, the standard source for Spain, offers statistics on a wide range of subject areas including: geography and climate; demography; agriculture, forestry and fisheries; industry; transport and communications; foreign trade; finance; prices and wages; employment; health; education; tourism; justice; religion; and housing. Publication was suspended between 1935 and 1942, and an 'edición manual' (pocketbook-size) was started in 1941 to provide a concise version of the *Anuario*, with some issues covering two years. The *Anuario* is supplemented by the monthly *Boletín Mensual de Estadística* (Monthly Bulletin of Statistics) (1939- .), and is divided into two parts: national statistics; and statistics for individual provinces.

684 **Demographic Yearbook.**
New York: United Nations Department of International Economic and Social Affairs: Statistical Office, 1948- . annual.

This large volume contains detailed statistics on population, including: natality; foetal mortality; infant mortality; maternal mortality; general mortality; nuptiality; and divorce. The text is in English and French.

685 **The Europa Yearbook: a World Survey.**
London: Europa Publications, 1926- . annual.

The section on Spain usually extends over thirty or forty pages, and provides a useful overall statistical analysis of the country. The information is revised annually, either directly from Spanish sources or from United Nations statistical data. There is an introductory survey listing details on: climate; language; religion; recent history; government; defence; economic affairs; transport and communications; social welfare; education; tourism; and public holidays. The statistical survey which follows includes tables on area and population; agriculture; industry; finance; trade; tourism; transport; mass media; and education.

686   **European historical statistics, 1750-1970.**
B. R. Mitchell.   London: Macmillan, 1975. 827p.
This work includes statistics on Spain which are particularly useful for the historical comparison of figures. The statistical information is based on Spanish sources published from 1849 to 1970, and topics covered include: climate; population; labour; agriculture; industry; trade; transport and communications; finance; prices; and education.

687   **Statistical Yearbook.**
New York: United Nations Department of International Economic and Social Affairs: Statistical Office, 1948- . annual.
This yearbook continues the *Statistical Yearbook of the League of Nations* (1926-44. annual). Statistics are included for member countries on: population; manpower; agriculture; forestry; fishing; industry; mining; manufacturing; construction; development assistance; trade; tourism; transport and communications; wages and prices; finance; energy; health; housing; science and technology; and culture. Parallel texts appear in English and French.

688   **Statistical Yearbook.**
Paris: United Nations Educational, Scientific and Cultural Organization, 1963- . annual.
An important work covering statistics on: education; science and technology; culture and communication; libraries and museums; the theatre; book production; newspapers and periodicals; the cinema; and radio and television. The data is supplied by over 200 member countries, in English, French and Spanish.

689   **World Health Statistics Annual.**
Geneva, Switzerland: World Health Organization, 1962- . annual.
A three-volume work which looks at all aspects of health and disease. Volume 1 includes vital statistics and causes of death; volume 2, infectious diseases; and volume 3, health personnel and health establishments. The main drawback with this work lies in the time lag, sometimes one of several years, between receiving the data and its actual publication.

Inventario de estadísticas de España: análisis documental de las publicaciones editadas desde 1960. (An inventory of statistics on Spain: a documentary analysis of works published since 1960.) *See* item no. 966.

Environment and Planning

690 **Regenerating Barcelona with parks and plazas.**
Peter Buchanan. *Architectural Review*, vol. 175, n. 1048 (June 1984), p. 32-46.

The author looks at recent strategy to renew the city, and appraises nine projects designed to provide Barcelona with an enhanced image and more open space through the creation of new squares and parks. There are currently over 160 such projects in motion. The article is excellently illustrated with colour photographs and several maps.

691 **National parks and reserves of western Europe.**
Eric Duffey, foreword by Sir Peter Scott. London: Macdonald, 1982. 288p. 10 maps. bibliog.

The chapter on Spain (p. 206-23) presents a most detailed guide for the zoologist, botanist and wildlife enthusiast, with beautiful illustrations, art-work and specially commissioned maps. The section opens with a general geophysical description of the country, its national parks and nature reserves, their wildlife and vegetation, and concludes by noting that Spain's efforts to protect the environment still lack the public support enjoyed by other countries. The book contains a glossary and map key, an index to the flora and fauna named in the text, and a list of the addresses of conservation organizations.

692 **Covadonga National Park, Asturias, Spain: its history, conservation interest and management problems.**
Miguel Angel García Dory. *Biological Conservation*, vol. 11, no. 2 (Feb. 1977), p. 79-85.

The Covadonga National Park was the first to be established in Spain (1918), and is one of the oldest in Europe. This article briefly describes the park's flora and fauna, and gives a general history of the location. The promotion of tourism in

Spain has led in recent years to the occupation of even the wildest and most remote areas, and the author stresses the importance of environmental protection, and the need to adopt basic reforms to achieve this.

693 **Urban development in southern Europe: Spain and Portugal.**
E. A. Gutkind. New York: Free Press; London: Collier-Macmillan, 1967. 534p. map. bibliog. (International History of City Development, vol. 3).

The cities of Spain 'occupy a special position' in the history of urban civilization, because they are 'historical records in stone of the two civilizations that have moulded Spanish history – Islam and Christianity'. This work attempts to describe the history, growth and topography of Spanish towns and villages in relation to geographic, economic and historic factors. It represents a standard work on the subject for Spain, and contains over 500 illustrations.

694 **Housing in Spain.**
John C. King. *Town Planning Review*, vol. 42, no. 4 (Oct. 1971), p. 381-403.

A discussion of housing needs in Spain under Franco, and their complementary provisions allied to the resources available for fulfilling housing programmes. The author tries to assess the relationship between housing, economic and social policies.

695 **Landscape planning in Spain.**
Landscape Planning, vol. 3, nos. 1-2 (Oct. 1976).

The whole issue of nearly 150 pages is given over to Spain, and discusses natural landscapes, nature conservation and land-use planning. The conclusions reached remain valid, and emphasize the need for short and long-term planning in a country with over 1,500 miles of coastline and a large tourist industry.

696 **Ecología y política en España.** (Ecology and politics in Spain.)
Miguel Anxel Murado (et al.). Madrid: H. Blume, 1978. 244p. bibliog. (Ciencia, Tecnología, Sociedad).

A detailed study of the current environmental problems in Spain, which looks at nuclear energy, fisheries, conservation, forests, and the contamination and exhaustion of resources. The book is the result of the work of a group of biologists, who studied as objectively as possible how some of Spain's most important natural resources had been administered under Franco. They note how these ecological problems only became serious causes for concern when they developed into public order problems, or when they diverted public attention away from even more serious matters.

Environment and Planning

697 **Planeamiento urbano en la España contemporánea (1900-1980).**
(Urban planning in contemporary Spain, 1900-80.)
Fernando de Terán.   Madrid: Alianza, 1982. 631p. maps. bibliog.
(Alianza Universidad Textos, no. 39).

A detailed study of urban and regional development in Spain throughout the 20th
century, which includes a chronological table of historical and urban planning
events in Spain from 1900 to 1980. It emphasizes the continuity and persistence of
virtually unaltered principles in Spanish urban planning over the years.

698 **Barcelona: planning and change 1854-1977.**
Martin G. Wynn.   *Town Planning Review*, vol. 50, no. 2 (Apr.
1979), p. 185-203.

An examination of the evolution of urban planning in Barcelona since the middle
of the 19th century, and an attempt to assess 'the value of some of the historical
perspectives relating to planning over the period as a whole'. The author stresses
the importance of early plans or 'ordenación', and in particular that of Ildefonso
Cerda which remained the official Development Plan for Barcelona for almost a
century. It is only in the last twenty-five years that more sophisticated plans have
appeared, such as those mentioned in Buchanan's article on environmental
planning in the city (q.v.). Wynn has also written an article entitled 'Peripheral
urban growth in Barcelona in the Franco era' (*Iberian Studies*, vol. 8, no. 1
(spring 1979), p. 13-28).

699 **Spain: urban decentralisation.**
Martin G. Wynn, R. J. Smith.   *Built Environment Quarterly*, vol.
4, no. 1 (Mar. 1978), p. 49-54.

A brief description of the 'evolution of a policy in Spain which attempts to deal
with urban congestion and the consequences of urban growth in major cities
through dispersing population and industry into new towns'. Particular emphasis
is given to case studies of urban decentralization from Madrid and Barcelona.

**The city and the grassroots: a cross-cultural theory of urban social
movements.**
See item no. 458.

Regional development policy and planning in Spain.
See item no. 598.

**Contradictions in living environment: an analysis of twenty-two Spanish
houses.**
See item no. 819.

Education

700 **The Spanish educational reform and lifelong education.**
Ricardo Díez Hochleitner, Joaquín Tena Artigas, Marcelino
García Cuerpo. Paris: United Nations Educational, Scientific and
Cultural Organization, 1978. 112p. (Experiments and Innovations
in Education, no. 31).

The same authors wrote *Education and work in the Spanish educational reform*
(Paris: UNESCO, 1981), both works being studies prepared for the UNESCO
Institute for Education in collaboration with the International Educational
Reporting Service. Their principal purpose was to describe the current education
system in Spain, and the causes and conditioning factors of Spanish educational
reform.

701 **Freedom and political power in the Spanish university: the
democratic movement under Francoism.**
Salvador Giner. *Western European Education*, vol. 10, no. 3 (fall
1978), p. 5-65.

This issue of the journal was inspired by a symposium on university autonomy
held in Madrid in March 1978. It was conceived at a time when Spanish education
was expected to be granted considerably more autonomy than it had previously
enjoyed, through the provisions of the new Higher Education Act which was then
being drafted. The article represents a comprehensive treatment of autonomy and
freedom in Spanish university life, and a detailed study of univerisities during the
period 1939 to 1977. Several statistical tables and a bibliography are included.

702 **International handbook of education systems: volume 1 Europe and Canada.**
Edited by Brian Holmes. Chichester, England; New York: John Wiley, 1983. 729p. bibliog.

The section on Spain (p. 589-614) provides a good general introduction to the Spanish education system, its administration and finance.

703 **Students and society in early modern Spain.**
Richard L. Kagan. Baltimore, Maryland; London: Johns Hopkins University Press, 1974. 278p. 8 maps. bibliog.

An excellent historical analysis of Spanish educational reform under the Habsburgs. It is the contention of this study that 'the rise of bureaucratic institutions in Spain in the years between 1500 and 1700, and the changes in Spanish society that this occasioned, were the most important and far-reaching influences upon Spanish educational history during that period'.

704 **Education for a changing Spain.**
John M. McNair. Manchester, England: Manchester University Press, 1984. 189p. map. bibliog.

An excellent comprehensive study of education and educational legislation in Spain, which underlines the fact that before 1970 there had been no major reform of the education system in over a century. The Education Act of that year (based on the *Libro Blanco* published in 1969) was intended to provide a more democratic and more technologically-based education for the young people of Spain to match the new needs of society. McNair provides a very full account of the provisions of the act, followed by chapters examining how each level of the education system, from pre-school to university, works, with details of curriculum, organization and management. The final chapters deal with the role of the Catholic Church in Spanish education, and the problems that regional autonomy poses for the system.

705 **Students and politics in contemporary Spain.**
José M. Maravall. *Government and Opposition*, vol. 11, no. 2 (1976), p. 156-79.

This article discusses how universities in Spain were put under the control of the Falange and the Catholic Church following the Civil War, and assesses the attempts by students to reconstruct democratic student organizations.

706 **Education in Spain.**
N. W. Newcombe. London: Harrap, 1977. 32p. (Discovering Spain).

Although mainly aimed at students of Spanish in English schools, this book gives a useful introduction to the education system in Spain, with particular reference to primary schools. For another study of the history and development of primary education in the first three decades of the 20th century, see David Van Holtby's *Society and primary schools in Spain, 1898-1936* (Ann Arbor, Michigan:

University Microfilms International, 1978). In September 1984 Spain's six million primary and secondary-school children were the subject of new developments in the education system, namely the abolition of homework.

707 **The universities of Europe in the Middle Ages, vol. II – Italy, Spain, France, Germany, Scotland etc.**
Edited by F. M. Powicke, A. B. Emden. London: Oxford University Press, 1936. new ed. 3 vols. bibliog.

This large and scholarly work, which was originally published in 1895, contains a chapter on Spain and Portugal (p. 63-114) by Hastings Rashdall. It provides a general introduction to the twelve Spanish universities of the Middle Ages, established between 1208 and 1500, amongst them the famous names of Salamanca, Alcalá de Henares, Valladolid and Barcelona.

708 **La educación en España: bases para una política educativa.**
(Education in Spain: bases for an educational policy.)
José L. Villar Palasí (et al.). Madrid: Ministerio de Educación y Ciencia, 1969. 244p.

Better known as the *White Book on Education*, this publication marked a turning point in national educational policy, and was the basis for Franco's Education Act of August 1970. It is a very wide-ranging and detailed study, covering all aspects of the Spanish education system: primary; junior; higher; women's; libraries; administration; and financing.

Manpower and education in Franco Spain.
See item no. 674.

Dictatorship and political dissent: workers and students in Franco's Spain.
See item no. 678.

The world of learning.
See item no. 895.

Science and Technology

709 **The Royal College of San Carlos: surgery and Spanish medical reform in the late eighteenth century.**
Michael E. Burke. Durham, North Carolina: Duke University Press, 1977. 215p. bibliog.

A superb, scholarly work focusing on the founding of the Royal College of Surgery of San Carlos in Madrid in 1788 by Antonio Gimbernat. The author describes the development problems (which were much the same as in other countries), namely financial constraints, and conflicts with the State and with physicians. The book also covers: the organization of the Spanish medical profession and its various institutions; the reform of medical education in universities and hospitals; the curriculum, staff and administration; and academic life as a whole. The work is based on extensive research into contemporary records.

710 **Spanish scientists in the New World: the eighteenth-century expeditions.**
Iris H. Wilson Engstrand. Seattle, Washington; London: University of Washington Press, 1981. 220p. 5 maps. bibliog.

This well-illustrated work examines two major Spanish enterprises undertaken during the final years of the 18th century, with the common objectives of scientific exploration, collection, and accurate reporting. The first, the Royal Scientific expedition to New Spain (1785-1800) established a Royal Botanical Garden in Mexico City, and provided scientists for work in Mexico, California, the Pacific northwest, Puerto Rico, Cuba and Central America. The second, the expedition of Alejandro Malaspina (1789-94) visited South America, Mexico and other areas in the Pacific. The book is essentially a study of the scientists and their work, and one which underlines the contributions of Spain, so often overlooked, in the realm of scientific achievement.

711 **The comparative reception of Darwinism.**
Edited by Thomas F. Glick. Austin, Texas; London: University
of Texas Press, 1974. 505p. bibliog. (Dan Danciger Publications).

This extensive study contains a chapter on Spain (p. 307-45) which discusses the
impact of Darwinism in the 17th century, and scientific development in the
country during the same period. It is the first comprehensive study of the subject
in English.

712 **The Spanish scientific community: a sociological study of scientific
research in a developing country.**
Pedro González Blasco. Ann Arbor, Michigan: University
Microfilms, 1977. 655p. bibliog.

One of the few studies of science and the scientific community in Spain, originally
presented by the author as his doctoral thesis at Yale University in 1976. It is
divided into four main sections covering: Spanish scientific research; the
framework of science; the scientists; and scientific output. An analysis of the
CSIC (National Science Research Council) is also included. The author has also
written *Historia y sociología de la ciencia en España* (A history and sociology of
science in Spain) (Madrid: Alianza, 1979).

713 **Planning for national technology policy.**
Edited by Alan Goodman, Julián Pavón. New York: Praeger,
1984. 439p. bibliog. (Praeger Special Studies).

A scholarly report on the Modeltec project, a three-year study to formulate a
national planning process for the technological development of Spanish industry.
The work provides an academic model for enabling and encouraging technological
development, and is divided into three sections. The first details the model itself;
the second discusses the broad issues in technological development; and the third
provides details of a large number of studies carried out in Spain.

714 **Science and the clergy in the Spanish Enlightenment.**
David Goodman. *History of Science*, vol. 21, part 2, no. 52 (June
1983), p. 111-40.

A brilliant assessment of the developments in science, and reactions towards
them, in 18th-century Spain, which stresses the attitude of the clergy. The author
notes how the scientific revolution of the 17th century affected Spain much less
than either France or Italy, and left it scientifically backward, as evidenced 'not
only in its univerisites, which were not unusual in resisting modern scientific
thought, but also in the paucity of Spanish cultivators of the new science'. Much
of the blame is laid on Philip II (1556-98) who imposed rigorous censorship in
order to protect Spain from Reformation heresy. The article also contains a list of
over 100 useful references for further study. For a more detailed analysis of Philip
II's ambivalent attitude toward science, see Goodman's article 'Philip II's
patronage of science and engineering' (*British Journal for the History of Science*,
vol. 16, part 1, no. 52 (Mar. 1983), p. 49-66).

Science and Technology

715 **Spanish science tries to grow up.**
Ros Herman. *New Scientist*, vol. 99, no. 1377 (Sep. 1983), p. 933-39.

A short but interesting article, which looks at how the socialist government has been attempting to stimulate the country's scientific research and development effort. It also provides a historical background to the neglect which science and scentific research have often experienced in Spain over the centuries.

716 **The Spanish contribution to world science.**
Pedro Laín Entralgo, José María López Piñero, translated from the Spanish by Daphne Woodward. *Cahiers d'Histoire Mondiale*, vol. 6 (1960), p. 948-68.

A lucid article which attempts to outline the scientific output of Spain from its early history up to the 20th century. It represents an excellent resumé of most aspects of Spanish science, technology and medicine.

717 **Ciencia y técnica en la sociedad española de los siglos XVI y XVII.**
(Science and technology in Spanish society during the 16th and 17th centuries.)
José María López Piñero. Barcelona, Spain: Labor Universitaria, 1979. 511p. bibliog. (Manuales).

A highly detailed analysis of the development of scientific activity in Spain during the 16th and 17th centuries, which tries to answer the question of why the 'scientific revolution' was delayed in Spain. The author, a prolific writer on Spanish science, has also written *Estudios de historia y sociología de la ciencia en España* (Studies in the history and sociology of science in Spain) (Barcelona: Ariel, 1979) in collaboration with José Jiménez Blanco and Pedro González Blasco; and a short article entitled 'The development of the basic sciences and their influence on clinical medicine in nineteenth-century Spain' (*Clio Medica*, vol. 8 (Mar. 1973), p. 53-63.

718 **Reviews of national science policy: Spain.**
Paris: Organisation for Economic Co-operation and Development, 1971. 123p.

A diagnosis and critical analysis of scientific research in Spain, and an examination of the chief demands on a new science policy when Franco was still in power.

719 **Guide to world science: volume 9, Spain and Portugal.**
Edited by Robert A. C. Richards. Guernsey, Channel Islands: Francis Hodgson (F. H. Books Ltd.), 1974. 2nd ed. 252p.

This work covers pure and applied sciences, engineering, medicine and, to a certain extent, the social sciences. The first part is an introductory study of: the organization of science in Spain; policy and finance; government science and technology; academic science and research; industrial research and development; agriculture and related sciences; medical sciences; nuclear sciences; aerospace sciences; sponsored and non-profit research; and societies, associations and information sources. The second part comprises a directory of the most important scientific establishments in Spain. Although now over ten years old, this book remains useful as one of the very few works in English covering the whole range of sciences in Spain.

Roman mines in Europe.
See item no. 162.

Spanish oil: a study of Spain's new oil frontier.
See item no. 624.

Bibliografía histórica sobre la ciencia y la técnica en España.
(A historical bibliography of science and technology in Spain.)
See item no. 968.

Literature

General

720 **Spanish literature: a brief survey.**
Nicholson Barney Adams, John E. Keller.   Paterson, New Jersey:
Littlefield & Adams, 1962. 206p. map. (The New Littlefield
College Outline College Series, no. 38).
This most competent and succesful work presents a succinct picture of Spanish
literature from the early Middle Ages to the 20th century.

721 **Writers in arms: the literary impact of the Spanish Civil War.**
Frederick R. Benson.   London: University of London Press; New
York: New York University Press, 1968. 345p. map. bibliog.
An examination of the influence of the war on European and American literature.
The author considers those writers who were active participants in the conflict,
and whose subsequent writings illuminated the various perspectives and ideologies
of the war. Ernest Hemingway, Arthur Koestler, André Malraux, Georges
Bernanos, George Orwell and Gustav Regler were among the major writers who
saw in the conflict a great cause with meaning far beyond the fighting in Spain,
and their writings influenced the 'conscience of Western man'. The work includes
a list of political abbreviations and their English equivalents, a chronology of the
war, and an extensive bibliography. In this area it is also worth consulting John
M. Muste's *Say that we saw Spain die: literary consequences of the Spanish Civil
War* (Seattle, Washington: University of Washington Press, 1966).

722 **Diccionario de literatura española.** (A dictionary of Spanish literature.)
Edited by Germán Bleiberg, Julián Marías Aguilera. Madrid: Revista de Occidente, 1972. 4th ed. 1,245p. 12 maps. bibliog.

A revised and enlarged edition of the original, which was first published in 1949. Over two dozen collaborating writers cover not only Hispanic literature, including sections on contemporary Catalan and Galician works, but also aspects of language and linguistics. The entries are reasonably concise, and those on the more important authors conclude with a list of further readings and critical works. There is also an 'A to Z' of writers and subjects, with a title index and a chronological table of literary and historical events in Spain from 711 to 1971.

723 **The literature of the Spanish people: from Roman times to the present day.**
Gerald Brenan. Cambridge, England: Cambridge University Press, 1953. 494p. bibliog.

One of the finest surveys of the literature of Spain through the ages, providing a detailed and well-written interpretation which is especially helpful to the novice. Brenan omits what he considers inferior, as his aim is to draw the attention of English and American readers to what was most worth reading in Spanish literature, and to help them to a better appreciation of it.

724 **The twentieth century.**
G. G. Brown. London: Ernest Benn; New York: Barnes & Noble, 1972. 176p. bibliog. (A Literary History of Spain).

Aimed primarily as a guide to the understanding and appreciation of Spanish literature, this work deals in turn with the novel, poetry and drama since the Civil War, set against social and political events. 'In short, what makes the twentieth century up to the Civil War a brilliant period for Spanish letters is what ultimately constitutes the greatness of any great period of literature: a substantial number of writers whose work merits lasting recognition and elicits lasting response precisely because it defies and transcends explanation and definition in terms of the circumstances in which it was produced'.

725 **Writers and politics in modern Spain.**
John Butt. London: Hodder & Stoughton, 1978. 76p. bibliog.

A concise commentary on the period from 1939 to 1960, which analyzes the interaction between politics and literature. The author contends that Spanish modernism was 'subverted from below' due to the rejection by writers of any kind of literature which smacked of 'élitism' or 'escapism'. As a result, the largely left-wing younger writers ignored most pre-Civil War Spanish literature in favour of 'socialist realist' poetry and prose. The resulting literary stagnation in the 1950s and 1960s was thus 'as much a result of the triumph of a long anti-modernist critical tradition as of the repressive policies deployed by the Franco regime'.

726 A new history of Spanish literature.
Richard E. Chandler, Kessel Schwartz. Baton Rouge, Louisiana: Louisiana State University Press, 1961. 696p. 2 maps. bibliog.

A comprehensive history of all the major Spanish writers and their works from the 11th century to 1960. The volume is particularly aimed at university students, but is presented in such a way as to be suitable for all interested readers. Both authors also edited *A new anthology of Spanish literature* (Baton Rouge, Lousiana: Louisiana State University Press, 1967), a work for undergraduate students which spans the period from el Cid to the present. Schwartz has also edited *Introduction to modern Spanish literature: an anthology of fiction, poetry and essay* (New York: Twayne, 1968), which covers 20th-century literature.

727 Eighteenth-century Spanish literature.
Ralph Merritt Cox. Boston, Massachussetts: Tawyne, 1979. 161p. bibliog. (Twayne's World Authors Series, no. 526).

A useful work on a lesser-studied period of Spanish literature. The author looks at the drama and poetry of the time, and attempts to show that 18th-century literature was quite varied in its scope, and that its main intent was didactic, i.e. to teach and reform.

728 The Middle Ages.
A. D. Deyermond. London: Ernest Benn; New York: Barnes & Noble, 1971. 244p. bibliog. (A Literary History of Spain).

Mediaeval Spanish language derived from a simplified popular form of Latin, whilst its literature evolved against the background of Moorish occupation and the Reconquest. The author analyses all the literary forms from the 11th to the 14th century, including lyrics, the epic (with special emphasis on the *Poema de Mío Cid* (Poem of the Cid)), learned prose, fiction, poetry and drama.

729 A history of Spanish literature.
Guillermo Díaz-Plaja, translated and edited by Hugh A. Harter. New York: New York University Press, 1971. 374p. bibliog.

An English translation of the original Spanish edition, presenting a chronological history of Spanish literature from the Middle Ages to 1970, and underlining how vast the Spanish contribution to European literature has been. It contains extensive quotations, and a bibliography listing English translations of classic Spanish drama, poetry and prose.

730 A new history of Spanish literature.
James Fitzmaurice-Kelly. Oxford, England: Humphrey Milford, 1926. 551p. bibliog.

This book was reprinted in New York in 1968 by Russell & Russell, having first appeared in 1898 under the title *A history of Spanish literature*. It is a classic work covering the period from early Spanish verse to the literature of the beginning of the 20th century. The author emphasizes the importance of France to the real beginnings of Spain's written literature, and notes how the earliest specimens of Spanish literature which are still extant are almost all written under French influence.

731 **The eighteenth century.**
Nigel Glendinning. London: Ernest Benn; New York: Barnes & Noble, 1972. 160p. bibliog. (A Literary History of Spain).

A well-balanced examination of the various forces which influenced Spanish writers of the period, and their reactions to foreign and national views of Spanish culture. The author emphasizes the importance of the composition and preferences of the 18th-century Spanish reading public in influencing what was written, when at the time a great many Spaniards were in fact illiterate. He has restricted the number of authors discussed rather than analyzed every single writer of the period, and has selected those major writers who best exemplify the literary feelings and atmosphere of the times.

732 **Spain and the western tradition: the Castilian mind in literature from el Cid to Calderón.**
Otis H. Green. Madison, Wisconsin: University of Wisconsin Press, 1963-66. 4 vols. bibliog.

This large scholarly work provides an 'interpretation of Spanish literary culture during five centuries on the basis of its dominant ideas'. Each volume in this very detailed contribution to Spanish mediaeval literature has its own index, and there is a cumulative index at the end of the entire study.

733 **Literature and inner exile: authoritarian Spain, 1939-1975.**
Paul Ilie. Baltimore, Maryland; London: Johns Hopkins University Press, 1980. 197p. bibliog.

This detailed and scholarly work, which at times makes difficult reading, jointly appraises the themes of literature and alienation. It discusses the many Spaniards who remained in the country after the trauma of the Civil War to experience what the author calls 'inner exile' (with geographical location sometimes being of secondary importance), made manifest in their disaffection for Francoist culture.

734 **The Golden Age: prose and poetry: the sixteenth and seventeenth centuries.**
Royston Oscar Jones. London: Ernest Benn; New York: Barnes & Noble, 1971. 233p. bibliog. (A Literary History of Spain).

This volume should be read in conjunction with the study by Edward M. Wilson, *The Golden Age: drama, 1492-1700* (q.v.), and is suitable for both specialist and non-specialist alike. It encompasses chivalresque, pastoral and picaresque novels, and the poetry of Garcilaso de la Vega and Luis de León, as well as important individual writers such as Miguel de Cervantes Saavedra, Baltasar Gracián, Luis de Góngora y Argote, and Francisco Gómez de Quevedo y Villegas.

735 **The origins of the Romantic movement in Spain: a survey of aesthetic uncertainties in the age of reason.**
Ivy Lilian McClelland.   Liverpool, England: Liverpool University Press, 1975. 2nd ed. 402p. bibliog.

The authoress is widely known for her contributions to Hispanic scholarship, and the purpose of this classic study is to analyze the trend of Spain's national Romanticism in the 18th and 19th centuries. Part 1 of the book is devoted to a review of literary theory, and examines the influence of Calderón and Lope de Vega. Parts 2 and 3 survey original works of Romantic literature.

736 **Surrealism and Spain: 1920-1936.**
Cyril Brian Morris.   Cambridge, England: Cambridge University Press, 1972. 291p. bibliog.

Surrealism had its centre in Paris, but the author traces the processes by which its influence reached Spain and was taken up by Spanish writers and artists. He discusses the major French works and the themes and techniques which appeared as a result in Spanish and Catalan, mainly in literature, but also in painting and films. One of the important features of this book is the collection of documentary materials on surrealism in Spain in the six appendixes, which includes lectures and other writings.

737 **This loving darkness: the cinema and Spanish writers 1920-1936.**
Cyril Brian Morris.   Oxford, England: Oxford University Press, for the University of Hull, 1980. 196p. bibliog. (University of Hull Publications).

The cinema aroused conflicting emotions in Spain at this time, and whilst many writers and critics delighted in the visual and imaginative stimuli presented to them, others saw it as a threat to the theatre, good writing and moral standards. Morris discusses how many writers thrived in this climate of controversy, and analyzes in particular the influence of the cinema on the poetry (the genre most affected) of Rafael Alberti, Luis Cernuda and Federico García Lorca.

738 **An introduction to Spanish literature.**
George Tyler Northrup.   Chicago: University of Chicago Press, 1960. 3rd rev. ed. 532p. bibliog.

This edition was revised by Nicholson B. Adams, and covers the whole field of Spanish literature from the earliest days up to 1960. When it first appeared in 1925 it received the following review in the *Bulletin of Spanish Studies*: 'It is superior to any Spanish history of literature in English. . . . It is put together carefully, it criticizes sanely, interprets liberally, and teaches understandingly'. This revised, enlarged and relatively up-to-date edition follows the same original pattern, with the author's purpose being to give the general reader and the university student an account of Spanish literature which will introduce him to its literary relevance and distinctive characteristics, through a survey of the evolution and development of the great genres.

739   **The Romantic movement in Spain: a short history.**
Edgar Allison Peers.   Liverpool, England: Liverpool University
Press, 1968. 230p. bibliog.

An abridged version of his two-volume work *History of the Romantic movement
in Spain* (Cambridge, England: Cambridge University Press, 1940). It has been
prepared with the non-specialist student of Spanish literature in mind, and
comprehensively covers the period from pre-1800 to the 1860s. The work is widely
accepted as an excellent study of a period which, although not particularly
outstanding in itself, was important for the ground it prepared for a far more
fruitful period of Spanish literature beginning around 1870.

740   **The 1898 movement in Spain: towards a reinterpretation.**
Herbert Ramsden.   Manchester, England: Manchester University
Press; Totowa, New Jersey: Rowman & Littlefield, 1974. 212p.
bibliog.

The novelists, poets, essayists and thinkers active at the time of the Spanish-
American War (1898), who restored Spain to a position of intellectual and literary
prominence that it had not held since the Golden Age of Spanish literature, were
labelled 'la Generación de Noventa y Ocho' (the Generation of '98), a term first
used by the writer and critic Azorín (the pen-name of José Martínez Ruiz, 1874-
1967). The defeat of Spain in the war led many writers to analyze, through their
work, Spain's problems and destiny. The Generation brought to the fore,
amongst other things, an awareness of foreign trends in literature, and through
that enabled the Spanish people to reassess their own values and awaken a
national consciousness, thus setting the mood for Spanish cultural development in
the 20th century. Ramsden's book aims to show that the Generation existed as a
significant grouping, and that its basic characteristics represent a pattern of
thought peculiar to the time, but not exclusively Spanish. He begins with a
comparative analysis of two key works: Miguel de Unamuno's *En torno al
casticismo* (On the Spanish way of life) and Angel Ganivet's *Idearium español*
(Spain: an interpretation), and proceeds to argue that the essential characteristic
of the 1898 Generation was its application of new methods, deriving from the
mainstream of European thought, to the age-old problem of Spain.

741   **Historia social de la literatura vasca.** (The social history of Basque
literature.)
Ibon Sarasola, translated into Spanish from the Basque by Jesús
Antonio Cid.   Madrid: Akal, 1976. 183p. map. bibliog. (Akal,
vol. 74, no. 59).

Originally published in Basque in 1971, this Castilian version is considerably
larger than the Basque original. It does not attempt to be comprehensive, but
merely gives a good introduction to the history, foundation and style of Basque
literature from the 16th century to the present. It is particularly useful for its
discussion of the major Basque writers of the 20th century and their works.

742 **The nineteenth century.**
Donald Leslie Shaw. London: Ernest Benn; New York: Barnes
& Noble, 1972. 200p. bibliog. (A Literary History of Spain).

The 19th century was one of the most important literary periods in Spain,
beginning with Romanticism and ending with the Generation of 1898, and this
work emphasizes the major writers, ideas and literary movements of the time.
The year 1898 witnessed the loss of the last vestiges of the Spanish empire, when
the Philippines, Puerto Rico and Cuba were forceably signed away, and a group
of young writers and intellectuals emerged (the Generation of '98) whose major
aim was the cultural and ideological regeneration of Spain. For a more detailed
study of the Generation see Shaw's *The Generation of 1898 in Spain* (London:
Ernest Benn; New York: Barnes & Noble, 1975), which includes an excellent
bibliography; and also Herbert Ramsden's *The 1898 movement in Spain: towards
a reinterpretation* (q.v.).

743 **A short history of Spanish literature.**
James R. Stamm. New York: New York University Press, 1979.
rev. ed. 285p. bibliog. (The Gotham Library).

A brief introduction to Spanish writing (first published in 1967) from its Latin and
Arabic beginnings, with particular emphasis on the 20th century. This is an
extremely useful book for the reader who requires a short overall survey, with the
aim of moving on to study some of the classic individual works available in
English translation (listed in the excellent bibliography).

744 **Catalan literature.**
Arthur Terry. London: Ernest Benn; New York: Barnes &
Noble, 1972. 136p. bibliog. (A Literary History of Spain).

Catalan is one of the three major Peninsular literatures, and has at certain times,
and to varying degrees, influenced Spanish literature. Information on Catalan
writers and literature in English is very sparse, and Terry has devoted most of the
book to literary developments and the major authors. Although it is particularly
useful for the specialist, it is also intended as a guide for the general reader with
some knowledge of Spanish.

745 **History of Spanish literature.**
George Ticknor. London: Trübner, 1863. 3rd ed. 3 vols.

A classic study of Spanish literature, which is based on the author's studies begun
in 1818 whilst travelling around Spain. This is a corrected and enlarged edition of
the original (1849), and although somewhat dated, it represents one of the first
thorough accounts of Spanish literature through the ages.

746 **The Oxford companion to Spanish literature.**
Edited by Philip Ward. Oxford, England: Oxford University
Press, 1978. 629p.

The author is a professional librarian who founded the Private Libraries
Association in 1956. He spent over twelve years preparing this book, which is a

well-produced encyclopaedic guide to Spanish writing (South American as well as Iberian), and a comprehensive reference guide to Spanish literature from Roman times to the present day. Regional literature (i.e. Basque, Catalan and Galician) is included, and excellent bibliographical information is provided within the individual entries, which are arranged in a single alphabetical sequence.

The rhetoric of humanism: Spanish culture after Ortega y Gasset.
See item no. 449.

A sourcebook for Hispanic literature and language: a selected, annotated guide to Spanish, Spanish-American, and Chicano bibliography, literature, linguistics, journals, and other source materials.
See item no. 959.

Manual of Hispanic bibliography.
See item no. 962.

Modern Iberian language and literature: a bibliography of homage studies.
See item no. 964.

M.L.A. International Bibliography of Books and Articles on the Modern Languages and Literatures.
See item no. 969.

Spanish and Spanish-American literature: an annotated guide to selected bibliographies.
See item no. 976.

The Year's Work in Modern Language Studies.
See item no. 977.

Novels

747 **The short story in Spain in the seventeenth century; with a bibliography of the novela from 1576 to 1700.**
Caroline Brown Bourland. New York: Burt Franklin, 1973. 217p. bibliog. (Burt Franklin; Research and Source Works Series; Selected Essays and Texts in Literature and Criticism; no. 192).

A reprint of the 1927 edition, which describes and analyzes the little-studied area of the short story before and after Cervantes. Over half the work is taken up with the bibliography of the 'novela', listing comprehensively the 17th- and 18th-century editions of the short stories written in Spain during the 17th century, exclusive of those of Cervantes. For the latter, references to bibliographies already existing have been given. The era of the short story in Spain began in 1613 with the 'Novelas ejemplares' (Exemplary novels) of Cervantes, and ended in effect around the middle of the century.

Literature. Novels

748 **The Spanish picaresque novel.**
Peter N. Dunn. Boston, Massachussetts: Twayne, 1979. 166p.
bibliog. (Twayne's World Authors Series, no. 557).
An analysis of the genre (so-called 'romances of roguery'), and an examination of its major works from *Lazarillo de Tormes* (1554) to *Estebanillo González* (1646). *Lazarillo* was the early form of the novel which established the genre, one which remained popular in Europe from 1550 to 1750. In Spain numerous successors followed this hugely successful original, e.g. Mateo Alemán's *Guzmán de Alfarache* (1599) and Francisco Gómez de Quevedo's *La vida del buscón* (The life of the swindler) (1626). All quotations are given in English, and useful plot summaries and criticisms are included.

749 **The modern Spanish novel.**
Sherman H. Eoff. London: Peter Owen, 1962. 280p. bibliog.
A comparative analysis of Spanish and other European novelists of the 19th and 20th centuries in the light of their common intellectual background. It probes deeply into the philosophical influence of science in fiction, and compares Spanish literature with works from England, France and Russia. Eoff demonstrates how Spanish intellectuals participated in contemporary European thought, and looks at the works of Spanish writers such as: José María de Pereda; Leopoldo Alas; Emilia Pardo Bazán; Vicente Blasco Ibáñez; Benito Pérez Galdós; Pío Baroja; Miguel de Unamuno; and Ramón J. Sender.

750 **The Spanish historical novel 1870-1970: a study of ten Spanish novelists and their treatment of the 'episodio nacional'.**
Madeleine de Gogorza Fletcher. London: Tamesis Books, 1973.
174p. bibliog. (Colección Tamesis: Serie A-Monografías, no. 32).
The work opens with an introductory chapter on the 'episodio nacional' (national episode) which developed into a new genre in the Spanish literature of the 19th and 20th centuries. It was basically a historical novel of the recent past, and the study covers the major writers in this style: Benito Pérez Galdós; Pío Baroja; Miguel de Unamuno; Ramón de María del Valle-Inclán; Ramón J. Sender and Max Aub; José María Gironella; Ignacio Agustí; Camilo José Cela; and Juan Goytisolo.

751 **Women novelists in Spain and Spanish America.**
Lucía Fox-Lockert. Metuchen, New Jersey; London: Scarecrow
Press, 1979. 347p. bibliog.
Twenty-two writers from 1630 to the present are included in this study, which aims to give the reader a better understanding of each individual novelist and Hispanic women in general, with emphasis on the feminine viewpoint rather than the literary aspects and merits of each writer. Each chapter follows a similar format: a brief biography of the writer and an analysis of one novel; commentary on the family, social class and the sexuality of the work; and an interpretation of the authoress's message from a feminine viewpoint. Unfortunately, there are some grammatical and printing errors, but as few books on this subject have been written, it still remains a valuable work.

218

752 **Literature and the delinquent: the picaresque novel in Spain and Europe 1599-1753.**
Alexander A. Parker. Edinburgh: Edinburgh University Press, 1967. 195p. bibliog. (University Lecture Series).

This is the definitive work on the genre, based on lectures delivered at the University of Cambridge in 1965. It presents a superb analysis of the Spanish origins of the modern European novel, and discusses the emergence of the picaresque novel in the social, religious, cultural, and literary conditions of Reformation Europe and Counter-Reformation Spain. Parker prefers the term 'delinquent' (an offender against the moral and civil law) to best express the 'pícaro' of Spanish 17th-century literature. The work is also invaluable for all students of English, French and German literature.

753 **The Spanish picaresque novel and the point of view.**
Francisco Rico, translated by Charles Davis with Harry Sieber. Cambridge, England: Cambridge University Press, 1984. 148p. bibliog. (Cambridge Iberian and Latin American Studies).

A translation of the third Spanish edition of 1982. The volume presents an overall picture of the picaresque genre in Spain, and its influence on the European novel, with emphasis on the two classic Spanish works *Lazarillo de Tormes* (anonymous) and Mateo Alemán's *Guzmán de Alfarache*.

754 **Spain's new wave novelists, 1950-1974: studies in Spanish realism.**
Ronald Schwartz. Metuchen, New Jersey: Scarecrow Press, 1976. 417p. bibliog.

This lengthy work covers the major trends and writers from the 1950s to the 1970s. It defines, criticizes and places in chronological perspective the developments in novel-writing in Spain during this period, and discusses the life and leading works of eighteen outstanding authors, with a view to defining the current position of the novel genre. There is an excellent bibliography covering each of the author's major works and the more important critical articles about them.

755 **The picaresque.**
Harry Sieber. London: Methuen, 1977. 85p. bibliog. (The Critical Idiom, no. 33).

This short introductory study is divided into two sections. The first considers the picaresque novel in Spain, its origins and definition, and the major works of the genre. The second looks at the picaresque novel in Italy, Germany, France and England.

756 **The Spanish pastoral novel.**
Amadeu Solé-Leris. Boston, Massachussetts: Twayne, 1980.
171p. bibliog. (Twayne's World Authors Series, no. 575).

Spanish pastoral novels were popular throughout western Europe in the 16th and 17th centuries, although pastoral literature in general was universally dismissed well into the 20th century as banal, false and artificial. The present work is inspired by the belief that there is a great deal more value in the Spanish pastoral novels than has hitherto been acknowledged, and aims to provide a concise, up-to-date survey dissecting, amongst others, Cervantes' *Galatea* and Lope de Vega's *Arcadia*.

Drama

757 **The Spanish sacramental plays.**
Ricardo Arias. Boston, Massachussetts: Twayne, 1980. 178p.
bibliog. (Twayne's World Authors Series, no. 572).

A detailed study of the 'auto sacramental' (sacramental, or mystery, play), the dramatic genre which reached its peak in the 17th century with the works of Pedro Calderón de la Barca. These short, allegorical plays were usually performed out of doors as part of the Corpus Christi feast day celebrations, and depicted different aspects of the mystery of the Holy Eucharist. Calderón took liturgical drama to new heights of artistic achievement before he was accused of showing irreverence towards the sacrament. In 1765 Charles III prohibited their performance by royal decree.

758 **The liturgical drama in medieval Spain.**
Richard B. Donovan. Toronto, Canada: Pontifical Institute of Mediaeval Studies, 1958. 229p. map. bibliog. (Pontifical Institute of Mediaeval Studies: Studies and Texts, no. 4).

A scholarly analysis of liturgical drama in Spain, and its relationship with the development of Spanish mediaeval drama and the liturgical drama of France. The author presents for the first time liturgical texts from Catalonia and the Balearics, and the work includes a detailed index and extensive quotations.

759 **The contemporary Spanish theater (1949-1972).**
Marion P. Holt. Boston, Massachussetts: Twayne, 1975. 189p.
bibliog. (Twayne's World Authors Series, no. 336: Spain).

This book represents the first inclusive study of post-Civil War Spanish drama. At the end of the war, theatrical production resumed in Madrid within days after the fall of the capital to the nationalists, but the artistic community itself had been decimated by the conflict. Ramón de María del Valle-Inclán had died shortly before the beginning of the war; Federico García Lorca had been killed in Granada; and Alejandro Casona was living in exile in South America. The year

1949 marked the approximate time when productions of the works of a new generation of aspiring playwrights began to appear, and this work deals with all the major writers of the period.

760   **Golden Age drama in Spain: general considerations and unusual features.**
Sturgis E. Leavitt.   Chapel Hill, North Carolina: University of North Carolina Press, 1972. 128p. (University of North Carolina: Studies in the Romance Languages and Literatures, no. 121).

This interesting and thoroughly entertaining work contains seventeen essays discussing many of the unusual aspects of Golden-Age theatre, including strip-tease, horror, justice, humour and animals. It emphasizes the role of the public in shaping Spanish plays, and their general appeal is obvious.

761   **Spanish drama of pathos 1750-1808.**
Ivy Lilian McClelland.   Liverpool, England: Liverpool University Press, 1970. 2 vols. bibliog.

Volume 1 is subtitled 'high tragedy', and volume 2, 'low tragedy'. The authoress surveys the dramatic aspect of Spain's movement towards modern thinking (or 'enlightenment'), and discusses the works of both the better- and lesser-known authors, scholars and dramatists, with special reference to the European context.

762   **Social drama in nineteenth-century Spain.**
J. Hunter Peak.   Chapel Hill, North Carolina: University of North Carolina Press, 1964. 168p. bibliog. (University of North Carolina; Studies in the Romance Languages and Literatures, no. 51).

A thorough analysis of a little-studied area of Spanish literature, which relates the 19th-century comedies of manners and social drama to the 'plays with a moral purpose' of the 16th and 17th centuries. The first and most important of the 19th-century social dramatists was Leandro Fernández de Moratín (1760-1828). Peak stresses the significance of Moratín's work, and considers that of other writers of the period.

763   **The Spanish stage in the time of Lope de Vega.**
Hugo Albert Rennert.   New York: Dover, 1963. 403p. bibliog.

A classic account of the 'Golden Age' of Spanish drama, and the playwrights of the 16th and 17th centuries, which was first published by the Hispanic Society of America in 1909. This edition is an unabridged and unaltered republication of that text, which only omits the 'list of Spanish actors and actresses, 1560-1680', which was appended to the original. In a similar vein, but far less detailed, is William Hutchinson Shoemaker's *The multiple stage in Spain during the fifteenth and sixteenth centuries* (Westport, Connecticut: Greenwood Press, 1973), in which the emphasis is on the methods of staging plays in Spain at this time.

764 **A history of the Spanish stage from medieval times until the end of the seventeenth century.**
N. D. Shergold.   Oxford, England: Clarendon Press, 1967. 624p. bibliog.

A fully illustrated and scholarly work on the history of the Spanish stage, covering all aspects of religious and secular drama. The main chapters deal with the buildings, stages, scenery, machines and actors, as well as the literary development and different themes and styles of Golden-Age drama. This lengthy volume also includes a glossary of theatrical terms, numerous footnotes, and an excellent bibliography.

765 **Modern Spanish rural drama.**
Barry Edward Weingarten.   Ann Arbor, Michigan: University Microfilms International, 1978. 378p. bibliog.

Originally presented as the author's PhD thesis at the University of Pennsylvania, the subject matter of this study ranges from the tragic and poetic elements in rural drama of the late 19th century, to specific studies on the work of Ramón de María del Valle-Inclán and the post-Civil War rural dramatists.

766 **The Golden Age drama 1492-1700.**
Edward M. Wilson, Duncan Moir.   London: Ernest Benn; New York: Barnes & Noble, 1971. 171p. bibliog. (A Literary History of Spain).

The drama of this period was one of the greatest and most influential in Europe, and was principally responsible for the development of a 'siglo de oro' (golden century) in Spain. The authors emphasize the importance of the main art forms of the time, the 'comedia' (play) and the 'auto sacramental' (sacramental, or mystery, play), whilst providing a detailed analysis of the works of the most famous writers (Juan del Encina; Lope de Rueda; Lope de Vega; Pedro Calderón de la Barca; and Tirso de Molina – the pseudonym of Fray Gabriel Téllez). They note how these Spanish dramatists wrote for an extremely wide range of society, and how from the middle of the 16th century companies of itinerant actors moving from town to town, performed their latest plays. From the 1590s onwards, however, Madrid became the centre of drama in Spain, and the provincial centres began to decline in importance.

767 **Spanish drama of the Golden Age.**
Margaret Wilson.   Oxford, England: Pergamon Press, 1969. 221p. bibliog. (The Commonwealth and International Library).

A highly readable introductory work to Spanish Golden-Age drama. The contents include chapters on the history of the Spanish theatre and the 'comedia' (play) from the 1580s to the death of Calderón in 1681, and the major playwrights and their works. This standard university text also includes translations into English of all the quotations used, and a list of the more important available English translations of the 'classics' of the period. It makes no claims to being comprehensive, but rather attempts to provide an overall picture of the literature of the time.

768 **A history of Spanish Golden Age drama.**
Henryk Ziomek.   Lexington, Kentucky: University Press of
Kentucky, 1984. 246p. bibliog.

Golden-Age drama came into existence in the last decades of the 16th century, and flourished for fifty years. This useful work presents an up-to-date survey of the history of the 'comedia' (play), with special emphasis on critical approaches developed during the past ten years. The author focuses on the work of the two geniuses of dramatic art, Lope Félix de Vega Carpio and Pedro Calderón de la Barca, whilst giving full credit to the host of lesser dramatists who followed in their paths. He also examines the profound influence of the 'comedia' on the literature of other cultures.

Staging in the Spanish theatre.
See item no. 856.

Bibliography of the drama of Spain and Spanish America.
See item no. 965.

Poetry

769 **Contemporary Spanish poetry (1898-1963).**
Carl W. Cobb.   Boston, Massachussetts: Twayne, 1976. 160p.
bibliog. (Twayne's World Authors Series, no. 373).

A useful introductory study of 20th-century Spanish poetry, with quotations in Spanish and corresponding English translations. An opening background survey is followed by a critical analysis of the major individual poets: Miguel de Unamuno: Antonio Machado; Juan Ramón Jiménez; Pedro Salinas; Jorge Guillén; Gerardo Diego; Federico García Lorca; Rafael Alberti; Vicente Aleixandre; Luis Cernuda; and the Generation of 1927 as a group (or 1925 – these poets actually began writing around 1920, but 1927 marks specifically the tricentennial of the death of Luis de Góngora, and it was a re-evaluation of his work that the Generation successfully undertook).

770 **The Spanish traditional lyric.**
Edited by John G. Cummins.   Oxford, England; New York:
Pergamon Press, 1977. 179p. bibliog. (Pergamon Oxford Spanish
Series).

Traditionally a lyric is a sung form of poem, and is closely connected with folk songs. The Spanish peasant has been instrumental in preserving much of Spain's lyric tradition. This work is divided into two parts: the first gives a representative selection of traditional lyric poems arranged by theme; the second, a series of examples of the use made of forms and themes by imitators from the 11th to the 20th century. It includes an index of first lines, and a useful bibliography.

771 **The post-Civil War Spanish social poets.**
Santiago Daydí-Tolson. Boston, Massachussetts: Twayne, 1983.
174p. bibliog. (Twayne's World Authors Series; TWAS 686).
The work aims to offer a critical literary interpretation of social poetry in post-war
Spain. 'Social poetry represents a view politically and aesthetically opposed to
that of the writers who supported Franco's "autocratic" rule, a form of protest
within the bounds which censorship imposed'. The author does not survey the
complete spectrum of social poetry of the time, but selects and considers only a
few poets, giving particular emphasis to Blas de Otero and Gabriel Celaya, the
two most prominent and characteristically 'social' poets of the period.

772 **Poetry of discovery: the Spanish Generation of 1956-1971.**
Andrew P. Debicki. Lexington, Kentucky: University Press of
Kentucky, 1982. 233p. bibliog.
The author is Professor of Spanish at the University of Kansas, and in the first
study of this Generation he examines the work of ten poets of the post-Civil War
period: Francisco Brines; Eladio Cabañero; Angel Crespo; Gloria Fuertes; Jaime
Gil de Biedma; Angel González; Manuel Mantero; Claudio Rodríguez; Carlos
Sahagún; and José Angel Valente. He particularly emphasizes the common
characteristics of language, images and metaphors shared by all of them. The
work also contains a useful bibliography covering the Generation as a whole, and
individual poets.

773 **Spanish writers of 1936: crisis and commitment in the poetry of the
thirties and forties: an anthology of literary studies and essays.**
Edited by Jaime Ferrán, Daniel P. Testa. London: Tamesis
Books, 1973. 141p. bibliog. (Colección Tamesis: serie A; no. 31).
This collection of studies stems in part from a symposium which was convened in
1967 at Syracuse University, New York, where some twenty Spanish writers and
American Hispanists presented a wide range of views on the literary ambience of
a relatively brief, but turbulent, period of Spanish literary history. The focus is
emphatically on the literary consequences brought about by the fundamental
changes in literary currents that were occurring in Europe, and the effects of the
upheaval caused by the Civil War in Spain itself.

774 **The early Spanish ballad.**
David William Foster. New York: Twayne, 1971. 220p. bibliog.
(Twayne's World Authors Series, no. 185).
A broad critical-analytical study of Spanish ballads of the 14th and 15th centuries.
The ballad tradition represents one of the primary literary forms of Spain, and her
own native ballads are generally termed 'romances'. All the works considered are
anonymous and unattributable to any known artist. The author hopes to justify
'the often expressed intuition that the ballads are in fact the best poetry of the
pre-Renaissance period in Spain'.

775 **Spanish poetry since 1939.**
Charles David Ley.   Washington, DC: Catholic University of
America Press, 1962. 273p. bibliog.
This volume is aimed both at the scholar and the interested layman. The author
examines and evaluates representative Spanish poets of the period 1939 to 1960.
He provides biographical and historical details and information, as well as a
selection of their works in Spanish with English translations.

776 **The dream-house (silent films and Spanish poets).**
Cyril Brian Morris.   Hull, England: University of Hull, 1977. 28p.
bibliog.
A brief investigation into the influence of the cinema on the Spanish poetry of the
1920s and 1930s. The silent films of Buster Keaton and Charlie Chaplin aroused
much enthusiasm, and undoubtedly influenced Spanish poets of the period.

777 **A generation of Spanish poets, 1920-1936.**
Cyril Brian Morris.   Cambridge, England: Cambridge University
Press, 1969. 301p. bibliog.
A critical study of the work of the 'Generation of 1927', which flourished between
the First World War and the Spanish Civil War. Morris treats the poets as a
group, and shows how although similar themes and attitudes were shared by them
all, each developed and gained an original style. The book contains numerous
quotations from their poems, with an English prose translation included. There is
also an excellent bibliography, black-and-white photographs of the poets,
comprehensive notes to the poems, and a glossary of Spanish terms.

778 **Studies of the Spanish mystics.**
Edgar Allison Peers.   London: Society for Promoting Christian
Knowledge, 1951-1960. 2nd rev. ed. 3 vols. bibliog.
A classic work, which is primarily concerned with the mystical aspect of the
writings, lives and personalities of seven of the greatest figures amongst the
Spanish mystics. Volume 1 discusses St. Ignatius of Loyola, St. Teresa, St. John
of the Cross, Fray Luis de León and Fray Luis de Granada; volume 2 considers
thirteen lesser-known writers; and volume 3 takes the study up to 1700, and
includes a lengthy bibliography and other information completed by an editor
after the author's death. For an interesting anthology of the prose work of the
Spanish mystics from the 15th to the 17th century, with some biographical
information included, see Kathleen Pond's *The spirit of the Spanish mystics* (New
York: P. J. Kennedy, 1958).

779 **Reality and the poet in Spanish poetry.**
Pedro Salinas, translated by Edith Fishtine Helman.   Westport,
Connecticut: Greenwood Press, 1980. 165p.
The work was originally published in 1940, and this edition is a reprint of that
published by Johns Hopkins Press, Baltimore (1966) in the series 'Johns Hopkins
Paperbacks'. Salinas (1891-1951) was the oldest member of the 'Generation of

1927', who pursued in his work a type of 'pure poetry'. Here he discusses some of Spain's most famous poems ('Poem of the Cid') and poets (Jorge Manrique; Garcilaso de la Vega; Fray Luis de León; St. John of the Cross; Luis de Góngora; and José de Espronceda), and tries to show how Spanish poetry, through the ages, 'has found for that insuperable problem of the two worlds, the poetic and the real, a series of solutions, each more beautiful than the other'.

780   **Spanish ballads.**
Edited by C. Colin Smith.   Oxford, England: Pergamon Press, 1964. 220p. bibliog. (Pergamon Oxford Spanish Series, no. 295).
A detailed examination of the ballad's relevance as a literary genre and a form of musical expression. The author considers the history of the Spanish ballads, their origin, development, form, structure, style, themes and sentiments, and provides examples of the texts of seventy ballads, with notes and partial translations.

781   **The victorious expression: a study of four contemporary Spanish poets.**
Howard T. Young.   Madison, Wisconsin; London: University of Wisconsin Press, 1964. 223p. bibliog.
A general study of the poetry of Miguel de Unamuno, Antonio Machado, Juan Ramón Jiménez and Federico García Lorca. The author has chosen these poets for their embodiment of the major themes and techniques of more than thirty years of Spanish poetry. A brief historical introduction is followed by details of their lives and major works, with original Spanish quotations and English translations.

Anthologies and translations

782   **Spanish poetry: from its beginnings through the nineteenth century: an anthology.**
Edited by Willis Barnstone.   New York; London: Oxford University Press, 1970. 526p. bibliog.
An excellent introduction to the history and development of Spanish poetry over the years, which presents a good selection of poems in Spanish of the more important writers. The anthology ranges from the jarchas (kharjas) which were written in Muslim Spain between the 11th and 13th centuries, to the poetry of the 19th century, and also provides brief biographical sketches of the poets.

783   **Modern Spanish theatre: an anthology of plays.**
Edited by Michael Benedikt, George Emanuel Wellwarth.   New York: Dutton, 1968. 416p.
An anthology of modern Spanish drama of the 20th century. Wellwarth also edited *Spanish underground drama* (University Park, Pennsylvania: Pennsylvania

State University Press, 1972), which is 'a presentation of the writings of a number of marginal playwrights' labelled 'underground dramatists' by Wellwarth himself.

784 **The Penguin book of Spanish verse.**
Introduced and edited by J. M. Cohen. Harmondsworth,
England: Penguin Books, 1960. rev. ed. 442p. (Penguin Poets, no.
D30).
One of the best anthologies of Spanish poetry from the 12th-century 'Poem of the Cid' to the 20th century, which includes plain prose translations into English. Two more useful poetry anthologies are: *An anthology of Spanish poetry: from its beginnings to the present day, including both Spain and Spanish America*, compiled and edited by John A. Crow (Baton Rouge, Louisiana: Louisiana State University Press, 1979), which is a bilingual collection from the mediaeval period to the present day for the general English-reading public; and *Spanish poetry: a selection*, edited by Eugenio Florit (London: Constable, 1971), which is an illustrated anthology of the writings of twenty-nine major Spanish poets from the 12th century onwards, and includes biographical details of the individual poets.

785 **Classic tales from modern Spain.**
Edited by William E. Colford. Woodbury, New York: Barron's
Educational Series, 1964. 201p.
A collection of sixteen short stories by leading 19th- and 20th-century authors, which includes several works appearing for the first time in English translation.

786 **The Penguin book of Spanish Civil War verse.**
Edited by Valentine Cunningham. Harmondsworth, England:
Penguin Books, 1980. 510p.
The first comprehensive collection of British poems concerned with the Spanish Civil War. Some very well-known literary figures (including W. H. Auden, Stephen Spender, Louis Macniece and George Orwell) are represented, as well as some lesser-known writers like Charles Donnelly, Clive Branson and Miles Tomalin. The book also includes supporting prose reports and reviews by the poets, and a selection of poems (notably Spanish 'romances') in translation. A very good introductory chapter portrays the war's relation to English literature, using material from the Archive of the International Brigade Association. Arthur Terry, who himself has edited an anthology of Spanish poetry (q.v.), commented in a review of the book: 'the most a writer can do in any war is to remain sane, articulate and self-aware. The fact that so many did so, on however modest a scale, under the privations and conflicting claims of the Spanish War more than justifies the present anthology, not only as an outstanding piece of historical reconstruction, but as a human document of absorbing interest'. For another work on the subject see Carlos Bauer's *Cries from a wounded Madrid: poetry of the Spanish Civil War* (Athens, Ohio: Swallow Press, 1984).

787 **Great Spanish short stories.**
Edited by Angel Flores. New York: Dell, 1962. 304p.
An anthology in English of seventeen writers, covering four centuries of the

development of the short story. Brief bibliographies of the authors are included. Flores has also edited: *Great Spanish stories* (New York: Modern Library, 1956), containing sixteen stories by Spanish writers of the past eighty years; *Masterpieces of the Spanish Golden Age* (New York: Rinehart and Co., 1957), comprising six early Spanish literary pieces dating from the middle of the 16th century to the middle of the 17th century; *An anthology of Spanish poetry from Garcilaso to García Lorca* (Garden City, New York: Doubleday, 1961), with selections in English spanning over four hundred years of poetry; and *Spanish drama* (New York: Bantam Books, 1962), an anthology of translations of ten major dramatic works from the 16th to the 20th century, by leading playwrights.

788 **Plays of protest from the Franco era.**
Translated, and with an introduction, by Patricia W. O'Connor.
Madrid: Sociedad General Española de Librería, 1981. 263p.
bibliog. (Modern Spanish Literature Series in English).

The translator is one of the leading authorities on the complex nature of Spanish censorship. The works included in this anthology are written by Spain's best-known serious dramatists, and are here published in English for the first time. The four selected works are: *The basement window* (El tragaluz) by Antonio Buero Vallejo; *The shirt* (La camisa) by Lauro Olmo; *The inkwell* (El tintero) by Carlos Muñiz; and *The guest* (El convidado) by Manuel Martínez Mediero. The format for each is the same: a brief synopsis of each play; biographical details about the dramatist; a short bibliography; and then the play itself.

789 **The Harrap anthology of Spanish poetry.**
Edited by Janet H. Perry. London: George G. Harrap, 1953.
467p. bibliog.

A representative selection in Spanish of poetry from the 12th century to the date of publication. The introductory chapter and notes are in English. Another anthology which has a similar time-span is *Ten centuries of Spanish poetry* edited by Eleanor L. Turnbull (Baltimore, Maryland: Johns Hopkins University Press, 1969), in which the texts are in Spanish with corresponding English translations and brief biographical sketches.

790 **The golden tapestry: a critical survey of non-chivalric Spanish fiction in English translation (1543-1657).**
Dale B. J. Randall. Durham, North Carolina: Duke University Press, 1963. 262p. bibliog.

A well-organized compilation, which provides a historical and critical examination of Spanish prose fiction during the 'Golden Age of English translation'. The year 1543 witnessed the first English printing of a Spanish narrative, and 1657 marks the year when the last of the great picaresque novels was translated into English. Between these years over a hundred English titles, editions and issues of translated Spanish fiction were produced. Randall's survey attempts to 'suggest the nature and extent of the Spanish fiction – especially the non-chivalric fiction – that was imported for Renaissance English readers'.

791 **The best of Spanish literature in translation.**
Edited by Seymour Resnick, Jeanne Pasmantier. New York:
Frederick Ungar, 1976. 304p. bibliog.

This is an abridged paperback edition of the comprehensive two-volume *Anthology of Spanish literature in English translation* (New York: Frederick Ungar, 1958). It presents an excellent selection of Spanish prose, verse and drama from the 12th century to the present, and includes brief biographical sketches and an author index. Resnick and Pasmantier also edited *Highlights of Spanish literature* (New York: Frederick Ungar, 1963), which is an anthology of works of prose and poetry, in Spanish (with English translations), from mediaeval times to the present. Resnick also edited *Selections from Spanish poetry* (Irvington-on-Hudson, New York: Harvey House, 1962), which is a collection of thirty-eight examples of classic poetry from the 12th century to the present in Spanish, with English translations.

792 **Roots and wings: poetry from Spain 1900-1975.**
Edited by Hardie St. Martin. New York: Harper & Row, 1976.
528p. bibliog.

A bilingual anthology of 20th-century poetry from more than twenty of the most important Spanish poets of the period. It opens with the works of Miguel de Unamuno, Antonio Machado and Juan Ramón Jiménez who were major writers and influences of the time. Unfortunately, no critical commentaries are given, although the introduction attempts to sum up the major themes of each poet, and the biographical and bibliographical notes contained at the end of the work give useful details about each one.

793 **An anthology of Spanish poetry 1500-1700.**
Edited by Arthur Terry. Oxford, England: Pergamon Press,
1965-68. 2 vols. bibliog. (Commonwealth and International Library
Series).

A valuable anthology, with historical and critical notes on the poets. Part 1 covers the period from 1500 to 1580, and consists of ninety-one poems by thirty poets from Garci Sánchez de Badajoz to St. John of the Cross. It includes a long introductory essay which covers the development of poetry and poetic theory in 16th-century Spain, and a glossary of archaic words and word forms. Part 2 (1580 to 1700) complements part 1, and looks at a further forty-two poets, from Miguel de Cervantes to Sor Juana Inés de la Cruz. Each volume is designed to constitute a self-contained work, and both are aimed particularly at university students of Spanish poetry.

794 **The Oxford book of Spanish verse: thirteenth century-twentieth
century.**
Edited by James Brande Trend. Oxford, England: Clarendon
Press, 1940. 2nd ed. 522p.

The original edition, published in 1913, was edited by James Fitzmaurice-Kelly. This second edition, revised by Trend, is now a standard work, and includes more examples covering the 19th and 20th centuries. There is an introduction in English, followed by the texts of the poems and ballads in Spanish. Over three hundred poems make up this excellent selection.

795 **Spanish poetry of the Golden Age.**
Edited by Bruce W. Wardropper.   New York: Appleton-Century-Crofts, 1971. 353p. bibliog.

A good selection of over 200 works from the leading Spanish lyric poets who wrote during the Golden Age of Spanish literature. The poems are in Spanish, with notes in English, and brief biographical sketches are included. Although aimed at students of Spanish poetry, the detailed notes make it accessible to those with a reasonable knowledge of Spanish.

796 **The new wave Spanish drama.**
Edited by George Emanuel Wellwarth.   New York: New York University Press; London: University of London, 1970. 321p.

The 'new wave' drama in Spain is recognized as having begun with Antonio Buero Vallejo's *Historia de una escalera* (Story of a staircase) (1949), and this anthology includes works by José Ruibal, José M. Bellido, Antonio Martínez Ballesteros and Alfonso Sastre. None of their plays had been performed in Spain when the book was written, as for the most part their publication and production there were forbidden because of their satirical and political comments.

A new history of Spanish literature.
See item no. 726.

Spanish plays in English translation: an annotated bibliography.
See item no. 970.

English translations from the Spanish, 1484-1943: a bibliography.
See item, no. 972.

The literature of Spain in English translation: a bibliography.
See item no. 973.

Spanish literature in Russia and in the Soviet Union 1735-1964.
See item no. 975.

The Arts

General

797 Moorish culture in Spain.
Titus Burckhardt, translated by Alisa Jaffa. London: Allen & Unwin, 1972. 219p. bibliog.

After the arrival of the Moors in 711, Arabic culture exerted great influence in Spain for over eight centuries. This book stresses the importance of Moorish contributions in the fields of painting and architecture, amongst others, and is beautifully illustrated.

798 Art treasures in Spain: monuments, masterpieces, commissions and collections.
Edited by Trewin Copplestone, Bernard S. Myers. London; Sydney, Australia: Paul Hamlyn, 1970. 175p. 2 maps.

This beautifully-illustrated book covers all types of art from the cave paintings of Altamira to modern work. Each section has been written by an expert on the subject and period.

799 The kings of Spain.
Frederic V. Grunfeld. Chicago: Stonehenge Press, 1982. 176p. 3 maps. bibliog. (Treasures of the World).

A lavishly illustrated book on some of the notable art treasures of several of Spain's most important rulers: Alfonso the Wise; Isabella and Ferdinand; Charles I; Philip II; and Philip V. The colour plates are outstanding.

800 **The arts of Spain.**
José María Gudiol Ricart.   London: Thames & Hudson, 1964.
318p.

The author's aim is to bring the reader 'closer to a world of art that is much less familiar than it should be, to a country rich in legend and history, and to a culture that was for centuries a bridge between the Atlantic and Mediterranean civilizations'. This variety of culture derives from Spain's location between Europe, Africa and the Americas, from numerous foreign invasions, changing styles, and the remarkable evolution of ideas. The work presents a comprehensive study of art, crafts, architecture, sculpture and culture generally, from prehistoric times up to 1960, and is supported by superb illustrations.

801 **Art and architecture in Spain and Portugal and their American dominions 1500-1800.**
George Kubler, Martin Soria.   Harmondsworth, England:
Penguin Books, 1959. 445p. 3 maps. bibliog. (The Pelican History of Art, no. Z17).

An indispensable and authoritative survey, which contains nearly 200 photographs of buildings, sculptures and paintings, as well as many figures and architectural drawings. It is still the best general study in this area in English, and achieves two principal aims: 'to respect regional groupings, even at the expense of nationalist sentiment; and to treat style as our most important concern'. Part 1 is a study of architecture; part 2 looks at sculpture; and part 3, painting.

802 **Early medieval art in Spain.**
Pedro de Palol, Max Hirmer.   London: Thames & Hudson, 1967.
500p. 4 maps. bibliog.

A beautifully-produced and illustrated historical survey of all phases of art and architecture in Spain from the time of the Visigoths to the end of the 13th century. Descriptive notes and genealogical tables are included.

803 **Spain – a history in art.**
Bradley Smith.   New York: Gemini-Smith, 1979. rev. ed. 296p.
bibliog.

A collection of photographs, paintings, sculptures, tapestries, murals, illuminations and 'objets d'art' which illustrate the pageant of Spanish history. The author is one of the world's outstanding photographers of art works, and his primary aim is to evoke the spirit of Spain and its people from the evolution of the Iberian Peninsula in prehistoric times to the end of the monarchy of Alfonso XIII in 1931. Each major section is introduced with parallel tables showing the art chronology and the historical chronology of the period.

804 **Iberian art.**
Miguel Tarradell. New York: Rizzoli International Publications, 1978. 111p. map. bibliog.
The short introduction is followed by a brief description of Iberian architecture, sculpture, painting and metalwork. The most important feature of this work is that it principally consists of colour and black-and-white illustrations (nearly 100).

805 **Spanish art: an introductory review of architecture, painting, sculpture, textiles, ceramics, woodwork, metalwork.**
Edited by R. R. Tatlock. London: B. T. Batsford, for the Burlington Magazine, 1927. 121p. map. bibliog. (Burlington Magazine Monograph, no. 2).
Although nearly sixty years old, this book contains some excellent colour and black-and-white illustrations representing a comprehensive history of all aspects of Spanish art. The prime objective of the volume is to encourage a closer and more detailed study of Spanish art, both on the part of those who know the country well, and on the part of interested readers. Each section has been written by an expert in a particular field.

Painting

806 **Images and ideas in seventeenth-century Spanish painting.**
Jonathan Brown. Princeton, New Jersey: Princeton University Press, 1978. 168p. bibliog. (Princeton Essays on the Arts, no. 6).
At the time he wrote this book, the author was the Director of the Institute of Fine Arts of New York University, and the work itself is based on the author's thesis at Princeton University in 1964. It is one of the few studies which relate important Baroque paintings and painters to their cultural environment. Part 1 provides a very detailed study of the artistic-literary academy of Francisco Pacheco, whilst part 2 deals with four major painters and their works (Velázquez, Zurbarán, Murillo and Valdés Leal). Brown, in conjunction with John Huxtable Elliott, also wrote *A palace for a king: the Buen Retiro and the court of Philip IV* (New Haven, Connecticut; London: Yale University Press, 1980), which looks at the King's patronage of the arts in the first half of the 17th century, and the collections built up by him in the Buen Retiro palace in Madrid.

807 **Spanish painting.**
Gotthard Jedlicka, translated from the German by J. Maxwell Brownjohn. London: Thames & Hudson, 1963. 204p.
This work represents a selection of some of the greatest and most famous of Spanish painters and paintings (El Greco; Jusepe de Ribera; Zurbarán; Murillo; Juan de Valdés Leal; Velázquez; and Goya), and captures the atmosphere and

motivating forces surrounding them. It also describes several of the general characteristics which epitomized Spanish painting between the 15th and 17th centuries, noting the importance of religious themes.

808 **Spanish painting: from the Catalan frescoes to El Greco.**
Jacques Lassaigne, translated by Stuart Gilbert. Geneva, Switzerland: Skira, 1952. 137p. map. bibliog. (Painting, Colour, History, vol. 6).

A translation of the French original. The volume provides an overall picture of the continuity of Spanish art over the years, rather than a study of specific painters. There are over seventy colour reproductions of the paintings, together with critical commentaries, biographical notes on the artists represented, and a large bibliography.

809 **Spanish painting: from Velázquez to Picasso.**
Jacques Lassaigne, translated by Stuart Gilbert. Geneva, Switzerland: Skira, 1952. 148p. bibliog. (Painting, Colour, History, vol. 8).

This work continues the study on Spanish painting begun in the previous entry, and follows a similar format.

810 **Spanish painting.**
John F. Moffitt. London: Studio Vista; New York: Dutton, 1973. 159p. bibliog.

A brief and somewhat sweeping survey of the history of Spanish painting, divided chronologically, from the earliest times to the present. The author emphasizes how Spain has made a major contribution to European culture through the works of El Greco, Velázquez, Goya, Dalí, Picasso and others, and points out how Spain gave rise to the solitary artistic genius rather than particular schools of painting. He sees the keynote of the Spaniard and of Spanish art as being the balance between the material and the spiritual.

811 **A history of Spanish painting.**
Chandler Rathfon Post, edited by Harold Edwin Wethey.
Cambridge, Massachussetts: Harvard University Press, 1930-66. 14 vols. bibliog. (Harvard-Radcliffe Fine Art Series).

An exhaustive, and now classic, study of Spanish art up to the middle of the 16th century, by the foremost historian of Spanish mediaeval and Renaissance painting. Each volume is devoted to a particular phase, and contains a bibliography and indexes of artists and places. Volume 11 contains an additional bibliography for volumes 1-10, and the final volume includes the author's personal biography and a bibliography of his works.

812 **Spanish drawings: from the tenth to the nineteenth century.**
Francisco Javier Sánchez Cantón. London: Studio Vista, 1965.
141p. bibliog. (Great Drawings of the World).
The author, one-time Director of the Prado Museum in Madrid, has made a careful selection, from collections both public and private all over the world, of Spanish works of art over ten centuries. Forty-seven artists are represented, including drawings by Goya, Velázquez and El Greco, together with brief biographies.

813 **Treasures of Spanish paintings.**
M. Wiesenthal. Barcelona, Spain: Geocolor, 1979. 95p.
A collection of over 100 colour plates of some of the most famous Spanish paintings, by Spain's outstanding artists. The accompanying text provides brief biographical details and critical comments on the artists' works.

Architecture

814 **History of Spanish architecture.**
Bernard Bevan. London: B. T. Batsford, 1938. 199p. 2 maps.
bibliog.
A competently-written, comprehensive survey of architecture in Spain through the centuries, which is as valuable for the general reader as it is for the subject specialist. This now standard work emphasizes the great contrasts in architectural styles, the products of the two distinct Christian and Moorish civilizations. It includes individual chapters on castles and cathedrals, and architectural drawings and illustrations.

815 **Architecture of Spain.**
Harold W. Booton. Newcastle upon Tyne, England: Oriel Press, 1966. 96p. map. (Oriel Guides).
An attractive pocket guide illustrating every style of architecture to be found in Spain. The work includes: a glossary of architectural terms; a brief outline of Spanish architecture; descriptions of styles, with numerous examples; a short guide to architectural tours in Spain; brief general information; and nearly 200 illustrations. This series is specifically intended for tourists, but is also useful for students of architecture.

816 **Spanish folk architecture: 1 – the northern plateau.**
Luis Feduchi. Barcelona, Spain: Editorial Blume, 1977. 373p.
bibliog. (New Image Collection).
Originally published in Spanish in 1974, this work represents the first of five projected volumes (and at the time of writing the only one to have appeared), and

covers the northern meseta plateau in general. Feduchi uses the term 'folk architecture' to encompass the architecture among the common people where 'each craftsman solves architectural problems in his own way, with his own building techniques and following his own sense of grace, beauty and composition . . . yet the houses of each region are all very similar since the work itself is impersonal and reflects the joint efforts of many different craftsmen'. Over 1,000 illustrations are included.

817 **The cathedrals of Spain.**
John Harvey. London: Batsford, 1957. 279p. map. bibliog.

'A wonderful and thrilling book . . . as a work of combined interest and erudition it is not likely to be equalled in our time' was Sachaverell Sitwell's comment on this work, which investigates all aspects of cathedral architecture in Spain. The author provides a historical and descriptive analysis by region, and includes all the relevant technical details concerning dimensions, as well as information about building dates and architects.

818 **Baroque in Spain and Portugal, and its antecedents.**
James Lees-Milne. London: Batsford, 1960. 224p. bibliog.

The author, who at the time of writing was architectural adviser to the National Trust, makes no claims to comprehensiveness in this work. Instead, he stresses the origins of the Baroque style in the Peninsula from 1680 to 1780, and notes the distinct regional variations.

819 **Contradictions in living environment: an analysis of twenty-two Spanish houses.**
David Mackay. London: Crosby Lockwood, 1971. 118p. map.

Mackay was joint architect for two of the buildings studied in this appraisal of house architecture in the Barcelona area. His principal objectives are to illustrate a selection of houses built in Spain during the decade 1960 to 1970, which he believes contributes to a critical interpretation of the living environment, and to try to explain his own critical approach to the houses. The book consists of a long introduction to the problems of the living environment, and an analysis of how they have been tackled in the design of Spanish houses. The remainder of the work consists of photographs, plans and descriptions of the twenty-two examples.

820 **Cathedrals and monasteries of Spain.**
Friedrich Rahlves. London: Nicholas Kaye, 1966. 310p. map. bibliog.

Translated from the French, this study moves through the architectural periods and styles from Visigothic times to the late Gothic period (15th century). Rahlves himself was an architect and historian, and he presents the results of his observations in an interesting and absorbing manner. Spain's most famous monastery-palace, El Escorial, has provoked much writing during its four centuries of existence, and one of the best and most detailed studies of its architectural history is George Kubler's *Building the Escorial* (Princeton, New Jersey: Princeton University Press, 1982). See also Mary Cable's *El Escorial*

(London: Reader's Digest Association, 1971), which contains beautiful photographs of the location and its treasures.

821 / **Moorish Spain: Cordoba, Seville, Granada.**
Enrique Sordo. London: Elek Books, 1963. 223p. bibliog.
This beautifully-illustrated work deals with the art and architecture of Moorish Spain (Al-Andalus), and traces the progress of Moorish art from the 8th to the 15th century. The three cities of southern Spain in the title are famous for their Moorish architecture and lasting Arab influence.

822 **Buildings in Spain.**
R. Tames. London: Harrap, 1977. 32p. (Discovering Spain).
A useful, but brief, introduction to Spanish architecture for the general reader, illustrated with photographs of some of the most impressive and interesting buildings in Spain. A brief historical survey is followed by sections on: Renaissance, Baroque and Rococo architecture; the Alhambra; the Escorial; the modern period; Antoní Gaudí (1852-1926); regional architecture; the post-Civil War building boom; Spanish houses; and the increase in building over the past two decades due to the huge influx of tourists.

823 **Spanish gardens: their history types and features.**
C. M. Villiers-Stuart. London: Batsford, 1936. 138p. bibliog.
The author notes how in Spain house and garden are closely interlinked, and attempts to illuminate the unique relation of Spanish gardens to garden craft in east and west. This evocative work provides closely-detailed descriptions of the gardens, which perfectly expose their variety and individuality. Another highly descriptive work on Spanish gardens is Rose Standish Nichols' *Spanish and Portuguese gardens* (Boston, Massachussetts; New York: Houghton Mifflin, 1924).

824 **Castles in Spain.**
Oliver Washburn. Berkeley, California: Robert R. Morgan, 1957. 320p. map.
A profusely-illustrated book which records a 17,000-mile tour of Spain through detailed descriptions of over 100 Spanish castles.

Decorative arts

825 **Hispanic furniture: from the fifteenth through the eighteenth century.**
Grace Hardendorff Burr. New York: Archive Press, 1964. 2nd ed. 231p. bibliog.
A beautifully-produced history of Spanish furniture from the Gothic to the end of the Rococo period, which is aimed at scholars, designers, dealers and collectors.

The author (formerly Curator of Furniture of the Hispanic Society of America museum in New York), looks in particular at the furniture of the 16th and 17th centuries, an important period when the cabinet-makers of Spain and Portugal developed the original style that distinguishes their work from that of the rest of Europe. There is also a section on Spanish and Portuguese colonial furniture.

826 Spanish interiors and furniture.

Photographs and drawings by Arthur Byne, with a brief text by Mildred Stapley. New York: Dover, 1969. 300p.

A one-volume unabridged reprint of the work originally published in three volumes (New York: William Helburn, 1921-25). It presents a history of all aspects of the subject, and contains a superb photographic collection of interior decorative schemes and furniture.

827 Spanish ironwork.

Arthur Byne, Mildred Stapley. New York: Hispanic Society of America, 1915. 143p. (Hispanic Society Publications, no. 89).

Spanish ironwork owes little to foreign influence, as practitioners of the art were almost invariably native born. The authors concentrate on the Gothic and Renaissance periods, and emphasize the influence of the Moorish occupation of Spain over seven centuries on all areas of the industrial arts. The volume contains over 150 illustrations of Spanish ironwork, and a catalogue of works in the collection of the Hispanic Society of America.

828 Spanish glass.

Alice Wilson Frothingham. London: Faber & Faber, 1964. 96p. map. bibliog. (Faber Monographs on Glass).

The authoress (one-time Curator at the Hispanic Society of America Museum) provides a full history of glassmaking in Spain from the mediaeval period to the middle of the 19th century, which includes both colour and black-and-white photographic examples of Spanish glassware. She stresses the influence of both the Arabs and the Romans, and highlights Catalonia's contribution to glassmaking: 'By the sixteenth century, the Catalans not only imitated but rivalled Venice in the excellence of their products and in variety of colour and design'. As in other areas of 'the industrial arts', Spain was very receptive to foreign influences, but also contributed many ideas of her own, so much so that Spanish glass remains unmistakable.

829 Renaissance sculpture in Spain.

Manuel Gómez-Moreno, translated from the Spanish by Bernard Bevan. New York: Hacker Art Books, 1971. 113p. bibliog.

This book was first published in Florence in 1931 by Pantheon-Casa Editrice. During the 15th and 16th centuries there was a demand in Spain for magnificent and ostentatious works of art, which initially showed great originality and religious influence. This excellent study provides good biographical, as well as critical, studies of Spain's major sculptors of the time.

830 **Spanish folk ceramics of today.**
José Llorens Artigas, José Corredor-Matheos, translated from the
Spanish by Martha Tennent. Barcelona: Editorial Blume, 1974.
2nd ed. 235p. map. bibliog. (Nueva Imagen).

An excellent work, which is beautifully illustrated. The authors' purpose is to 'call
attention, above all, to the cultural testimony of this art', and they proceed to
describe the techniques employed by Spanish potters, which are gradually being
overtaken by modern automated methods.

831 **Hispanic lace and lace making.**
Florence Lewis May. New York: Hispanic Society of America,
1939. 417p. map. bibliog. (Hispanic Notes and Monographs;
Peninsular Series).

A full and interesting study of the growth and development of the art of lace-
making in Spain, Portugal and Latin America. It contains a map showing the
centres of lace-making in the Peninsula, and over 400 black-and-white illustrations
of lace.

832 **Silk textiles of Spain: eighth to fifteenth century.**
Florence Lewis May. New York: Hispanic Society of America,
1957. 286p. bibliog. (Hispanic Notes and Monographs: Peninsular
Series).

There are very few sources in English on the subject, and this is the most useful.
The author provides many detailed descriptions of specific textiles, and the work
contains numerous reproductions of details from them. An excellent bibliography
is included.

833 **Jewels in Spain 1500-1800.**
Priscilla E. Muller. New York: Hispanic Society of America,
1972. 195p. bibliog. (Hispanic Notes and Monographs: Peninsular
Series).

An excellent, fully-documented history, and the only one in English, of secular
and religious jewellery and the leading jewellers and their patrons, spanning three
centuries. At this time the goldsmith's art was at its best, and numerous
illustrations provide beautiful examples to complement the text.

834 **The Golden Age of Hispanic silver, 1400-1665.**
Charles Oman. London: HM Stationery Office, 1968. 70p. map.
bibliog.

A detailed catalogue and description, containing nearly 200 black-and-white
plates, of the impressive Victoria and Albert Museum collection. The text gives
its history, and a basic introduction to Hispanic silver. The collection's two special
claims for consideration are that the examples are mostly of very fine quality, and
are representative of most of the important centres of silverwork in Spain and
Portugal during this period.

835 **Spanish folk crafts.**
Maria Antonia Pelauzy, translated from the Spanish by Diorki.
Barcelona, Spain: Editorial Blume, 1978. 238p. map. bibliog.
(Nueva Imagen).

An extremely interesting and detailed study covering all the regions of Spain, and all aspects of Spanish handicrafts. The emphasis is on the influence of various peoples and cultures, which has enriched and sustained the tremendous beauty and diversity of Spanish folk arts in general. The work also includes a glossary of commonly-used terms, an index of places, a short bibliography, and a list of Spanish museums connected with folk art.

836 **Spanish Romanesque sculpture.**
A. Kingsley Porter. New York: Hacker Art Books, 1969. 2 vols. in 1. bibliog.

A comprehensive study of sculpture in Spain during the 11th and 12th centuries, and one which assesses the continuity of the art in Spain over the years.

837 **Castilian sculpture: Gothic to Renaissance.**
Beatrice Gilman Proske. New York: Hispanic Society of America, 1951. 525p. bibliog. (Hispanic Notes and Monographs: Peninsular Series).

A detailed discussion of Gothic and Renaissance Castilian sculpture centred on Burgos and Toledo. Over 300 black-and-white photographic examples of the art are included.

838 **Spanish leather: a history of its use from 800 to 1800 for mural hangings, screens, upholstery, altar frontals, eccelsiastical vestments, footwear, gloves, pouches and caskets.**
John W. Waterer. London: Faber & Faber, 1971. 130p. bibliog. (Faber Monographs on Furniture).

The author was honorary Secretary of the Museum of Leathercraft in London. In this attractive book he studies the origins of the art in Moorish Spain, its subsequent development within the Peninsula, and its spread to other parts of Europe. He lays particular emphasis on the importance of leather in interior decoration.

839 **Early Spanish manuscript illumination.**
John Williams. London: Chatto & Windus, 1977. 117p. map. bibliog.

A superbly-illustrated history of early mediaeval illumination from the 7th century, when Spain's artistic traditions were based on the legacy of the ancient world, to around 1100, when its traditions were once more joined to those of Europe. Most of the manuscripts used as examples for illumination were created in monasteries in the 10th century, in the Christian kingdoms of north central Spain. This beautifully-produced work will be of value to the interested general reader and the specialist alike.

Music and dance

840 **Dances of Spain.**
Lucile Armstrong. London: Parrish, 1950. 2 vols. 2 maps.
bibliog. (Handbooks of European National Dances).
These illustrated books describe regional dances, costumes and music, and also provide detailed descriptions and steps for some of the more important dances. Volume 1 covers the south, centre and northwest of Spain; volume 2, the northeast and east.

841 **Andalusian dances.**
José Manuel Caballero Bonald, translated by Charles David
Ley. Barcelona, Spain: Editorial Noguer, 1959. 2nd ed. 62p.
A comprehensive study of the dances of Andalusia, with sections on classical, theatrical and flamenco dances. There is also information on the history of the dances, as well as lists of the different types and styles, and descriptions of the most representative forms.

842 **The music of Spain.**
Gilbert Chase. New York: Dover Publications, 1959. 2nd ed.
383p. bibliog.
Together with Livermore's work (q.v.), this is the standard text on Spanish music and its history. It presents a concise, yet comprehensive, account of all aspects from the Middle Ages to the 20th century, and discusses over 400 composers and their works, as well as Spain's contribution to world music.

843 **Music in eighteenth century Spain.**
Mary Neal Hamilton. Urbana, Illinois: University of Illinois,
1937. 283p. bibliog. (Illinois Studies in Language and Literature,
vol. 22).
This work has been published as a *University of Illinois Bulletin* (vol. 35, no. 8), and has also been reprinted as a separate monograph (New York: Da Capo, 1971). The very detailed and scholarly text covers both secular and sacred music, and includes early music scores transcribed into modern notation.

844 **The dance in Spain.**
Anna Ivanova. New York: Praeger, 1970. 202p. bibliog.
An interesting analysis (and one of the best in English) of Spanish dancing over the centuries, by a ballerina attempting to teach a Spanish folk-dancing group ballet. She discusses all aspects of dance, including ballet, the new 'danceologies', national dance, and the influence of flamenco, and ensures that the work is suitable not just for dance specialists, but also the general reader.

845 **Manuel de Falla and the Spanish musical renaissance.**
Burnett James. London: Gollancz, 1979. 172p. bibliog.

'A work that offers many mature insights and fills a definite gap in musical literature'. The author sees Falla as 'the most complete representative of the Spanish mind and spirit in music', but the book covers more than simply Falla and his work. It surveys Spanish music from its beginnings, its folk origins and foreign influences, and compares it with musical development in other countries.

846 **A short history of Spanish music.**
Ann Livermore. London: Duckworth, 1972. 262p. bibliog.

This standard work traces the chronological development, both national and local, of Spanish music, and provides a thorough description of the lives and works of the major composers. There is a comprehensive glossary of musical expressions in English, eight pages of photographic illustrations, and a chapter on Spanish music in Latin America.

847 **The Spanish Baroque guitar: with a transcription of De Murcia's 'Passacalles y obras'.**
Neil D. Pennington. Ann Arbor, Michigan: UMI Research Press, 1981. 2 vols. bibliog. (Studies in Musicology, no. 46).

A revised version of the author's thesis (University of Maryland, 1979), which provides a comprehensive study of the guitar and guitar music in 17th and 18th-century Spain, and discusses its place in Spanish society during the Baroque era.

848 **A history of Spanish piano music.**
Linton E. Powell. Bloomington, Indiana: Indiana University Press, 1980. 213p. bibliog.

This excellent book represents the first comprehensive survey of solo piano music in Spain from the 18th century to the present day, and includes chapters on: piano music from 1740 to 1840; Isaac Albéniz; Enrique Granados; Manuel de Falla; Joaquín Turina and Federico Mompou; the influence of the guitar; and developments since the Second World War. A glossary of Spanish musical terms is included.

849 **Spanish cathedral music in the Golden Age.**
Robert M. Stevenson. Westport, Connecticut: Greenwood Press, 1976. 523p. bibliog.

A reprint of the original 1961 edition (Berkeley and Los Angeles: University of California Press), which deals with the music of the major composers of the period: Cristóbal de Morales; Francisco Guerrero; Juan Navarro; Tomás Luis de Victoria; and others.

850 **Spanish music in the age of Columbus.**
Robert M. Stevenson. The Hague: Martinus Nijhoff, 1960. 335p. bibliog.

A detailed and scholarly analysis of Spanish music up to 1530, with frequent reference to its earlier musical influences. Numerous extracts from original sheet music are also included.

851 **Catalan songs.**
  Edited by Ivor Waters, chosen and translated by Mercedes Waters, Elvira Heredia. Chepstow, Wales: Ivor Waters, 1981. 43p.
A collection of Catalan popular songs with English translations. The tunes of folk songs are generally superior to the words, and the compilers regret that they have been unable to print the music as well.

Theatre and cinema

852 **Theatre in Madrid: the difficult transition to democracy.**
  Phyllis Zatlin Boring. *Theatre Journal*, vol. 32, no. 4 (Dec. 1980), p. 459-74.
A study of the theatre since the death of Franco, which tries to explain why the post-Franco period has been one of confusion for playwrights and playgoers alike. The article also discusses how tradition was, and still is, a great influence in Spanish society and the theatre. Despite the relaxation of censorship, many traditional theatregoers were unprepared for, and unwilling to pay to see, new avant-garde theatre with nudity and anti-religious, anti-Franco or anti-army sentiments. The authoress emphasizes throughout that 'the future of the stage will largely mirror the path taken by Spanish society as a whole'.

853 **García Lorca: 'La Barraca' and the Spanish national theater.**
  Suzanne Wade Byrd. New York: Ediciones Abra, 1975. 142p. bibliog.
'Over the last forty years nationalization of the theatre in Spain has achieved outstanding results. Under patronage of the Ministry of Information and Tourism, Spanish theatre receives increasing emphasis financially and culturally'. Madrid's Teatro Español (Spanish Theatre) is the national theatre, and was officially designated as such in 1909. Federico García Lorca activated and directed the theatre company 'La Barraca' as part of the 'cultural missions' (libraries, travelling museums and theatre companies) aimed at imparting cultural enlightenment to the illiterate masses in Spain's rural regions. Lorca in fact named the company 'La Barraca' (hut or cabin) after the name of the rustic dwellings of Valencian farmers, and the word was also used to describe the van which housed the itinerant performers. His direction was aimed at achieving artistic innovation and dramatic excellence.

854 **International film guide 1985.**
  Edited by Peter Cowie. London: Tantivy Press, 1984. 480p.
The section on Spain (p. 274-78) offers a brief sketch of the Spanish film industry.

The work is published annually, and provides updated information on major new and forthcoming films. A recent royal film decree, which substantially modifies the structure of the industry, officially became law in February 1984.

855 **New cinema in Spain.**
Vicente Molina-Foix. London: British Film Institute, 1977. 55p.

The author, a Spanish film critic, novelist and lecturer, studies cinema in Spain since the Civil War, and provides excellent sections on film censorship regulations. He gives a brief historical guide to the problems and prejudices which beset the film industry under Franco, which nevertheless produced a great number of excellent films during this period. The most famous Spanish film director, Luis Buñuel (1900-83) spent a large period of his life in Mexico, and made many of his films in France. His succession of acclaimed productions began in 1928 with 'Un chien andalou' (An Andalusian dog), and ended in 1977 with 'Cet obscur objet du désir' (That obscure object of desire). Numerous books have appeared on Buñuel's life and works, including Francisco Aranda's *Luis Buñuel: a critical biography* (London: Secker & Warburg, 1975), and the director's autobiography *My last breath* (London: Cape, 1984).

856 **Staging in the Spanish theatre.**
Edited by Margaret A. Rees. Leeds, England: Trinity and All Saints' College, 1984. 120p. bibliog.

A collection of four of the papers presented at the College in November 1983. They discuss the Spanish theatre, its drama, production and direction from the 16th to the 20th century, through specific studies of individual plays and playwrights.

857 **Diccionario del cine español, 1896-1965.** (A dictionary of the Spanish cinema, 1896-1965.)
Fernando Vizcaíno Casas. Madrid: Editora Nacional, 1970. 3rd ed. 359p. bibliog.

A collection of about 1,500 brief biographies of personalities in the Spanish film world, by the versatile author of many large-selling works. The book also includes the names of directors and actors from outside Spain who have worked on Spanish films.

This loving darkness: the cinema and Spanish writers 1920-1936.
See item no. 737.

The contemporary Spanish theater (1949-1972).
See item no. 759.

A history of Spanish Golden Age drama.
See item no. 768.

The dream-house (silent films and Spanish poets).
See item no. 776.

Folklore, customs and costume

858 **Folklore y costumbres de España.** (Folklore and customs of Spain.)
Edited by F. Carreras y Candi. Barcelona, Spain: Alberto
Martín, 1931-33. 3 vols. bibliog.
A standard and comprehensive work by various contributors, which is beautifully
illustrated. Volume 1 covers origins, mythology, the land and bullfighting; volume
2, song and dance; and volume 3, the sea, the home, and religious customs.

859 **Folklore research around the world: a North American point of
view.**
Edited, with an introduction, by Richard M. Dorson.
Bloomington, Indiana: Indiana University Press, 1961. 197p.
bibliog. (Indiana University Folklore Series, no. 16).
Also published in the *Journal of American Folklore* vol, 74, no. 294 (Oct.-Dec.
1961). The chapter on Spain (p. 50-57) is entitled 'Folklore study in Spain' by
Frances Gillmor, and describes the resources (bibliographical, physical and
human) open to the student of folklore in Spain. The background information
provided is very useful, if brief.

860 **Spanish fiestas: (including romerías, excluding bull-fights).**
Nina Consuelo Epton. London: Cassell, 1968. 250p. map.
An illustrated, comprehensive and classified collection of 'fiestas' (festivals)
throughout the Spanish year. It was the first book in English to explain their
significance in detail, and describes a hundred of the most colourful and
interesting. An index is also provided.

861 **A book of the Basques.**
Rodney Gallop. New York: Benjamin Blom, 1971. 294p. bibliog.
The aim of this easy-to-read book is to provide a greater insight into the life of the
Basques, their civilization, traditions and customs. It looks at the whole area of
Basque culture, and the customs which make it so distinct. There are chapters on:
the origins and history of the people; their character, language and literature;
folk-songs; folk-tales and proverbs; folk-dances; the arts; 'pelota'; and customs
generally.

862 **El folklore español.** (Spanish folklore.)
Edited by José Manuel Gómez-Tabanera. Madrid: Instituto
Español de Antropología Aplicada, 1968. 455p. 3 maps.
A comprehensive study of all aspects of Spanish folklore, from regional dress and
Spanish proverbs, to marriage and burial rites.

863 **The regional costumes of Spain: their importance as a primitive expression of the aesthetic ideals of the nation.**
Isabel de Palencia.   London: Batsford, 1926. 160p.

Palencia was an ardent liberal, and in 1936 was appointed Minister of Spain to Sweden. This work contains over 200 plates, including some in colour, portraying Spaniards in regional costume. The text intermingles descriptions of the costumes with details of popular customs and festivals.

864 **Costume of the western world: the dominance of Spain 1550-1660.**
Brian Reade.   London: Harrap, 1951. 27p. bibliog. (Costume of the Western World Series, no. 4).

This short work describes how the Spanish overtook the Germans and Italians to become leaders of fashion by 1550, with France the only serious competitor. By 1620 Spain's influence on European costume began to decline in proportion to the ascendancy of France and Holland, and after the accession of the Bourbon dynasty in 1700 French styles were adopted by all but the country people.

Entertainment in Spain.
See item no. 880.

Food and Drink

865 Dining in Spain: a guide to Spanish cooking with recipes from its most distinguished restaurants.
Gerrie Beene, Lourdes Miranda King.   Rutland, Vermont: Charles E. Tuttle, 1969. 197p.

A unique cook-book, with recipes from Madrid restaurants and others in the provinces. It includes all the most famous Spanish dishes, and an introduction describing dining customs, basic ingredients, and the wines of Spain.

866 Spanish cookery.
Ursula Bourne.   London: Futura, 1974. 182p.

The authoress has travelled all over the Iberian Peninsula collecting recipes from every region. The ingredients are set out in the margins, with instructions on the pages proper.

867 Spanish cooking.
Elizabeth Cass.   St. Albans, England: Mayflower Books, 1976. 204p.

This book is intended to provide a general idea of the principles of Spanish cooking, and contains an introductory section on such topics as herbs and flavourings, types of sausages, wines and liqueurs, and cheeses. Recipes supplied by Spanish restaurants are included.

868 Sherry.
Rupert Croft-Cooke.   London: Putnam, 1955. 232p.

A detailed history of the exploitation of sherry, the techniques involved in its making, and a description of the vineyards and bodegas of the famous firms. The

247

author has also written *Through Spain with Don Quixote* (New York: Knopf, 1960), a travel account following in the footsteps of Don Quixote and Sancho Panza. Another useful general work on sherry is simply called *Sherry* by Manuel María González Gordon (London: Cassell, 1972).

869 The cooking of Spain and Portugal.
Peter Steinam Feibleman and the editors of Time-Life Books. Amsterdam: Time-Life International, 1970. 208p. map. (Foods of the World).

The author lived in Spain for eight years, and travelled the entire Peninsula whilst preparing this study. The result is an outstanding work, which is more than a mere recipe book. The book takes us on a journey through the regions of Spain, and expounds the variations in cooking. Indexes in English, Spanish and Portuguese are provided.

870 The International Wine and Food Society's guide to Spanish cookery.
Mary Hillgarth. London: David & Charles, 1970. 200p.

The authoress has lived in Spain for many years, and the 400 recipes she describes emphasize the variety and individuality of Spanish cooking. There is also an introductory chapter on the culinary influences of the Roman, Moorish and French occupations.

871 Sherry.
Julian Jeffs. London: Faber & Faber, 1982. 3rd ed. 314p. 2 maps. bibliog. (Faber Books on Wine).

The author worked for a leading wine-shipper, and lived in the town of Jerez de la Frontera, from which sherry took its name. The book begins with the historical background to sherry, and goes on to describe every stage in the preparation of the wine. This expanded and updated edition also contains a new chapter on recent developments.

872 Spanish regional cookery.
Anna MacMiadhacháin. Harmondsworth, England: Penguin, 1976. 263p. map.

The authoress has travelled extensively throughout Spain, and has collected over 300 recipes for this book. She explains the background to, and individuality of, each region's food, and how distinct it is from the typical tourist menu. This excellent illustrated collection was compiled over a period of more than twenty years, and includes short notes on the regions of Spain and covers: weights and measures; special kitchen equipment; ingredients; and Spanish wines.

873 Sherry and the wines of Spain.
George Rainbird. London: Michael Joseph, 1966. 4 maps. 224p. bibliog.

An easily understandable expert account, which offers a short history of Spanish wines as a whole, and devotes the rest of the text to sherry and wines of all the important wine regions. The author has tried to avoid using wine jargon, and this is one of the reasons why the book is so suitable for any interested reader.

874 Paradores of Spain: their history, cooking and wines.

Jan Read, Maite Manjón. London: Macmillan, 1977. 224p. maps.

Jan Read is a prolific writer on Spain and Spanish cooking and wines, and the major part of this book is devoted to recipes from a wide choice of paradores. The word 'parador' derives from the Arabic 'waradah' meaning 'a halting place'. There are over thirty converted castles, monasteries and baronial houses in Spain, forming part of a network of nearly 100 government-run hotels and restaurants, strategically placed in areas of the country where ordinary hotel facilities are not available. There is a growing demand for parador holidays, where families can travel around the whole of Spain seeing a great deal more than most tourists. The book is therefore particularly valuable for the prospective tourist, and provides a list of paradores, albergues (inns), refugios (winter sports centres) and hosterías (restaurants).

875 The wines of Spain.

Jan Read. London: Faber & Faber, 1982. 267p. 4 maps. bibliog.

Spain has more land under vines than any other country in Europe. This attractively-written and fully illustrated book describes new trends in Spanish wine production, and introduces the reader to a wide range of wines from the lesser-known regions. Read has also written a work on the most famous wine-producing region of Spain: *Wines of the Rioja* (London: Sotheby, 1984).

876 Food and drink in Spain.

D. J. Wiltshire, G. M. Wiltshire. London: Harrap, 1979. 32p. 2 maps. (Discovering Spain).

A brief, illustrated introduction to food and drink in Spain, emphasizing the regional differences, which are mainly due to climatic and agricultural variations. The book also contains several recipes for some well-known Spanish dishes.

Sports and Recreation

877 **Deporte y Estado.** (Sport and the State.)
Luis María Cazorla Prieto. Barcelona, Spain: Editorial Labor,
1979. 320p. bibliog. (Politeia, no. 5).
The author was a member of the Organizing Committee of the 1982 football
World Cup in Spain. In this book he attempts to clarify the whole nature of sport
in Spain, and its political relationship. The work is divided into four main sections
covering: the economic and social importance of sport; different types of sporting
activity; sport and the State; and sport and politics. There is also an appendix on
the organization and financing of the 1982 World Cup. For a more specific study
of the same subject see Nicola Goward's 'Sport and politics in post-Franco Spain:
the Barcelona Football Club' *Iberian Studies*, vol. 10, no. 1 (spring 1981).

878 **Or I'll dress you in mourning.**
Larry Collins, Dominique Lapierre. St. Albans, England:
Mayflower Books, 1969. 346p.
The exciting story of the rise to fame of El Cordobés (Manuel Benítez Pérez),
who was born in 1936, and began his career in 1959. He became Spain's most
highly-paid bullfighter, and was renowned for his exceptional reflexes and
courage.

879 **Encyclopaedia of bullfighting.**
Barnaby Conrad. London: Michael Joseph, 1962. 271p. bibliog.
The author, a prolific writer on bullfighting, spent six years working on this
volume. He has tried to include all the terms, biographies and technical aspects
about which any reader with a basic interest in the spectacle would wish to know.
The main encyclopaedic section is an 'A to Z' of all these facts, and is followed by
a chart of 20th-century matadors, and the first full translation into English of the
rules of bullfighting.

880 **Entertainment in Spain.**
J. G. Escribano, S. Escribano. London: Harrap, 1977. 32p.
(Discovering Spain).

A light-hearted introduction to Spanish entertainment, which will be of interest to anyone looking for a basic understanding of the most popular pastimes and leisure activities of the Spanish people, as well as some of their unique customs.

881 **El fútbol, sin ley.** (The lawless world of football.)
Julián García Candau. Madrid: Ediciones Penthalón, 1980. 180p.
(Debate).

An enlightening and entertaining study of football, its role in society since the Civil War, and its relationship to politics in Spain. The title refers to the fact that, since 1939, football has existed outside official legislation. With the arrival of democracy all federations and sports groups have been ordered by the Consejo Superior de Deportes (Higher Council for Sport) to reconcile their statutes and regulations with the Physical Culture and Sport Law. There are two excellent appendixes on football terminology and an anthology of poems about football and footballers.

882 **The bullfight.**
Doddy Hay. London: New English Library, 1976. 128p. bibliog.

Bullfighting, though one of the 'sports' most misunderstood by non-Hispanic people, is an intrinsic part of Spanish culture. Hay, a freelance journalist living in Spain, attempts to present the bullfight in all its aspects, from its historical origins through Christian and Moorish hunting of the bull, to its present-day colourful 'spectacle of courage'. The primary aim of the book is 'to give the reader the "feel" of the bullight by tracing in words and pictures its origins, history and traditions and by telling some stories of the men who have shaped its development throughout the centuries'.

883 **Death in the afternoon.**
Ernest Hemingway. London: Jonathan Cape, 1932. 358p.

The best study of the Spanish bullfight in both emotional and aesthetic terms, and one of the first, and often reprinted, English-language studies of the subject to appear. Hemingway also wrote the classic English-language novel about the Spanish Civil War *For whom the bell tolls* (London: Jonathan Cape, 1941), which captures the essence of Spain during the bitter and agonizing struggle.

884 **The complete aficionado.**
John McCormick, Mario Sevilla Mascareñas. London:
Weidenfeld & Nicolson, 1967. 276p. bibliog.

A highly detailed work, 'addressed to the large public that has already made an acquaintance . . . with the art of "toreo" '. Spanish words and phrases are translated and defined, and the study includes numerous sketches on the technical movements and positions of the modern matador.

251

Sports and Recreation

885 **The bulls of Iberia: an account of the bullfight.**
Angus MacNab.   London: Heinemann, 1957. 264p.

A lavishly illustrated history and study of the bullfight, as a public performance and a national spectacle.

886 **Sobre el tapete verde: a handbook of Spanish cards.**
Alberta Wilson Server.   Mexico City: Editorial Cultura, 1962.
122p.

An interesting handbook which includes sections explaining: the make-up of the Spanish pack; card-playing terms; special vocabularies for specific card games; and descriptions of some typical Spanish card games. Those using this guide are expected to have a basic knowledge of Spanish.

887 **Bull fever.**
Kenneth Tynan.   London: Longmans, Green, 1966. 2nd ed. 169p.

The narrative takes the form of a journey through Spain from north to south, with descriptions of several 'corridas' (bullfights) seen en route. The author, a well-known drama critic who died in 1980, focuses on the rivalry of two leading matadors, one representing the romantic and the other the classic method of bullfighting.

The Enchanted Mountains: a quest in the Pyrenees.
See item no. 30.

Libraries, Museums and Archives

888 **Libraries and archives of Madrid.**
James W. Cortada. *Journal of Library History*, vol. 9, no. 2
(Apr. 1974), p. 176-86.
A brief discussion of the numerous libraries and archives in the capital, some of
which are among the oldest in the western world.

889 **The state of information science in Spain.**
Emilia Currás. *Journal of Information Science*, vol. 2, no. 6 (Dec.
1980), p. 315-17.
Information science experienced a good deal of reorganization after Franco's
death, and this article briefly outlines the changes which took place. It also
includes descriptions of Red Inca (the national information network) and SEDIC
(The Spanish Society for Documentation and Scientific Information).

890 **University libraries in Spain and Portugal.**
Javier Lasso de la Vega. *Library Trends*, vol. 12 (Apr. 1964),
p. 539-49.
Although somewhat out-of-date, the basic history and administrative procedures
of university libraries have not changed. At the time of writing this article, the
author was Professor of Librarianship and Documentation at the University
Library, Madrid, and here he discusses the organization, access, classification
systems and financing of university libraries in general. Surprisingly, at the time
that the author wrote this article there was no building in Spain constructed
specifically and functionally for the purpose.

891 **Nueva guía de las bibliotecas de Madrid.** (A new guide to the
libraries of Madrid.)
María Isabel Morales Vallespín (et al.).   Madrid: Asociación
Nacional de Archiveros, Bibliotecarios y Arqueólogos
(ANABAD), 1979. 350p.

A work which contains details of over 250 libraries in Madrid and which provides
information about: addresses; special subjects; history; the availability of
material; catalogues; publications; and opening hours. Part of the book is
dedicated solely to the libraries of State organizations. In fact, nearly all of the
libraries described are more or less directly under official organization, as private
enterprise in Spain has shown little interest in this area.

892 **Museums of the world.**
Munich, GFR; New York; London: K. G. Saur, 1981. 3rd ed.
622p. (Handbook of International Documentation and
Information, vol. 16).

The section on Spain (p. 314-31) provides a full list of museums by city and town,
together with details of addresses, type of museum, the year of founding,
collections and facilities.

893 **The Prado.**
Francisco Javier Sánchez Cantón, translated from the French by
James Cleugh.   London: Thames & Hudson, 1971. rev. ed. 261p.
(The World of Art Library).

The author was Assistant Director of the Prado from 1922 until 1960, when he
was appointed Director, and was responsible for the large-scale changes and
improvements which took place at that time. The Prado is filled with collections
formed in the course of three centuries by the Habsburg and Bourbon kings of
Spain, and is one of the world's greatest art galleries. It was commissioned in 1787
by Charles III, and was opened to the public in 1819 as the Royal Museum of
Painting, becoming the National Museum of the Prado in 1868. A historical
background to the museum itself is followed by vivid descriptions of the
masterpieces it contains, from the Italian, Spanish, Flemish, German, French and
Dutch schools of the 14th to the 18th centuries. The whole work is magnificently
illustrated.

894 **The new guide to the diplomatic archives of western Europe.**
Edited by Daniel H. Thomas, Lynn M. Case.   Philadelphia:
University of Pennsylvania Press, 1975. 441p. bibliog.

The section on Spain by Lino G. Canedo (p. 275-313) looks at the following
archives: General Archive of Simancas; National Historic Archive (Madrid);
General Archive of the Indies (Seville); Archive of the Ministry for Foreign
Affairs (Madrid); Archive of the Crown of Aragón (Barcelona); other smaller
archives; military centres; and private archives. The lay-out of information for
each centre is standard, providing: details on the history of the major

depositories; descriptions of the organization, arrangement and classification of records; administration and use of documents; and available services (reference, duplicating, etc.).

895   **The world of learning 1984-85.**
London: Europa Publications, 1984. 1,853p.

An annual publication which provides a comprehensive and up-to-date directory of educational, cultural and scientific institutions all over the world. The section on Spain (p. 1,066-101) gives the names, addresses and other useful details of Spanish universities, academies, learned societies, research institutes, libraries, archives, museums, polytechnics and colleges.

The Book Trade

896 **Edición y comercio del libro español, 1900-1972.**
(The Spanish publishing and book trade, 1900-72.)
Fernando Cendán Pazos.   Madrid: Editora Nacional, 1972. 445p.
(España en Tres Tiempos).
A detailed and fully documented history of the book trade, which includes
sections on censorship, publishing, commercial structure, and a survey of Spanish
reading habits.

897 **Literature and the book trade in Golden-Age Spain.**
D. W. Cruickshank.   *Modern Language Review*, vol. 73 (Oct.
1978), p. 799-824.
The author's intention 'is to examine a literary movement in terms of the
influence upon it of the printing press'. He therefore relates printing to, among
other things, literature in general, education, the illiteracy level, and economic
conditions.

898 **Publishing in Spain.**
H. R. Lottman.   *Publishers Weekly*, 12 June 1978, p. 37-50.
A report by an international correspondent on the political and social
transformations in Spain, and the economic consequences of the new freedom to
the publishing industry. Lottman visited the publishing capitals of Barcelona and
Madrid where, since Franco's death, the book trade has experienced many
changes. He also looks at the major publishing houses, and comments on their
policies and future plans.

899 **A descriptive catalogue of printing in Spain and Portugal 1501-1520.**
F. J. Norton. Cambridge, England: Cambridge University Press, 1978. 581p. bibliog.

This catalogue 'is intended to cover not only the works which have survived from the period 1501-20, but also those lost editions of which a reliable record, however brief, has come to my notice'. It does not include printing outside the kingdoms of the Peninsula in the languages of Spain and Portugal, but nevertheless contains nearly 1,400 items arranged under an alphabetical listing of printing centres.

900 **Printing in Spain: the first hundred years.**
Graham John Shields. *Spanish Studies*, no. 5 (summer 1983), p. 13-18.

A brief examination of the introduction and growth of printing in Spain between the 1470s and 1570s, with particular emphasis on how the fears of the Spanish church and State led, in 1490, to the Inquisition's involvement in, and censorship of, the trade as a whole.

The Press

General

901 **Anuario de la Prensa Española.** (Yearbook of the Spanish Press.)
Madrid: Editora Nacional, 1943- . irregular.

Edited for the Ministry of Information and Tourism, the title of this publication belies its regularity. It provides detailed information on Spanish newspapers and periodicals, including address, personnel, format, size and number of copies printed.

902 **Press censorship in Spain and Portugal.**
Alberto de Caravalho, A. Monteiro Cardoso. *Index on Censorship*, vol. 1, no. 2 (summer 1972), p. 53-64.

A useful overview of the problems of censorship in Spain under the Franco régime. The authors are lawyers practising in Portugal, who compiled a comparative survey of censorship, and the article also discusses the press laws of both countries. Also worth reading is 'The press and censorship in Franco Spain' by John Ll. Hollyman (*Iberian Studies*, vol. 3, no. 2 (autumn 1974), p. 60-69), which briefly studies press censorship from 1940 to 1973, and the Press Law of 1966.

903 **The Spanish media since Franco.**
William Chislett. . London: Writers & Scholars Educational Trust, 1979. 37p.

A well-documented discussion of the press under and after Franco, and Spanish television and radio since his death. It recounts how Franco controlled the media, and how substantial changes have taken place in press, television and radio since that time. The number of Spaniards who read newspapers is low, and correspondingly the influence of television and radio is considerable.

904   **Historia del comic español, 1875-1939.** (A history of the Spanish
      comic, 1875-1939.)
      Antonio Martín.   Barcelona, Spain: Editorial Gustavo Gili, 1978.
      245p. bibliog. (Colección Comunicación Visual).
A thoroughly entertaining analysis of the different stages which the Spanish comic
went through before acquiring its own real separate identity. It grew from a
satirical publication into a filler in the children's press, until eventually in the
1930s it became a fully-developed means of mass communication.

905   **The press and the rebirth of Iberian democracy.**
      Edited by Kenneth Maxwell.   Westport, Connecticut; London:
      Greenwood, 1983. 195p. bibliog. (Contributions in Political
      Science, no. 99. Global Perspectives in History and Politics).
Obviously mass communication played a critical role in the complex process of
political change in Spain, and *El País* (The Nation), one of Europe's finest daily
newspapers, became a symbol of the transition to democracy. A leading Spanish
newspaper man claimed that 'Our task was fundamental; on one side, to inform
the public of the crisis of Franquism, about debates and tensions in government
. . . on the other side, using the game of words we had used for years, we
informed the public about Europe and the defence of democracy'. This useful
book analyzes the changes which took place as regards the press following the
transition, and the final section looks at how well-informed the United States and
western Europe are about current conditions in Spain and Portugal.

906   **The history makers: the press of Europe from its beginnings
      through 1965.**
      Kenneth E. Olson.   Baton Rouge, Louisiana: Louisiana State
      University Press, 1966. 471p. bibliog.
This work contains a chapter on Spain entitled 'A breath of freedom comes at
last: the press of Franco's Spain' (p. 270-84), which recounts the history of the
Spanish press from the 1470s to the 1960s. The author emphasizes Franco's
control during the dicatatorship, and indicates that the new Press Law of 1965-66
represented a partial relaxation of the strict censorship.

907   **The Spanish press 1470-1966: print, power and politics.**
      Henry F. Schulte.   London, Chicago: University of Illinois Press,
      1968. 280p. bibliog.
A wide-ranging history of the Spanish periodical press from its beginnings to
Franco's new 'liberal' Press Law of 1965-66 mentioned in the previous entry.
Particular attention is paid to the 'predominant role' of censorship during the
Franco régime.

908 **Prensa y sociedad en España (1820-1936).** (Press and society in Spain, 1820-1936.)
Manuel Tuñón de Lara (et al.), edited by Manuel Tuñón de Lara, Antonio Elorza, Manuel Pérez Ledesma. Madrid: Editorial Cuadernos para el Diálogo, 1975. 290p. 5 maps. bibliog. (Colección ITS).
Another detailed examination of the press, its effects on society, and influence on 19th- and early 20th-century Spain. The contributors concentrate on the following areas: the Madrid daily press from 1850 to 1875 and 1873 to 1887; the Madrid press in general from 1858 to 1909; the Carlist press; the liberal press; the Barcelona daily press from 1895 to 1910; and individual weeklies and journals.

Newspapers

909 **ABC.**
Madrid: Prensa Española, 1905- . daily.
The leading monarchist newspaper, which was founded by Torcuata Luca de Tena, and immediately converted from a weekly to a daily. It has strong contacts with the establishment, and contains a great deal on Spain's diplomatic and economic relations. Circulation is approximately 125,000, and it is one of the three major papers which can be readily obtained outside the region. *ABC Los Domingos* (ABC on Sunday) is the weekly colour magazine, and has a circulation of around 270,000. A Seville edition of the paper was founded in 1929, and now has a circulation averaging 62,000.

910 **El Alcázar.** (The Fortress.)
Madrid: DYRSA, 1936- . daily.
Founded in Toledo during the siege of the alcázar, this newspaper moved to Madrid in July 1939. It is a right-wing paper, with an average circulation of around 95,000.

911 **As.** (Ace.)
Madrid: Semana, 1967- . daily.
The leading sports paper, with a circulation of 150,000.

912 **El Correo Catalán.** (The Catalan Post.)
Barcelona, Spain: Fomento de la Prensa, 1876- . daily.
A well-established regional paper, with a circulation of nearly 40,000 on weekdays, and 60,000 on Sundays. It has lost some ground due to the publication of *El País* (The Nation) (q.v.) in Barcelona since 1982, and due also to the founding of *Avui* (Today) (Barcelona: Prensa Catalana) in 1976, a daily paper in

Catalan with a circulation of 80,000. The largest-selling daily in Barcelona is *El Periódico* (The Newspaper) (Barcelona: Ediciones Zeta, 1978- .), which sells 170,000 copies a day.

913 **El Correo Español – El Pueblo Vasco.** (The Spanish Post – The Basque People.)
Bilbao, Spain: Bilbao Editorial, 1938- . daily.

El Correo Español was founded in 1937, whilst *El Pueblo Vasco* began in 1910. In 1938 they amalgamated to produce what has become one of the leading independent Basque dailies, with a circulation of over 80,000.

914 **Diario 16.** (Daily 16.)
Madrid: Información y Revistas, 1976- . daily.

An evening liberal-conservative newspaper, with a circulation of around 125,000.

915 **Diario de Barcelona.** (The Barcelona Daily.)
Barcelona, Spain: Publicaciones de Barcelona, 1792- . daily.

The senior member of the Spanish press, and one of the oldest newspapers in the world. During the Civil War it was printed in Catalan. It has a circulation of around 30,000.

916 **Diario Vasco.** (The Basque Daily.)
San Sebastián, Spain: Sociedad Vascongada de Publicaciones, 1934- . daily.

A liberal paper with a circulation of around 62,000. Aside from the *Hoja del Lunes* (Monday News-sheet) (San Sebastián: Asociación de la Prensa, 1930- .) with a circulation figure of 67,000, other important dailies of the region are *Egin* (Fact) (San Sebastián: Orain, 1977- .), a radical nationalist Basque daily which is often used as a platform by ETA and which sells around 50,000 copies a day and *El Correo Español – El Pueblo Vasco* (The Spanish Post – The Basque People) (q.v).

917 **Hoja del Lunes.** (Monday News-sheet.)
Madrid: Asociación de la Prensa, 1930- . weekly.

No newspapers are published in Spain on Monday except the *Hojas del Lunes* of the different provinces. They are published by the Press Associations which only exist in towns where there are one or more dailies. These Associations are long-established institutions (dating back to the 19th century) to which all active journalists belong. All the profits of the Madrid paper go to the Social Security Fund of the Association of Madrid Journalists. Circulation is around 170,000.

918 **Iberian Daily Sun.**
Madrid: Majorca Daily Bulletin, 1969- . daily.

An English-language daily, with a circulation of about 5,500. Another such paper is the *Majorca Daily Bulletin* (Palma de Mallorca: Pedro A. Serra Bauzá, 1962- .), which has a circulation figure of 6,500.

The Press. Newspapers

919   **Marca.** (Score.)
      Madrid: MCSE, 1938- . daily.

One of the leading daily sports papers, with a circulation approaching 100,000. During the 1950s and 1960s newspapers in Spain devoted practically no space to political news and less to local and national news. Cultural, religious and sports news was given much more prominence, a fact which accounts for the success of sports dailies such as this, which in the mid-1960s had the third-highest circulation of any daily newspaper in Spain.

920   **El Mundo Deportivo.** (Sports World.)
      Barcelona, Spain: El Mundo Deportivo, 1906- . daily.

The leading Barcelona sports daily, with a circulation of 71,000.

921   **El País.** (The Nation.)
      Madrid: PRISA, 1976- . daily.

El País has become one of Europe's leading newspapers, and the most prestigious within Spain. It is a strongly liberal daily, with a highly respected editor (Juan Cebrián Echarri), and provides excellent coverage of international affairs. Since 1984 a weekly international edition has been published, giving a round-up of events around the world. Its own weekly magazine *El País Semanal* (The Nation Weekly), published on Sundays, has a circulation of over 470,000, whilst the daily paper is bought by nearly 300,000 people. Since 1982 it has been printed simultaneously in Barcelona, and at the end of 1984 it began publishing a microform edition with subject and chronological indexes.

922   **La Vanguardia Española.** (The Spanish Vanguard.)
      Barcelona, Spain: Talleres de Imprenta, 1881- . daily.

By the beginning of the 20th century *La Vanguardia* (as it was called up to 1939) had grown into a national newspaper, after pioneering the granting of fringe benefits to newspaper employees (paid vacations, sickness pay and pensions). It is a monarchist paper which has a highly professional approach, and good foreign and national news coverage. The circulation figure is around 275,000.

923   **Ya.** (Now.)
      Madrid: Editorial Católica, 1935- . daily.

One of Madrid's more successful dailies, which was founded by a group of Catholics. It is still a church-oriented, right-wing paper, which generally gives a good press to the United States. It contains a large amount of advertising to fund its independence, and has an average circulation of 115,000 Mondays to Fridays, and 185,000 at the weekends.

Periodicals

924 **Actualidad Económica.** (Economic News.)
Madrid: Punto Editorial, 1958- . weekly.
A respected and influential magazine, covering present-day business and economic affairs. It has a circulation of 28,500.

925 **Cambio 16.** (Change 16.)
Madrid: Información y Revistas, 1976- . weekly.
A highly successful news magazine, which is a valuable source for public comment on individuals from all areas of Spanish life. It provides reliable information on economics and current trends, and has a circulation of around 175,000. The title of the magazine stems from the fact that it was founded by a group of sixteen people at a time of political change in Spain.

926 **Ciudadano.** (Citizen.)
Madrid: Alfonso S. Palomares, 1978- . monthly.
This very useful publication is Spain's leading consumer magazine (the equivalent to *Which?*), and is full of news and surveys.

927 **Diez Minutos.** (Ten Minutes.)
Madrid: Editorial Gráficas Espejo, 1951- . weekly.
A popular general-interest magazine, with a circulation of 425,000.

928 **¡Hola!** (Hello!)
Madrid: Hola, 1944- . weekly.
An extremely popular and illustrated general-interest magazine, with a circulation of 470,000.

929 **Insula.** (Island.)
Madrid: Ediciones de Insula, 1946- . monthly.
A scholarly magazine which reviews all areas of the arts, literature and science. In 1955, when philosopher José Ortega y Gasset died, the Ministry of Information and Tourism issued an order outlining coverage of his death, and restricting newspapers to 'three articles relative to the death of Ortega y Gasset: a biography and two commentaries'. *Insula* exceeded the authorized number of pages in issues devoted to the writer, and was consequently closed down. However, it reappeared in 1957, and now has a circulation of about 5,000.

930 **Interviú.** (Interview.)
   Barcelona, Spain: Ediciones Zeta, 1978- . weekly.

Often described as a 'male-interest' magazine due to its glossy centrefold, it offers a mixture of sex and political scandal from contributors who are in the main freelance journalists. It has become one of the leading Spanish weeklies, and carries news, features, and interviews with popular stars from television. Its circulation is over 500,000.

931 **El Jueves.** (On Thursday.)
   Barcelona, Spain: Ediciones el Jueves, 1979- . weekly.

A satirical magazine, with a circulation of 82,000.

932 **Sal y Pimienta.** (Salt and Pepper.)
   Barcelona, Spain: Ediciones Zeta, 1979- . weekly.

A general-interest magazine, with a circulation of 140,000.

933 **Semana.** (This Week.)
   Madrid: Semana, 1942- . weekly.

An illustrated general-interest magazine, with a large circulation of 340,000.

English-Language Periodicals

934 Anglo-Spanish Society Quarterly Review.
London: Anglo-Spanish Society, 1957- . quarterly.
A publication which promotes Anglo-Spanish friendship. It covers all aspects of Spanish culture and, besides the numerous articles, contains news, readers' correspondence and crosswords.

935 Bulletin of Hispanic Studies.
Liverpool, England: Liverpool University Press, 1923- . quarterly.
This journal was founded in 1923 by Edgar Allison Peers, and was originally entitled *Bulletin of Spanish Studies*. It is devoted to the study of the languages, literature and civilization of Spain, Portugal and Latin America, and includes articles, reviews of books, and reviews of reviews.

936 Hispanic Review.
Philadelphia: Department of Romance Languages, University of Pennsylvania, 1933- . quarterly.
A journal devoted to research in the Hispanic languages and literatures, with articles in English and Spanish. It also contains regular book reviews, and lists of books received. The index to volumes 1 to 25 (1933-57) was issued as a supplement to volume 25 (1958).

937 Iberian Studies.
Keele, England: University of Keele, 1972- . bi-annual.
The main aim of this journal is to encourage free and responsible discussion of the Spanish and Portuguese social scenes, mainly of the 19th and 20th centuries. Subject areas include anthropology, economics, geography, history, politics and sociology, but not language or literary studies. At the end of each issue there are

reviews of recently-published books on Spain. Lately there has been a problem of time-lag in publication.

938 **Spanish Studies.**
London: Olga Kenyon, 1979- . annual.

A journal comprising short articles on contemporary Spanish literature, history and politics, written in Spanish or English. A future aim is to publish the poems of contemporary Spanish and Latin American poets.

939 **Vida Hispánica: Journal of the Association of Teachers of Spanish and Portuguese.**
York, England: Association of Teachers of Spanish and Portuguese, 1953- . 3 times per year.

Presents articles and news on all aspects of Hispanic civilization, language-teaching and linguistics, written in English, Spanish or Portuguese. The aims of the Association are: the encouragement of interest in, and knowledge of, the languages and culture of the Spanish and Portuguese-speaking peoples of the world; the development of living contact with these peoples; and the improvement in Great Britain and Ireland of the teaching of these languages. There are also book reviews, lists of books received, and an annual listing (each May) of doctoral theses completed and in progress. The equivalent journal in America is *Hispania: a journal devoted to the interests of the teaching of Spanish and Portuguese* (Cincinnati, Ohio: American Association of Teachers of Spanish and Portuguese, 1917- . quarterly).

Broadcasting

940　**La radiofusión española.** (Spanish radio broadcasting.)
　　Anibal Arias Ruiz.　Madrid: Publicaciones Españoles, 1972. 2nd
　　ed. 93p. bibliog. (Temas Españoles, no. 530).
This work attempts to give the reader an insight into the birth, development and overall history of Spanish broadcasting. It provides details on all the broadcasting stations, and contains illustrations of the first radio transmitters in Spain. The author also wrote *La televisión en España* (Television in Spain) (Madrid: Publicaciones Españoles, 1970) in the same series.

941　**La 'trastienda' de TVE.** (Behind the scenes at TVE.)
　　Juan Felipe Vila-San-Juan.　Barcelona: Plaza y Janes, 1981. 244p.
TVE (Spanish Television) is the State-run national television company, broadcasting on two channels. Television first appeared in Spain in Madrid in 1956, but took about seven years to reach all parts of the country. Interestingly, in 1966 television licences were abolished, since so few Spaniards bothered to pay their fees anyway. This is a well-written, entertaining and informative history of the first twenty-five years (1956-81) of TVE. The author himself worked with the company from 1960, and has been responsible for numerous programmes. He relates how television in Spain has dealt with many of the major events that have occurred over the twenty-five years, and offers a fascinating insight into the organization and workings of Spanish television.

The Spanish media since Franco.
See item no. 903.

Encyclopaedias and Directories

942 **Who's who in Spain . . .: a biographical dictionary containing about 6,000 biographies of prominent people in and of Spain and 1,400 organizations [sic].**
Edited by S. Olives Canals, S. S. Taylor. New York: Intercontinental Book and Publishing Co., 1963. 998p.

Unfortunately, no later edition has appeared to date, but this work remains useful for the information it provides on prominent Spaniards of the 20th century, and because it is the only English-language biographical dictionary on Spain. Data on individuals includes: present occupation; date and place of birth; education; career; address; awards; memberships; publications; recreations; and family. There is also a large directory section of organizations, associations and institutes by category (p. 929-98).

943 **Directory of the Spanish industry, export and import.**
Madrid: Prodei, 1984. 19th ed. 1 vol.

An irregular publication, but one which more recently has appeared annually. It contains useful general information about Spain; a list of trade marks; an alphabetical index of the main commodities produced and exported; and an 'A to Z' classification of the main goods with which Spain is currently trading, or hoping to trade with. It also lists more than 15,000 Spanish trading firms, with commercial references.

944 **Gran enciclopedia Rialp.** (The great Rialp encyclopaedia.)
Madrid: Ediciones Rialp, 1971-76. 24 vols.

A well-produced, scholarly encyclopaedia, compiled under the direction of expert subject committees. All the articles are signed, and have full bibliographies which emphasize Spanish-language materials. The reader is helped to form his own judgement on things, events and ideas, and the work as a whole 'without falling into partiality or localism aims to reflect the idiosyncrasies of the Spanish speaking peoples and their particular modes of thought and life'.

945 **Gran enciclopedia de España y América.** (The great encyclopaedia of Spain and America.)
Coordinated by José María Javierre.   Seville: Autor-Editor,
1983- . 10 vols.

A detailed and scholarly work, which covers all areas of Hispanic life and culture. Volumes 1 and 2 study anthropology and population; volume 3, geography; volumes 4 to 6, history; volumes 7 to 9, folklore, literature and art; and volume 10, economics.

946 **Kompass (Spain): register of Spanish industry and commerce.**
East Grinstead, England: Kompass, 1984. 16th ed. 2 vols.

An annual publication which provides details of suppliers of individual products and services for 24,000 companies, classified by an easy-to-use system. Volume 1 deals with products and services, and volume 2 covers firms.

The world of learning.
See item no. 895.

Anuario de la Prensa Española. (Yearbook of the Spanish press.)
See item no. 901.

Bibliographies

General

947 **Bibliografía Española.** (Spanish Bibliography.)
Madrid: Dirección General de Archivos y Bibliotecas, 1958- .
annual.

Unfortunately, bibliographic control in Spain leaves a great deal to be desired. Three of the major bibliographic publications of Spain have all experienced problems over the past couple of years. *El Libros en venta* (Books in Print) (q.v.) has had publication delays; *El Libro Español* (Spanish Books) (q.v.) has resorted to uncumulated monthly issues which are cumbersome to use; and this publication (*Bibliografía Española*) is way behind, and in 1984 the last available volume was for 1978. Nevertheless, when it does appear, it is a useful and well-indexed work. Based on copyright deposit, it is updated by the monthly *Boletín mensual* (Monthly bulletin) (Madrid: Instituto Bibliográfico Hispánico, 1969- .). The annual volumes contain all the cumulated information from these bulletins, together with notification of new periodicals, names of publishers, and collections of books and pamphlets.

948 **British Bulletin of Publications on Latin America, the Caribbean, Portugal and Spain.**
London: Hispanic and Luso-Brazilian Council, 1949- . semi-annual.

The Council was founded in 1943 to stimulate understanding between Britain, Spain, Portugal and Latin America in the fields of culture, languages, and economics. This useful bulletin aims to inform readers of recently-published books in English about the geographical areas listed in the title. Each entry has a short descriptive annotation, and a selection of recent periodical articles is also included.

949 **Latin America, Spain, and Portugal: an annotated bibliography of paperback books.**
Compiled by Georgette Magassy Dorn. Washington DC: Library of Congress, 1976. 2nd rev. ed. 323p. (Hispanic Foundation Bibliographical Series, no. 14).

A very valuable and easy-to-use work, which lists 2,202 titles within three sections: Latin America; Spain and Portugal; and dictionaries, grammars, readers, and textbooks. The emphasis is on literature and history, and there is also a list of publishers and booksellers, and a subject index.

950 **A selected bibliography on Spanish society.**
Henk Driessen, Donny Meertens. Amsterdam, The Netherlands: Anthropological-Sociological Centre, University of Amsterdam, 1976. 81p. (Papers on European and Mediterranean Societies, no. 6).

A helpful, but by no means comprehensive, study with most of the cited works in Spanish, and others in English, German, French and Dutch. The scope of the work is extensive, and all areas of Spanish life and culture are touched upon to some degree.

951 **Manual bibliográfico de estudios españoles.** (A bibliographic guide to Spanish studies.)
Fernando González-Ollé. Pamplona, Spain: Ediciones Universidad de Navarra, 1976. 1,375p.

The author's aim is to cover as wide an area of Spanish life and culture as possible, and he does so by reference to over 30,000 works in English and Spanish, covering twenty-two subject areas, including: bibliography; journals; biography; history; empire; religion; law; sociology; geography; economics; education; science; the media; linguistics; literature; art; sport; and folklore. It is particularly easy to use due to its excellent indexing and good cross-referencing from section to section.

952 **El Libro Español.** (Spanish Books.)
Madrid: Instituto Nacional del Libro Español, 1958- . monthly.

This bibliographic tool is a mixture of *The Bookseller* and the *British National Bibliography*. It was formed by the merging of the Institute's *Bibliografía Hispánica* (Hispanic Bibliography) (1942-1957. monthly) and *Novedades Editoriales Españoles* (New Spanish Publications) (1958-63. monthly). *El Libro Español* appears in two parts: one contains articles and notes on new publications and the book trade in general, whilst the second provides bibliographic information on the previous month's new books. It lists these in Dewey Decimal Classification order, and provides further access through an author-title index. Publishers' names and addresses are also included. As the monthly bulletins are not cumulated, it can be a time-consuming exercise to check each year's volumes.

953 **Libros en venta en Hispanoamérica y España.** (Books in print in
Hispanic America and Spain.)
Buenos Aires: Bowker, 1974. 2nd ed. 2 vols.

First published in 1964, this work lists around 150,000 titles in print issued by
Spanish and Hispanic-American publishers, available up to the end of 1972.
Works in Basque, Catalan and Galician are also included. Annual supplements
have appeared covering up to 1982, and the next annual volume for 1983-84 is due
to be published in May 1985.

954 **Libros Españoles: ISBN.** (Spanish Books: ISBN.)
Madrid: Instituto Nacional del Libro Español; Agencia Española
del International Standard Book Number, 1978- . annual.

A continuation of *Libros Españoles: Catálogo ISBN* (1973- .). The 1978 volume
listed more than 100,000 Spanish books in print, providing full bibliographic
details in its subject-title indexes. It also gives complete details (address, phone
number, ISBN prefix) for all publishers. At present this work represents the most
up-to-date and useful of the four principal Spanish bibliographies. The latest
three-volume set covering the year ending June 1984 was due for publication in
December 1984.

955 **Manual del librero hispano-americano; Bibliografía general
española e hispanoamericana desde la invención de la imprenta
hasta nuestros tiempos, con el valor comercial de los impresos
descritos.** (A handbook of Spanish publications for the bookseller.
A general Spanish and Hispanic-American bibliography from the
invention of the press to the present, including the commercial
value of the cited books.)
Antonio Palau y Dulcet. Oxford, England: Dolphin, 1981. 2nd
ed. 28 vols.

A monumental work, and the most complete bibliography of Spanish publications
up to the 20th century. The twenty-eight volumes are arranged by alphabetical
sequence, as is the index of titles-subjects. The second edition is an entirely new
work, since the amount of material has been more than doubled and brought up
to date.

956 **Spain, the country, her history and culture.**
Ian Robertson. London: National Book League, 1970. 40p.

Somewhat out of date now, but a work which retains its usefulness in that it is one
of the few separately-published English-language bibliographies available, and
many of the books listed are standard works. Quality and availability are the
author's foremost considerations in this selection.

957 **Latin America, Spain and Portugal: a selected and annotated bibliographical guide to books published in the United States, 1954-1974.**
Compiled and annotated by Alva Curtis Wilgus. Metuchen, New Jersey; London: Scarecrow, 1977. 910p.

The sections on Spain cover: travel and geography; history; government and politics; foreign relations; the economy; society; language; literature; the arts; biographies; and bibliographies. It is a useful volume for students, academics, librarians, and the general reader. Unfortunately, numerous typographical errors in many entries detract from the reasonable standard maintained within each section, and the section headings provide a false impression of a wider range of subjects covered than is actually the case. The works cited are mainly American publications, and although the sections covering travel and literature in translation are particularly helpful, others, such as foreign relations, are very limited in scope and number. The annotations are deliberately brief, and quite often do not help in determining the value of a particular work.

Spain: a companion to Spanish studies.
See item no. 148.

Subject

958 **Romance linguistics and the Romance languages: a bibliography of bibliographies.**
Kathryn F. Bach, Glanville Price. London: Grant & Cutler, 1977. 194p. (Research Bibliographies and Checklists, no. 22).

The Ibero-Romance section (p. 67-107) lists over 130 items on Spanish, Catalan and Spanish-American journals, grammar, syntax and dialects, with brief critical and descriptive annotations. The arrangement within sub-sections is basically chronological, and cross-references appear at the head of each chapter, section or sub-section. This study has proved an extremely valuable reference book for Spanish language and linguistics mainly because of the well-annotated entries and the clearly organized format. It is also useful in that it includes items which, although not specifically prepared as formal bibliographies, are useful sources of bibliographical references.

959 **A sourcebook for Hispanic literature and language: a selected, annotated guide to Spanish, Spanish-American, and Chicano bibliography, literature, linguistics, journals, and other source materials.**
Donald W. Bleznick. Metuchen, New Jersey; London: Scarecrow, 1983. 2nd ed. 304p.

This invaluable work aims to be 'a practical guide to bibliography and other basic materials which would serve budding and even mature Hispanists in literary and linguistic research', and attempts to identify essential books and journals in the areas most central to that research. The study contains 1,410 items, and is not merely a bibliography of bibliographies, but also provides information on every kind of book available for literature and language studies and other related fields. An author and title index is included together with a list of selected publishers and book dealers.

960 **A bibliographic guide to Spanish diplomatic history, 1460-1977.**
Compiled by James W. Cortada. Westport, Connecticut; London: Greenwood Press, 1977. 390p. bibliog.

'Spain has participated in worldwide activities, in various ways and with fluctuating importance, since her earliest days'. There has been a tremendous upsurge over the past few years in the study of Spain's role in international affairs, for the following reasons: there has been easier access to archives and libraries in Spain; more diplomatic files on important topics like the Second Republic and the Franco régime (early days) have become available; and there has been a greater realization of the importance of the strategic position of Spain in the Mediterranean. This detailed work contains thousands of references to Spain's foreign relations over 500 years, organized chronologically and then by country.

961 **A bibliography of Hispanic dictionaries: Catalan, Galician, Spanish, Spanish in Latin America and the Philippines.**
Maurizio Fabbri. Imola, Italy: Galeati, 1979. 381p. (Biblioteca Spicilegio Moderno; Collana Bibliografica, no. 1).

This excellent study represents the first comprehensive attempt to provide a complete and current bibliography of dictionaries of Spanish. It lists some 3,500 dictionaries, vocabularies, glossaries and work-lists of a general character, as well as texts dealing with technical and scientific languages and their highly specialized terminology. Entries are arranged by author, and there are author, language and subject indexes.

962 **Manual of Hispanic bibliography.**
Compiled by David William Foster, Virginia Ramos Foster. New York; London: Garland, 1977. 2nd ed. 329p. (Garland Reference Library of the Humanities, vol. 85).

This bibliography 'represents an attempt at providing Spanish and Spanish-American literary scholars with a comprehensive bibliographical guide to primary and important secondary sources of investigation'. It includes annotated listings of both literary and national bibliographies, as well as works relating to literary resources. It is arranged in four parts with separate sections under the four main headings of: general bibliographies; bibliographies of Spanish literature; bibliographies of Spanish-American literature; Spanish-American national bibliographies. An author, corporate entry, and short title index is included. This second edition contains 1,050 items, as opposed to the first edition's 796.

963 **Bibliography of the Spanish Civil War 1936-1939.**
Juan García Durán. Montevideo: Editorial El Siglo Ilustrado,
1964. 559p. (Instituto de Historia de la Guerra Civil Española, no.
1).

A massive work which contains over 6,200 entries on all aspects of the war. This
is the first serious attempt to gather together all types of material – books,
journals, newspapers and films – on the conflict in one bibliography. The original
intention of the author was to provide a major source of research on the civil
war's political, social, economic and ideological background and aftermath, and it
is particularly useful for the references to publications which appeared in France,
Spain and Britain during and immediately after the war itself.

964 **Modern Iberian language and literature: a bibliography of homage
studies.**
Herbert Hershel Golden, Seymour O. Simches. Millwood, New
York: Kraus Reprints, 1971. 184p.

A reprint of the original 1958 edition (Cambridge, Massachussetts: Harvard
University Press). It is a bibliography of nearly 500 items comprising the most
important articles in *Festschriften* and homage publications, relating to Spanish
and Portuguese languages and literature from 1500 onwards. The linguistic
sections were updated by David S. Zubatsky in 'Hispanic linguistic studies in
Festschriften: an annotated bibliography (1957-75) (*Hispania*, vol. 60 (1977),
p. 656-717), which also includes some items missed by Golden and Simches.

965 **Bibliography of the drama of Spain and Spanish America.**
Raymond Leonard Grismer. Minneapolis, Minnesota: Burgess-
Beckwith, 1967-69. 2 vols.

Volume 1 (A to L) and volume 2 (M to Z) together contain about 7,000 entries
arranged by author, and include useful reviews of the published editions of plays.
Grismer also began work on the unfinished *A new bibliography of the literatures
of Spain and Spanish America; including many studies on anthropology,
archaeology, art, economics, education, geography, history, law, music, philosophy and other subjects* (Minneapolis, Minnesota: Perine Book Co., 1941-46,
vols. 1-7 (A-Cez)), which was intended to replace the author's two earlier
volumes of bibliography published in 1933 and 1935.

966 **Inventario de estadísticas de España: análisis documental de las
publicaciones editadas desde 1960.** (An inventory of statistics on
Spain: a documentary analysis of works published since 1960.)
Barcelona, Spain: Consorcio de Información y Documentación de
Cataluña, 1975. 595p.

An in-depth analysis, which contains nearly 600 publications, indexed by author,
title and subject. It is an excellent source for all the major statistical publications
of Spain.

967 **Official publications of western Europe; vol. 1: Denmark, Finland, France, Ireland, Italy, Luxembourg, Netherlands, Spain and Turkey.**
Edited by Eve Johansson.   London: Mansell, 1984. 313p.
The section on Spain (p. 183-243) has been written by someone who works in the official publications section of the National Library in Madrid. There is no official printer for government publications in Spain like Britain's HMSO, and this is the first up-to-date general guide on the subject in English. It is particularly useful as the bibliographic control for this area is, on the whole, very poor.

968 **Bibliografía histórica sobre la ciencia y la técnica en España.**
(A historical bibliography of science and technology in Spain.)
José María López Piñero (et al.).   Valencia; Granada:
Secretariado de Publicaciones de la Universidad, 1973. 2 vols.
(Cuadernos Hispánicos de Historia de la Medicina y de la Ciencia,
XIII, Serie C).
An impressive source for books and articles on the evolution and development of science and technology in Spain from the 18th century to the 1970s. Volume 1 covers, for example, mathematics, astronomy, geology, mineralogy, botany, biology, zoology and metallurgy. Volume 2 deals with biographies, arranged in chronological groups from antiquity to the present day, and is indexed by subject and by biographer.

969 **M.L.A. International Bibliography of Books and Articles on the Modern Languages and Literatures.**
New York: Modern Language Association, 1921- . annual.
One of the standard bibliographical sources for tracing articles and books on Spanish language and literature. This publication has provided the widest coverage in the field since 1956 when it commenced international coverage. Since 1981 it has been organized in five volumes which include author and subject indexes. Entry selections are made from numerous book sources and from a basic master-list of periodicals.

970 **Spanish plays in English translation: an annotated bibliography.**
Edited by Robert A. O'Brien.   New York: Las Americas, 1963.
82p.
Contains information on the translation of plays into English from the times of early drama up to the 20th century. The work also includes notes on individual plays and dramatists, and although very useful, it is unfortunately badly printed.

971 **Guide to the law and legal literature of Spain.**
Thomas Waverly Palmer.   Westport, Connecticut: Hyperion
Press, 1979. 174p.
A reprint of the original 1915 edition (Washington DC: Government Printing Office), prepared by the Library of Congress 'to meet the growing demand on the part of lawyers, legislators and students for a knowledge of the law and legal

institutions of foreign countries'. Although very dated, it still represents one of the few English-language sources for the student of comparative law and anyone interested in the history of Spanish law, and contains a large glossary of Spanish legal terms.

972 **English translations from the Spanish, 1484-1943: a bibliography.**
Remigio Ugo Pane. New Brunswick, New Jersey: Rutgers University Press, 1944. 218p. (Rutgers University Studies in Spanish, no. 2).

An unannotated, alphabetical listing of 2,682 items of Iberian literature and history. A review, with corrections and additions to this work by W. K. Jones, was published in *Hispanic Review* (vol. 13 (Apr. 1945), p. 174-77).

973 **The literature of Spain in English translation: a bibliography.**
Compiled and edited by Robert S. Rudder. New York: Frederick Ungar, 1975. 637p.

The fullest bibliography of its kind, which aims to bring to attention all that can be found of the literature of Spain in English, and is especially useful to scholars, librarians, students, translators and publishers. The book is arranged by periods from the Middle Ages to the 20th century, and within each period authors are listed alphabetically.

974 **Bibliografía de la lingüística española.** (A bibliography of Spanish linguistics.)
Homero Serís. Bogotá: Instituto Caro y Cuervo, 1964. 981p.
(Instituto Caro y Cuervo. Publicaciones, no. 19).

A massive study which looks at all aspects of Spanish language, including dialects, South-American Spanish, and the teaching of the language. A number of the items are annotated, and many references to book reviews are provided, as well as a lengthy index and a detailed table of contents.

975 **Spanish literature in Russia and in the Soviet Union 1735-1964.**
Ludmilla Buketoff Turkevich. Metuchen, New Jersey: Scarecrow, 1967. 273p.

A partly-annotated bibliography of works by Spanish authors, and of critical works about these writers, arranged alphabetically by Spanish name. It contains 1,792 entries, and emphasizes that a huge amount of Spanish literature has been translated into Russian. The section on Cervantes and Don Quixote takes up 100 pages of the book!

976   **Spanish and Spanish-American literature: an annotated guide to selected bibliographies.**
Hensley C. Woodbridge.   New York: Modern Language Association of America, 1983. 74p. (Selected Bibliographies in Language and Literature, no. 4).

A bibliography of bibliographies, arranged chronologically by periods for Spanish literature, and by country for Latin America. This current and extremely useful study concentrates on works published since 1950, and includes an index of authors.

977   **The Year's Work in Modern Language Studies.**
Cambridge, England: Modern Humanities Research Association, 1931-40, 1950- . annual.

Each volume provides a critical survey of work done in modern languages and literatures. Large sections are given over to evaluating the year's developments and publications in Spanish language and literature, as well as Catalan studies from mediaeval times to the present. Author and subject indexes are included. Volume 11 spanning the years 1941 to 1949, was published as a composite volume.

Sociology in Spain.
See item no. 476.

Library catalogues

978   **Catalogue of the library of the Hispanic Society of America.**
Boston, Massachussetts: G. K. Hall, 1962. 10 vols.

A massive catalogue (over 100,000 entries) for every book printed since 1700, and housed in this prestigious library. Manuscripts, most periodicals, and pre-1700 books are not included, and the emphasis of the collection is on the art, history and literature of Spain, Portugal and colonial Hispanic America. The first supplement of four volumes was published in 1970.

979   **A short title catalogue of Spanish and Portuguese books, 1601-1700, in the library of the British Musuem (The British Library, Reference Division).**
Valentine Fernande Goldsmith.   Folkestone, England: Dawsons of Pall Mall, 1974. 250p.

A catalogue of: 'books written wholly or partly in Spanish or Portuguese, no matter where published' and 'books, in no matter what language, published or printed at any place which today forms part of Spain or Portugual'. This work continues chronologically the Museum's *Short-title catalogue of books printed in*

Spain and of Spanish books printed elsewhere in Europe before 1601 by Henry Thomas (London: British Museum, 1921).

980 **Hispanic and Luso-Brazilian Councils, Canning House Library, London. Author and subject catalogues.**
Boston, Massachussets: G. K. Hall, 1967. 4 vols.
This library contains over 30,000 Spanish, Latin American and Portuguese books, mostly of the 19th and 20th centuries. Philosophy, religion, education, history, economics, the arts, and language and literature are among the wide range of subjects covered. The library also houses important cultural and economic periodicals. The first supplement was published in 1973.

Theses

981 **Theses in Hispanic studies approved for higher degrees by British universities to 1971.**
C. A. Jones. *Bulletin of Hispanic Studies*, vol. 49 (Oct. 1972), p. 325-54.
A list of theses approved for higher degrees since 1913, the majority of which are devoted to literature and history. However, language, Spanish-Arabic studies, education, religion, politics and economics are all represented, and there is also an index of authors. This study has been updated by F. W. Hodcroft for 1972-74 (vol. 52 (1975), p. 325-44), and by D. Mackenzie for 1975-78 (vol. 56 (1979), p. 283-304).

982 **Tesis Doctorales Aprobados en las Universidades Españoles durante el Curso.** . . . (Doctoral theses approved for higher degrees by Spanish universities during the year. . . .)
Madrid: Centro de Proceso de Datos, Ministerio de Educación y Ciencia, 1976/77. annual.
This work represents the Spanish national thesis bibliography, and stems from a government decree that such a catalogue should be compiled. As such it is the first of its kind in Spain, and all universities except Valencia and Granada are included. It lists 563 theses by faculty within university, and then by author and subject.

Vida Hispánica: Journal of the Association of Teachers of Spanish and Portuguese.
See item no. 939.

Index

The index is a single alphabetical sequence of authors (personal and corporate), titles of publications and subjects. Index entries refer both to the main items and to other works mentioned in the notes to each item. Title entries are in italics. Numeration refers to the items as numbered.

flamenco 56
flora 109, 111–112
food and drink 56
geography 56, 62
gypsies 369
history 56
insects 106
plants 109
population 56
regionalism 373
reptiles 106
social change 481
social structure 459
sport 56
Andalusia 29, 56, 62
Andalusian dances 841
Andalusian dog (film) 855
Andalusian flowers and countryside 109
Andalusians 373
Anderson, C. W. 582
Andorra
  guidebooks 89
Andrade, J. M. 561
Anger 4
Angling (see Fishing)
*Anglo-Spanish Society Quarterly
  Review* 934
Animals (see also Fauna)
  in drama 760
Anna, T. E. 314
Another sword for St. James 179
Anthologies 726, 790-791
  drama 783, 787–788, 791, 796
  philosophy 445
  poetry 780, 782, 784, 786–787, 789,
    791–795, 881
  short stories 785, 787, 790
*Anthology of Spanish literature in
  English translation* 791
Anthology of Spanish poetry 1500–1700
  793
*Anthology of Spanish poetry: from the
  beginnings to the present day,
  including both Spain and Spanish
  America* 784
*Anthology of Spanish poetry from
  Garcilaso to García Lorca* 787
Anthropology (see Social anthropol-
  ogy)
Anticlericalism 429, 442–443
  Barcelona 443
Anticlericalism: conflict between church

  *and State in France, Italy, and
    Spain* 442
La antropología médica en España 496
Anual, Battle of (1921) 253
Anuario de la Prensa Española 901
Anuario Estadístico de España 683
AP (Alianza Popular) 527, 529
Apparitions
  religious 424, 426
*Apparitions in late medieval and
    Renaissance Spain* 424
*Appleton's new Cuyás English-Spanish
    and Spanish-English dictionary*
  410
Applied arts (see Crafts)
Apprentices of freedom 267
Approaches to the history of Spain 150
*Aproximación al derecho constitucional
    española: la constitución de 1978*
  541
Arabs (see Moors)
Aragón 173, 186
  banking history 608
  dialect 389
  history 154
  land reform 470
Aranda, F. 855
Arango, E. R. 501
Aranguren, José Luis 449
Araujo García, C. 419
Arcadia 756
Archaeological sites 119, 122, 126
  Altamira 59, 115, 798
  Balearic Islands 125
  Canary Islands 160
  Ribadesella 115
  wrecks 120–121
Archaeology 114–122, 124, 126, 167
  Balearic Islands 125
  bibliographies 965
  Canary Islands 160
  Copper Age 118
  Iron Age 113
  North Africa 118
  Portugal 116, 118–119, 126
  Stone Age, 118, 123
  western Europe 118
*Archaeology under water: an atlas of
    the world's submerged sites*
  121
Architecture 19, 36, 92, 96, 800,
    804–805, 814–815, 818, 822

283

287

291

Columbus: the story of Don Cristóbal
Colón, Admiral of the Ocean and
his four voyages westward to the
Indies according to contemporary
sources 328
Comedias (see Drama: 16th and 17th
centuries)
Comics 904
Coming of the Spanish Civil War:
reform reaction and revolution in
the Second Republic 281
Comintern 263, 274, 283
Comintern and the Spanish Civil War
263
Comintern army: the International
Brigades and the Spanish Civil
War 283
Commerce 615, 621
18th century 626
Commercial law 615
Communications 52, 310, 663, 685
Catalonia 60
statistics 683, 686–688
Communism and political change in
Spain 530
Communism and the Spanish Civil
War 266
Communist parties of Italy, France
and Spain: postwar change and
continuity: a casebook 525
Communist Party (see PCE)
Communist Party in Spain 511
Communists 247, 262, 266, 508,
511–512, 515, 519–520, 525, 530
Communists in Spain: study of an
underground political movement
520
Companies
accounts 609
Companies, Multinational
investment in Spain 592
Companion guide to Madrid and
central Spain 84
Companion guide to the south of Spain
92
Companya catalana (see Catalan
Grand Company)
Comparative reception of Darwinism
711
Comparing nations: the use of quantita-
tive data in cross-national research
475

Complete aficionado 884
Compromising relations: kith, kin and
class in Andalusia 459
Concise history of Spain 139, 144
Concise history of the Spanish Civil
War 273
Concise Spanish grammar 403
Concordats
1953 427, 431
Congress of Deputies (see Cortes)
Connell, T. 400
Conquest and commerce: Spain
and England in the Americas
329
Conquistadores 326
Conrad, B. 879
Consejo Superior de Deportes (Higher
Council for Sport) 881
Conservation 691–692, 695–696
Conservative politics in western Europe
526
Conservatives 526, 529
Constitución española: edición
comentada 536
Las constituciones de España 537
Constituciones y períodos
constituyentes en España
(1808–1936) 542
Constitutional history 537–538, 540,
542, 544
Constitutionalism and statecraft during
the Golden Age of Spain: a study
of the political philosophy of Juan
de Mariana, S. J. 215
Constitutions 17, 309
1808 542, 544
1812 158, 537, 544
1834 544
1837 544
1845 542, 544
1856 544
1869 542, 544
1873 544
1876 227, 250, 542, 544
1931 538–539, 542, 544
1978 290, 308, 536–537, 539,
541–543, 668
Construction industry 643
statistics 687
Consumer advice
periodicals 926
Consumer protection 554

El Pinar
  social change 454
Elections 279, 504, 508, 528
  1977 509, 533, 541
  1979 507, 541
  trade unions 671, 673
  statistics 532
Electoral participation: a comparative analysis 532
Electronics industry 639, 643
Elliott, J. H. 201–204, 806
Ellis, H. 5
Elorza, A. 908
Embleton, C. 65
Emden, A. B. 707
La emigración española a Bélgica en los últimos años 376
Emigración española a Europa 382
La emigración española a Francia 380
La emigración española en la encrucijada: marco general de la emigración de retorno 377
Emigración española en Europa 382
Emigration 348, 453, 600
  statistics 380–382
  to Australia 379
  to Belgium 376
  to Britain 381
  to Europe 382
  to France 377, 380, 382–383
  to Germany 377, 382
  to Latin America 374, 378, 577
  to Mexico 375, 478
  to the Netherlands 382
  to Switzerland 377, 382
  to the United States 374, 378
L'emigration Basque 374
Emperor Charles V: the growth and destiny of a man and a world-empire 192
Empire 173, 181, 189, 201–202, 240–242, 315–316, 318, 341–342, 801
  administration 327, 329, 338
  Africa 341
  architecture 801
  art 801
  Athens 344
  bibliographies 951
  Canary Islands 320
  Caribbean 343, 346
  Ceuta 340

Chaffarine Islands 340
  cost of maintaining 591
  Cuba 315, 335, 566, 742
  Europe 341
  Italy 327
  justice 323
  Melilla 340
  Mexico 221, 334
  Morocco 317
  Naples, Kingdom of 327
  Netherlands 194, 212, 325, 336–337
  Pacific 319, 345
  Peñón d'Alhucemas 340
  Peñón de Vélez de la Gomera 340
  Peru 221
  Philippines 334, 742
  Portuguese 316, 333, 345
  Puerto Rico 335, 742
  race relations 323
  religion 422
  Sardinia 327
  scientific expeditions 710
  Sicily 327
  Spanish America 175, 182, 185, 187, 200, 212, 216, 251, 314, 316, 321–324, 326, 328–331, 333–335, 338–339, 341–343, 346, 564
  trade 329, 616, 622
  Western Sahara 332
Employment
  statistics 683
  women 676
Employment of women in Spain 676
En torno al casticismo 740
Enchanted Mountains 30
Enchanted Mountains: a quest in the Pyrenees 30
Encina, Juan del 766
Encyclopaedia of bullfighting 879
Encyclopaedias 944–945
  bullfighting 879
  literature 746
Energy industry 638
  statistics 687
Engineering 162, 719
English translations from the Spanish, 1484–1943: a bibliography 972
Engstrand, I. H. W. 710
Enlargement of the European Community: case-studies of Greece, Portugal and Spain 619
Enlightenment 238, 437, 761

K

L

315

Mexico City
  Royal Botanical Garden 710
Michelin Green Guide: Spain 93
Michener, J. A. 39
Middle Ages 728
Middle East
  relations with Spain 571
Migration, External (see Emigration)
Migration, Internal 347, 351, 453, 456
  Galicia 353
*Migration, kinship, and community:
  tradition and transition in a
  Spanish village* 456
Miguel, J. M. de 476, 496, 498–499
El milagro turístico 80
*El militar de carrera en España: estudio
  de sociología militar* 562
Los militares en la transición política
  565
Military bases
  American 572, 581
Military-civil relations 230, 560, 563,
  565, 568–569
Military orders (see also Calatrava,
  Alcántara, Santiago) 180
Miller, T. 183–184
Mineral resources 162, 631
Mineralogy
  bibliographies 968
*Miners against fascism: Wales and the
  Spanish Civil War* 271
Minet, G. 576
Mining 162, 601, 631
  statistics 687
Ministerial administration 555
Miño, River 29
Minorca (see also Balearic Islands)
  climate 98
  economics 98
  fauna 98
  flora 98
  geology 98
  guidebooks 90, 98–99
  history 98, 157
  topography 98
Minorca 98
Mitchell, B. R. 686
Mitchell, D. 277
*MLA International Bibliography of
  Books and Articles on the Modern
  Languages and Literatures* 969
Mocatta, F. D. 357

Modeltec project 713
*Moderates and conservatives in western
  Europe: political parties, the
  European Community and the
  Atlantic alliance* 529
*Modern Iberian language and litera-
  ture: a bibliography of homage
  studies* 964
Modern Spain 1788–1898 241
Modern Spain 1875–1980 231
Modern Spanish novel 749
Modern Spanish rural drama 765
*Modern Spanish theatre: an anthology
  of plays* 783
Moffitt, J. F. 810
Moir, D. 766
Molina, Luis de 208
Molina, Tirso de 766
Molina-Foix, V. 855
Molina Negro, F. 663
Mompou, Federico 848
Monarchomachs 215
Monarchy 540–541, 554
Monasteries 820
Monasterio de San Lorenzo el Real del
  Escorial (see Escorial, El)
Monastic history 421
Mondragón 625, 627, 641
Mondragón 1980 627
Mondragon: an economic analysis 641
Monetary policy
  15th century 595
*Money, prices and politics in fifteenth-
  century Castile* 595
Monopolists and freebooters 345
Monteiro Cardoso, A. 902
Montero, M. 158
Montes de Toledo 483
Montevideo 374
Montserrat 60
Moore, C. 94
Moore, C. H. 298
Moorish architecture 797, 821
Moorish art 797
Moorish culture in Spain 797
*Moorish Spain: Cordoba, Seville,
  Granada* 821
Moors 50, 145, 168–169, 179, 187, 190,
  372, 623, 797
  architecture 797, 821
  art 797
  economic policy 593

N

Nadal Oller, J. 352, 585–586, 603
Names 385
Nansa valley
  religion 426
Naples, Kingdom of 327
Napoleon I, Bonaparte 233, 235, 244,
  248
*Napoleon and the birth of modern
  Spain* 244
Narrow gauge railways 654
Nasrids 179
National parks 691
  Covadonga 692
*National parks and reserves of western
  Europe* 691
Nationalists 285, 287
Nationalities 320
  Basques 355, 359–361, 365, 367, 371,
  373
  Catalans 362–363, 365, 368, 370, 373
  Galicians 354, 371, 373
NATO 529
  relations with Spain 302, 307, 569,
  573, 578
Natural resources 696
Naturalist in Majorca 107
Nature protection 691–692, 695
Naval Air Service 561
Naval law 566
Navarre (see also Basque Provinces)
  57, 242, 360
Navarro, Juan 849
Navigation 128, 616
Navy 559, 569
  history 559, 566
Naylon, J. 62, 79
Neal, W. K. 634
Nebrija, Antonio de 187
Negrín, Juan 258
*Neighbors: the social contract in a
  Castilian hamlet* 465
Neoscholasticism 448
Netherlands 194, 212, 336–337
  government publications 967
  independence 325
  investment in Spain 613
  Spanish immigrants 382
Neuman, A. A. 366
New anthology of Spanish literature 726
*New bibliography of the literatures of
  Spain and Spanish America;
  including many studies on
  anthropology, archaeology, art,
  economics, education, geography,
  history, law, music, philosophy
  and other subjects* 965
New Castile 27, 58
  religion 425
New Castile 58
New cinema in Spain 855
*New guide to the diplomatic archives of
  western Europe* 894
New history of Spanish literature 726,
  730
*New Mediterranean democracies:
  regime transition in Greece, Spain
  and Portugal* 312
New wave Spanish drama 796
New World (see America, Spanish)
New world in our hearts 514
New Yorker 46
Newcombe, N. W. 706
Newspapers 643, 902–903, 905–907,
  909–923
  directories 901
  statistics 688
Newton, M. T. 664
Nichols, R. S. 823
Nicolini, G. 122
Nineteenth century 742
*El niño en la cultura española: ante la
  medicina y otras ciencias; la
  historia, las letras, las artes y las
  costumbres* 491
Noel, C. C. 437
Noreña, C. G. 450
North Africa 332
  archaeology 118
  relations with Spain 571
North Atlantic Treaty Organization
  (see NATO)
Northern Spain 44
  guidebooks 86
Northrup, G. T. 738
Norton, A. 557
Norton, F. J. 399, 899
Norway 381
*Not on Queen Victoria's birthday: the
  story of the Rio Tinto mines* 631
Novedades Editoriales Españoles 952
Novelas ejemplares 747
Novels 749, 751, 754

319

Rocroi, Battle of (1643) 318
Rodríguez, Claudio 772
Rodríguez, E. A. 401
Rof Carballo, Juan 449
Roglić, J. 49
Rokkan, S. 371, 475, 528
Roman, M. 600
Roman Catholic Church (see Catholic Church)
Roman mines in Europe 162
Roman Spain 50, 119, 122, 124–125, 162, 165, 167, 171
architecture 167
Roman Spain: an introduction to the Roman antiquities of Spain and Portugal 167
Romance linguistics and the Romance languages: a bibliography of bibliographies 958
Romances 774, 786
Romano, V. 672
Romans in Spain 217 B.C.–A.D. 117 165
Romantic in Spain 32
Romantic movement 735, 739, 742
Romantic movement in Spain: a short history 739
Romerías 860
Ronda 84, 459
Roots and wings: poetry from Spain 1900–1975 792
Rose, R. 532
Rose for winter: travels in Andalusia 35
Roth, C. 372, 441
Rowdon, M. 341
Rowe, D. T. 42
Rowse, A. L. 217
Royal College of San Carlos: surgery and Spanish medical reform in the late eighteenth century 709
Royal Corps of Engineers 564
Royal Museum of Painting (see Prado)
Royal Scientific Expedition 710
Royal vendetta: the crown of Spain 1829–1965 226
Rubio, J. 380
Rubottom, R. R. 572
Rudder, R. S. 973
Rueda, Lope de 766
Ruibal, José 796
Ruiz, D. 161
Ruiz-Ocaña Remiro, C. 569

Rule, J. C., 222
Rural Catalonia under the Franco regime: the fate of regional culture since the Spanish Civil War 363
Rural drama
20th century 765
Rural sociology 453–454, 456–457, 462, 464–465, 467, 473, 483
Rushworth, J. 618
Russell, P. E. 148
Russia (see also USSR)
navy 566
Spanish literature 975

S

Sahagún, Carlos 772
St. James 44, 179
St. Martin, H. 792
Sal y Pimienta 932
Sala, M. 65
Salamanca University 707
Salic Law 254–255
Salinas, Pedro 769, 779
Salis, C. E. de 585
Salisbury, W. T. 302
Salmon, E. D. 342
Salomon, H. P. 372
Salter, C. 18
Sampedro, J. L. 619
San Carlos, Royal College of Surgery of (Madrid) 709
San Martín
social change 473
San Sebastián 44
Sánchez Cantón, F. J. 812, 893
Sánchez de Badajoz, Garci 793
Sánchez López, F. 382
Sánchez Robayna, D. 611
Santa Hermandad 487
Santander 59
Santiago de Compostela 44, 54
Santiago, Order of 180
Sanz del Río, Julián 447
Sarasola, I. 741
Sardinia 327
Sastre, Alfonso 796
Sauer, C. O. 343

327

Map of Spain

This map shows the more important towns and other features.

FRANCE

PYRENEES

ANDORRA

Fuenterrabia
Echalar
Ibao · Bidassoa
Mondragón
Muréiaga
Guernica
Sebastian
Sebastian

BASQUE · Pamplona
PROVINCES NAVARRE
Logroño
a Rioja

Ibieca ·
· Huesca

Gerona ·

Costa Brava

R. Ebro
Soria ·
Zaragoza Lérida ·
ARAGON

Montserrat
CATALONIA
· Barcelona

Tarragona

Costa Dorada

Valdemora ·
enares
uadalajara
alá
e
nares

La Alcarria

· Teruel

MINORCA

MAJORCA

· Cuenca

Castellón de la
Plana

Palma

BALEARIC ISLANDS

CASTILE

Mancha

Albacete ·

VALENCIA

Levant

GULF OF
VALENCIA CABRERA
· Valencia

IBIZA

· Alicante

FORMENTERA

MURCIA
Murcia ·

MEDITERRANEAN SEA

NEVADA
nada
Yegen
ujarras
Almeria
del Sol

· CHAFFARINE IS. ALGERIA
elilla

| | Land over 2000m |

0   100   200 km